THE POLITICS OF MEMORY IN

POSTWAR EUROPE

# The Politics of Memory in Postwar Europe

RICHARD NED LEBOW, WULF KANSTEINER,

AND CLAUDIO FOGU, EDITORS

Duke University Press    Durham and London    2006

© 2006 Duke University Press
All rights reserved
Printed in the United States of America on acid-free paper ∞
Designed by C. H. Westmoreland
Typeset in Adobe Minion by Keystone Typesetting, Inc.
Library of Congress Cataloging-in-Publication Data appear
on the last printed page of this book.

TO CAROL, SONJA, AND ELISA

# Contents

# Preface

Many developments in life are the result of fortuitous confluences, and this project is one of them. In 1999 we, the three editors of this volume, came together under the same roof: the Mershon Center at Ohio State University. Ned was the center's director, Claudio an assistant professor in the department of history, and Wulf a postdoctoral fellow. A number of lunchtime talks and dinners led to a commitment to produce a collection of essays on the memory of Nazism and the Holocaust in Europe; it would be unlike any other, exploiting recent research in disparate disciplines to open a channel of communication between historians working on collective memory and social scientists studying the nature of individual and collective identities and processes of democratization. Our starting point would be a set of commonly formulated research questions that would guide national case studies. We would bring all the participants together to discuss the questions and their cases. The case studies in turn would allow the editors to offer generalizations of a substantive and theoretical nature.

Our common interests in memory and identity both facilitated and hindered our collaboration. It prompted us to work toward the goal of a comparative study that would explore the similarities and differences in how European countries had addressed their respective roles in World War II and what internal conflicts had arisen concerning these constructions of the past. Ned was particularly interested in the implications of this process for democratization and relations with neighbors. Claudio and Wulf wanted to use the findings to evaluate the field of collective memory studies. All of us were keen to understand what light these conflicts shed on the relationship between memory and identity. We began with an exploration of what we meant by "memory" and "identity," which quickly revealed a considerable gulf in how we framed these concepts and thought about making connections between them. As we drafted our research agenda we succeeded in bridging some of our differences but also took advantage of the value of multiple perspectives. To profit fully from this tension and to explore possible ways of resolving it, at least in part, we asked Wulf to prepare an essay on memory as understood by historians and applied to World War II. On the social science side, we agreed to circulate a treatment of the problem of identity, in the process of being drafted for another project by our Ohio State colleagues Marilynn Brewer and Richard Herrmann. We would digest and thrash through both treatments, and send them on, along with the research questions, to the scholars invited to participate in the project.

We then set about selecting appropriate scholars for our study. We wanted to involve young scholars from Europe, so we recruited Heidemarie Uhl from Austria, Annamaria Orla-Bukowska from Poland, and Regula Ludi from Switzerland. Tom Wolfe, a young political scientist from the United States, agreed to write the chapter on the Soviet Union/Russia, and Joe Golsan, a senior U.S. scholar in the field of French cultural studies, covered France.

At that point we needed to finance the project adequately and involve a wider scholarly community in organizing the discussion workshops. We were very fortunate to find in Friedrich V. Kratochwil (Fritz), a visiting professor at Mershon, an ideal and energetic collaborator. Ned and Fritz wrote a grant application to the German American Academic Council, which gave us money to hold our first conference-workshop on the politics of memory; the Hanns Seidel Foundation, having been approached by Fritz and his colleague James Davis, invited us to hold our conference at their Alpine retreat in Wildbad Kreuth. At the conference, which took place in October 2001, we collectively critiqued draft chapters and reformulated the original set of questions based on the preliminary findings of the case studies. A second workshop met at La Jolla in April 2002 and was generously funded by the Mershon Center. For both conferences we invited additional experts to critique our drafts: Dorothy Noyes, a folklorist and professor in the English department at Ohio State; Alex Stephan, an Ohio Eminent Scholar and professor of Germanic languages and literature, also at Ohio State; Martin Heisler of University of Maryland's political-science department; Harald Welzer, a social psychologist at the Kulturwissenschaftliche Institut in Essen; and Bernhard Giesen, a macrosociologist at the University of Konstanz. All five provided extraordinarily helpful feedback on the essays and the broader project. We hope that an echo of their contributions can also be found in the comparative-theoretical essays that frame our volume.

There are several other people we would like to thank. Rick Herrmann and Marilynn Brewer gave us an early, and very helpful, draft of their joint authored piece on identity. Matthew Keith, administrator of the Mershon Center, helped to organize the conferences and to work out complicated accounting arrangements with our German partners. Eli Lebow did a fine job of retranslating and editing Heidemarie Uhl's essay. Peter J. Verovsek provided invaluable assistance in compiling the bibliography and finalizing the manuscript. Valerie Millholland of Duke University Press displayed an early and unflagging interest in our project, and we are indebted to her and her colleagues at the press for bringing the project to fruition. Ned would like to acknowledge the assistance he received from Janice Gross Stein, who provided extensive feedback on the first draft of his introductory chapter, and from Martin Heisler, who did the same for the revised version.

Finally, we would like to thank our contributors for their enthusiasm, their diligence in meeting deadlines, their thoughtful comments on our drafts, and their willingness to rewrite in response to feedback from editors and external reviewers. Working with our contributors made the project not only intellectually stimulating but good fun.

CLAUDIO FOGU

WULF KANSTEINER

NED LEBOW

RICHARD NED LEBOW ✳

# The Memory of Politics in Postwar Europe

Footfalls echo in the memory
Down the passage which we did not take
Towards the door we never opened
Into the rose garden
—T. S. Eliot, "Burnt Norton"

In April 2005 the College of Cardinals elected a German pope—Cardinal Joseph Ratzinger—who had been a member of the Hitlerjugend and briefly served in the Wehrmacht. The new pope was controversial in Europe—for his ultraconservative religious views, not for his German past. It was widely accepted that he bore no personal responsibility for the crimes of the Nazi era. Just about every youth of his age had been enrolled in the Hitlerjugend, and he had deserted the German army to return to the seminary. Jewish authorities praised him for encouraging his predecessor's official recognition of the church's historical role in fanning anti-Semitism and for his efforts to establish more fraternal relations with the State of Israel and Jewish communities in Europe.

At the same time as the College of Cardinals was deliberating, Chinese demonstrators, egged on by their government, were throwing stones at the Japanese embassy in Peking and consulates elsewhere in China, attacking Japanese businesses, and generally protesting Japan's efforts to obtain a permanent seat on the United Nation's Security Council. The demonstrators and the Chinese government had become doubly enraged by the nearly simultaneous publication of a Japanese textbook that sought to downplay or discredit the atrocities, including the Rape of Nanjing, that Japanese occupation forces had committed in China and elsewhere in Asia. The textbook, like most in Japan, also put a favorable gloss on Japan's invasions of China and Southeast Asia, characterizing them as acts of anticolonialism and as economically beneficial for those who had been occupied.[1]

The two events in two different regions of the world were closely related, even if diametrically opposed in their symbolic value. The election of a German pope, and one, moreover, who had worn a military uniform, would have been hard to imagine in the absence of a decades-long effort by successive German governments to come to terms with the past and accept their responsibility for the horrendous suffering the Nazis had inflicted on Europe. The Chinese government was not shy about comparing the German and the Japanese politics of memory. Chinese officials praised Germany for acknowledging its Nazi past, for paying billions of dollars in reparations to victims or their families, and for the increasingly forthright approach of its school curriculum. They noted the visits Chancellor Willy Brandt and President Richard Weizsäcker had made to Auschwitz, as well as their seemingly heartfelt apologies for Germany's crimes. Had the Japanese behaved this way, one Chinese official said, we would view them and their claims for a Security Council seat differently.[2]

These events clearly highlight the positive side of Germany's struggle to overcome its past. But that struggle is far from complete, not only in Germany—hate crimes have reached an all-time high in the former East Germany—but in Europe more generally, where the past continues to weigh on the present in unfortunate and unhelpful ways. On 28 February 2002 Chancellor Gerhard Schröder canceled his visit to Prague to protest Czech prime minister Milos Zeman's branding of ethnic Germans, expelled at the end of World War II, as "Hitler's fifth column." The week before, Prime Minister Victor Orban of Hungary said that neither the Czech Republic nor Slovakia should be admitted to the European Union until they revoked a 1945 decree stripping ethnic Germans and Hungarians of their citizenship in retaliation of their support for Nazi Germany.[3] In September 2004 the Polish parliament unanimously passed a resolution demanding reparations from Germany.

How should one understand such statements and actions? Are they throwaway lines intended to placate aging émigré constituencies? Do they reflect something more sinister: a revival of national assertiveness kindled by still-rankling memories of past wrongs in which all parties concerned consider themselves the victims? And what about the undeniable rise of anti-immigrant and anti-foreigner sentiment through Europe? Is this the last gasp of old ethnic antagonisms fueled by the unfreezing of politics in the east and high unemployment in the west brought about by both the collapse of Communism and an economic downturn? Or does it signal a rebirth of xenophobia, fueled by illegal immigration, Islamic fundamentalism, and opportunistic politicians like Jean-Marie Le Pen of France, Jörg Haider of

Austria, and the late Pim Fortuyn of Holland? What do these events, and the ways in which governments and people respond to them, say about the emerging identity and politics of the European Union?

A growing literature explores these problems and how European public opinion and governments respond to them. Rather than engage these themes directly, the essays in this volume explore the context in which such issues play out and responses to them develop. Even the most cursory review of European policies about national identity, ethnic conflict, immigrants, and antidemocratic politicians and parties indicates the extent to which these issues are refracted through the lenses of the 1930s and World War II. These points of reference appear quite independent of the political views and policy preferences of those involved. To be sure, the widespread appeal to the history of this period is at least partly rhetorical and invoked to sell or justify policy preferences reached for other reasons. However, historical references have been so rife and taken for granted that it is not unreasonable to infer that understandings of the past have provided an important frame of reference for judging the meaning of these events and issues, and for formulating responses to them.

An understanding of the past not only helps us interpret the present; it tells us who we are. Shared experiences and memories, and the values and commitments they create and sustain, provide distinctive identities to individuals and communities.[4] Seminal works on nationalism by Hans Kohn, Carleton J. H. Hayes, and Karl W. Deutsch all maintain that a shared past, whether based on territory, language, religion, history, or some combination of these, is the foundation of nationality.[5] Deutsch defines a people as "a community of complementary habits of communication" and emphasizes the ways in which stylized representations of the past shared by a community create a "we feeling" among its members.[6] At least as far back as Herodotus, students of community have recognized the largely mythical nature of the founding sagas of communities and how these myths and later events have been woven into master narratives to "invent" a people and provide them with a distinctive and uplifting history.[7] Individual identity appears to be shaped by an analogous process; Ernst Kris and Erik Erikson contend that people construct narratives of their pasts to shape and justify their lives and their responses to contemporary challenges.[8]

Historians, political scientists, psychologists, and psychiatrists now recognize that collective and individual memories are social constructions. Both kinds of memory not only run on parallel tracks but also have a dense net of switches connecting them. Historians of collective memory have sought to map such systems in individual countries with regard to specific events (e.g., World Wars I and II and the Holocaust). Political scientists have analyzed the construction of national memory, and psychologists have studied some of the processes that mediate between national and individual memories. One of the most striking findings of this research is the extent to which individual memories are shaped through interactions with other people and reflect, and often reinforce, dominant discourses of society. Those discourses and their contents, in turn, are generally created by elites and counter-elites to justify themselves and to advance their political, economic, and social goals. It is at once a top-down and a bottom-up process. In both directions, and at every level, the construction of memory is infused by politics.

This volume explores the politics of memory in postwar Europe with several goals in mind. Our objective is to better understand the timing, nature, and evolution of debates about the roles that European states played in World War II, not only as an end in itself but in the context of a controlled, comparative analysis that allows more general observations about the process by which political memories emerge, are contested, and take root. Such comparative analysis also offers insight into the emergence and content of postwar national identities, which are based in part on shared constructions of the past. These questions are addressed in seven country case studies—France, Germany, Italy, Switzerland, Austria, Poland, and the Soviet Union-Russia—and a final chapter in which the findings of these country studies are then used to evaluate the longstanding debate in the humanities about the relationship between memory and history.

Memories and the policy lessons they generate or sustain shape our responses to the present. They also influence external perceptions of and responses to a nation, and accordingly have powerful implications that extend beyond national borders. One of the most remarkable and least expected features of postwar Europe has been the ability of former enemies to put aside their historical animosity to cooperate in a series of economic, military, political, and cultural projects. The success of these supranational projects has led to the forging of new identities that extend beyond traditional ethnic and national boundaries.

European cooperation was inspired by visionaries, motivated at the outset by a range of national and common interests, and energized and supported by a powerful third party, the United States. To take root, cooperation needed extensive backing beyond the narrow elites who brought these projects into being. Popular support was not merely the result, as some have suggested, of a positive feedback cycle in which the economic benefits of cooperation prompted further efforts at integration. Nor was it primarily the result of institutions that reshaped the interest calculations of actors, although this process was not insignificant. Leaders and the public alike made—and continue to make—judgments about the character, goals, and reliability of other national partners. Trust and empathy were critical components of these relationships, just as they are in interpersonal relations. Democratization was an important pillar of cross-national trust. So, too, were the judgments that leaders and publics made about how their putative partners had addressed their pasts. It is hard to imagine that Germany's neighbors would have bound their economies to a Germany in which the rule of law was threatened by authoritarian political movements, or one in which a leading party was committed to revanchist territorial goals, or even a Germany in which the political and intellectual elite refused to acknowledge the special burden placed on them by the crimes of the Nazi era. Facing up to history and democratization are closely related; several recent studies of postwar Germany argue that the former is an important requirement of the latter.[9] If so, the politics of memory, democratization, relations with neighbors, and European integration are all integrally connected and best analyzed as components of a larger interactive system.

This volume represents a multinational and multidisciplinary collaboration that brings together scholars from Austria, Germany, Italy, Poland, Switzerland, and the United States in the fields of critical and literary studies, history, sociology, political science, and psychology. To avoid producing a Tower of Babel, we developed a kind of common language and set of concepts. At the same time, we wanted to reap maximum benefit from our cultural and disciplinary diversity. Early on, we discovered two kinds of tensions that needed addressing: first, that between the national focus of case-study authors and the comparative perspective of the authors of the "bookend" chapters; second, that between disciplines, the important cleavage being less between individual fields of study than between humanists and social scientists.

Regardless of their discipline, all seven case-study authors are specialists in the history, politics, and culture of a particular country; their propensity was to describe the unique paths of their countries and account for them largely with reference to the idiosyncratic political and cultural attributes of the societies in question. The editors were certainly interested in describing the range of national diversity but also were committed to discovering what experiences and patterns might be more widely shared. We wanted our case-study authors to develop a "double vision" that would enable them both to describe and interpret national experiences as informed insiders and to use analytical categories that would facilitate comparisons across cases.

After struggling with the issue, we hit on Alexis de Tocqueville's *Democracy in America*—a single-country study whose questions derive from a comparative framework—as a model. Tocqueville's framework remained implicit but nevertheless provided a template that helped him distinguish the particular from the general, gave him latitude to explore the idiosyncratic in some detail, and allowed him to compose his analysis as an artful narrative. Inspired by Tocqueville, we drew up a list of research questions based on the premise that postwar elites sought to impose interpretations of their country's role in World War II that were self-justifying and supportive of their domestic- and foreign-policy goals. We recognized that the needs of self-justification and policy are not always consistent and may have posed difficult choices for some elites in some countries. Nor did we expect elite constructions to be consensual or unchallenged. Members of the governing elite may disagree among themselves, especially in cases where self-justification and more practical political and policy concerns tug in different directions. (President François Mitterrand's address of 12 September 1994, a self-exculpatory speech about his role in World War II that was televised to the French nation, offers a striking example of how long such efforts can continue and how divisive they can become even within leadership circles.)[10]

Counter-elites and diverse groups in society have different needs and interests, and are likely to construct the past in a manner that supports those interests. Depending on the nature of the regime and the broader political culture, proponents of contrasting conceptions of the past may engage in open conflict with each other and seek wider support for their own interpretations and agendas. We encouraged our case-study authors to identify and track such conflicts, their timing, the arenas in which they played out, how they evolved, the extent to which they were intra-elite or involved the clash of top-down and bottom-up perspectives, and to make informed judgments about the reasons behind the patterns they observed. In doing so, they observed the interaction between history and the politics of history, which in the end determine what history becomes and what becomes history.

The second tension, again, emerged between humanists and social scientists. Humanists value historical description as an end in its own right, and one that requires a different notion of conceptual sophistication than commonly employed in theory building. They embed arguments in a narrative structure, which is entwined with and grows out of the evidence that is presented. While none of the participating social scientists are of the neopositivist persuasion, they are nevertheless accustomed to framing problems in the form of hypotheses and propositions, and collecting and organizing data in a manner that facilitates evaluation. Both the humanists and social scientists among us worried that humanists who read this book would skim through the introduction and theoretical conclusion and concentrate on the case studies and the Claudio Fogu–Wulf Kansteiner chapter on the implications of those analyses for the study of collective memory. We were also concerned that all but the most dedicated social scientists might read the bookend, theoretical chapters and gloss over, even ignore, the "data" chapters unless they had a special interest in a particular country. After two rounds of workshops and revisions, we believe we have struck a balance that makes the case studies and comparative chapters entirely interdependent. We also have chosen to eschew in this introduction the standard format and language of neopositivist social science, advancing no propositions and avoiding terms like *independent and dependent variable*, *covariance*, or even *testing*. Instead, we have chosen to follow the tradition of Verstehen, an approach to social science that bridges more easily to the humanities. Thus, we have attempted to identify the dimensions and processes in terms of which the European politics of postwar memory might best be understood, and to show the relevance of these politics to democratization, relations between neighbors, the formation of collective identity, and the emergence of the European Union.

Toward these ends, we begin with a discussion of memory, as it is the cornerstone around which our intellectual edifice is built. We use *memory* in a double sense: to refer to what people remember—or more accurately, what they think they remember—and to describe efforts by individuals, groups, and states to foster or impose memory in the form of interpretations and commemorations of their country's wartime role and experiences. We then take up the range of roles that historians use to describe the experiences of different European countries between 1939 and 1945; these roles offer a benchmark against which to assess the role characterizations offered by participants in the postwar debates over World War II and its meaning. Of course, many role categories are possible: victor-loser and perpetrator-victim, for example, are but two of many continuums along which states might be arrayed. Any role definition inevitably collapses a multiplicity of diverse experiences and contradictory understandings into a single, simplified national categorization. In this essay we refer to both the range of competing understandings and dominant national ones, where they exist, in keeping with our focus on national states and the politics of their institutional memory. We describe four dimensions—they might also be conceived of as tensions—in terms of which any analysis of the politics of memory must be examined: (1) contrasting understandings of what event or time period is being represented or contested; (2) domestic and international inputs into the construction of memory and identity at all of these levels; (3) purpose and emergence, that is, the extent to which dominant discourses are the outcome of purposeful designs or the largely unintended, system-level consequences of interactions among a large number of agents; and (4) the national "languages" and cultures through which disputes about memory and identity are refracted. We end the chapter with some general observations about the relationship between war and the formation of national forms of memory and identity.

## Memory

Memory mediates between the present and the past. It lays the past to rest or keeps it alive; it binds communities together or keeps them from forming or tears them apart. We first needed a clear idea of what the word *memory* means. In the literature of memory, analysis occurs at three different levels: collective (the purview of sociological and cultural-historical inquiry), individual (the purview of psychologists and psychiatrists), and institutional (the purview of political scientists and historians). This section of the chapter provides an overview of these three conceptions, and explains why we will frame memory primarily, though by no means exclusively, at the institutional level.

*Collective memory* builds on the pioneering work of Maurice Halbwachs, a French sociologist and student of Durkheim. Halbwachs, like his mentor and in opposition to Bergson and Freud, held that individual memory was socially determined.[11] Durkheim and Halbwachs argued that memory was "created" through communications with other members of society and thus was a heavily stylized reflection of the dominant discourses of society. Collective memory, they contended, helped individuals to find meaning in their lives and to create bonds of solidarity with other people. Collective memory and its ritualization in turn formed the core of communities. Halbwachs, the Russian psychologist Lev Vygotsky, and the American psychologist F. C. Bartlett all emphasized the role of everyday communication in shaping memory and memory's consequent dependence on language, social discourses, and the relationships people have established.[12] Their works thus challenge the tradition in psychology of studying adult memory as an individual, context-free process.

Research lends increasing support to the framing of memory as a social phenomenon. On the neurological level, one's ability to store, recall, and reconfigure verbal and nonverbal stimuli is mediated by patterns learned from one's personal and cultural environments.[13] So, too, are the language and narratives that one uses to describe memory and make it plausible and significant to others. Memory adapts itself to the conventions of the age. In the process more general memories are typically simplified and condensed in their representation; their detail is reduced, with emphasis placed on those aspects that allow the memories to be assimilated to broader narrative schemes.[14] "Flashbulb memories" are a case in point: although reported in exquisite detail, people's recollections of what they were doing, for example, when they first received news of Pearl Harbor, the Kennedy assassination, or the fall of the Berlin Wall often prove to be inaccurate.[15] Why? Because flashbulb memories are not actually established at the time but only later when the significance of the event for society has been established.[16] Current events broadly affect the way in which people remember earlier events. Commemorations of past events lead people to make upward revisions in memories about the event or the individuals involved.[17] They appear to help people cognitively assimilate such events, which precludes the need to ruminate further about them. Conversely, when people talk less about an event, they remember it to a greater extent, dream about it more, and feel it more intensely.[18]

Collective memory is a useful but tantalizingly elusive concept because it is so difficult to apply with precision. This has not deterred historians from studying it at the family, professional, generational, ethnic, class, national, and regional levels. Scholarship on collective memory has tended to focus on catastrophes and their related traumas: slavery, Fascism, World War II, the Holocaust, and postwar genocides and human rights abuses.[19] Holocaust memory studies have become such a cottage industry that a burgeoning secondary literature of "anti-memory" and metacriticism has emerged.[20] Some critics of collective memory studies have suggested that emphasis on the subjective and socially constructed nature of memory encourages the belief that history itself is the product of unconscious selection biases and socially conditioned interpretation.[21] More sympathetic critics—among them, Claudio Fogu and Wulf Kansteiner—have raised methodological concerns, contending that the connections between collective and individual memory are poorly theorized, that collectivities may respond very differently than individuals to traumas and other life experiences, and that the important relationship between memory and identity has been largely neglected.[22]

The collective-memory approach is the only one of the three that attempts to bridge levels of analysis. Most studies of individual memory assume not only that people are more or less interchangeable but that their processing of memories and construction of life narratives is independent of culture, class, generation, and other social identifications or processes. Institutional memory recognizes interaction between institutional and individual memory, and frames it as a top-down process: elite constructions of memory shape the memories of groups and individuals. Many discussions of institutional memory treat this process as unproblematic. However, it is notoriously difficult to determine the actual effects of attempts to influence public opinion even in micro cases, as Kansteiner observes with respect to the German television series, *Holocaust*.[23] On a macro level these effects are even harder to assess. There is ample impressionistic evidence of success and failure, often within the same case, and lots of unsubstantiated speculation about the reasons for these alleged effects.

Communist rule in Eastern Europe offers a good illustration of several of these problems. Germans who grew up in East and West Germany have developed understandings of Germany's role in World War II and of the German past more generally that are strikingly different. (Public-opinion polls indicate that a significant percentage of East Germans believe that their country fought on the Soviet side in World War II!) East and West Germans also hold different historical memories, which some analysts suggest might explain greater hostility in the former East Germany toward Jews and immigrants.[24] The German case, and parallel developments in Eastern Europe as a whole, can be read as strong evidence for both the success and failure of institutional efforts at socialization. Extensive indoctrination in schools, by the media, and through commemorations and monuments failed to eradicate individual and group memories at odds with the official view. These alternate memories, and the proscribed interpretations of history they sustain, survived in the niches of the impoverished civil society.[25] Such memories were more readily sustained in Poland than in most of the rest of Eastern Europe because of the semi-independent role of the Catholic Church, but even in the absence of such institutions, nonconforming memories have survived and been reinforced when dissidents have exploited official discourses for their own ends. In the Soviet Union, for example, historians, social scientists, writers, and artists created works that superficially reproduced, even appeared to reaffirm, the official discourse and its associated interpretations, while actually subverting them in subtle ways.[26] Readers, viewers, and audiences became highly sophisticated in their ability to pick up these cues and to read, so to speak, between the lines. In the Soviet Union's last decade the practice of "double discourse" grew increasingly overt, with social scientists sometimes able to criticize openly existing assumptions or policies provided they began and ended their books and articles with appropriate genuflections to the Marxist canon.

At the other end of the spectrum lies *individual memory*, what individual people remember, or think they remember, about their pasts. Individual memories are richly documented in memoirs, autobiographies, and interviews, and are popularly held to be the only authentic kind of memories. We all tend to measure the accuracy of other accounts of the past, especially second-hand ones, against the benchmark of what we ourselves remember—with the bedrock belief that our memories are correct. This is a dubious assumption, as suggested by research on flashbulb memories, wherein an individual can recall in considerable detail his personal circumstances at the moment he received news of a shocking event.[27] Studies of flashbulb memories, witnesses at crime scenes, autobiographies, and laboratory experiments indicate that first-hand accounts are notoriously unreliable. The problem of recall aside, narratives of the past are not static but evolve and are subject to change with each retelling. Psychologists have discovered multiple "remembered selves," whose evocation depends on the nature of the trigger and the social milieu in which the person is situated at the time.[28]

Experience is a highly subjective representation of internal and external stimuli, and memory is an abstract recording and reordering of select experiences. Individual memory can misrepresent experience in three fundamental ways. First, an individual experiences only a subset of the stimuli to which he is subjected, remembers only a portion of those experiences, and retains a sharply declining fraction of memories over time. Second, memory is highly selective; there are distinct biases in what we remember or choose to remember. Third, the details of memory are often inaccurate and out of sequence. Studies suggest diverse psychological reasons for biased and inaccurate representation, and two theories of human need that address some of those reasons are germane to the process of relating individual memory to broader social and political processes. Psychologists find it useful to distinguish among *episodic memory* (recall of a past event), *autobiographical memory* (recall of an event that plays a significant role in a person's life), and *life narrative* (a series of autobiographical memories that serves as an important means of self-definition).[29] Extensive research on the subjective nature of all three kinds of memory has led some psychologists to question the utility, and even the epistemological status, of "original events." Derek Edwards and Jonathan Potter suggest that reality is not a stable phenomenon that can be used to validate memories but is instead established by memories. This postmodern approach to memory dovetails nicely with historical research on collective memory but remains highly controversial in the field.[30]

Much of Freudian psychoanalysis revolves around the problem of trauma, and its practitioners therefore tend to conceptualize the narratives that people construct about themselves as motivated in the first instance by their need to suppress recall of painful experiences. In support of this interpretation, psychoanalysts point to the seamless, stylized, and quasi-fictional nature of so many life narratives, to the propensity of such narratives to break down in the course of analysis, and to the emergence of alternative narratives once traumas have been confronted. Healthy people change their narratives as they mature and face new challenges. According to the influential psychoanalyst Ernst Kris, narratives evolve to help people shape and justify their responses to the challenges they meet. Since World War II was undeniably traumatic for millions of people, many of them still in the formative stages of their lives, psychoanalytic literature on trauma and memory might be of some use in understanding individual responses to the war, and perhaps collective ones as well.[31]

Drawing again on Freud, psychiatrists have approached the study of memory in terms of the assumption that people need to justify their lives to themselves. Erik Erikson contends that everyone goes through a life cycle.[32] Between the ages of twelve and nineteen, from adolescence to early adulthood, one works toward developing a single, integrated identity and personality. Erikson suggests that memories from these years are the most important, and overwhelming evidence indicates that people can recall more personal and political memories formed from the ages of twelve to nineteen than from any other period in their lives.[33] Beginning at about the age of twenty, one confronts the next challenge: developing close friendships and intimate relationships. Around the age of forty, one begins to look back at one's life to find meaning and validate one's life choices.[34] This may in part explain a widely documented phenomenon in which commemorations of dramatic and traumatic events appear in profusion approximately twenty-five years after they have occurred.[35] (Of course, those who have reached their forties also often have the wealth, political clout, and leisure to indulge in commemoration.)[36] In keeping with the need for self-validation, there is some evidence indicating that people rewrite their personal histories to make themselves more important actors or to justify their political and personal choices. People sometimes use counterfactuals to place themselves at the center of decisions in which they took no part, or to allege that they urged courses of action that (they contend in retrospect) would have been more successful than the courses of action actually adopted.[37]

*Institutional memory* describes efforts by political elites, their supporters, and their opponents to construct meanings of the past and propagate them more widely or impose them on other members of society. The modern incarnation of this process was exemplified in the French Revolution. Supporters considered it a defining moment for France and a worldwide opportunity to redefine the purpose of government such that it would enable human beings to realize their full potential—a revolution in the best sense of the word. Opponents portrayed it as a revolt against the best traditions of France that would lead to anarchy and dictatorship, and leave few, if any, enduring, positive results. At least until the Fifth Republic, the principal cleavage in France was between those who traced their lineage to the Revolution of 1789 and those who were united by their rejection of it and the Enlightenment. And, in a wider sense, the French Revolution remains a contested symbol of the Enlightenment among intellectuals in all countries.

The French Revolution and its aftermath offer a veritable laboratory of contestation, illustrating how groups with different political agendas use every means at their disposal to disseminate and empower their versions of the past and to limit the ability of their opponents to do the same. From 1870 onward, pro-Revolution political forces successfully used their control over education, public holidays, and official commemoration—the Vichy interregnum aside—to propagate their point of view. More recently, in heated debates regarding school curricula, many French schoolteachers opposed the teaching of world history on the grounds that it diminished the importance of the French Revolution (which suggests a certain insecurity among the seemingly dominant pro-Revolution forces).[38] Controversy over how to understand such events as the Vichy regime and the war in Algeria is even more intense, and not unrelated to older struggles, for instance, about the meaning of the French Revolution as Richard Golsan convincingly demonstrates.

The contestation of historical memory is visible and relatively easy to study in France because it is an open society—in contrast to the former Soviet Union, Castro's Cuba, or North Korea. In these and other authoritarian regimes, while quasi-public debates about the past often take place during leadership battles, the victors, once in power, almost invariably attempt to enforce their own self-serving interpretations of the past—as exemplified by Nikita Khrushchev's famous 1956 assault on Stalin and the "cult of personality." In George Orwell's *1984*, Big Brother and his propagandists—could Big Brother himself have been just another one of their fabrications?—frequently rewrote the past to make it consistent with Oceania's ever-shifting alliances. The hero of the novel is an isolated, free-thinking man who comes to realize that state pronouncements bear little, if any, relationship to the truth; he is ultimately discovered by the thought police and sent away for "reeducation." Although Orwell suggests that totalitarian regimes can successfully manipulate their citizens' understanding of the present and past, the history of self-styled Communist regimes indicates that mind control is far more difficult to achieve than he surmised.[39] Even in the absence of a functioning civil society, East Europeans, especially in Poland, where the church remained robust, kept alive alternative conceptions of history that fueled political opposition and ultimately emerged triumphant in 1989.[40] Early on in the Cold War, Czeslaw Miłosz described the concept of Ketman, wherein of necessity one protects one's true convictions by denying them in word and deed, and how it allowed East Europeans to develop inner lives rooted in dissident interpretations of history while outwardly complying with Communism.[41]

Ketman notwithstanding, a decade of post-Communist history in Eastern Europe suggests that Communist regimes did successfully indoctrinate several generations of their citizens with respect to certain key events—most notably, World War II and the Holocaust. From the Communist perspective, World War II was caused by monopoly capitalism, so East German workers could consider themselves victims, not perpetrators. Furthermore, by identifying Jews murdered in the East not as Jews but as citizens of their home countries, then toting up the war's victims by nationality, Communist regimes could argue that the Holocaust was a non-event, which freed East Europeans of any need to consider their share of responsibility for genocide.[42] The national case studies on Germany, Poland, and the Soviet Union-Russia indicate that such conspiracies of silence about Jewish victims continued well into the post-Communist era, but are now increasingly being confronted.

Despite its uncertainties, institutional memory remains the most appropriate analytical category for our study since we are interested in studying the *politics* of memory, which is played out in the first instance in the political arena. Whereas most psychological approaches to the study of memory, whether at the level of individual, group, or society, often do not take context into account, political explanations assume that context is the most important factor shaping the responses of societies, groups, and perhaps even individuals. In its most stringent formulation, political analysis begins with the Gramscian assumptions that discourses shape the way people think and express themselves and determine the boundaries of what is acceptable, and that leaders shape and control these discourses. Michel Foucault suggests that history be conceptualized as a series of archeological strata, each of which constitutes a different "discursive formation," or set of rules for thinking and speaking about the world. These strata have sharply defined boundaries, testifying to the "ruptures" that mark sudden shifts in political and social discourse.[43]

Contributors to this volume favor a weaker form of the political approach relaxing its two core assumptions: We accept the premise that, just like discourses, institutionalized forms of memory are important but not all-controlling and that leaders exercise only imperfect control over institutional memory. All contributors reject the notion that institutional memories— and the interpretations of the past they enable and sustain—are effective mental shackles, recognizing instead the capacity of the human imagination, given sufficient political and social incentive, to devise new ways of thinking and framing problems and to develop new languages to express them. Furthermore, public memories and the historical narratives they support, which were difficult to manipulate even in the age of print and *samizdat*, are presumably even more difficult to control in the age of the Internet.

The national case studies in this volume suggest that changes in discourse tend to be gradual, rather than marked by sharp breaks, as assumed by scholars such as Foucault. Multiple memorial discourses coexist at any given time, in various degrees of correspondence and conflict with one another, and there is diversity within as well as across discourses. Any one discourse, moreover, can sustain more than one understanding of the past such that even when hegemonic discourses prevail, as in the former Soviet Union, opponents may be able to gnaw at them from within. Following the weaker form of the political approach, the authors of our country studies have looked for conflicts about the degree to which institutionalized memories and their associated readings of history and commemorations of the past can serve as a means of identifying and tracking larger conflicts in society. The national case studies confirm that institutionalized memories are not all-determining and that their creators and proponents may become just as constrained by them as those on whom they are foisted. Such constraints operate at both the political and cognitive levels. In Germany the Christian Democratic Union (CDU), its Bavarian ally, the Christian Social Union (CSU), and the Social Democratic Party (SPD) all fostered a nationalist discourse to attract the votes of German expellees (*Vertriebenen*) from the east. The three parties refused to renounce Germany's claim to the lost territories, sponsoring maps that described the German Democratic Republic (DDR) as "central Germany" and used the prewar, or even pre-1914, borders in the east. Konrad Adenauer, first prime minister of the Federal Republic of Germany (FRG), also envisaged this nationalist discourse and its attendant commemorations and rituals as a means of integrating those expelled from former German territories into the still-fragile West German democratic order.

Subsequent generations of CDU politicians took the postwar nationalistic discourse at face value and were unable to find more productive ways of dealing with the DDR in the 1960s after the Berlin Wall went up or a decade later when the Cold War entered a new, less intense phase. Social Democrats Willy Brandt and Egon Bahr crafted Ostpolitik, an innovative and conciliatory strategy for normalizing relations with Eastern Europe, which their conservative opponents found difficult even to imagine. Those who could were initially reluctant to espouse policies at odds with the existing discourse for fear of the political price they would pay. In the Gorbachev era, the West German left became the victim of this discourse. Throughout the 1980s the political and cultural representatives of the German left, following the lead of Jürgen Habermas, espoused a postconventional identity based on the democratic principles of Western constitutions and devoid of any nationalistic elements. Having convinced themselves that West Germans largely embraced this formulation, left-wing politician and intellectuals were blindsided by the outpouring of nationalist and pro-unification sentiment following the breach of the Berlin Wall.


Roles and Identities

Role definitions are central pillars of identity, and identity and memory are mutually constitutive. Understandings of roles help shape identities, just as identities shape roles. A rationalist might assume that nations in the unquestioned role of victor would have the least need to remake their national identities in the aftermath of war, although they might celebrate and commemorate that victory in ways to reinforce or strengthen their identities. That same rationalist might further assume that nations in the role of loser would be likely to be governed by new regimes and that, whether put in power through the ballot box, revolution, or the bayonets of victors, such regimes would have strong political incentives to distance themselves from their predecessors to legitimize themselves in the eyes of their compatriots and neighbors. Losing nations would likely have to placate victors and neighbors to regain their trust, gain readmission into the international community, and avoid onerous obligations and restrictions.

The aftermaths of the Napoleonic Wars and World War I support these two propositions. After Napoleon's defeat, the Bourbons, restored to the throne by allied bayonets, made strenuous efforts to revitalize prerevolutionary values and conceptions of citizenship. Two of the victorious allies—Prussia and Austria-Hungary—had reluctantly introduced reforms to mobilize popular support for their war against France but, after winning the war, repudiated most of these reforms and endeavored to reaffirm and strengthen traditional identities and political arrangements. During and after World War I, all of the principal losers—Germany, Austria-Hungary, and the Ottoman and Russian Empires—lost their empires or significant territory, underwent regime changes, and struggled to create postwar identities. Under the leadership of Kemal Ataturk, Turkey made a reasonably successful transition from multi-ethnic empire to secular, national state. The Soviet Union attempted to substitute class identities for national ones (with somewhat less success) and to legitimize itself as the leader of proletarian internationalism. Newly created republics in Germany and Austria tried, unsuccessfully in the long run, to legitimize themselves and new understandings of the national community in the face of considerable domestic opposition from both extremes of the political spectrum.

The actors in all these struggles mobilized history as a weapon, and the interwar period witnessed intense and unresolved debates about who had been responsible for war and defeat and about what kinds of historical commemorations and symbols were acceptable (in Germany, for example, the new national flag was anathema to conservative nationalists). Historical controversy over responsibility for the outbreak of war—the *Kriegsschuldfrage*—was a central feature of international relations of the interwar period. At Versailles, the Allies justified reparations on the grounds of German responsibility for the war. The socialist government in Berlin, supported in this instance by conservatives, made the case for German innocence and embarked on the extensive (and very selectively edited) publication of diplomatic documents in support of its contention. The principal victors—France, Britain, and the United States—were under no such pressure to redefine themselves; they had only to defend their allegations of German responsibility and did so through publications from their own archives. Yet four years of costly war and the Great Depression a decade later exacerbated internal conflicts in victor nations, in France becoming sufficiently acute to call into question the primacy of national identities over class identities. Among the losers and victors alike, unresolved issues about the past and its representation became sources of deep internal division and a major contributing cause of World War II.

With regard to the two "rationalist" propositions—that victor nations tend to reinforce their existing national identities and that loser nations tend to struggle to redefine themselves in order to rehabilitate their international standing—World War II is more anomalous. Among the three principal European losers—Germany, Austria, and Italy—only Germany undertook anything approaching a soul-searching confrontation with its past, and that reckoning, as Wulf Kansteiner argues, began only after a decade of near denial.[44] Austria, in sharp contrast to Germany, still labors to come to terms with the consequences of World War I, as Heidemarie Uhl demonstrates. Japan, the other great loser of the war, appears to have sustained its official and unofficial policies of denial into the sixth postwar decade, as is evident in recent Japanese literature and pronouncements about the Nanjing Massacre, school texts, and "comfort women."[45] Of three principal victors, two—the United Kingdom and the United States—reveled in this role.[46]

The Soviet Union stood alone among the victors of World War II—and those of World War I and the Napoleonic Wars—in its efforts to use the lessons of the war to restructure its identity. This began during World War II when Communist officials urged the Soviet people to repel the German invasion in the name of Holy Mother Russia, a shift from Communism to nationalism as the basis for identity and sacrifice that, as Thomas Wolfe reports, was sustained throughout the war and the entire Soviet era. It survived Khrushchev's attack on Stalin and the cult of personality, the purge of Marshal Georgiy Zhukov and efforts to revitalize the Communist Party. If anything, emphasis on the war and the sacrifice it entailed was strengthened during the Brezhnev era to placate the military establishment and compensate for the failure of the Soviet economy to compete with the West. By the 1980s, the "Great Patriotic War" may have become the principal prop of legitimacy for the Soviet regime. However, its utility declined sharply as the wartime generation aged, retired, and died off.

World War II presents us with the phenomenon of countries with "in-between" roles. France, Italy, Austria, and Yugoslavia encapsulated multiple roles—loser, occupied country, collaborator, resistor, victor—some of them simultaneously. Occupation exacerbated class and ideological divisions as some groups in these countries collaborated actively with the Nazis, while others resisted in underground and partisan movements. In France the cleavage was primarily class-based. In Italy, while class was also important, it was somewhat blurred by ideologies that cut across class lines. In Yugoslavia loyalties were divided almost entirely along ethnic lines, although Tito's Serb-dominated Communist partisans claimed to act in the name of all Yugoslavs and Tito himself was a Croat. By virtue of their wartime division, all three countries might have been expected to have a more difficult time in coming to terms with the past and healing, or learning to live, with still-festering wounds. However, as Richard Golsan and Claudio Fogu suggest, this process was somewhat eased in France and Italy by the efforts of postwar politicians to wrap themselves in the mantle of the resistance. As many of their claims were questionable, it seems that something resembling a tacit conspiracy to tiptoe quietly around the past developed between major forces on the right and left. Only decades later did wartime issues became prominent, and in quite different contexts in both countries. Yugoslavia, too, managed to suspend reckoning with the past for many decades, but for different reasons. Tito's partisans, having emerged victorious from the Yugoslav civil war and the war against the Germans, found themselves in the difficult position of consolidating their rule while being on the front lines of the Cold War. Tito had strong incentives to downplay past differences, and his regime set about propagating the myth of multi-ethnic resistance to foreign invaders. After Tito's death in 1980, this myth was challenged more openly, and ethnic tensions therefore intensified. When the Cold War ended, ethnic divisions were exploited by former Communists seeking to legitimize themselves under the banner of nationalism, which quickly led to secession and a brutal civil war.

All occupied countries suffered terribly in wartime, but some of them, like Holland, Belgium, and Denmark, had had less problematic political histories. Like all occupied countries, they had local collaborators, some of whom went off to fight on the Eastern Front, and mixed track records with regard to protecting Jewish citizens and Jewish refugees who sought their protection. Both France and Italy, although invaded, were occupied for only part of the war. Poland, however, suffered the longest occupation of any European country. The German invasion of Poland on 1 September 1939 began World War II in Europe, and Poland was occupied for more than five years. For almost two of those years—from Soviet intervention in Poland on 17 Sep-

tember 1939 to the German invasion of the Soviet Union on 21 June 1941—
Soviet forces occupied the eastern third of Poland. The Red Army returned
in 1944, and for most Poles, its reentry constituted another occupation. Poles
consider their country the greatest victim of the war and are proud of the
roles they played, first as resistors against the German and Soviet invasions,
then as partisans or participants in the heroic but ultimately unsuccessful
Warsaw uprising that began in August 1944. Many Poles went into exile and,
as members of the British or Soviet forces, fought the Germans. But there
are darker aspects to Polish wartime history: a mixed record with regard
to its Jewish citizens (that continued well after 1945), internecine warfare
among partisan groups of different ethnic backgrounds, and ethnic cleansing of Ukrainians in disputed territories. History is written by the victor, and
postwar Polish history reflected the Soviet version of events. Any collective
and official reckoning with the past could therefore only begin in 1989, and
as Annamaria Orla-Bukowska argues, Polish willingness to face the complexity of the past is now under way and critical to the consolidation of
liberal democracy.

Then there were neutral countries. Like occupied countries, they accom-
modated themselves in quite different ways to the initial success of German
arms. Franco's Spain was deeply indebted to Fascist Italy and Nazi Germany
for military support during the Spanish Civil War, and was wooed by Hitler
after his conquest of France. Franco opted for neutrality, allowed his country to become a safe haven for Jews and other refugees, and moved closer to
the Allies as the tide of war shifted. Ireland and Sweden were neutral as well
and provided valuable commodities (agricultural produce and iron) to Britain and Germany, respectively. Switzerland was famously neutral in both
world wars and avoided occupation although it was surrounded by Germany, Italy, and Vichy and occupied France. In fact, as Regula Ludi shows,
the Swiss made neutrality a pillar of their national identity, and the dominant, but not unchallenged, view of Swiss wartime history was that neutrality allowed the country to avoid invasion and, via the Red Cross, to
alleviate suffering in occupied countries. In the last decade, controversy
about Switzerland's financial and economic relations with Nazi Germany,
response to Jews seeking refuge, and the postwar failure of its banks to safe-
guard and leave untouched funds deposited by Hitler's victims has garnered
headlines in Switzerland and abroad. Ludi analyzes this controversy, situates
it in Switzerland's ongoing internal debate about its wartime role, and exam-
ines its implications for Swiss democracy and relations with other countries.

Three preliminary conclusions emerge. First, contestations about historical memory revolve around definitions of wartime roles. The role descriptions offered by dominant elites in many countries in the early postwar period are often strikingly at odds with their depictions by historians.[47] The initial response of postwar elites everywhere was to portray their countries and citizens as victims; this was true even of Germany (East and West), the Soviet Union, and Italy, those countries generally held responsible for the war.[48] Countries with a record of collaboration, like France and Hungary, emphasized the role of their resistance movements. In France, Yugoslavia, Norway, and Poland, resistance became the principal frame of reference for wartime histories, commemoration, and public memory. Neutral countries stressed their work on behalf of victims and the constraints under which they operated. Meanwhile, everyone blamed the Germans for the Holocaust, the Germans blamed the Nazis, and the Nazis blamed Hitler.

Second, most countries and their intellectuals propagated narrowly self-serving interpretations and memories of their past. More than half a century has elapsed since the end of World War II, and almost every country has undergone some kind of wrenching public debate about its role(s) in that conflict and the atrocities for which its government or nationals were responsible. In some countries controversy surfaced early on; in others it took decades. The catalysts for such debates were diverse, as were the fora where they took place. In some countries external events, such as the Eichmann trial, stimulated national debate and introspection; in others, internal developments, such as controversial memoirs, television series, and court cases, were responsible. The ensuing debates varied in their intensity and in the extent to which they involved political and intellectual elites and caught the attention of the wider public. Intellectuals invariably spearheaded these debates, and even when they were not members of younger postwar generations, their support came overwhelmingly from the younger population. The incentive for change and reformulation of memory was bottom up in the sense that it originated with people who were for the most part far from the levers of political power. It was nevertheless largely intra-elite, as the professors, artists, journalists, playwrights, filmmakers, and students who instigated or supported efforts to revisit and rewrite history were educated, comparatively well-to-do, and well endowed with resources.

Third, beginning with the Napoleonic Wars but in intensifying degrees through the two world wars, all national-identity debates have been shaped by postwar concerns, have played into national politics in generally different ways, and have had varied and often unpredictable longer-term consequences.

## Dimensions

### *What Is the Past?*

This volume begins with the end of World War II on the assumption that most, if not all, participant nations and many neutral ones viewed the postwar period as the beginning of a new era, one, moreover, whose domestic and international stability depended on coming to terms with the past, or at least suppressing some of the acute conflicts to which it had given rise. That past, of course, means different things to different peoples and nations. For Germans, Italians, and Austrians, World War II was only the last and most horrifying stage of a troubling past. In Germany the relevant past comprised the twelve years of the Nazi era, from January 1933 to May 1945. To what extent had German history followed a special path (*Sonderweg*)? Was Nazism an extension of previous German developments or a radical departure from them? Debate also centered on Germany's responsibility for the war and the need to make moral and material amends (*Wiedergutmachung*). Italians in turn speak of the *ventennio nero*, the two decades of fascist rule from 1922 to 1943. Like the Germans, they differ among themselves about the extent to which Fascism was the natural outgrowth of earlier political, economic, social, and intellectual developments, or an aberration —an unfortunate "parenthesis," in the words of Benedetto Croce.

For many countries, the troubling part of the past was largely coterminous with the war. In Poland, the relevant past began with the German invasion of 1939, although it did not end with "liberation" by the Red Army in 1944–1945. France and Britain declared war in response but were not seriously militarily engaged until the German invasion of Denmark, Norway, Holland, Belgium, and France in the spring of 1940. With the exception of Britain, all these countries were occupied, along with most of Eastern Europe, the Balkans, and the western regions of the Soviet Union. Citizens in these lands had to accommodate their occupiers to some extent or to risk their lives in diverse forms of resistance. Most Jews had no choices, although a minority survived by fleeing, joining the resistance, going into hiding, or passing as Christians. In many occupied countries the war exacerbated existing political and ethnic divisions, all the more so when those divisions led opposing groups to make different choices about resistance and collaboration. This pattern was most evident in Yugoslavia where Croats and Serbs fought each other, the former in quasi-alliance with the Wehrmacht, the armed forces of Nazi Germany. In France many on the right supported the

Vichy regime, while the left became the backbone of the resistance. This conflict never escalated into a civil war, in part because the resistance also attracted many non-Communists while the Gaullist opposition in exile drew support from across the political spectrum. In Yugoslavia and France—and almost everywhere else to some degree—postwar governments and peoples had to find ways of leaving these conflicts behind. The construction of memory was an important tool toward this end; it was sometimes used to resolve or ease internal conflicts by openly confronting the past but was more often employed to sweep the past under the rug, where it remained ominously present but blessedly out of sight.

Although Austria belonged with Germany and Italy—and arguably, the Soviet Union—in the category of perpetrator, Austrians successfully portrayed themselves as an occupied country and victim of the Nazis. They did so with the complicity and assistance of the United States, which was keen to enlist Austrian support for its side of the Cold War. According to Heidemarie Uhl, the decisive historical event for postwar generations in Austria was not World War II but the collapse of the Austrian Empire in 1918. It is only recently that the order of priority is in the process of being reversed. Prewar history did not begin in 1939, 1933, or even 1922; of necessity, attempts to understand World War II and the events that led up to it must reach further back into the past. In Germany and Italy debates about their Nazi and fascist pasts problematized their respective periods of unification and ultimately led to unseating of triumphalist interpretations by more critical revisionist ones. Fogu observes that the Great War was absolutely central to how Europeans framed the problem of the past because it established a high degree of generational consciousness. "Generational-synchronic" identities not only competed with "historical-diachronic" ones, but they also encouraged successive generations—including postwar ones—to perceive "events" as historic and to organize them in epochs bounded by watersheds. History became increasingly generational, but this mode of constructing history freely crossed generational lines. Although the generational framework of history was most pronounced in Western Europe, generations were almost universally important in determining what made it on to the historical agenda and how it was understood.

The politics of memory functioned somewhat differently in the east. In Poland, as Orla-Bukowska reports, there is little evidence of "generational history" or of any sharp generational divides. The Polish experience is characterized by a certain unity across generations that derives from a common understanding of Poland and Poles as martyrs and from a related effort to understand Poland's experience in World War II as an extension of earlier partitions of Poland and unsuccessful rebellions to restore unity and independence. In the Soviet Union, Tom Wolfe argues, the sense of the past was shaped primarily by Marxist discourse, which conceived of time and its significance in different ways than it was constructed in other countries. Soviet discourse was also less tolerant of "blank spots," historical discontinuities and ambiguities, which significantly influenced understandings of the past, not only in the Soviet Union but also in post-Soviet Russia. This may explain, Wolfe suggests, why the Soviet Union, and later Russia, experienced no war-criminal trials, no "blockbuster" revisionist histories about the war, no television series or *Historikerstreit* that challenged conventional understandings and engaged the public in rethinking their country's wartime experiences and their relevance to contemporary politics.

*Domestic vs. International*

Because the politics of memory takes place primarily within countries, this volume structures itself around national case studies. Although each case is idiosyncratic, the politics of memory is shaped by political and psychological processes that to some extent transcend national and cultural boundaries. One national experience sheds light on another, and collectively, they illuminate the underlying processes.

Comparative studies are essential for a second, historically substantive reason. States are not hermetically sealed units but permeable to varying degrees to external developments. Kansteiner suggests that Germany's public engagement with the Holocaust was jump-started by the 1961 trial of Adolf Eichmann in Jerusalem. The American miniseries *Holocaust*, produced in 1978, and Claude Lanzmann's nine-and-a-half-hour documentary, *Shoah*, produced in 1985, played on movie and television screens across Europe, where they had profound effects. *Holocaust* was featured on Austrian state television in March 1979 and was accompanied by intensive media coverage of the "Final Solution" and Austria's role in bringing it about. For the first time, Uhl notes, "icons of destruction" lodged themselves in the Austrian consciousness and encouraged a series of cultural and political projects that had broad public appeal and encouraged more openness about the past. Orla-Bukowska attributes similar effects in Poland to the airing of the Lanzmann documentary.

Public opinion did not regard all outside influences as benign. Austrians reacted defensively, as Uhl describes, to revelations about President Kurt

Waldheim's activities during World War II. In Switzerland, according to Ludi, the debate about the Swiss role in World War II was already under way, prior to U.S. pressure on the country and its banks to conduct an honest accounting of the assets of depositors who had perished in the Holocaust. Outside pressure nevertheless intensified and influenced the course of that debate. Poland experienced something similar when Carmelite construction of a convent at Auschwitz in 1986 provoked protests from Israel and Jewish communities around the world and put the "Jewish Question," and, by extension, the complexities of Poland's wartime role, on the public agenda. Both Switzerland and Poland greeted foreign allegations and pressure with incomprehension and anger, in Switzerland because such charges clashed with the national self-image of being benign humanitarians who had used their wartime neutrality to help others, in Poland because being the target of accusations reinforced the Polish self-image of martyrdom—once again the world was ignoring their wounds and betraying them in the interests of others.

In a more diffuse but nevertheless significant way, international developments that had nothing to do with the politics of memory shaped the context of those politics throughout Europe. Most notably, the Cold War froze the possibility of bottom-up politics in the East and led Soviet-sponsored regimes to impose Soviet-dictated narratives of World War II. In East Germany the Cold War provided a convenient mechanism by which Germans, even those who were privately anti-Communist, could avoid their past. In Austria it had the same effect. Wrapped in the mantle of victimhood—a role definition propagated by Austrian leaders and encouraged by Washington as part of its Cold War political strategy—the Austrians had little incentive to engage in the kind of painful introspection that occurred across the border in the Federal Republic. Although Austria was the most extreme case, other Western countries likewise took advantage of the Cold War to shelve uncomfortable discussion of the past. The end of the Cold War and the collapse of the Soviet Union, by contrast, served as catalysts for a reconsideration of wartime issues, East and West. Even in Switzerland, Ludi reports, these events shattered the framework of national identity and made a reassessment of collective memory inescapable. So, too, has the desire of so many ex-Communist countries to join the European Union: membership rules required those countries to demonstrate their commitment to democracy and, in so doing, to become more open in confronting their respective pasts.

Influences external to a nation can be conceptualized as international, transnational, and cross-national. "International" describes the actions and interventions of other states, as in the several examples cited above. "Transnational" characterizes the efforts of nongovernmental organizations, organized religion, and professional groups like historians and political scientists. "Cross-national" describes more diffuse interactions, among them the conversations and experiences of citizens who travel abroad, exposure to interpretations of the past, and debates about the past conducted by foreign media—always significant among neighbors who share a common language and now increasingly common given the growth of English as the lingua franca of Europe.

*Purpose and Emergence*

The politics of memory describes a process that involves large numbers of actors, some of them private individuals, some government officials. These actors have access to a wide range of resources and mobilize them to achieve goals that may be discrete or quite diffuse. They act in a political and cultural setting where other influences, many of them unpredictable or unforeseen, help shape the consequences of their behavior and the ways in which debates evolve. Such a complex and open-ended process may produce short- and long-term outcomes at odds with the expectations of key actors, as happened when efforts in the FRG to foster a particular view of the past to win the support of German expellees established a cognitive framework that had profound and unanticipated implications for future policy toward the German Democratic Republic. In France, General de Gaulle's postliberation decision to remain silent about the role of Vichy and to nationalize the resistance likewise had unexpected outcomes, as Golsan describes. Because the Free French Forces were an insufficient political basis for a postwar regime, de Gaulle decided to promote a generous, collective vision of France's struggle for liberation—a politically expedient move, and one that abetted national recovery by encouraging French citizens to form a positive image of themselves. The myth of France's "national resistance" was reaffirmed in 1958 after de Gaulle's return to power and again in 1964, with the transfer of the resistance martyr Jean Moulin's ashes to the Panthéon. Given the myth's psychological and political utility, efforts to challenge it and reexamine the past appeared unpatriotic, and post-Gaullist forgetting took on a long life of its own. Choices open and foreclose other, future choices, or at least make some paths easier or more difficult to tread. In a world of open systems and imperfect information, it is never possible to do more than make educated guesses about the consequences of one's actions. The politics of memory is thus unpredictable and path-dependent.

*Language and Culture*

The construction of the past and contestation of those narratives are political processes that take place in a broader linguistic and cultural setting. That setting can make contestation more or less likely and determine the domains in which it occurs, the form it takes, and the kinds of people and groups who participate. In some countries—Germany and Italy, for example—the elite press both is widely read and gives serious and sustained coverage to historical debates, facilitating a sophisticated discussion of controversial issues beyond a narrow circle of intellectuals. Elite media can nevertheless engage in conspiracies of silence to keep questions out of the public eye, as it did for decades in France with regard to that country's wartime treatment of its Jewish residents and citizens. Or, as Fogu demonstrates, foreign media can propagate a falsely benign image of a people, as with its *brava gente* depiction of Italians, which effectively discouraged thorough investigation of the criminal and otherwise shady aspects of that country's past.

The Federal Republic has gone further than its neighbors in confronting its past for many reasons. One of them, Kansteiner suggests, is its long-standing cultural practice of using the past as a resource to frame thought about the present. This goes back at least as far as the late eighteenth century and early nineteenth, when German idealists and romantics (e.g., Hölderlin, Schelling, Hegel) sought to use their highly stylized understanding of ancient Greece as a model for contemporary ethics, aesthetics, and politics.[49] Debates about Wilhelminian Germany and Germany's "special path" of historical development were a critical component of political debates during the Weimar era. Postwar debate about the Nazi period and the Holocaust, as part of a continuing effort to come to terms with the past (Vergangenheitsbewältigung) continued this pattern. In Italy, by contrast, there was no equivalent tradition. Italian culture is characterized by the recurrent appropriation and transfiguration of long-standing metaphors, tropes, and discursive structures to frame discussion of the present. Italians, Fogu contends, are drawn to metaphors and respond to new challenges by transforming old vocabularies to reframe the past. Italian historical culture can be read as a succession of metaphors and discourses, encouraging epochal analogies rather than cross-epochal comparisons.

As these examples make clear, each country's language and culture is more than a setting in which contestations of the past take place; they are key to understanding the often idiosyncratic ways in which the past has been constructed and contested in their respective countries. At the same time, cultural forms are to some degree malleable; for example, as Uhl reports, critical journalism, never an Austrian tradition, nevertheless emerged in that country in the 1970s and contributed, along with increasing Austrian confidence in the national identity, to a new willingness to confront the past.

## Memory, Identity, War

Identity and memory, as they relate to each other and to contestations about national roles in World War II, are difficult to capture analytically because they reside at multiple levels. Individuals have multiple identities, some of which are collective (e.g., as members of families, professions, regions, nationalities, ethnic groups and religions); such social, professional, political, and cultural groups have identities in turn, making the representation of identity something like a set of Russian *matruska* dolls, where bigger dolls have smaller ones nested within them.

Memory is equally layered, residing at three levels, each of which interact with each other. The synergies and conflicts among levels of memory can be played out at both conscious and unconscious levels. Our project focuses primarily, though not exclusively, on institutional memory given the nature of the problem we are examining. We recognize, as do our authors, that this level of analysis offers at best an incomplete explanation for the politics of memory, and for this reason, the national case studies dip into collective and individual memories. Scholars must ultimately find more systematic ways of integrating studies of memory across levels of analysis and relating them to identities at these same levels; drawing on the findings of the national case studies, Fogu and Kansteiner critically examine existing approaches and offer a number of thoughtful suggestions in this regard.

Complexity and layering notwithstanding, the national case studies offer some provisional observations about the substantive relationship between memory and identity, and between both of them and the war in general. Perhaps the most important of these is what appears to be the primacy of identity. In many of the countries the need to build or sustain a national identity, for psychological as well as political reasons, has been a powerful drive. It has shaped and repressed memory, history, and their representations to suit its needs. Political authorities, often with the support of public opinion, have ignored, isolated, ridiculed, and even punished individuals or groups who have questioned key features of the national myth, voiced memories, raised memorials, or produced histories, exhibits, documentaries, plays, or novels that questioned representations of the past on which such myths were based. Only when people have begun to feel more secure about their national identities have they been willing to look more openly at their pasts and even to question the historical interpretations and other representations that sustain them.

A robust national identity is only one component of internal security, just as internal security is only one component of national security. The latter includes foreign security, which may find expression in bloc solidarity, as it did on both sides of the Cold War divide. As people feel less threatened by past and present enemies, domestic or foreign, they feel more secure in their own identity. In Western Europe perceptions of threat have diminished for numerous reasons, including the presence of U.S. military power, decades of unrivalled economic growth, and the "domestication" of West Germany in a Western Europe whose states and peoples are increasingly bound together by a dense network of political, economic, and cultural institutions. In the past two decades the end of the Cold War, German unification, the dissolution of the Soviet Union, the eastward expansion of democratic forms of government, and entry of most European countries into the North Atlantic Treaty Organization (NATO) and the European Union (EU) have further eased perceptions of threat. However, ethnic wars in the former Yugoslavia, illegal immigration, and the more recent threat of Islamic terrorism have given rise to new fears, and continuing ethnic conflicts in places like Spain and Northern Ireland sustain old ones. So identity and memory, which have done so much to shape the politics of postwar Europe, have been equally influenced by its politics.

This volume's sample of seven countries indicates that problematic identities have diverse causes. Italy and Germany are unusual in Western Europe because of their late unification. National identity preceded national unity, and to some degree remained distinct, perhaps even aloof from, identification with the state. In Italy the divide between national and state identities was due to the problematic nature of the Italian State under both Mussolini and the ever-shifting coalitions and short-lived governments that characterized the postwar republic. Many postwar Italians have been downright scornful of their national government and have sought refuge from it above and below: both by supporting the European project and by flaunting regional and local identities. The extent to which Italians identified as Italians was based on a benign image of a people made distinctive by their values and way of life. Fogu describes the unifying self-image of Italians as good people (brava gente) motivated by individual and collective desires to make a good impression (*fare bella figura*). Ceaselessly propagated by the media—and by Italy's liberators and many former victims of Fascism—this image became deeply embedded in Italian consciousness and memories. Not incidentally, it allowed Italians to distance themselves from and deny responsibility for the imperialism, anti-Semitism, and brutality of the Mussolini era.

Although the FRG was significantly larger in territory and population than the German Democratic Republic and claimed to be the successor state to the former Reich, it was still something of a rump state in competition for decades with its eastern counterpart. Both states claimed to be the true representative of the German people, with leaders of both political entities encouraging their citizenry to develop a state-based identity in addition to the preexisting national one. The national identities remained fragile, though, and authorities on both sides of the German border sought to buttress them through manipulation of the German past. After forty years of division, half of it as the hottest battleground of the Cold War, the terrain of memory came to resemble nothing less than a battlefield crisscrossed by deeply dug trenches and scarred by the detritus of unsuccessful offensives by the two sides. Not surprisingly, Germans, like Italians, became major supporters of European integration—with important differences. For Italians, integration was primarily strategic, designed in part to limit and circumvent the power of their national government. For Germans, the appeal was at least as much the identity it conferred; it enabled them to transcend, at least in part, their Germanness by building a new, shared identity with former enemies that would also make their identification as Germans more acceptable to themselves and their neighbors.

Austria was one of two rump states of a former empire, Hungary being the other. Unlike the two Germanys, there was little antagonism between the two states or peoples in the postwar period—in contrast to their intense conflict during the waning decades of the Austro-Hungarian Empire, the post World War I Austrian civil war, and in the period leading up to and after the *Anschluss*. For much of the Cold War, Austria was neutral and Hungary the most economically innovative member of the Council for Mutual Economic Cooperation (COMECON); they envisaged themselves as a bridge between East and West. Austrians were nevertheless more closely linked to Germany by language and culture (or, at least, to Bavarians), and most had welcomed unification with Germany in 1938. Postwar Austrians faced a triple challenge to their identity: division, the country being divided into U.S. and Soviet zones of occupation until 1955; the need to discover and define who they were in the absence of their former empire; and to do this while distancing themselves from Germany, past and present.[50] Like the Italians, many Austrians sought refuge in a benign cultural image, that of a happy, largely rural people distinguished by local costumes and customs. The bitter memories they dwelled on were not the Nazi years but the destruction of the "two hearts" of Vienna—the State Opera and St. Stefan's Cathedral—destroyed, respectively, by Allied bombs and the artillery of retreating ss units. Not surprisingly, Austrian reconstruction of the past played fast and loose with what many non-Austrians considered the "facts" of the case.

Initial efforts by Europeans to avoid addressing a past at once threatening and at odds with the general thrust of postwar identity construction led to the adoption of a range of common strategies; the most widespread of these was what we might call quarantine. This consisted of marking off the war, the fascist period, the era of collaboration, or whatever events were troubling as special epochs characterized as extraordinary, as diverging from the "normal" trajectory of the nation. This strategy was first embraced by conservative Germans but quickly adopted by French and Italians. Golsan describes how the years between 1940 and 1944 came to be considered "*les années noires*" (the Dark Years) and the Vichy regime an anomaly or aberration. In Austria the Nazi era was described as the "Nocturno," and all evildoing was blamed on Hitler and "his" Nazis. Austrians overlooked the warm welcome Hitler had received when he marched into Vienna and the ongoing support that Anschluss and the Nazi regime received from the Austrians until almost the bitter end.

A related strategy involved denial of any national responsibility for the Holocaust. This was widespread throughout Europe, with the FRG being the most important exception. Other exceptions were Denmark and Bulgaria, who could legitimately claim to have protected their Jewish communities, neutrals like Sweden and Spain, who took in Jews during and after the war, and Great Britain, which was never occupied. Despite official acknowledgment of responsibility for the Holocaust and acceptance of the need to pay reparations, the West German public did not begin to confront this part of their past until the late 1960s. In East Germany this never occurred. In France many of those responsible for the deportation of one-third of the country's Jews were protected by the highest authorities. In Austria the returning trickle of Jews was unwelcome, and the sight of Jews in newsreels, according to Uhl, provoked anti-Semitic outbursts in theaters, including cries of "gas them." Hostility to Jews was also marked in Poland, the site of the largest number of German death camps and, along with the Soviet Union, one of the two countries with the largest prewar Jewish populations. Jews were murdered in Poland after the war was over, and many more were expelled or hounded to leave, not only in the immediate postwar years but again in 1968. While this volume is about the politics of postwar memory, not about the Holocaust, one of the more interesting—and revealing—features about national debates is how the destruction of European Jewry is—or is not—addressed.

A third common strategy was to downplay collaboration and emphasize resistance, portraying the latter, when possible, as a national effort. In Italy, where national resistance became a national myth, this myth intersected nicely with Italian narratives of the Holocaust, which emphasized the role of Italian soldiers, guerrillas, and ordinary civilians in saving Jews. The Jewish communities in both countries, perhaps feeling vulnerable, more or less went along with this narrative. In Poland resistance was central to national identity, but the Warsaw Uprising of 1944 was neither officially commemorated nor featured in the educational curriculum while the Communists were in power; the 1943 Warsaw Ghetto Uprising, on the other hand, fared better because it concerned atrocities committed by the Germans. In Austria the resistance was emphasized in the early postwar years but was then shelved. In the Soviet Union, according to Wolfe, a more ambiguous and contentious narrative emerged about the role of soldiers and civilians caught behind enemy lines.

Change came about when governments and peoples felt secure enough to allow national myths to be challenged or more contentious discourses about the past to emerge. Although outside pressure sometimes served as a catalyst, its influence should not be overvalued. In the FRG, to be sure, international pressure was important at the outset, but at the time, West Germany was making the transition from occupied country to independent state. Kansteiner suggests that German willingness to accept responsibility for the Holocaust and pay reparations to Israel and individual survivors was also internally motivated; it was part of conscious strategy by the Adenauer government to gain legitimacy and support for the new West German State. In Austria and Poland outside pressure was fiercely resisted. Uhl and Orla-Bukowska recount the hostility provoked by U.S. censure of Austrian president Kurt Waldheim and by the ongoing criticism that Jews from many countries leveled against the Polish historical narrative, which portrayed Auschwitz as a site of Polish suffering while relegating Birkenau and Jewish extermination to the sidelines. As Ludi describes, similar hostility greeted U.S. pressure on Switzerland and its banks to do a fair accounting of the money deposited by Jews who were murdered during the war and to repay it with interest to surviving members of their families. Despite a hostile reaction throughout most of Switzerland, including the elite press, U.S. pressure was largely effective and led to agreements with the banks, in part, as Ludi suggests, because historians and the Swiss media had already begun to problematize the country's wartime role, including its less-than-welcoming response to Jews seeking refuge. This implies that international pressure may be most effective when it comes *after* national populations have already begun to look into some of the darker corners of their past.

Most of the national case studies in this volume suggest that change is related to demography. The wartime generation appears to have had a very different set of political and psychological needs than the generations that followed. Those needs more or less precluded any honest public discussion of national wartime roles and activities by a majority of the population. To be sure, some groups and individuals favored, even pushed for, such a debate, but they were marginalized, and sometimes even punished judicially. Subsequent generations confronted different sets of problems and, as Erikson suggests, used history as a resource to confront them. This often involved focusing on different aspects of the past and developing different interpretations about them. In Germany, where generational cohorts are an accepted category of analysis, scholars and journalists have long been struck by the shift in interest and understandings of the war associated with the generation of the 1960s, many of whom were the sons and daughters of veterans or had lost a parent in the war. Since they had no first-hand memories of the Nazi era and were the first beneficiaries of growing German affluence, the 1960s generation had strong incentives to rebel against their parents and the generational values and beliefs they shared. The 1960s witnessed a youth rebellion on many fronts, and attempts to foster a more honest discussion of the past were by no means the most dramatic. Such efforts held out the prospect of considerable hedonic gain. Not only was Germany's wartime role an issue on which their parents were vulnerable, but by publicly condemning and distancing themselves from the Nazi past, 1960s youth sought to gain widespread European acceptance for themselves and their country.

The crucible of war was a dominant cultural icon and prop for the Soviet regime through the 1960s. The Soviet historical narrative emphasized the suffering of the Soviet people and treated the war as part of the continuous revolutionary heritage that had begun in 1918. The former generated affect that could be translated into political support, and the latter provided a framework for establishing a common identity that transcended national differences. The centrality of the war experience weakened in subsequent decades, precipitously so in the late 1980s. Glasnost and downgrading of the war experience—natural bedfellows, so to speak—created space for other groups, including dissidents, to articulate new relationships to the past that helped them define who they were and justify their political agendas. Like Kansteiner, Wolfe distinguishes between the generation that experienced the war directly and those that came later. But in the Soviet Union, unlike in Germany, it was not the first postwar generation that was politically important. Members of the Soviet Union tended to take seriously the Communist Party's claims that the war was an integral part of the revolutionary legacy and that to understand it as such confirmed one's Soviet identity. The break came with the second postwar generation: those born after 1960 and coming of age in the late 1970s and 1980s. For them the war was "twice removed," and they perceived the wartime narratives propagated by their parents, grandparents, and the media as naïve and self-serving. In large numbers, they rejected the party's claim that victory validated its rule and the socialist system.

Almost across the board, films, plays, and television series were catalysts for revisiting the past, as exemplified by the influence of the documentary *Shoah* and the mini-series *Holocaust* in Germany, Austria, and Poland. In Austria Thomas Bernhard's controversial and widely publicized play, *Heldenplatz*, accomplished the same end. Performed in Vienna in 1988 on the fiftieth anniversary of the Anschluss, it depicted the humiliation of Jewish citizens in the streets of the city in the aftermath of the Nazi takeover and the amusement that provided for some of their neighbors. In Italy, beginning in the 1970s, a wave of now famous directors—Federico Fellini, Lina Wertmüller, Bernardo Bertolucci, and Pier Paolo Pasolini—introduced new layers of complexity in the representation of Fascism and suggested certain continuities between Fascism and postwar regimes. In the mid-1970s television began to address these themes and soon became the dominant medium for transforming Italian understandings of the past while using these understandings to problematize the present. In France *Le chagrin et la pitié* (The Sorrow and the Pity), which was completed in 1969 but not shown in France until April 1971, exposed the Gaullist myth (France united in its resistance) and offered an alternative narrative (France united in its cowardice). Beginning in the early 1980s a spate of films about the "Dark Years"

appeared, including *Shoah* (1985), *Au revoir les enfants* (1987), *Une aff∣*
*femmes* (1988), *Docteur Petiot* (1990), and *Hotel Terminus* (1993). Sup∣
mented by new critical histories, they had a significant impact on Frei∣
opinion.

In Western Europe films, plays and novels were commercial ventures,
independent of government control, which may be why they spearheaded
the challenge of national myths. In some countries this was still an uphill
battle: *The Sorrow and the Pity*, for example, played in the FRG, Switzerland, the Netherlands, and the United States before it could be released in
France, where negotiations with French television dragged on interminably
and constituted what the film's director, Marcel Ophuls, called "censorship
through inertia." Television and the mainstream press were even more cau-
tious, perhaps because the former is often owned or regulated by the government, and the latter, in some countries, mouthpieces for political parties. A
notable exception was Austrian state television's decision to show *Holocaust*
in 1979. In the eastern bloc, with the possible exception of Poland, where
*Holocaust* was shown on television, government-controlled media struggled
to maintain traditional myths and meanings of the war.

While the collapse of Communism was certainly a precondition for meaningful change in the east, regime change and the concomitant beginnings of
freedom of expression by no means led automatically to serious efforts to
rethink the past. Progress in this regard has been uneven. In almost every
country at least one political party has attempted to situate itself within the
national tradition and lay claim to be its truest representative. These parties
propagate narrow, nationalist readings of the past and strenuously oppose
more open discussions in the media and schools. But there are also bright
spots: in post-Soviet Russia, as Wolfe reports, the appeal of liberal reformers
derives at least in part from their *lack* of connection with any Soviet or
Russian past.

The signs of change—East and West—have much in common, with two
particularly distinguishing features: (1) attempts to incorporate "dark" periods of history, formerly blocked off and even repressed as anomalous, into
national history and consciousness; and (2) attempts to confront participation in the Holocaust and, more generally, the prewar, wartime, and postwar
treatment of Jews and other persecuted minorities in one's country. These
challenges are not the same, but they are connected, as recent developments
in France illustrate. In 1998 France's highest court handed down a controversial decision that for the first time acknowledged responsibility for the
crimes of Vichy. The judges made the French government responsible for

half the damages that Maurice Papon was ordered to pay the Jewish community, because he was acting in his capacity as a French official when he ordered the roundup of Jews in the Bordeaux region.[51] Papon was nevertheless released from prison in September 2002, when the court ruled that he was too old and ill to serve his sentence. These two streams of "nonhistory" are also coming together in the East. In May 2001 leaders of the Polish Catholic Church, led by Cardinal Jozef Glemp and one hundred bishops, recognized that Poles were not only victims but also perpetrators. In a well-publicized ceremony they apologized for Polish participation in the 1941 massacre of hundreds of Jews in a northeastern town of Jedwabne and for similar acts elsewhere in the country.

The politics of memory in postwar Europe has an obvious starting point (1945), some critical turning points (among them, 1968, 1979, 1991), but no endpoint. While there are undeniably distorted constructions of World War II and the events leading up to it that still need to be confronted, discredited, and replaced, there is no objective truth or reading of the past to take their place. Nor do the same aspects of the past have enduring relevance; they change as a function of contemporary problems and needs. For both reasons, the politics of memory will be a salient feature of the European landscape for many decades to come.

## Notes

1  Norimitsu Onishi, "Protests over History Texts," *New York Times*, 1 April 2005; Norimitsu Onishi, "In Japan's New Texts, Assertions of Rising Nationalism," *New York Times*, 17 April 2005; Joseph Kahn, "No Apology from China for Japan Protest," *New York Times*, 18 April 2005; Jim Young, "A Hundred Cell Phones Bloom," *New York Times*, 25 April 2005; Howard W. French and Joseph Kahn, "Thousands Rally in Shanghai, Attack Japanese Consulate," *New York Times*, 16 April 2005.

2  Joseph Kahn, "If 22 Million Protest at UN, Japan Won't," *New York Times*, 1 April 2005; Joseph Kahn, "Chinese Pushing and Supporting Japanese Protests," *New York Times*, 15 April 2005.

3  Steven Erlanger, "More Fallout from 1945," *New York Times*, 1 March 2002.

4  For some of the relevant anthropological literature, see Malinowski, "The Role of Myth in Life"; Sapir, "Language"; Basso, "Stalking with Stories"; Herdt, *Guardians of the Flutes*; Gross and Barnes, *Talk that Talk*.

5  Hayes, *Essays on Nationalism*; John, *Prophets and Peoples*; Deutsch, *Nationalism and Social Communication*.

6  Deutsch, *Nationalism and Social Communication*, 81.

7   See Herodotus, *The Histories*, on the founding myths of peoples of the ancient world; Freud, *Moses and Monotheism*; Anderson, *Imagined Communities*.

8   Erikson, *Childhood and Society*; Kris, *Selected Papers of Ernst Kris*.

9   Dubiel, *Niemand ist frei von der Geschichte*; Assmann and Frevert, *Geschichtsvergessenheit/Geschichtsversessenheit*; Marcuse, *Legacies of Dachau*; Moeller, "What Has Coming to Terms with the Past Meant?"

10   See Golsan, *Memory, the Holocaust, and French Justice*, especially his introduction.

11   See Halbwachs, *Les Cadres sociaux de la memoire*; Halbwachs *La Topographie legendaire des Evangiles en Terre Sainte*; Alexandre, *La Memoire collective*, a posthumous collection of Halbwachs's writings; and Hutton, *History as an Art of Memory*, 73–90, which offers a good discussion of Halbwachs work and his reception.

12   Vygotsky, *Mind in Society*; Bartlett, *Remembering*.

13   Schacter, *Searching for Memory*; Schacter, *The Cognitive Neuropsychology of False Memory*.

14   Allport and Postman, *Psychology of Rumor*; Bartlett, *Remembering*; Singer, *Repression and Dissociation*; Rubin, *Remembering Our Past*; Conway et al., *Theoretical Perspectives on Autobiographical Memory*; Conway, Gathercole, and Cornoldi, *Theories of Memory*.

15   Neisser, *Memory Observed*.

16   Bohannon and Symons, "Flashbulb Memories."

17   B. Schwartz, "The Social Context of Commemoration."

18   Wegner, *White Bears and Other Unwanted Thoughts*; Pennebaker and Harber, "A Social Stage Model of Collective Coping."

19   See, for example, Peitsch et al., *European Memories of the Second World War*; Deak et al., eds., *The Politics of Retribution in Europe*; Suedfeld, *Light From the Ashes*; Yoneyama, *Historical Traces*; Molasky, *The American Occupation of Japan and Okinawa*; Osagie, *The Armistad Revolt*; Berry and Berry, *Genocide in Rwanda*; Beckwith, *Charting Memory*; Bradley and Cahill, *Habsburg Peru*. For an introduction to the field of historical-memory studies, see Olick and Robbins, "Social Memory Studies." For a sympathetic critique, see Kansteiner, "Finding Meaning in Memory."

20   See, for example, Peter Novick, *The Holocaust in American Life*; Cole, *Selling the Holocaust*; Finkelstein, *The Holocaust Industry*; Bartov, *Mirrors of Destruction*; Diner, *Beyond the Conceivable*.

21   Burke, "History as Social Memory," 98; Lowenthal, *The Past Is a Foreign Country*, 214; and Megill, "History, Memory, Identity," 37–62.

22   An exception is J. Assmann, "Collective Memory and Cultural Identity" and *Das kulturelle Gedächtnis*. Assmann contrasts everyday communications, which are strongly influenced by contemporary memory of the events in question and have a life span of eighty to one hundred years, with cultural memory. The latter consist of the corpus of texts, images, and rituals specific to a society and whose stabilization—here historians play an important role—serves to maintain a society's self-image.

23  Kansteiner, *Finding Meaning in Memory*.

24  These comparisons are complicated by the existence of other key differences—most notably, economic—between the territories and populations of the former East and West

25  Lévesque, *The Enigma of 1989*; Thomas, *The Helsinki Effect*, chaps. 5–7, on how Helsinki and then Gorbachev created conditions under which civil society could be resurrected and mobilized for political purposes.

26  For evidence of how this worked in the Soviet bureaucracy and institutes, see Evangelista, *Unarmed Forces*; English, *Russia and the Idea of the West*.

27  Brown and Kulik, "Flashbulb Memories"; Bohannon and Symons, "Flashbulb Memories."

28  Neisser, "John Dean's Memory"; Spence, *Narrative Truth and Historical Truth*; R. T. White, "Recall of Autobiographical Events"; Polkinghorne, "Narrative and Self-Concept"; Neisser, *The Perceived Self*; Neisser and Fivush, *The Remembering Self*.

29  Robinson, "Sampling Autobiography"; Brewer, "What Is Autobiographical Memory?"; Neisser, "Self-Narratives"; Barclay, "Composing Protoselves through Improvisation."

30  Edwards and Potter, "The Chancellor's Memory"; Edwards, Potter, and Middleton, "Toward a Discursive Psychology of Remembering"; Gergen, "Mind, Text, and Society." For the critics who think this is throwing out the baby with the bathwater, see Baddeley, "Is Memory All Talk?"; Hyman, "Multiple Approaches to Remembering"; Neisser, "The Psychology of Memory and the Socio-Linguistics of Remembering."

31  Breuer and Freud, *Studies in Hysteria*; Kris, *Selected Papers of Ernst Kris*; Horowitz, *Stress Response Syndromes*; Silver, Boon, and Stones, "Searching for Meaning in Misfortune"; Pennebaker, "Confession, Inhibition and Disease."

32  Erikson, *Childhood and Society*.

33  Franklin and Holding, "Personal Memories at Different Ages"; Fitzgerald, "Vivid Memories and the Reminiscence Phenomenon"; Conway, *Autobiographical Memory*; Conway and Rubin, "The Structure of Autobiography Memory"; Rubin, Wetzler, and Nebes, "Autobiographical across the Lifespan"; Schuman and Scott, "Generations and Collective Memories."

34  Erikson, *Adulthood*.

35  Pennebaker and Banasik, "On the Creation and Maintenance of Collective Memories," on memories and commemorations of the King and Kennedy assassinations; Adams, "War Stories." The trauma hypothesis suggests that such delayed commemorations indicate that after twenty-five years people are prepared to confront an event in a way they were not previously.

36  Pennebaker and Banasik, "On the Creation and Maintenance of Collective Memories."

37  Portelli, "Uchronic Dreams."

38  Jacques Hymans, "What Counts as History and How Much Does History Count?"

39 Orwell, *Nineteen Eighty-four*.

40 Lévesque, *The Enigma of 1989*; Thomas, *The Helsinki Effect*.

41 Milosz, *The Captive Mind*.

42 Herf, *Divided Memory*, especially chap. 5.

43 Foucault, *The Archaeology of Knowledge*, 31–38, 126–31, 166–77.

44 On Germany's denial period, see Mitscherlich and Mitscherlich, *The Inability to Mourn*; Moeller, "War Stories"; Dubiel, *Niemand ist frei von der Geschichte*.

45 Hein and Selden, *Censoring History*; Saburo, *Japan's Past/Japan's Future*.

46 U.S. and U.K. commemorations of Victory in Europe Day and Victory in Japan Day are uncontroversial, and the film and publishing industries of both nations continue to produce a stream of movies and books about the war, few of which attempt to problematize anything other than personal experiences of combatants. As the political reaction to the Enola Gay exhibit at the National Aerospace Museum made very clear, the wartime generation and their political backers will tolerate no tampering with the official and flattering image of America's role as selfless liberator in World War II. One telling sign of the need to hold on to this image is the way in which American depictions of the war changed to accommodate the civil-rights movement. Sometime in the late 1960s, comic books that featured war stories introduced the historical anachronism of integrated World War II platoons. More recently, films and television documentaries have dealt more honestly with the problem of prejudice, showcasing the accomplishments—and struggles against prejudice—of Japanese American soldiers and African American aviators in the European theater of operations. The plight of noncombatant Japanese Americans in internment camps has also received considerable attention and a belated official apology from the U.S. government. All of this suggests that the commitment to civil rights trumps the otherwise still-powerful need to maintain a pristine image of America's role in World War II and that the ongoing reexamination of racial relations in wartime—as well as in the history of baseball and American music—has been and is being used to foster and strengthen that commitment.

47 An obvious exception is the Soviet Union and Marxist historians, in East and West, who portrayed it as a victim in support of the Soviet line that the capitalist states bore total responsibility for the war.

48 Mitscherlich and Mitscherlich, *The Inability to Mourn*; Moeller, "War Stories."

49 D. J. Schmidt, *On Germans and Other Greeks*.

50 In 1956 the first survey of Austrians about their identity revealed that 49 percent of Austrians considered themselves a distinct people, while 46 percent considered themselves Germans. See note 16 in Uhl's essay.

51 "France Responsible for Reparations," *New York Times*, 13 April 1998.

HEIDEMARIE UHL ✻

# From Victim Myth to Co-Responsibility Thesis

NAZI RULE, WORLD WAR II, AND THE HOLOCAUST

IN AUSTRIAN MEMORY

## The Theory of Victimization as the Foundational Narrative of the Second Republic

On 19 August 1945 the Memorial to the Fallen Soldiers of the Red Army raised by the Soviet occupation forces was unveiled at Vienna's Schwarzenbergplatz. The ceremony, just a few months after the end of World War II, offered representatives of the three founding parties of the Second Republic the opportunity to express their views on the years of National Socialist (Nazi) rule. Leopold Figl, who later became chancellor, explained that "the people of Austria have spent seven years languishing under Hitler's barbarity. For seven years the Austrian people was subjugated and suppressed; no free expression of opinion, no confession of an idea was possible, as people were forced into blind servitude by a reign of brutal terror and violence."[1]

Figl's speech exemplifies Austrian self-portrayal within the framework of the theory of victimization. This theory became the foundation for the interpretation of history incorporated into Austria's Declaration of Independence, adopted by representatives of the Socialist Party (SPÖ), the People's Party (ÖVP) and the Communist Party (KPÖ) on 27 April 1945. These parties formed the provisional government that announced the restoration of the Democratic Republic of Austria and the annulment of Nazi Germany's *Anschluss* (annexation) of Austria. "The Democratic Republic of Austria has been restored and is to be refurbished in the spirit of the constitution of 1920. The annexation forced upon the Austrian people in the year 1938 is henceforth declared null and void," they announced in articles 1 and 2 of the declaration. At the same time, regarding the question of Austrian co-responsibility for the Nazi regime, the declaration quoted verbatim from the Moscow Declaration of 30 October 1943, in which the Allied foreign ministers described Austria as "the first free country which fell victim to Hitler's aggression" and the March 1938 Anschluss as "forced upon the Austrian people, who were rendered helpless" by a "large-scale military intervention."[2]

The Declaration of Independence, however, also addressed the question of the military service of Austrians in the German Wehrmacht (armed forces). This was a point of some delicacy, as the so-called co-responsibility clause of the Moscow Declaration noted that "Austria shares some of the responsibility for its participation in the war on behalf of Hitler-Germany." The provisional government took pains to counter this accusation by referring to the "fact that the Nazi reign of Adolf Hitler's Third Reich led the Austrian people, who had been rendered powerless and were bereft of any free will, into a senseless and pointless war of conquest, which no Austrian ever wanted any part of."[3] It was through these passages in the Declaration of Independence that the so-called victim theory found its fundamental formulation, its first "antifascist" variant. According to the victim theory, Austria had been occupied by force in March of 1938, and the years from 1938 to 1945 counted as foreign rule. A patriotic Austrian resistance made itself felt, despite brutal suppression. The Austrian soldiers in Hitler's army were pressed into service "under duress, facing unprecedented terror," and were compelled to fight "on the other side" in the war.[4]

This interpretation permeated the political symbolism and the representation of the Nazi era in all areas of public life during the period immediately following the end of the war. It found one of its earliest expressions in the Austrian state's coat of arms, established on 1 May 1945: the eagle adopted from the First Republic was now furnished with chains burst asunder, "in memory of the reacquisition of Austrian independence and the restoration of statehood."[5]

The erection of memorials to the victims of the struggle for freedom, both in Vienna and in the provinces, was intended to strengthen the "victim" conception of history.[6] So was the federal government's 1946 publication of the *Red-White-Red Book* (*Rot-Weiß-Rotbuch*), which was intended to provide an argumentation strategy for the victim theory through "official source materials" and so to bolster Austria's "claim to the status and favorable treatment of a 'liberated state' within the terms of the Moscow declaration." The book placed special emphasis on the "resistance of the Austrian people against their Nazi oppressors," because international public opinion was still widely influenced by the "optical delusions and acoustic deceptions of Nazi propaganda."[7] This was a reference to widely reproduced pictures of the triumphant reception of the Wehrmacht in Vienna and, above all, to images of a rally at Vienna's Heldenplatz during which Adolf Hitler had proclaimed the "entry of my homeland into the German empire" before a jubilant sea of faces.[8]

And yet the *Red-White-Red Book* claimed that the Austrian resistance had had to "put up with far greater difficulties" than comparable movements. "It needs to be re-iterated over and over just how exceedingly aggravating the circumstance of the linguistic kinship between the occupants and the occupied really was. A further difficulty lay in . . . the thoroughness, with which, particularly in Austria, all leading positions of any kind, both in government and in the economy, were cleansed of all Austrian patriots and filled with Germans from the Reich."[9] A chapter entitled "Austrians and the War" explained that "the attitude of the Austrian population towards 'Hitler's War' was one of disapproval from the very outset, unless one held hopes for its end as sole possibility for deliverance from the Nazi yoke." In addition, it claimed, each Austrian participant in the war was able to confirm that "the treatment of Austrians in the German armed forces was an especially rough and discriminatory one, so that for most of them it was only allied captivity that finally marked the end of their sufferings."[10]

The interpretation of National Socialism as a foreign tyranny also lay at the base of the semi-official antifascist exhibition *Lest We Forget* held at the Viennese Artists' House in 1946.[11] Intended for the general public, the exhibition developed memorable images of the criminal character of the Nazi regime. "Fascism Is Death" read the motto on one wall display, where the ghost of German Fascism raised a threatening hand in a Hitler salute over icons of Austrian national identity (such as the destroyed St. Stefan's Cathedral and the Vienna Opera House). However, in such representations of Fascism and suppression, of resistance and deliverance, a new form of the victim theory was already beginning to insinuate itself, one which would become more important to the theory's semantics than the antifascist forms of expression. A series of charity stamps created for the exhibition by the painter Alfred Chmielowski offered variations on the motifs of crushing Fascism and of the resurgence of a free Austria. However, he also gave victim status a new connotation, a Catholic connotation, in the image of St. Stefan's Cathedral, burning and wearing a crown of thorns—emblematic of Catholic Austria as a victim of the Nazi regime.[12] It was not the antifascist resistance itself so much as the image of the burning cathedral that took hold as the symbol of victim status in the visual memory of the Second Republic. The extermination of Austrian Jews, on the other hand, found no reflection in the pictorial motifs of the stamp series. A section of the exhibition was, of course, devoted to the persecution of the Jews, but such acts were attributed to German or Prussian Fascism, as indeed were Nazi crimes generally. Fascism was interpreted as being "un-Austrian" in itself, standing in contradiction to the Austrian national character.[13]

In the Austrian narrative of the postwar era, emphasizing things Austrian —accepted today as a matter of course, at least from the perspective of a secure national identity—was at least as important as disavowing collusion with the crimes of National Socialism. However, it was the very lack of such national identity that had brought about the downfall of the First Republic, "The State that Nobody Wanted."[14] The questions of whether an Austrian nation even existed and what its characteristics might be were highly contentious issues in the first couple of postwar decades, given the prevalence of pan-Germanic attitudes.[15] In 1956 the first survey on Austrian national identity asked, "Are you personally of the opinion that we are a group of the German people, or are we an Austrian people of our own?" In response, 49 percent answered that the Austrians were a separate people, while 46 percent claimed membership in the German people.[16] Not until the 1960s did Austrian self-confidence reassert itself sufficiently to allow one to speak of a separate Austrian national identity.[17]

However, the Austrian "invention of a tradition" had abandoned anti-Fascism as an underlying motif of the Austrian national character by 1948– 1949, if not earlier. By that time, Communists had claimed the concept of anti-Fascism, a decisive change in that direction occurring as early as the first elections for the National Council in late autumn of 1945, when the conservative People's Party achieved an absolute majority and the Communist KPÖ, with about 5 percent of the vote, made a much poorer showing than expected. *The Book of Austria*, published in 1948 on a government initiative, compiled a set of clichés that later became part of the self-image of the Second Republic; these included the invocation of the cultural heritage of a once great nation and a predominantly rural and conservative idea of "the people," which was distinguished not by political or social structures but by traditional costumes and local customs. The Nazi era was consigned to history as an "Austrian Nocturno."[18] "Vienna's most bitter days" occurred not in 1938 but at the end of the war, when the "two hearts" of the city were destroyed: the Vienna Opera House, destroyed by allied bomber squadrons, and St. Stefan's Cathedral, set ablaze by the artillery fire of retreating ss units.[19]

The construction of the Austrian nation as a nation of culture, inhabited by an easygoing, friendly, happily singing, and peaceful people, was also designed to underpin the demand for the departure of the occupying powers. This is nowhere expressed more clearly than in the official propaganda film *1 April 2000*, a "utopian satire" (as official genre classification would have it) conceived in 1948 and completed in 1952. In the film, set in the year 2000, the Austrian government cancels the controlling agreement with the occupying powers and consequently has to answer for itself before an international tribunal meeting in Vienna for its "breach of the world peace." The government successfully refutes the accusations, however, by providing proof of *a thousand years* of peaceful history and by the powers of persuasion offered by a visit to a *Heurigen* (beer garden). Finally, in the ceremonial hall of the National Library, an agent of the tribunal comes across the Moscow declaration of 1943, providing irrefutable proof of Austrian innocence: "Austria has been unjustly accused, and its freedom was already guaranteed back then."[20]

## The Victim Thesis in the Politics of History during the First Postwar Decade

The propaganda film *1 April 2000* was primarily a foreign-policy ploy to accelerate the restitution of state sovereignty. But in Austria itself the politics of history had already shifted. The years 1947–1949 form a clear caesura in how Austria dealt with the Nazi past: while the immediate postwar years had been characterized by measures of denazification and criminal prosecution of Nazi crimes, the politics of integration with regard to former Nazis now came to the foreground.[21] The Lesser Incrimination Amnesty of 1947 amnestied some 90 percent of the 550,000 Austrians affected by de-Nazification and also reinstituted their right to vote.[22] From the 1949 elections onward, courting the (not insignificant) voting power of the *Ehemaligen* ("erstwhiles," or former Nazis) became a constant of the Second Republic's political culture.

With the escalation of the Cold War and the shift from anti-Fascism to anti-Communism, Austrian semantics of victimization began changing key a very short time after the war.[23] In the following years two variants of the victim myth developed. The first, with reasoning based on the precepts of constitutional law and the Declaration of Independence, interpreted the 1938–1945 occupation as a tyranny forced on the "Austrian people," a stance which dominated how Austria represented itself to the outside world. The second, aimed at the integration of society within Austria itself, extended victim status to all Austrian men and women—including those who had not been direct victims of the Nazi regime. Former Nazis themselves were categorized as "seduced" or "deceived" victims of "unfortunate times" who had been subjected to the further injustice of denazification. Parallel to this, the glorification of the antifascist liberation struggle, which had been used to legitimize the new Austria in the immediate aftermath of the war, was now defamed as Communist and thus unpatriotic.[24] In conjunction with their increasing detachment from the Communist KPÖ, the representatives of the ÖVP and SPÖ also withdrew from the Concentration Camp Association, which was a nonpartisan organization, though in the light of its People's Front strategy, it was Communist-dominated. ÖVP and SPÖ founded their own organizations, the ÖVP-Fellowship of the Victims of Political Persecution and the Federation of Socialist Freedom Fighters and Victims of Fascism.[25]

In turn, surviving Austrian Jews, although they contemplated a return to Austria, were confronted with largely unmitigated anti-Semitism. The renowned concentration-camp survivor and Nazi prosecutor Simon Wiesenthal recalled how Viennese cinema audiences reacted to a newsreel report on the arrival of Jewish emigrants from Shanghai: when "the commentator noted that these were 'Jews returning to Austria, to take part in rebuilding their homeland,' raucous laughter arose from the audience, along with the exhortation to 'Gas 'em!' "[26] The issues of reparation and the restitution of Jewish property could not be resolved; the Council of Ministers agreed to "let the matter drag on and on."[27] By contrast, the grief suffered by the general populace as a consequence of Allied military actions during the war—be it through bombings, or the "defense of the homeland" and the "fulfillment of one's duty" in the wartime military—was turned into an integrative conception of history, with which even former Nazi sympathizers could identify. This transference of victim status from the martyrs of the resistance and the subjects of racial persecution to the Austrian public at large found its symbols in the emotionally staged readmission to the "homeland" of the "returnees," the returning Austrian soldiers. Radio broadcasts reported on the arrival of prisoner-of-war transports and on the welcome speeches given by high-ranking politicians. The "homecomings" of the returning soldiers were continuously present in the visual and discursive repertoires of the postwar era, as "standardized martyr-images of ragged soldiers behind barbed-wire fences were beginning to out-distance the public visual representations of Nazi victims by 1947 at the latest." The men who had been in Soviet captivity were now presented as the "true" victims.[28]

No corresponding measures were taken for the return of the emigrants.

Viktor Matejka, Vienna's Communist city councilor for culture and public enlightenment, who motioned that "all of the highest authorities . . . should inform all our emigrants, at least theoretically, that they would again be cordially welcomed in their liberated home country," only managed to get himself shown what he called "the coldest shoulder of my life."[29]

At the same time, the Austrian federal government used the appeal for victim status on the basis of constitutional law as an argument against the presence of the occupying powers. If Austria, as laid down in the Moscow Declaration, had been occupied in 1938 and freed by the Allies in 1945, then why would the "Austrian people" continue to be unjustly denied its freedom? This reproach formed a constant drone underlying all political discourse during the period from 1945 to 1955, when Austria was divided into four zones of occupation and the inner city of Vienna was jointly controlled by the four victorious powers.[30] The metaphor "Four Guys in a Jeep" came to symbolize Austria's role in the Cold War—a bridge between the East and the West.

The concept that one foreign rule had been superseded by another (and the implied identification of the Nazi regime with the postwar occupiers) characterized political discourse starting at the end of the 1940s. When the Austrian State Treaty, which granted Austria its independence, was signed on 15 May 1955, Foreign Minister Figl spoke of "seventeen years of a long and thorny road of bondage" coming to an end.[31]

The contradictions between the reasoning put forward in the victimization thesis and historical reality are obvious, even flagrant. In particular, the victim theory disavows Austrians' widespread enthusiasm for "affiliation" with the German empire, the high proportion of Nazis in the Austrian population, and identification with wartime military service in the German armed forces. Taking recourse to the Moscow Declaration was merely a rationalization, as the decisions of that conference of foreign ministers were not intended to provide a framework for postwar reconstruction of Austria; the declaration was a (fairly ineffective) propaganda instrument, intended to strengthen any Austrian resistance.[32] Nevertheless, the claim to victim status on the basis of international law became the central strategy in the negotiations for the Austrian State Treaty, with particular emphasis placed on the "Austrians, but not Austria" argument, which claimed that, since there had been no state and no Austrian government, there could be no Austrian responsibility for the crimes of the Nazi regime.

The Austrian government raised an analogous argument with regard to the question of reparation payments. After the Jewish Claims Conference concluded its agreement with the Federal Republic of Germany, which had passed the Federal Restitution Act in 1953, it made similar demands on Austria. The government retreated to the position that Austria was not obligated under international law to make any payment for damages sustained, as it had been a country occupied by the Germans; the government also claimed that Austria carried no moral responsibility, since the crimes against Jews were committed by Germans. The Committee for Jewish Claims on Austria was told, "All the grief suffered by the Jews during this time was inflicted on them by the Germans and not by the Austrians; Austria was not to blame for any of these evil things, and where there is no guilt, there is also no obligation for reparations."[33] Only after international public opinion and the Allied Council pressured the government did it finally agree to a payment of damages—but without acknowledging any responsibility.[34]

Regarding Austria's participation in the war, the government maintained that Austrians, like inhabitants of other occupied areas, had been forced "to serve in the hateful war machine."[35] The Austrian government was not only able to prevail with this reasoning but even succeeded in having the co-responsibility clause thrown out in the last round of negotiations.[36]

With the signing of the Austrian State Treaty, Austria had finally become "free," as Foreign Minister Figl put it in his legendary speech. Figl's presentation of the signed contract from a Belvedere Palace balcony became one of the most widely reproduced images of the Austrian success story—in fact, according to recent surveys, it was the only significant identity-bequeathing event of the Second Republic.[37]

Although the "historical fiction" of having been the "first victim" lost its pragmatic justification once the Austrian State Treaty was signed, the official self-portrayal continued to be based on the victim myth, which successfully marked—until the Waldheim controversy—the largely unquestioned, positive image of Austria as an "Island of the Blessed."[38] (These words, widely attributed to Bruno Kreisky, were in fact used by Pope Paul VI to describe Austria on the occasion of his visit in 1967.) International attention concentrated on the German Federal Republic, which, as the successor state to the Third Reich, was liable for the consequences of the Nazi war and policies of destruction and thus had to provide proof of its democratic learning processes under the public's critical gaze.[39] Austria, by contrast, continued to present itself as an "occupied country," despite the high proportion of Austrian Nazis (some 688,000 people, or 8.2 percent of the total population, were members of the Nazi Party in 1942), the expulsion of about 130,000 Austrian Jews, the extermination of another 65,000 Jews, and the leading role Austrians played in the Nazi occupation- and terror-machine.[40] A whole lineup of native Austrians who helped organize the Final Solution were later perceived to be Germans instead, including Ernst Kaltenbrunner (second to Himmler in the ss command from 1943 onward), Adolf Eichmann, Odilo Globocnik (responsible for Operation Reinhard, which had 1.9 to 2.2 million Jewish victims), and Franz Stangl (commander of the Sobibor and Treblinka extermination camps).[41] The arrest and conviction of Adolf Eichmann in 1961 was a key event for the German process of coming to terms with the past and initiated the prosecutions of ss crimes before German courts (the Auschwitz trials), which were intently followed by the public.[42] By contrast, in Austria similar trials, wherein witnesses for the prosecution were frequently mocked, led to disgraceful acquittals.[43]

Nevertheless—even though or perhaps because its presentation of history had so little in common with the historical truth and the experiences of the majority of Austrians—the victim theory dominated the official handling of the Nazi era up to the 1980s. Unlike in Germany, where the Nazi period became "normatively internalized" as a negative-reference event, National Socialism became "externalized" in Austria as a phase of foreign rule standing outside Austrian history and for which Austria bore no responsibility.[44] The same applied to Austrian perceptions of World War II. In a standard history book, *History of Austria*, the authors Ernst Joseph Görlich and Felix Romanik observed, "The Second World War belongs to world history, but is not really part of any Austrian tradition. It was no Austrian war; Austria did not participate in it *as a state*."[45] However, this line of reasoning soon contradicts another, equally widespread perspective on the issue: "No such thing as a 'defense of the homeland' existed. The Austrian patriot would even have had to tell himself that only by defeating Hitler could he harbor any hopes for the restoration of the Austrian state. That this was not clearly understood at first by hundreds of thousands of Austrians is to be explained by the circumstances of the times and the massive Nazi propaganda, but it cannot change anything about the historical fact."[46]

From this and similar analyses, it appears that within Austria a conception of history had taken hold during the two postwar decades that contradicted the antifascist variant of the victim theory as it had been formulated in 1945.[47] The interpretation of the years from 1938 to 1945 as a time of tyranny, the positive view of the Austrian resistance, and the rejection of Hitler's war retained little relevance as historical reference points in the new Austria—the strategies of both major parties at election times involved wooing "the old and the new Nazis" and thus made necessary certain historical and political revisions. Critical voices were already beginning to warn of neo-Nazi activities and resurgent tendencies toward a "re-Nazification."[48]

Clearly, all that was left of the victim theory by the 1950s and 1960s was its capacity to elide from "Austrian history" the years from 1938 to 1945 and so to project blame and responsibility for Nazi crimes onto Germany. Thus, the emphasis on suppression and resistance, which had been essential for the antifascist variant of the victim theory, could also be avoided; touching on these sensitive issues might have stirred up the conflicts between advocates and opponents of the Nazi regime within Austrian society, conflicts that were by no means dormant.[49]

This screening-out process was most apparent in school textbooks, which asserted that Austrian history terminated with the "end of independent Austria" on 12 March 1938 ("on that day our country lost its freedom and independence").[50] The textbooks covered the years of World War II as German or international history. According to *Times, Peoples and Cultures*, a widely distributed history book issued in 1957 and intended for use in public schools, Austrian history resumed on 27 April 1945 or even in March of that year, when "Soviet troops from the east crossed the Austrian border."[51] (Note the paradox of referring to an Austrian border while claiming the nonexistence of an Austrian nation.) In effect, the "Collapse of Nazi Rule," as the book claimed in a heading above the first paragraph of the chapter "The Second Republic of Austria," led to the rise of "Chaos, Destitution and Horror as Consequences of the War." Not surprisingly, "soon all order dissolved. Grocery storage depots were plundered, people were robbed and murdered, the life of the individual counted for nothing anymore. This is how Austria experienced the horrendous end of the Total War."[52] The image of the year 1945 was not dominated by liberation from a criminal regime but by the suffering caused by Allied troops.

## Commemorating the Dead as an Antithesis to the Victim Theory

The arguments presented for the victim thesis describe only one aspect of Austria's policy on history: the official self-portrayal, particularly in foreign-policy presentations but also in schoolbooks and other semi-official publications. Yet a change of attitude about the "Austrian Nocturno" was noticeable in public discourse just a few years after the end of the war. The escalation of the Cold War, along with an increasingly relaxed relationship with the Western Allies, had an integrative effect inside Austria itself. Even former Nazis could sympathize with anti-Communism and the *Feindbild* (identification of the enemy) as applied to the Soviet Union. However, the most significant factor in reorienting discourse on history was the policy for reintegrating former Nazi sympathizers. The more the two major parties attended to their voting power, the more they distanced themselves from the resistance fighters and victims of Nazism—not least in their own ranks. A short time before his death, the socialist Josef Hindels related how prominent politicians were calling on concentration-camp survivors to "stop talking about the horrors of the concentration camps, because people do not wish to hear that sort of thing anymore."[53]

Concurrent with the wooing of former Nazis were discernible changes in policies on history, especially the history of the resistance movement on the one hand and Austrians' military service in the German armed forces on the other. The invocation of the Austrian struggle for freedom, which had served at the end of the war as the solemn legitimation of the new Austria supported by all elements of society, began within a few years to change into a politically labeled understanding of history on the domestic plane, which limited itself in essence to the organizations of resistance fighters, to parts of the Socialist Party, and particularly to the Communist KPÖ. These changes were most visible in the distribution of memorials: outside Vienna, establishing monuments to the resistance came to be politically risky, if not impossible to achieve. By the mid-1950s memorials to "victims of Fascism" were considered to be instruments of "Communist propaganda," as Gustav Canaval expatiated in 1954 in the *Salzburger Nachrichten* newspaper.[54] However, a broad movement for the establishment of monuments in memory of those who had served and died began around 1950. The new culture of commemoration was by no means accepted unquestioningly; it was seen quite clearly as a paradigm change in views of the Nazi era and simultaneously as antithetical to the victim theory's appraisal of the resistance. "From now on," as one newspaper editorial on the commemoration of the dead asserted in 1949, the soldiers who fell in World War II would "also occupy a place of honor in the memory of our people," and not just as victims of the war—"it is simply not true that all of those hundreds of thousands were lured to their deaths by some crafty system"—but "as heroes [who died] in the performance of their duties, and with courage."[55]

The war memorials raised during this phase must be viewed not just as commemorative tokens of respect for the fallen but also as a public commitment to the soldiers and hence as a sign of the rehabilitation of the surviving participants of the war as a political presence. From 1949–50 onward this category of memorial developed to some extent into the norm of collective commemoration, as during the 1950s almost every community set up a war memorial or expanded the existing memorial to the dead of World War I. The inspiration for this memorial movement came from the Kameradschaftsbund, a veterans' association, and its precursor organizations, in which participants of the two great wars joined forces and set themselves the task of "creating a positive image of the soldier of the Second World War."[56] The public support that greeted this concern became visible through the memorials; they served as an expression of the sentiment that "the homeland, by restoring and redesigning its war memorials, once again stands by its sons, who fell in the ultimate battle," as stated at the official dedication of the cenotaph in Graz in 1951.[57] The Kameradschaft associations welcomed the "about-face" in attitudes toward wartime service: "While in 1945 and after the soldier was slandered in every conceivable way, and the soldierly performance of duties was derided as a crime, while desertion and the murder of one's own comrades were praised as heroic deeds, now at last a healthy perspective is once again prevailing in Austria."[58]

Politicians of all parties during this phase—sometimes even for entirely tactical reasons, motivated by electioneering considerations—publicly advocated a full rehabilitation of the Wehrmacht soldiers. In public commemorations, consecrations of memorials, and other declarations, leading provincial politicians, as well as representatives of the federal government, paid their respects to the men who had died as soldiers. These men were "protecting our Fatherland in battle" and were prepared "to risk their lives in the fulfillment of their duty," as the provincial governor of Styria, Josef Krainer, explained at the unveiling of the *Memorial to the Dead, Admonition to the Living* at the state capital, Graz, in 1961.[59]

The local memorials to the war dead did not, therefore, function solely as places of mourning and commemoration for relatives and fellow-citizens, but rather set the tone for a deeply "patriotic" understanding of history. The war memorial, usually raised at a central location or in the vicinity of a church, is one of the most prominent public-space fillers in many parts of Austria, particularly in rural regions and small towns. The hegemonic position of the commemoration of those killed in action rests in particular on the support of practically all political and social powers (political parties, unions, schools) and specifically the Catholic (or Protestant) Church. The Catholic Church strove to win back former Nazis—which meant in turn that a culture of commemorating religiously motivated resistance was seen as a threat to this compromise. This is what confronted local initiatives for the rehabilitation of the conscientious objector Franz Jägerstätter, executed in

1943, when their efforts were rejected by the church at every level. Jägerstätter became known to the general public in Austria only through the investigative work of Gordon C. Zahn, first published in German in 1967.[60] As the *Linzer Kirchenblatt* (Linz Church Journal) observed: "Zahn marvels at the fact that church authorities were still hesitant even in 1946 to hold Jägerstätter up as *the* hero. Yet any such move would have offended the sensibilities of tens of thousands of POW's who were gradually returning home between 1945 and 1948; it also would very much have let them doubt the wisdom of their church."[61]

Given the denial of honorable remembrances of the victims of the Nazi regime, war memorials embody the dominance of a historical narrative that reduces Nazi rule solely to the timeframe of World War II (1939–1945, as the numerals inscribed on the war memorials indicate) and to the grief experienced at the "front" and back in the "homeland." Experiences that diverged from this consensus and thus called for other forms of commemoration were not readily given space, or were refused it outright, as happened in the 1950s and as amply proved by the difficulties surrounding numerous "belated" memorials raised since the 1980s; such belated memorials were raised to commemorate, for example, victims of the local resistance, a concentration-camp subsidiary in town, the expulsion of a town's Jewish population, or a death-march of Hungarian Jews during the final weeks of the war.

Opposition to the victim theory and support for the Nazi war policy, which to some extent determine the ideological context of Austria's culture of commemoration, are expressed clearly in the supraregional provincial memorials erected in honor of the war dead. The Borderland Honor Memorial, erected in 1963 at Riegersburg Castle in Styria, placed the military service of World War II in an "eternal struggle against the assault from the East," in which the soldiers had had "to give their lives for the preservation of Christian culture and the freedom of the West."[62] The Memorial to the Returnees, consecrated at the Ulrichsberg in Carinthia in 1959, was (until very recently) the site of remembrance celebrations attended by former members of the Weapons SS from all over Europe, who were addressed by high-ranking Austrian politicians such as the Carinthian provincial leader Jörg Haider. As the designation of this monument indicates, its purpose is not limited to commemorating the fallen soldiers but is also to open up a political stage for those who have "returned home." Fittingly enough, a manifesto character can also clearly be ascribed to "Legacy of the Returnees," an inscription at the base the Ulrichsberg cross: "Behold Fatherland, this is what we have brought back to you: our loyalty, our courage, our love, consecrated by the sacrifice of tens of thousands. It will have to mean much to you, today and for ever more."[63]

During these same years, monuments to the victims of the Holocaust— such as the monument at the Ebensee concentration-camp cemetery and the gravesite of Jewish concentration-camp prisoners at St. Florian—were destroyed or else purged of the no longer timely terminology of anti-Fascism.[64] Thus, for example, in 1955 the Tyrolean state government removed the commemorative plaque for the resistance fighter Franz Mair, which had been unveiled in May of 1946 at the Innsbruck Landhaus (provincial house of representatives) because its wording was said to cause offense. The original wording read: "After seven years of suppression the flag of Austria was hoisted again on this house.[65] On the 1st, 2nd and 3rd of May [1945] men of the Austrian resistance were at this site fighting for the freedom of Tyrol. In the struggle for the Landhaus Professor Franz Mair was killed." The new inscription described the event only in the vaguest of terms and, to top it off, proved almost illegible: "Before this house in May of 1945, Professor Dr. Franz Mair fell in the fight for the freedom of Tyrol." Government officials justified the removal of the plaque by claiming that German tourists had complained about the text; the Catholic newspaper *Volksboten*, however, conjectured that former Nazis had brought their influence to bear. The plaque had to be replaced again, following protests from the Catholic side; in the new text the word *suppression* was replaced by the term *bondage*.[66]

Since the beginning of the 1950s a contradictory understanding of history emerged and exfoliated into a doublespeak which would become characteristic of a specifically Austrian policy on history. To the outside world Austria presented itself as the first victim of the war and, pointing to the Austrian resistance, as an anti-Nazi state. Within Austria itself, however, moves to keep alive the memory of the resistance and, more specifically, of the crimes of the Nazi regime were marginalized or slandered as "Communist-inspired," as was evident in the marginalization of the memorial site at the former concentration camp in Mauthausen.[67] During the negotiations for the Austrian State Treaty, Austrian politicians demanded deletion of the complicity clause, with the understanding that Austrians had been forced, just like the inhabitants of other occupied territories, "to serve in the hateful war machine"; afterward, politicians honored, via war memorials, former Wehrmacht soldiers for their performance of wartime duties and their willingness to sacrifice their lives in defense of the homeland. If, however, the question of responsibility for the crimes of the Nazi regime came up—as when material compensation was demanded for Jewish victims of the Nazis—the official strategy was to withdraw by pointing to the legal constructions of the victim theory, whereby from March 1938 onward no Austrian state and no Austrian government had existed.

Such contradictions were reflected in the very different perceptions of Austria at home and abroad. The successful Hollywood epic on the fate of the emigrant von Trapp family, *The Sound of Music* (1965), both epitomized and popularized, especially in the Anglo-American world, an image of Austria in which patriotic sentiments were coupled with an anti-Nazi stance. In Austria itself the film was practically ignored; in Salzburg it was pulled after just three days.[68] The narrative and visual repertoire of the still-fragile "imagined community" of the Austrian nation preferred to orient itself along ostensibly apolitical, harmonious, and consensual images of present and past realities, images of the kind projected in the popular homeland films of the 1950s and in the Sissi films on the life of the Hapsburg empress Elisabeth (1955–1956), played by the sixteen-year-old Romy Schneider.[69]

## Transformations of the Victim Thesis in the 1960s and 1970s

By the 1960s, in the context of general social change, Austrian understanding and awareness of history also inevitably experienced a partial transformation. With the generation change, new models of politics emerged in both of the major parties, and dividing lines between political camps no longer held fast. *Modernization* and *democratization* became the buzzwords of a reform phase, which was characterized domestically by the end of the Grand Coalition, and by single-party majority governments, first the Conservatives (from 1966), and then the Socialists (from 1970, the "Kreisky era"). The increasing self-assurance of the Austrian sense of identity, the politicization of the academic youth, and the emergence of a new brand of critical journalism all contributed to a lasting change in the conditions framing Austrians' historical consciousness.[70]

These transformation processes reached high visibility when some of the traditional political precepts relating to Austria's recent history came to bear on the establishment of new commemorative sites, which led to a series of scandals. The first of these scandals, which gave rise to a media uproar on Austria's failure to "come to terms" with its own past, occurred in 1961. While the Eichmann trial of the same year aroused only a slight resonance in Austria, the play *Der Herr Karl* (Mr. Karl) triggered a storm of protest.[71] The title character, an obsequious conformist, established an archetype that is to this day synonymous with the average, opportunistic Austrian and his cynical attitudes after 1945. *Der Herr Karl*, written by Helmut Qualtinger and Carl Merz and broadcast on 15 November 1961 on Austrian state television, was a play for solo performer that brought on an unexpectedly furious defensive response. The eminent critic Hans Weigel, writing in the newspaper *Kronen-Zeitung*, commented, " 'Mr. Karl' just wanted to kick a certain type of person in the shin, and now a whole nation is yelling 'Ouch!' "[72] Merz and Qualtinger had committed an offense against a taboo of the postwar era: the "Commandment of Silence," a "silencing order" valid only for discourse that took place in the public sphere.[73] Everyday communications were not covered by this taboo, but they also followed the needs of defense and displacement of a society of perpetrators. If crimes and victims were mentioned, it was only in terms of the negative effects of the war on the local population—Allied bombings, war crimes of the Allies and the partisans, captivity in the Soviet Union, expulsion of the Sudeten Germans, and the lootings and rapes committed by the "Russians" in the first few weeks after the end of the war.[74]

By the mid-1960s, following the éclat of the Tara Borodajkewycz affair, a series of changes began to appear, even within the official discourse on remembrance. Borodajkewycz, a professor of modern history at Vienna's University of World Trade, had been in the habit of making pan-Germanic and anti-Semitic remarks in his lectures. Socialist students had protested these remarks for many years but had found little support, even within their own party. The scandal proper was touched off by an essay Borodajkewycz wrote for a supplement of *Das Parlament* (Parliament), a weekly journal published in Bonn and a semi-official organ of the FRG's Federal Center for Political Education. Borodajkewycz had been invited, on the occasion of the twenty-fifth anniversary of the start of World War II, to contribute an essay from the perspective of an Austrian historian. Some of his comments—such as "It is only a small part of the overall German disaster, that we German Austrians have lost the larger Fatherland for the second time within a single generation"—led to a parliamentary inquiry, motioned by several SPÖ members of the Austrian House of Representatives.

A televised press conference in March 1965 finally escalated the issue into a full-blown scandal. In the press conference Borodajkewycz prided himself, among other things, on having joined the Nazi Party voluntarily, and many of his students cheered him on with applause and laughter. His statements and the students' conduct resulted in demonstrations both for and against the professor (supporters shouted "Hurrah for Auschwitz!"); in the course of the demonstrations a convicted right-wing extremist killed Ernst Kirch-weger, who had been a Communist resistance fighter.[75] The resulting shock, caused by the first casualty of a political clash of opinions in the Second Republic, had a "cathartic effect" on Austrian society.[76] Kirchweger's funeral was interpreted as a declaration of an official Austrian anti-Nazi stance and as a clear denouncement of the *Ewiggestrigen* (followers of an evil regime, stuck forever in the past): 25,000 people took part in the funeral procession, which started out at the Heldenplatz and then went along Vienna's major artery, the Ringstrasse. With the exception of some ÖVP politicians—chief among them, the federal chancellor Josef Klaus—the entire federal govern-ment participated in this event, which was seen as "drawing Democratic Austria closer together."[77] Special attention was focused on the participation in the march of Franz Jonas, the Socialist candidate for the federal presi-dency. From 1949 to the time of the march, pandering to former National Socialists (now euphemistically called "Nationals," meaning adherents to a pan-Germanic nation) had been accepted as a promising election strategy; by participating in the march, however, Jonas unequivocally condemned Borodajkewycz's conduct. The ÖVP candidate, Alfons Gorbach, did not par-ticipate in the funeral procession but merely expressed regrets over the clash, without commenting on its cause. Jonas's subsequent election victory was seen as an indication that expressing one's belief in an independent Austria was no longer an act of political daring.[78]

This commitment to Austria was also confirmed in April 1965 on the twentieth anniversary of the Austrian Declaration of Independence, when a special space dedicated to the Austrian struggle for freedom was opened in the exterior gate tower of Vienna's Hofburg Palace—the first site devoted to the resistance to be officially dedicated by the Republic of Austria. Political declarations regarding this anniversary contained clear words against down-playing National Socialism, precipitated, in part, by the clash during the demonstrations for and against Borodajkewycz.[79] In his much-noted speech at the joint festive session of the National and Federal Councils in parlia-ment, National Council president Alfred Maleta (ÖVP) stated, "We will not allow anyone to set fire to the house we have built." Maleta confirmed his resolution to "integrate the former Nazis into the democratic community." But he added with unmistakable clarity, "We have pardoned individuals, but we do not share their conception of the history of the Nazi past."[80]

The remembrance room dedicated to the "victims of the struggle for Austria's freedom," as the inscription reads, is situated in the immediate vicinity of the heroes' monument of the corporative state, dedicated in 1934 to the military victims of World War I and re-dedicated after 1945 to include the fallen soldiers of World War II. In opening the new remembrance site, representatives of the spö and the övp confirmed a unanimous commitment to the resistance as the historical legitimation of the Second Republic and in so doing gave the political victims of the Nazi regime the same official recognition as fallen Wehrmacht soldiers for the first time. As a sign of the official Austrian stance, this memorial site marks the end of a phase during which the Austrian government, even at the federal level, formulated the conception of history primarily by obliging the former Nazis. It also represented a renewal of the consensus between the political elites of the two major parties—specifically, between associations of political-persecution victims affiliated to the parties, including the kpö—regarding the victim theory. The memorial at the Hofburg Palace was a visible sign of the fact that official Austria had at the national level come to an understanding of history that fully incorporated the liberation struggle. (At the provincial level, the tradition of commemorating solely the war dead continued to dominate the culture of remembrance.) At the same time, the two separate memorials— the remembrance room and the heroes' monument which also had separate memorial services at state ceremonies—became symbols of the divergent cultures of remembrance. They also symbolized the contradictory historical narratives which had emerged in the remembrances of the struggle for freedom on the one hand and the fallen Wehrmacht soldiers on the other; these narratives have continued—in many cases, to this day—to structure the public culture of commemoration.

In the 1970s a newly formulated victim theory consolidated itself as the operative conception of official Austria's history; the new formulation used the resistance movement as the historical reference point of the Second Republic, despite the prevalence of opinions which doubted the existence or at least the legitimacy of such a resistance. The publications of the veterans' associations made no secret of their stance on this issue; but the presence of the war memorials and the rituals commemorating the war dead ("honoring of the heroes") had already made the "fulfillment of one's duties" in the German armed forces seem the defining Austrian behavior during the Nazi era.

This transformation process manifested itself, for instance, in the establishment of a museum at the Mauthausen memorial compound. In 1964 the Council of Ministers approved the project, and on 3 May 1970, on the twenty-fifth anniversary of the camp's liberation, the museum at Mauthausen was opened by the recently elected federal chancellor, Bruno Kreisky; for a long time it was almost the only permanent exhibit on 'the history of National Socialism in Austria.[81]

The institutional crystallization point for the preservation of the memory of the Austrian struggle for freedom was the Documentation Archive of the Austrian Resistance, founded in 1963, on the twenty-fifth anniversary of the end of Austrian independence, by scholars interested in contemporary history and by a number of former resistance fighters.[82] In 1970, researchers at the archive started compiling a documentation on "Resistance and Persecution in Vienna, 1934–1945." It was hoped that the archive would close what many felt was a gap in historical research—not just relatives to the levels of investigation attained in other European countries and cities—and that it would provide "a basis for contemporary historical studies and civics education."[83] The topic held "a certain national significance," since the resistance to the Nazi reign of force "was not only a moral rehabilitation of Austria, but in view of the Moscow declaration of October 1943, in which the Allies had called upon Austria to make an independent contribution towards her own liberation, it also held eminent political value."[84] No less important was the intention to have "that fateful impression of Vienna, of a city welcoming the Nazi *Anschluss*, which was created in March of 1938 and which still has not been effaced, corrected by providing an abundance of authentic counter-evidence."[85] The authors of the documentation, however, also saw their work as a historico-political intervention aimed at "lifting the frequently disputed or minimized resistance . . . once and for all from the twilight of doubt and placing it on the solid ground of indisputable fact."[86]

In school textbooks, too, the resistance became the preferred topic about the years of Nazi rule, which were otherwise "excised" from Austrian history, although in the interest of a well-meaning political balance, textbooks pointed out that "representatives of all political camps" had supported this patriotic Austrian resistance movement.

The "Austrian resistance," therefore, was unable to gain recognition as a general reference point of an official interpretation of history until the 1970s—all the while being faced with the widespread historical distortions of the Ehemaligen, who had either minimized the resistance or else denied its legitimacy outright as a "betrayal of the Fatherland." From today's perspective the invocation of the Austrian resistance can be seen as an element of the victim theory and as thus designed to disguise the Austrian share in the perpetration of Nazi crimes, but in the 1970s "resistance" was a political battle cry—a call for a historical enlightenment that strove to install a new historical point of reference—against the prevailing conception of history perpetuated by the Ehemaligen. This was precisely the point, too, of emphasizing a resistance movement supported "by all the political camps." The fact that the burden of the resistance against the Nazi regime was essentially carried by the Communists alone was negated by the construction of an "all-Austrian resistance," as was the question of whether there was a specifically Austrian resistance at all—or whether it had instead been part of an overall anti-Nazi resistance.[87]

However, the Nazi era played only a subordinate role in the strategies the two major parties (SPÖ and ÖVP) used in the politics of history. The central question instead concerned the faults and the failures of the First Republic. At the start of the 1970s a historians' commission was brought in to "clear up" a backlog of controversial topics, such as the establishment of the dictatorship of the Corporative State through the Christian-Social Party, the precursor organization of the ÖVP, and the coincident suppression of the Social Democratic February Revolt of 1934. The Nazi era, by contrast, was interpreted in terms of a positive foundational narrative of the Second Republic, as a time of catharsis, during which the hostile political parties of the First Republic, subjected to the fate of joint persecution, buried the hatchet on the courtyards of the concentration camps, while at the same time a large part of the population, finding out what the "German" rulers were really like, discovered a sense of their Austrian national identity.

But even with the reorientation of the official conception of history that made the Austrian resistance a central focus of commemoration, the counternarratives of a widespread "everyday Fascism" remained largely untouched. This became apparent in a further historico-political scandal. In 1975 Simon Wiesenthal, head of the Jewish Documentation Center of the Association of Jewish Victims of the Nazi Regime and internationally known as the "Nazi hunter" whose organization had famously succeeded in tracking down Adolf Eichmann, publicly pointed out that the FPÖ chairman Friedrich Peter had been a member of the First SS Infantry Brigade—an infamous unit responsible for war crimes in the hinterland of the Eastern Front. This led to a smear campaign against Wiesenthal, with Federal Chancellor Bruno Kreisky siding with Peter and even insinuating that Wiesenthal had, among other things, been a Nazi collaborator. Peter refused to accept any blame for his actions and defended himself by arguing, "I merely fulfilled my duty."[88] The affair surrounding his war record did not at first "cause any serious damage" to Peter's career. But in 1983, when Peter, following the formation of an SPÖ-FPÖ coalition, strove to become third National Council president, an emphatic resistance formed. Thousands of signatories—

among them prominent scholars, artists, and politicians—placed personally paid-for newspaper advertisements expressing their opinion that "the choice of Friedrich Peter as Third President of the National Council or his admission into the Federal Government would be detrimental to Austria's standing in the world. It is a contradiction of the values which form the basis of the parliamentary republic."[89]

There is no clear answer as to how this fundamental reversal of opinion within Austrian society came about. One element, certainly, was the generation change: the educational socialization of postwar generations had taken place within the context of the victim thesis. Another element, whose impact should not be underestimated, was the miniseries *Holocaust*, presented on Austrian state television from 1 to 4 March 1979, which was accompanied by intense media coverage relating to the Nazi Final Solution. It was in connection with *Holocaust* that the question of "Austria's participation in the Final Solution" was publicly discussed for the very first time, while the repertoire of knowledge and images of the "civilization breakdown of Auschwitz" were widely communicated in newspaper serials, TV documentaries, and the like that examined the Final Solution.[90]

Following the media event of *Holocaust*, visual "icons of destruction" began to lodge themselves in public memory banks of the Nazi era.[91] Since the 1960s, these visual narratives had crystallized in historically and politically enlightened projects and in presentations of history intended to have a broad appeal (such as the popular television series by Hugo Portisch and Sepp Riff on the history of the Second Republic, *Austria II*, which attained "ratings like a murder mystery" in 1982).[92] The storyline of the TV program followed the new, critically reworked formulation of the victim theory, starting with the Anschluss, which was presented as a military occupation ("*Panzers* on Vienna's *Ringstrasse*").[93] The Heldenplatz photographs were barely in evidence now, and only in reference to Nazi propaganda, which was purported to have shown only Nazi sympathizers and none of the "opposition to Hitler," which had "already disappeared into prison beforehand."[94] Similarly sparse was the use of pictures of the pogromlike excesses perpetrated by Austrians against their Jewish fellow citizens—and when these pictures did appear, they were usually furnished with an "externalizing" context, the outrages they depicted being attributed to "the Nazis." In the 1967 *Illustrated History of Austria*, under the caption of "anti-Semitic activities of the Nazis," photos show youths wearing swastika-emblazoned armbands in the act of labeling Jewish businesses, but there are no photographs of the humiliation of Jewish citizens.[95] Identity-enhancing pictorial motifs, however, concentrated on the Austrian resistance: the "women and men of the resistance" had provided "their own contribution to the deliverance of Austria, as demanded by the Allies"—or so it was claimed in "Heading for the Abyss: Austria's Way 1918–1945," a pamphlet intended for use in schools and published in 1978.[96] The executions of the Wehrmacht officers Major Karl Biedermann, Captain Alfred Huth, and Lieutenant Rudolf Raschke during the final battles for Vienna in April 1945 found their way into schoolbooks, teaching materials, and accounts of history, as did "05," the coded symbol of the Austrian resistance engraved on St. Stephan's Cathedral. So did the Mauthausen concentration camp, which was now placed in the general context of the Austrian history of suffering. The conclusive image of Austrian suffering was formed chiefly by the photographs which the postwar consensus used in order to present Austria as a victim of the war: the destructive bombing raids, the blazing St. Stephan's Cathedral, desolate people rambling through a landscape of ruined buildings. Under the signal clause of a critical reinterpretation of the past, these pictures were integrated into an antifascist narrative, according to which Hitler's Germany—and not the Allied war effort—bore responsibility for this destruction. The final photographic sequence of the pamphlet "Heading for the Abyss," for example, featured three pictures of a destroyed Vienna, followed by the text: "Marking the end of Hitler's reign, millions of people were dead, cities and entire countries destroyed. Those who had survived faced a world in ruins—but also a new beginning, for which the end of National Socialism was the precondition."[97]

Within the framework of a newly rephrased victim theory—as a critical counternarrative to the widespread positive appraisals of the Nazi era in the discourse of "everyday Fascism"—and through the interjection of the TV series *Holocaust* into the Austrian awareness of history, those arguments and critical attitudes that opposed glossing over the Nazi past were strengthened and thus were able to fashion the background to the critical opposition in the Waldheim conflict.

## Change of Direction in 1986: Erosion of the Victim Thesis and Austria's Acknowledgment of Responsibility for Nazi Crimes

Integration-enhancing narratives regarding the innocence of one's own people and the projection of guilt onto Germany were not exclusive to Austria but a common phenomenon throughout postwar Europe. The erosion of these political myths since the 1980s marked the end of the postwar era.[98]

From Victim Myth to Co-Responsibility   61

The Austrian variant of this European process was exemplified in the Wald-heim case: not until the 1986 debate regarding the war record of Kurt Wald-heim, the ÖVP candidate for the federal presidency and a former general secretary of the United Nations, was Austria finally confronted with "its own" Nazi past.[99] Waldheim's remark on the performance of his duties—"I did nothing more during the war than did hundreds of thousands of other Austrians, which was to fulfill my duties as a soldier"—threw the contradic-tions of the Austrian conception of history into stark relief, in particular its central conundrum: how to judge Austrians' military service in the German Wehrmacht.[100] Since the 1986 turning point, the question of "Austrian mem-ory" and the highly selective "specifically Austrian way of remembering and forgetting" have featured prominently in Austria's political culture and con-tinue to be renegotiated in historical and political conflicts about a range of political issues.[101]

The explosive force of the Waldheim controversy and the affective charge of the debate rest on a number of different elements; unlike the "historians' dispute" blowing up in the *feuilletons* (cultural pages) of German news-papers during that same year, the highly incendiary question of what atti-tude Austrians took toward their wartime military service affected the back-ground and experiences of a substantial part of the population, and not just the so-called war generation alone but also their children and grand-children. In addition, the performative context of the debate—an election campaign—exacerbated the potential for conflict. A not-unimportant role might also have been played by the widely published photograph of Wald-heim wearing the uniform of a Wehrmacht officer at an airfield in the Balkans: it evoked images of the Holocaust, clearly lodged in people's con-sciousnesses through publications such as *Yellow Star*[102] or, more particu-larly, through the broadcast of *Holocaust*. German soldiers were no longer seen as unfortunate victims of Allied war actions (as in the pictures of soldiers at Stalingrad or the photographs of returning POWs); instead, they were seen as active perpetrators.

The Waldheim controversy split the country at the seams. The anti-Semitism which bubbled to the surface—Waldheim sympathizers assumed Jewish circles to have pulled the strings behind the "campaign"—as well as the justifications for Wehrmacht service that appeared in newspaper com-mentaries and letters to the editor caused the "Island of the Blessed" to be cast in the shadow of "Fascism." Austria was seen as a paradigmatic case of "forgetting" and "suppression" on the European landscape of remembrance.

And yet, since the shock of the Waldheim controversy, new ways of interpreting the Austrian past have come to bear. On the level of political discourse, statements by leading representatives of the republic suggest an erosion of the victim thesis in favor of a modified "co-responsibility thesis," which features a self-critical distancing from the manner in which Austria had previously dealt with the past. On 8 July 1991 the federal chancellor, Franz Vranitzky, speaking before the National Council, acknowledged "the share of responsibility for the suffering imposed on other people and peoples, not by Austria as a nation, but nonetheless by citizens of this country."[103] Similar statements were made during the state visits of the federal president and the federal chancellor to Israel.

Austrian admissions of the dark side of its own past proceed from the assumption that although the State of Austria may have been the "first victim," there were among Austrians both victims and perpetrators—in fact, "some of the worst thugs of the Nazi dictatorship," as President Thomas Klestil declared before the Knesset in 1994.[104] The acknowledgment of co-responsibility implies that National Socialism is a part of Austria's "own" history and that the Second Republic bears at least a moral responsibility for the Austrian share of Nazi crimes with regard to the extermination and expulsion of Austria's Jewish citizens.

This admission and the associated apology to the victims are the essential elements of the co-responsibility thesis, which has the support of a wide societal and political consensus. In 1993, during the first state visit of an Austrian federal chancellor to Israel, Vranitzky stated in effect that Austria bore collective responsibility for the crimes of National Socialism; that statement was received with approval, with 81 percent of those surveyed agreeing completely or partly and only 17 percent reacting negatively.[105]

In diametrical opposition to it stood (disregarding the extreme right wing) the FPÖ's perspective on history. This so-called Liberal Party, under the direct or, more recently, camouflaged chairmanship of Jörg Haider, has continued to cling—whether for reasons of political expediency or from biographically determined conviction—to an interpretation of the Nazi past that was first developed in the 1950s.[106] Its statements have been accordingly marked by a lack of distance with regard to Nazi propaganda and policies. During a session of the Carinthian provincial parliament in 1991, Haider praised the "proper job creation program" of the Nazi era. The Liberal Party has used anti-Semitic "allusions," lapsed into abusive language, and reinterpreted Nazi war policies as based on a resistance struggle fought by the Christian West or as a "defense of the homeland." Speaking to an assembly of World War II veterans at an Ulrichsberg remembrance celebration in Carinthia in 1990, Haider explained, "Your sacrifices will be seen in the right light within a few years because the overall development of this Europe of today will make it clear that the foundations for peace and liberty were laid out by you."[107] Five years later, at a get-together of former members of the Weapons ss in the Carinthian town of Krumpendorf, Haider expressed his appreciation for the loyalty and respectability of those present.[108]

However, after the change of direction in 1986, the transformation from externalizing to internalizing the Nazi period as the historical reference point of a "negative memory" was broadly completed, at least on the level of official memory. This new way of seeing also appeared in signs of the cultural memory. In November 1997 all of the political parties in parliament (including the FPÖ) sent a "clear sign" regarding the European Year against Racism and Xenophobia by designating May 5, the day when the Mauthausen concentration camp was liberated, as Remembrance Day for the victims of Nazi atrocities.[109] The establishment of the Holocaust Monument at Vienna's Judenplatz and other local initiatives for memorials to the victims of the Nazi regime, many of them dedicated specifically to the memory of Jewish victims, as well as activities such as the rebuilding of the Graz Synagogue, show that the Co-Responsibility Thesis has not been limited to official Austria or to Vienna but has also become capable of achieving a political majority in smaller communities.[110]

Acknowledgment of co-responsibility for the crimes of the Nazi regime was also a necessary condition for material compensation, as were transnational debates on how to deal with the "guilt of nations" and Austria's accession to the European Union: "a forceful Vergangenheitsbewältigung may well be part of the hidden agenda of the *acquis communitaire* and Europe's new value system."[111] In 1995, on the occasion of the fiftieth anniversary of the Second Republic, the National Fund of the Republic of Austria for Victims of National Socialism was established. In connection with demands for the restitution of property confiscated from Jews—and in particular with the "art-robbery debate" triggered in January 1998 by the confiscation of two Egon Schiele paintings from an exhibition in the Museum of Modern Art in New York—the Historians' Commission was formed in autumn 1998 and charged with conducting research into the entire complex of enforced alienation of property on the territory of the Republic of Austria during the Nazi period and any compensation paid by the Republic of Austria since 1945.

The new conception of history also changed how the events of March 1938 were interpreted: if the victim thesis was a "historical lie," then how was the Anschluss to be judged?[112] From this perspective, the photographs of jubilant throngs celebrating the Anschluss at Vienna's Heldenplatz and of the pogromlike riots against the Jewish population of Vienna directly after the invasion of the German troops do indeed turn into visual testimonies against the victim myth, just as they provide evidence of an Austrian "society of perpetrators." In the visual narrative based on critical analysis of the Nazi past, as is now being established in historiographical works and in textbooks, the pogrom following the Anschluss has been moved to the center of the picture. The humiliation of Jewish Viennese is now seen as the specifically Austrian contribution to the Nazi politics of annihilation; these events came to symbolize the guilty entanglement of the entire Austrian nation in the expulsion and extinction of the Jewish population.

The cheering at Heldenplatz and the Anschluss pogrom dominate the pictorial memory of the Anschluss today; they also form the central focus of artistic attempts to come to grips with the Austrian Nazi past. Thomas Bernhard's controversial play *Heldenplatz* was performed at the Burg theater in the autumn of 1988, the fiftieth anniversary and commemorative year of the Anschluss, but the rioting that had been feared due to polemics in the media failed to materialize. The most powerful sense of indignation has been triggered by images of the humiliation of Jewish citizens in the streets of Vienna, a motif that has been seized on in many forms of artistic expression—Maria Lassnig's painting *1938*, for example, or the "Jew scrubbing the streets," the controversial central detail of the *Monument against War and Fascism* by Alfred Hrdlicka, a large-scale memorial project at Albertinaplatz in the city center of Vienna, which expressed a new "politics of commemoration."

This new historical narrative did not experience any fundamental change through the political upheaval of the year 2000. However, with the formation of a coalition government by the övp and the fpö, the question of how to handle the past did acquire a new relevance: the fpö's policy on history was explicitly the opposite of the victim-centered policy of commemoration that had developed since the 1980s. The question of 2000 was "Are we all Nazis?"[113] In view of the election victory of Haider's fpö, which had emerged from the National Council elections of 1999 with about 27 percent of the vote (making it the second most powerful political party), this question was not only discussed in the local media but was also what the European and international public wanted an answer to.

Concern over the consequences of government participation by the fpö, a "populist right-wing party with radical elements," was also present in the preamble to the government's inaugural declaration (demanded by President Thomas Klestil), which presented Austria's self-critical discourse on remembrance as one of the foundations of its canon of democratic political values.[114] Austria's responsibility "for the light and dark sides of its past and the actions of all Austrians, whether good or evil" was written into it, as was the commitment of the federal government "towards a critical reconciliation with the Nazi past."[115] Austria's international reputation as a "Naziland" required urgent measures on historical policy to avert what was turning into a national political disaster. It was all the more astounding, therefore, that in November 2000 Federal Chancellor Wolfgang Schüssel explained to the *Jerusalem Post* that "the sovereign Austrian state" had not only "been the first victim of the Nazi regime," but also that "the Austrians themselves . . . had been its first victims."[116]

Given international criticism of Austria, negotiations for material reparations became a priority for the new government. The institution of the Reconciliation Fund for the compensation of Nazi forced labor in 2000 and the successful conclusion of an agreement on the restitution of so-called Aryanized assets in 2001 were also representative of the new government's historical policy: it was not the Social Democrat–led governments, in office since the 1970s, but the controversial ÖVP-FPÖ coalition that finally succeeded in resolving the prior failures of the politics of restitution.[117]

The form of the official Austrian remembrance, as expressed in the rituals and symbols of commemoration, did not change much with the arrival of the *Wende* (turning point) coalition of the ÖVP and the FPÖ despite the government's efforts to strengthen a patriotic Austrian commemorative culture.[118] Anniversary Day on 5 May continues to be celebrated with a solemn commemorative session in parliament, though it is barely noticed by the public.

But a new set of controversies have gained some purchase on Austrian memory. In connection with the debates around the Wehrmacht Exhibition, which was shown in revised shape in spring 2002 in Vienna, the 8th of May— which, though it marked the end of World War II, had previously played hardly any role in Austrian historical culture—became the starting point for a series of conflicts on whether the end of the war was a "liberation" or a "defeat."[119]

The developments in historical policy since the political "turning point" in Austria indicated the fact that negotiations regarding the interpretation of the Nazi past have by no means come to an end but are carried out in ever-changing configurations. Since the demarcation of the fault-line toward the end of the 1980s, a departure from the victim myth and a commitment to the co-responsibility thesis have largely prevailed in the historical policies of official Austria, while in discourse among the public and in the media, new perspectives on the society of perpetrators have replaced the image of the first victims. Through a new "culture of remembrance" Austria has positioned itself in the mainstream of European (indeed, international) commemorative culture, which is defined by a changeover from the postwar political myths toward an alignment with a global culture of commemoration of the Holocaust.[120] At the same time, this new Austrian remembrance continues to be challenged by "counter-memories" of the Nazi era, which remain effective past the generational threshold.

But perhaps a long-term reorientation of Austrian memory will not, in fact, have its beginnings in the current conflicts in historical policy, which have turned memories of the Nazi past into a battlefield between political groups and between the generations, but rather in the memory of local "perpetrator history" being overwritten by a positive, patriotic jubilee historiography: in connection with the 2005 celebrations for the fiftieth jubilee of the Austrian State Treaty, for the first time since the change of direction in 1986 the history of the Second Republic will again be told, throughout the media, as a success story.

*Translated by Tom Appleton and Eli Lebow*

Notes

1  Cited in "Mahnmal unerbittlicher Gerechtigkeit," *Das Kleine Volksblatt*, 21 August 1945.

2  "Proclamation of 27 April 1945," *Staatsgesetzblatt für die Republik Österreich*, 1 May 1945.

3  Ibid. Regarding the wording of the victim theory in the Declaration of Independence, see Bischof, "'Opfer' Österreich?"

4  Leopold Figl, cited in "Mahnmal unerbittlicher Gerechtigkeit," *Das Kleine Volksblatt*, 21 August 1945.

5  "Gesetz von 1. Mai 1945 über Woppen, Farben, Siegel und Embleme der Republik Österreich," *Staatsgesetzblatt für die Republik Österreich*, 1 May 1945, 13. See also Spann, "Staatswappen und Bundeshymne der Republik Österreich"; Leser and Wagner, *Österreichs politische Symbole*; Diem, *Die Symbole Österreichs*, 124–25.

6  Dokumentationsarchiv des österreichischen Widerstandes, *Gedenken und Mahnen in Wien 1934–1945*; Uhl, *Steinernes Bewusstsein*.

7 Bundeskanzleramt, *Rot-Weiss-Rot-Buch*, 3.

8 Dokumentationsarchiv des österreichischen Widerstandes, *"Anschluß" 1938*, 340. See Stachel, *Mythos Heldenplatz*, 5–26.

9 Bundeskanzleramt, *Rot-Weiss-Rot-Buch*.

10 Ibid, 94–95.

11 Kos, "Die Schau mit dem Hammer."

12 Gemeinde Wien, " '*Niemals vergessen!*' " illustrations section.

13 See Hurdes, "Von Friedrich bis Hitler."

14 See Andics, *Der Staat, den keiner wollte*.

15 For a discussion of the conflicting concepts between a German nation of culture and Austrian patriotism in cultural policies after 1955–56, see Pape, *Ungleiche Brüder*, 401–41.

16 See Bruckmüller, *Nation Österreich*, 61.

17 See Bruckmüller, *Österreichbewußtsein im Wandel*, 15. By 1993 popular support of the Austrian nation had reached 80 percent.

18 See Marboe, *Das Österreich-Buch*, 535–40. The ambivalent semantics of liberation are evident in wordings such as "The enemies of the front were friends at heart, destroying only to free us."

19 Ibid., 540. In fact the roof of the cathedral caught fire from flying sparks. See Mayer, *Lexikon der populären Irrtümer Österreichs*, 226–27.

20 Steiner, "Kostümierte Interessen," 171.

21 On denazification in general, see Stiefel, *Entnazifizierung in Österreich*; Garscha, "Entnazifizierung und gerichtliche Ahndung von NS-Verbrechen," 852–83. On the basis of guilty verdicts by people's courts some thirty death penalties had been carried out by 1948 (see Kuretsidis-Haider, "Verdrängte Schuld, vergessene Ahndung," 98).

22 It was in an effort to attract this voter potential that the SPÖ assisted in setting up the Verband der Unabhängigen (VDU, or Federation of Independents, the precursor organization to the FPÖ), founded especially to appeal to Nazi supporters. The SPÖ has for some years been going through intense soul searching in an effort to exorcise the "brown stains" in its party history, particularly with regard to the Federation of Socialist Academicians' (BSA) courting of erstwhile Nazis. See Neugebauer and Schwarz, *Der Wille zum aufrechten Gang*.

23 See Bischof, *Austria and the First Cold War, 1945–55*.

24 See Molden, *Der Ruf des Gewissens*.

25 See B. Bailer, *Wiedergutmachung kein Thema*, 45–48.

26 Cited in Helga Embacher, *Neubeginn ohne Illusionen*, 126. See also Hanisch, "Der Ort des Nationalsozialismus in der österreichischen Geschichte"; Bukey, *Hitlers Österreich*; Bukey, *Hitler's Austria*; Thomas Albrich, "Holocaust und Schuldabwehr."

27 From a verbal statement by Internal Affairs Minister Oskar Helmer at the 132nd Ministerial Council Session of 9 November 1948, regarding a point on the agenda relating to funds from nonheritable properties (Knight, *"Ich bin dafür, die Sache in die Länge zu ziehen,"* 197).

28  Hornung, "Trümmermänner," 247–48.

29  Matejka, *Widerstand ist alles*, 192.

30  See, for instance, Federal Chancellor Leopold Figl's 1948 New Year's address and Federal President Karl Renner's 1950 New Year's address (in Jochum and Olbort, *80 Jahre Republik*, 57–58 and 60–62, respectively).

31  Cited in ibid., 76.

32  Bischof, "Die Instrumentalisierung der Moskauer Erklärung nach dem 2. Weltkrieg"; Keyserlingk, *Austria in World War II*.

33  Jellinek, "Die Geschichte der österreichischen Wiedergutmachung," 398.

34  See B. Bailer, *Wiedergutmachung kein Thema*, 77–98; Bailer-Galanda, *Die Entstehung der Rückstellungs- und Entschädigungsgesetzgebung*. For a comparative analysis of the restitution policies in Austria and the Federal Republic of Germany, see Forster, *Wiedergutmachung in Österreich und der BRD im Vergleich*.

35  Cited in Csáky, *Der Weg zu Freiheit und Neutralität*, 130.

36  Gerald Stourzh, *Um Einheit und Freiheit*, 4:519–20.

37  See Brix, Bruckmüller, and Stekl, "Das kulturelle Gedächtnis Österreichs," 14; Breuss, Liebhart, and Pribersky, *Inszenierungen*, 306–14; Uhl, "Der Staatsvertrag."

38  Johnson, *Die österreichische Nation, die Moskauer Deklaration und die völkerrechtliche Argumentation*, 50.

39  Bergmann, Erb, and Lichtblau, "Die Aufarbeitung der NS-Zeit im Vergleich."

40  See Botz, "Eine deutsche Geschichte 1938 bis 1945?"

41  See ibid., 28; Safrian, *Die Eichmann-Männer*.

42  See Assmann and Frevert, *Geschichtsvergessenheit/Geschichtsversessenheit*, 144.

43  Tramontana, "Spruch heil: NS-Prozesse in der Zweiten Republik"; Grabitz, "Die Verfolgung von NS-Verbrechen in der Bundesrepublik Deutschland, der DDR und Österreich."

44  M. Rainer Lepsius, "Das Erbe des Nationalsozialismus und die politische Kultur der Nachfolgestaaten des 'Großdeutschen Reiches.'"

45  Görlich and Romanik, *Geschichte Österreichs*, 551.

46  Ibid.

47  See Hacker, *Warnung an Österreich*.

48  Ibid., 9.

49  Pelinka, "Der verdrängte Bürgerkrieg."

50  Utgaard, *Remembering and Forgetting Nazism*; Berger et al., *Zeiten Völker und Kulturen*, 4:172.

51  Berger et al., *Zeiten Völker und Kulturen*.

52  Ibid., 4:189.

53  Hindels, "Nazivergangenheit und Gegenwart," 22. See also Manoschek, "Verschmähte Erbschaft."

54  G.A. Canaval, "Paulus und das geistige KZ," *Salzburger Nachrichten*, 27 March 1954.

55  "Helden und Opfer: Totengedenken im vierten Jahr nach Kriegsende," *Murtaler Zeitung*, 29 October 1949, p. 3.

56 "Zeitgemäße Aufgabenstellungen," *Kleine Zeitung*, 27 September 1977, p. 16.

57 "Dem Andenken der Gefallenen," *Kleine Zeitung*, 5 June 1951, p. 4.

58 "Ehrenrettung des Soldaten," *Sonntagspost*, 30 November 1952, pp. 8–9.

59 "Zehntausend auf dem Karmeliterplatz bei der Enthüllung des Grazer Ehren- und Mahnmales," *Tagespost*, 24 October 1961. See also Uhl, "Gedächtnisraum Graz."

60 Zahn, *In Solitary Witness*.

61 Franz Vieböck, cited in Putz, " 'Zuviel der Mahnung' " (forthcoming).

62 "Grenzland-Ehrenmal feierlich geweiht," *Kleine Zeitung*, 29 September 1959.

63 Fanta and Sima, "*Stehst mitten drin im Land.*" The ensemble on the Ulrichsberg now referred to as the "Memorial to the Returnees of Europe" or the "European Memorial" is the best-known memorial site of its kind on Austrian soil, familiar both inside Austria itself and to some extent also abroad.

64 See Seiler, "Im Labyrinth der Geschichtspolitik."

65 Cited in "Dem Fremdenverkehr geopfert," *Der Volksbote*, 30 November 1957, p. 5. See also Uhl, "Konkurrierende Gedächtnislandschaften."

66 See "Dank an Innsbruck," *Die Furche*, 5 March 1958, p. 2.

67 Perz, *Die KZ-Gedenkstätte Mauthausen 1945 bis zur Gegenwart*.

68 See Strasser, " 'The Sound of Music,' Ein unbekannter Welterfolg."

69 Breuss, Liebhart, and Pribersky, *Inszenierungen*, 281–83.

70 See Hanisch, *Der lange Schatten des Staates*, 456–57.

71 Wassermann, "Zuviel Vergangenheit tut nicht gut!" 28–67.

72 Helmut Qualtinger, " 'Der Herr Karl' und andere Texte fürs Theater," 361. Hans Weigel, as cited in Garscha, "Die verhinderte Re-Nazifizierung," 34.

73 Ibid.

74 Ibid.

75 On this point, see Kasemir, "Spätes Ende für 'wissenschaftlich' vorgetragenen Rassismus."

76 Ibid., 497.

77 Ibid.

78 Kasemir, "Spätes Ende für 'wissenschaftlich' vorgetragenen Rassismus."

79 "Das Vermächtnis der Toten: Aufruf an die Jugend," *Volksblatt*, 28 April 1965.

80 Alfred Maleta, "Wir lieben dich, Vaterland!" *Wiener Zeitung*, 28 April 1965, 1–2.

81 Another, smaller, permanent exhibition was installed at the Documentation Archive of the Austrian Resistance in Vienna.

82 Bailer-Galanda, "Wolfgang Neugebauer."

83 *Widerstand und Verfolgung in Wien 1934–1945*, 2:5.

84 Ibid.

85 Ibid.

86 Ibid., 1:5.

87 See Neugebauer, "Widerstand und Opposition"; Hanisch, "Gab es einen spezifisch österreichischen Widerstand?"

88 Cited in Böhler, " 'Wenn die Juden ein Volk sind, so ist es ein mieses Volk.' "

89   Advertisement in *Profil* 20 (16 May 1983): 47, cited in Böhler, " 'Wenn die Juden ein Volk sind, so ist es ein mieses Volk,' " 525.

90   The cover story of the 13 March 1979 edition of *Profil* was devoted to the topic of "Austria's Part in the Final Solution." The cover illustration showed the red-white-and-red flag fitted with the Nazis' Jewish star. See also Diner, *Zivilisationsbruch*; Marchart, Öhner, and Uhl, " 'Holocaust' Revisited."

91   See Brink, *Ikonen der Vernichtung*.

92   Bacher, "Die Gegenwart leben helfen," 7.

93   See, for example, Göhring and Stadlmann, *Start in den Abgrund*, 40–41; see also Zippe, *Bildband zur Geschichte Österreichs*, 228–29. The Anschluss is illustrated with images of the invasion by German troops, with captions reading, for example, "German troops marching on Ringstrasse." Pictures of the mass assembly on the Heldenplatz, by contrast, are not featured.

94   Göhring and Stadlmann, *Start in den Abgrund*, 44.

95   Zippe, *Bildband zur Geschichte Österreichs*, 231. In Göhring's and Stadlmann's *Start in den Abgrund* reference is made to Austrians' participation, which is not, however, interpreted as any active collaboration with the Nazis. The Austrians are depicted as innocent bystanders: "During the first days after the annexation, Jews were obliged to clear the streets of Austrian political slogans, sometimes with the use of a toothbrush. Unfortunately one has to admit that these excesses of the National Socialists took place under the applause of a crowd of sensation-seeking onlookers" (53).

96   Göhring and Stadlmann, *Start in den Abgrund*, 78.

97   Ibid., 80.

98   See Judt, "Die Vergangenheit ist ein anderes Land."

99   See Mitten, *The Politics of Prejudice*; Wodak et al., *"Wir sind alle unschuldige Täter"*; Gehler, "Die Affäre Waldheim." A commission of historians cleared Kurt Waldheim of any suspicion of having committed any war crimes in February of 1988.

100   Kurt Waldheim in an election booklet of April 1986, cited in Neues Österreich, *Pflichterfüllung*.

101   Kannonier-Finster and Ziegler, "Einleitung und Ausgangspunkte," 21–26. A great number of books have been published on this issue, including Pick, *Guilty Victim*; Pelinka, *Austria*; Bischof and Pelinka, *Austrian Historical Memory and National Identity*.

102   Schoenberner, *Der gelbe Stern*.

103   Vranitzky cited in Betz and Sprengnagel, *Kontroversen am Österreichs Zeitgeschichte*, 576.

104   "Last der Geschichte, Chancen der Zukunft," *Der Standard*, 16 November 1994, p. 27.

105   "Hohe Zustimmung für Vranitzky-Worte," *Der Standard*, 16 June 1993.

106   Regarding Haider's socialization against a right-wing conservative background characterized by National Socialist views and attitudes, see Zöchling, *Haider*. See also Höbelt, *Defiant Populist*; Wodak and Pelinka, *The Haider Phenomenon in Austria*.

107   Cited in Czernin, *Wofür ich mich meinetwegen entschuldige*, 26.

108   Czernin, "Die Folgen von Krumpendorf," 11. As for Jörg Haider's perception · of history, see also Bailer-Galanda, *Haider wörtlich*.

109   "Federal Council Determines May 5 as Commemorative Day against Violence and Racism."

110   See Wiesenthal, *Projekt*. Regarding the opening of the Graz Synagogue on 9 November 2000, see: http://graz.at/.

111   Elazar Barkan, *The Guilt of Nations*.

112   Menasse, *Das Land ohne Eigenschaften*, 15.

113   Landsgesell, "Sind wir Nazis?"

114   This was the characterization of the FPÖ in the "Weisenbericht" (Wise Men's Report), a document published by an expert commission set up to evaluate the Austrian situation. The complete document can be found in "Dokumentation," *Wiener Zeitung*, 12 September 2000; see http://www.wienerzeitung.at.

115   Ibid.

116   "Das erste Nazi-Opfer," *Die Presse*, 10 November 2000, p. 7.

117   See Eizenstat, *Imperfect Justice*. For a comparison of Austria's restitution policies in an international context, see Rathkolb, *Revisiting the National Socialist Legacy*.

118   See Bischof, "Victims? Perpetrators? 'Punching Bags' of European Historical Memory?"

119   See Heer, Manoschek, Pollak, and Wodak, *Wie Geschichte gemacht wird*, 269–84; Höllwart, Martinez-Turek, Sternfeld, and Pollak, *In einer Wehrmachtsausstellung Erfahrungen mit Geschichtsvermittlung*; Lahodynsky, "Trend zum Revisionismus," 20, 28–32.

120   See Levy and Sznaider, *Erinnerung im globalen Zeitalter*.

RICHARD J. G(

# The Legacy of World War II i

MAPPING THE DISCOURSES OF MEMORY

In his recent study on the postwar legacy of Nazi occupation in France, Belgium, and the Netherlands, Pieter Lagrou asserts that, especially in comparison with East European countries, the respective histories of the three West European nations in question were not greatly affected or altered by the experience of war between 1940 and 1945.

> Did the Second World War fundamentally affect the history of Belgium, France, and the Netherlands? Was it a turning point, an experience that created something substantially new? Seen from a continental perspective, this seems doubtful. The war did not redraft the frontiers of these countries. Most of their displaced populations returned to the places from which they came. There were casualties but their numbers did not exceed 2% of the population.[1]

For those familiar with French politics and culture since the liberation and especially during the last twenty to thirty years, Lagrou's observation may well come as a surprise. Regardless of the relatively small impact of the war on France's borders and population, there is no doubt that what are widely referred to as *les années noires*—the Dark Years between 1940 and 1944—have quite literally haunted the nation. The history and memory of the period have produced a seemingly endless stream of political and judicial scandals and generated a long series of controversial films and books, which have attempted to expose, or, alternatively, to come to terms with the realities of that troubled past. Such has been the nation's obsession with the history and memory of the war—and especially the collaborationist Vichy regime—that in his classic 1987 study of the memory of the Dark Years, Henry Rousso described this obsession in terms of a psychological malady: the "Vichy Syndrome."[2] In 1994, at the moment when the extent and duration of President François Mitterrand's service to Pétain's regime was the focus of national and international attention and the source of hand-wringing d outrage in France, the American historian Robert Paxton wryly observed that the Vichy past interested the French more than money or sex.[3]

While the national obsession with Vichy and the Dark Years seems to be fading in the new millennium, it is clear that the history and memory of the period have not been—and may never be—completely integrated into the continuum of the nation's past. But this is perhaps to be expected if, as Gérard Noiriel argues, the Vichy past, like the French Revolution itself, constitutes less a particular historical period or moment among others than a turning point or break (*coupure*) between historical epochs.[4] As such, regardless of the historical realities—and continuities—it embodies, Vichy may always be perceived as an anomaly or even an aberration. Moreover, to the degree that over the last two decades the name "Vichy" has come to evoke France's shameful complicity with the Nazi Final Solution, it will in all likelihood continue to form part of the timeless "negative myth" at the heart of postmodern European identity: the Shoah itself.[5]

The groundwork for this essay's examination of the legacy and memory of Vichy in postwar France has already been laid in Rousso's *The Vichy Syndrome*, a work which has inflected virtually every study of the Vichy period and its memory, published both in France and abroad, over the past fifteen years. Drawing inspiration from the classic Freudian model of trauma, repression, and the return of the repressed, Rousso described the memory of Vichy in terms of four chronological phases. The first phase, covering the years 1944 to 1954, he labeled "Unfinished Mourning," a decade when the French were forced to deal with their own internal divisions and at least some of the realities of their complicity with the Nazis. A second phase, "Repressions," spanned the years from 1954 to 1971 and witnessed the relative effacement of the memory of Vichy in a national context dominated by new concerns, in particular the turmoil surrounding decolonization and Charles de Gaulle's return to power. The second period of Gaullist hegemony (1958–1970) was, moreover, dominated by the famous "Gaullist Myth of Resistance," which encouraged the belief that the vast majority of the French were *résistants* and that only a few marginal sorts and traitors collaborated with the Germans.

The third phase of the Vichy Syndrome, which Rousso labeled "Broken Mirror," lasted from 1970 to 1974 and was ushered in by the generational shift in perspective heralded by the student revolts of May 1968 and, where the history and memory of the occupation were concerned, by the 1970 release of Marcel Ophuls's groundbreaking documentary, *The Sorrow and the Pity*, a film which literally blew the lid off the Gaullist myth of resistance. De Gaulle's resignation from the presidency in 1969 also had a tremendous impact.

The fourth and final phase, "Obsessions," began in 1974 and has been characterized by an unremitting series of mostly political and judicial scandals and controversies relating to the Vichy past; it has also been dominated increasingly by what Rousso calls "Jewish Memory," the memory of the persecution of the Jews at the hands of the Vichy regime, especially in the context of French complicity in the Nazi Final Solution.

Although even the revised version of *The Vichy Syndrome* ends with the year 1991, Rousso's 1994 *Vichy: An Everpresent Past*, coauthored with Éric Conan, brings the Obsessions phase into the mid-1990s by emphasizing, among other things, the controversy surrounding the commemoration of the infamous Vel d'Hiv roundups of July 1942—when Paris police, acting on the orders of Vichy police chief René Bousquet, rounded up for detention and deportation some 13,000 Jews as part of France's active role in carrying out the Final Solution—and the trial of the former *milicien* Paul Touvier on charges of crimes against humanity. *Vichy: An Everpresent Past* also calls for a moratorium on scandal-mongering where the Vichy past is concerned, a penchant Rousso and Conan consider to be unfortunately all too natural, given the 1990s obsession with the Dark Years. Their plea, however, went largely unheeded because the scandal surrounding François Mitterrand's Vichy past erupted at precisely the moment the book was published, plunging the nation even deeper into an obsession with Vichy that did not cool down until the Maurice Papon trial ended in April 1998.

For at least some historians and commentators on the period, the medico-psychoanalytical metaphor used in *The Vichy Syndrome* now seems outmoded, and may perhaps have overdetermined Rousso's reading of the memory of the period as a kind of fluctuating, long-term psychological malady. Moreover, in choosing to compare the memory of the period to an illness, Rousso unwittingly managed, according to Nicholas Wiell, to give the memory of Vichy a certain perverse cachet that served to keep it in the public eye and thereby to sustain it artificially.[6]

Whatever one may think of Rousso's medico-psychoanalytical metaphor, however, there is no doubt that his division of the memory of the Vichy period into a series of distinct phases is not only historically legitimate but remarkably helpful as an analytical tool for contextualizing specific events. Moreover, the division of the memory of the period into the phases Rousso delineates also makes it possible to establish important links between the ways in which Vichy and the occupation are remembered at specific moments during the postwar period and the nation's sense of its own identity and well-being at that moment. For example, the predominance of the Gaullist myth in the public psyche during the Repressions phase overlaps not only with a fairly positive national self-image but, generally speaking, with the long period of economic prosperity known as *les trente glorieuses*. Conversely, the intensification of the Vichy Syndrome in the late 1980s and 1990s during the Obsessions phase marks a low ebb in national self-esteem and coincides with increasing internal dissensions over immigration—which stimulated the growth of the extreme right in the form of Jean-Marie Le Pen's National Front—as well as increasing insecurity over economic problems like unemployment. Moreover, the intensification of France's preoccupation with the criminality of Vichy anti-Semitism, accompanied as it was by a renewed *mise-en-cause* of the resistance, especially during the Moulin and Aubrac affairs, also contributed to a strong sense of national malaise.[7] As Robert Paxton observed in the American edition of *Vichy: An Everpresent Past*, a crucial component of France's positive postwar image derived from the contributions of the resistance and the Free French to the Allied war effort, and from the French nation having sat at the table of the victors.[8] These accomplishments were, of course, being buried under the weight of guilt and shame produced by a relentless focus on the memory of Vichy in the 1990s.

Though Rousso's four phases of memory as elaborated in *The Vichy Syndrome* are useful, this does not mean that they cannot be modified as a result of further developments or further research. Nor does it mean that the phases of the memory of Vichy cannot be reconfigured according to different criteria with equally useful results. For example, in his introduction to his 2001 collection of essays, *Vichy: L'événement, la mémoire, l'histoire*, Rousso himself argued that, without abandoning his overall scheme, one useful revision of the Obsessions phase was to divide it into two parts. Beginning in 1987 with the trial of Klaus Barbie, one could speak of a "Second Purge" (the first having occurred immediately after the war) which continued through the Papon trial eleven years later. Rousso also affirmed that one could reconfigure the memory of the war not in terms of the four phases of the Vichy Syndrome but in terms of a series of binary oppositions that serve to highlight the ways in which the fundamental antagonisms were viewed during successive periods of the postwar era. Before the 1970s, the basic conflict was perceived in terms of patriots versus traitors. During the 1970s, with the publication of Robert Paxton's *Vichy France: Old Guard and*

*New Order*, with its emphasis on Vichy's own reactionary ideology and willing complicity with the Nazis, and of Zeev Sternhell's account of an indigenous French Fascism in *Neither Right nor Left*, the conflict came to be viewed in terms of a confrontation between fascists and antifascists. Finally, in the 1980s and 1990s, with the awakening of Jewish memory, the basic opposition came to be seen in moral terms, as a struggle between what Rousso calls "the Just" and "the others."

Like Rousso's four phases of the memory of Vichy, the oppositions just described serve to illuminate changing perspectives on les années noires and are also based on an exhaustive knowledge of the historical, political, and legal changes, as well as shifts in France's ideological climate in the postwar period. Nevertheless, it is possible to explore the memory of Vichy in different contexts, for example, in how it has been represented in literature, where the paradigm is quite different. In his book on the memory of Vichy in literature, Alan Morris argues that while the Gaullist myth of resistance may well have held sway in public and political discourse especially during Rousso's Repressions phase, that myth was constantly challenged in novels about the war from the liberation on. Literary debunking of the myth received attention, according to Morris, only in the wake of May 1968 and with the arrival of a new generation of writers, in particular Patrick Modiano, who also challenged the resistance myth albeit from a different perspective.[9] From Morris's point of view, there was no Repressions phase in literature. I would add, moreover, that because the novels most closely associated with the Broken Mirror phase—Modiano's occupation trilogy, *La place de l'Étoile*, *La ronde de nuit*, and *Les boulevards de ceinture*—dealt for the most part with Jewish memory, they could be considered to be quite representative of the Obsessions phase as well. In literature, there was no clear boundary between the Broken Mirror and the Obsessions phases.

Given these variables—and the multiple configurations of the memory of the Dark Years in postwar France they allow for—what is in fact the best way to analyze that memory, to give it coherence without betraying its complexities and contradictions? Despite the usefulness of Rousso's four phases of memory, which rely essentially on a straightforward chronological progression in which all discourses are fused into one, it is at least equally useful to separate out these different discourses—political, legal, cinematic, and literary—in order to trace their *internal* evolutions. This enables a somewhat more composite picture of the memory of the war in France while making it possible to analyze more closely the ways in which these multiple memories coincide with, overlap, and, on occasion, contradict each other.

Political Memory: Mythmaking, Forgetting, Deheroizing

From the standpoint of a strictly political discourse, the memory of the Dark Years can be divided into three basic activities. While these activities correspond roughly to Rousso's chronology, they can be linked more precisely to three postwar periods: the two eras of De Gaulle's leadership; the "quietist" presidencies of Georges Pompidou and, to a certain degree, of Valéry Giscard d'Estaing; and the gradual deheroization of the resistance myth, which began under Giscard and culminated in the scandal over François Mitterrand's Vichy past in the fall of 1994.

*Gaullist Mythmaking*

In discussing what is now generally referred to as the Gaullist myth of resistance and its genesis in the postliberation period, it is important to stress that the myth did not grow exclusively and unproblematically out of the Gaullists' efforts to legitimize their own authority in the post-Liberation period. Claims for ownership of the legacy of resistance to Nazi and Vichy hegemony were also made by former internal résistants in an effort to validate the postwar leadership role they sought to play. Admired for their courage and their actions during the war, they were nevertheless unable to gain support from the general population in their efforts to establish themselves as a postwar political elite. Not only were they attacked by the neo-Vichy right for their *résistantialisme*—their bravado and "opportunism" in purportedly joining the conflict only in the final days of the war—but their role was diminished, although not entirely dismissed, by the Gaullists themselves.

The Gaullist myth of resistance emphasized an impersonal national rebellion against the Nazi invader spearheaded not by internal résistants but by de Gaulle and his Free French, who lived in exile, of course, during most of the war. To gauge the extent to which, during the immediate postwar years, de Gaulle himself attempted to minimize the role of the internal resistance's contribution to the struggle—and especially its Communist and leftist constituencies—Pieter Lagrou points to the make-up of those elected to the Order of the Companions of the Liberation by de Gaulle on his resignation from the provisional government in January 1946. Of the 1,036 new members, more than three-fourths were from the Free French Forces, and among those left out were Communist and leftist resistance heroes such as Raymond Aubrac, Pierre Villon, and Maurice Kriegel.[10]

Despite de Gaulle's—and the Gaullists'—efforts to appropriate the mantle of leadership for the liberation of France, he and his supporters were not blind to the necessity of including the vast majority of the French in the great epic—or, more accurately, the great myth—of France's resistance and especially its "self-liberation." As Lagrou pointed out, "The amalgamation of colonists and exiles that made up [de Gaulle's] Free French Forces was not a firm basis on which to build a new regime. De Gaulle was thus forced to promote a generous and collective vision of the French struggle for liberation, to pass over in silence the role of Vichy and of the Allies, and to nationalize the contribution of the resistance movement on French territory."[11] But the launching of the Gaullist myth of resistance was not simply a politically expedient move to consolidate de Gaulle's power and that of his followers; it was also crucial to the national recovery and to France's capacity to view itself in a positive and independent light. Lagrou observed that being liberated is not the same as liberating oneself. It is "too passive a mode to celebrate the recovery of national independence, and gratitude is a weak basis for national identity."[12]

After De Gaulle's resignation in 1946, those who followed him into power were certainly not Gaullists, nor were they particularly inclined to celebrate his and his followers' accomplishments. For De Gaulle himself, 1946 marked the beginning of a long period of exile from power, broken only by the general's return during the Algerian crisis in 1958. As for his successors in the 1940s and 1950s, preoccupations other than the memory of the war and the wounds and scars it left took center stage. When the Repressions phase got under way in the turning-point year of 1954 (following the 1953 amnesty laws for the crimes of treason and collaboration with the Nazis), the memory of Vichy and the Dark Years became less insistent and less visible not because the conflicts which characterized the period had been finally resolved but because other matters imposed themselves more urgently on the national conscience. These included the failure of the French military at Dien Bien Phu and the subsequent loss of France's Indochinese colonial possessions. In Algeria tensions were rising, and many of those in favor of *Algérie française* were former resisters who laid claim in their new struggle to the legacy of wartime resistance against the Nazis. This gave a new and highly problematic charge to the ideal of resistance, one which did not lend itself to a cooling of passions where the memory of the Dark Years was concerned.

Nevertheless, despite the strategic and troubling manipulation of the memory of the Dark Years and especially the legacy of the resistance in postwar crises like Algeria, the validity and legitimacy of the resistance myth went unchallenged, and its positive valency was confirmed, for example, by the eagerness of the supporters of a French Algeria to use it.

Following De Gaulle's return to power in 1958 and his largely successful resolution of the Algerian crisis, the Gaullist myth quite naturally took on a new luster, and renewed efforts were made to consolidate the myth of a quasi-universal and undivided resistance and to downplay the role of and support for Pétainism and collaboration. At the same time, responsibility for the violence and brutality of the period needed to be placed squarely on the shoulders of the German invader. The quintessential expression of these aims was the transfer of the ashes of the resistance martyr Jean Moulin, for all intents and purposes tortured to death by Klaus Barbie, the ss intelligence chief in Lyons, to the Panthéon in the heart of the Latin Quarter, where the remains of France's national heroes are interred. Rousso noted that the idea for this originally came from resistance groups and politicians on the left, but that the matter was taken in hand by de Gaulle's minister of culture, the former novelist, Communist fellow traveler, and resistance leader André Malraux, and that the final decree authorizing the transfer was made by the head of state himself. Two days of public ceremonies in December 1964 (the second day was broadcast on French national television) concluded with Malraux's famous eulogy to the résistants, whom he described as "the people of the night." The symbolism was clear. Not only was the idea of a "nation of resisters" reconfirmed, but Moulin—the epitome of *all* national resistance, internal as well as external—had been appropriated by the Gaullists.

### Post-Gaullist Forgetting

Despite the obvious success of the 1964 consecration of the memory of Jean Moulin, in the late 1960s the national consensus concerning the Dark Years began to crumble, especially with regard to the myth of a universal French resistance to Nazism. For Rousso, what initiated the process, what initially "cracked the mirror," so to speak, were the student revolts and strikes of May 1968. A challenge in the first instance to an outmoded and rigid education system and curriculum, the protests were also clearly directed at Gaullist authority. Taken as a whole, they constituted an act of defiance against the older—wartime—generation. A troubled past that had been largely passed over in silence by the parental generation was no longer taboo. As Rousso observed, "the repudiation of a certain type of society" implicitly entailed the rejection of "a certain vision of [that society's] history."[13] With de

Gaulle's definitive withdrawal from power the following year, the path was clear to dismantle the myth of resistance once and for all.

Pierre Nora, for one, challenged the notion that May 1968 constituted a deathblow to the resistance myth and to France's complacency concerning its wartime past. For Nora, the process began with the 1967 Six Day War in Israel and its awakening of Jewish memory in France. Whatever the case may be, those who followed de Gaulle in the French presidency had little interest either in resuscitating the resistance myth and its fading glories or in leading the nation in a collective soul-searching over the realities of the Dark Years. It is in this sense that Georges Pompidou and Valéry Giscard d'Estaing fostered a kind of forgetfulness or "quietism" that sought either to put the past behind or defuse its more troubling ideological valences. Despite his Gaullist lineage, Pompidou despised the bravado of résistantialisme, and in one instance at least sought unsuccessfully to put the Vichy past behind and bury its animosities. That gesture ricocheted: in both the short and long term, it did perhaps more to stir up the memories and animosities of the Vichy period than any other single action.

In November 1971 Pompidou quietly pardoned Paul Touvier, a former member of Vichy's paramilitary and fascistic police, the Milice, on the recommendation of some of his closest advisors. Protected and hidden for years by high-ranking officials of the Catholic Church, Touvier had been responsible during the war for, among other crimes, the arrest and murder of Jews and resistance fighters. Pompidou's pardon of Touvier was in fact not for the crimes he had committed during the war—the statute of limitations had run out on the death sentences handed down for war crimes in 1946 and 1947—but for what are known as accessory penalties. These prevented Touvier from claiming his inheritance in the Lyons region from whence he came. But when Touvier's pardon and the full extent of his wartime activities were revealed in an article by Jacques Dérogy in the magazine *L'Express* in June 1972, public outrage was intense. In an effort to calm tempers and justify his pardon, in September 1972 Pompidou held a press conference and expressed the view that the time had come for the nation to "draw a veil over the past, to forget a time when Frenchmen disliked one another, attacked one another, and even killed one another."[14] Pompidou's speech had precisely the opposite effect. In the end, his pardon of Touvier certainly did more to remove the veil, to expose and indeed revive old rancors than it did to put the past to rest. Touvier became an international celebrity of sorts and was forced to go into hiding once again until he was arrested for good in Nice in 1989. By then—and as a direct result of the scandal surrounding Pompidou's pardon—Touvier had long since been charged with crimes against humanity.

## Deheroizing the Past: From Giscard to Mitterrand

Despite the outcome of the Touvier pardon, the fact remains that Pompidou's intention in the entire affair was, as he put it, to draw a veil of forgetfulness over the Vichy past. This was something his successor, Valéry Giscard d'Estaing, did not discourage, given his strong family links through his father, uncle, and grandfather to the Vichy regime. But the form of forgetfulness that characterized Giscard's years in power was not an effacement of the past but a curious and vaguely perverted form of remembering that in effect sought to defuse the real ideological issues of the war in favor of a more anodyne and "chic" cult of some of its more superficial manifestations. These were the years of the *mode rétro* (which also included the final years of Pompidou's presidency). For Rousso, these years form part of the Broken Mirror and Obsession phases, but I think it is important to distinguish them from the memory of the war in the 1980s and 1990s because they represent more of an *évasion*, to use the French expression, than a real effort to fully expose or to come to terms with the hard realities of the Dark Years.

Broadly speaking, the mode rétro consisted of a fascination with the forties that was all too evident in a range of cultural objects, including novels and films. It also manifested itself in a palpable obsession with memorabilia from the period, including swastikas and old magazines like the Nazi photography magazine *Signal*. The fad was hardly innocuous. In a 1981 essay in *Le Débat* Pascal Ory condemned the perversity of the mode rétro in diabolical terms.[15] He labeled it *rétro satanas* (although, it must be said, he benefited from the fascination with the period and contributed to it by publishing a popular and successful book on collaboration, *Les collaborateurs*, in 1976). In his 1982 *Reflets du nazisme* Saul Friedländer examined works such as Michel Tournier's 1970 novel *Le roi des aulnes* and, to a lesser extent, Louis Malle's 1974 film *Lacombe Lucien*, and argued that while both works successfully exposed a hitherto unnoticed feature of Nazism—the link of kitsch and death in the Nazi sensibility—they, especially Tournier's novel, were at the same time troublingly uncritical of the linkage they revealed. Both works in fact displayed a disturbing fascination with their discovery and, in Friedlander's opinion, even seemed to be seduced by it.[16]

Of all the commentaries on the mode rétro, none was more condemnatory or astute in its assessment of the phenomenon—and its connection with France in the seventies—than Michel Foucault's analysis presented in an interview published in the *Cahiers du cinéma* in the summer of 1974.[17] According to Foucault, the demise of Gaullism and the election to the presidency of Valéry Giscard D'Estaing—a man of suave elegance with strong links to Vichy—marked the end of the grand, ideologically grounded narratives of the occupation fostered by Gaullists (but not personally by Georges Pompidou), most notably the myth of universal resistance and struggle against Fascism. In their place "Giscardism" offered a watered-down version of the past, according to which collaboration and resistance were less conscious political or ideological choices than matters controlled by external circumstances or even chance. A perfect illustration of this perspective could be found, according to Foucault, in Louis Malle's film *Lacombe Lucien*, whose ignorant peasant protagonist falls in with the German police (who are nevertheless Frenchmen in the film) because his bicycle has a flat tire and he is caught out after curfew. An effective minion of Nazi authority and brutality, Lucien has no comprehension of the ideological issues at stake and serves his masters primarily out of a taste for power. And yet Lucien is disturbingly sympathetic and even seductive, and the spectator cannot help but feel a twinge when he learns at the end of the film that Lucien has been executed for collaboration.

For Foucault the case of *Lacombe Lucien* was suggestive in the first instance of the mode rétro's penchant to eroticize power, and not just any power, but Nazi and Fascist power in particular. This, he argued, was linked to the person of Giscard himself. More significant, the mode rétro's debunking of the vision of the Dark Years as a period of great and indeed crucial ideological confrontations sat better with a bourgeoisie that, Foucault asserted, had always been uncomfortable with resistance heroism and had always preferred *attentisme* or a fairly subdued Pétainism. In a 1978 discussion of his own wartime adolescence, Louis Malle, echoing Foucault's assessment of bourgeois attitudes, commented on his own wealthy bourgeois family's class-based and "refined" Pétainism, and its view at the time that resistance was essentially *déclassée*.[18]

If the commentaries by Ory, Friedländer, and Foucault succeeded in capturing the perverse climate of the mode rétro and the peculiar form of forgetting they embody and that characterized the Giscard years and Giscardist attitudes, the arrival to power of François Mitterrand at the outset of the 1980s appeared, at least initially, to herald the return of the power and prestige of resistance, if not of the resistance myth itself. Although by no means a Gaullist, Mitterrand could certainly claim the mantle of the resistance—from the Left. Already in the early eighties, at least one of his actions suggested a desire to symbolically resanctify resistance martyrs, so to speak, by arranging for the extradition from South America and for the trial on charges of crimes against humanity of Jean Moulin's killer, Klaus Barbie.

What appeared, at least, to be Mitterrand's effort to revitalize, or revalorize, the legacy of the resistance, and its implicit condemnation of Vichy—and all that Vichy represented—did not last long. From 1987 on, Mitterrand annually placed a bouquet on the tomb of Pétain to honor "the victor of Verdun." For many, especially Jewish groups, this was a remarkably insensitive gesture, given Pétain's anti-Semitic policies under Vichy. In a speech made in July 1992 at the commemoration of the fiftieth anniversary of the Vél d'Hiv roundups, Mitterrand disavowed any responsibility on the part of Republican France for Vichy, its anti-Semitism, and its participation in the Final Solution. This assertion outraged many, especially in light of the fact that it was the Third Republic that voted itself out of existence and granted full powers to Pétain in the summer of 1940.

But all of these gestures paled in comparison with the scandal following revelations in Pierre Péan's 1994 biography of Mitterrand, *Une jeunesse française: François Mitterrand 1934–1947*. Péan's book revealed not only that Mitterrand's service to Vichy—which while generally known was not considered troubling because of his later role in the resistance—had lasted much longer than he had previously admitted but also that he had been a right-wing activist before the war and a convinced Pétainist well into the occupation. Indeed Mitterrand, it turned out, had won the régime's highest honor, the *francisque*.

Attempting to do damage control, Mitterrand agreed to be interviewed on French television in September 1994, but what he said only made matters worse. He admitted that René Bousquet, chief of Vichy police and organizer of the Vel d'Hiv roundups, had been a personal friend. Mitterrand also stated that he considered Bousquet a man of "exceptional stature" and confirmed that he had intervened behind the scenes to have legal proceedings involving charges of crimes against humanity halted against him on the grounds that Bousquet had already stood trial for "all his crimes" in 1949. But perhaps the icing on the cake was Mitterrand's misunderstanding of Vichy's 1940 and 1941 anti-Jewish statutes, which, he claimed, only applied to foreign Jews (as though that made them any less reprehensible).

In many ways, it is possible to see in François Mitterrand's trajectory a kind of mini-version of Rousso's Vichy Syndrome. From the myth of largely unalloyed resistance (Péan's book confirms the degree of Mitterrand's expediency in moving into the resistance) to a return of the repressed Vichy past, the memory of Mitterrand's Dark Years underwent a remarkable transformation during his presidency, and in its final stages coincided almost precisely with Rousso's Obsession phase at its most intense. But in terms of the longer term political (presidential?) memory of Vichy, it is in my opinion more representative of the gradual deheroization of the memory of Vichy that began with the mode rétro and the cultural politics of the Giscard era. Apart from a kind of hiccup of the revalorization of the resistance myth at the outset of Mitterrand's presidency, the three essential stages of the political memory of Vichy can be summed up in terms of myth-building, amnesia, and deheroization.

## Literature and Film: Demythification, Revolt, Repetition

The general evolution of the representation of the Dark Years in literature and film does not fit comfortably into Rousso's four phases of the memory of the Vichy past, nor does it coincide neatly with the three phases of political memory I proposed above. Instead, literary, cinematic, and documentary representations of the war fall into three of their own phases—demythification, revolt, repetition—the first two phases being, from an artistic point of view, the most vibrant. Generally speaking, the demythification phase runs from the liberation to the end of the 1960s and is best exemplified in works like Marcel Aymé's *Uranus* and Louis-Ferdinand Céline's German Trilogy. The revolt phase includes Patrick Modiano's early novels, Marcel Ophuls's documentary *Le chagrin et la pitié*, and Malle's *Lacombe Lucien*, whose scenario, significantly, was coauthored by Patrick Modiano. The repetitions phase can be said to include the majority of the novels and films produced in the 1980s and 1990s, although the degree of repetitiveness is occasionally offset by the artistic quality of the work itself.

### Demythification

Of the novels, literary essays, and plays written in the aftermath of the Dark Years that challenge, in one way or another, the myth of a universal French resistance during the war, perhaps none was more acerbic or broader in the scope of its attacks on French hypocrisy than Marcel Aymé's 1948 novel, *Uranus*. In the novel Aymé voiced a harsh critique of postliberation French bad faith and amnesia. His targets included Communists, Gaullists, resisters of the final hour, as well as *attentistes*. But Aymé's major target, manifest from the outset of the novel, was the hypocrisy and dishonesty of the myth of a universal French resistance to Vichy and the Germans. Taking a post-dinner stroll in the partially destroyed village of Blémont (bombed not by the Germans but the Allies), the engineer Archambault meditates bitterly on his fellow citizens' deliberate forgetfulness of their earlier Pétainism and either their current silence or their pretense of having been in the resistance. This "wave of hypocrisy," supported by the press and the authorities, was literally unfurling throughout France, affecting millions of lives and propagating a "colossal lie." For Archambault, this hypocritical amnesia is nothing less than a "cancer" on French society as a whole.[19]

Aymé's perspective was seconded in Céline's postwar trilogy, especially *D'un château l'autre* and *Nord*, novels that traced the flight of the author as well as other French collaborators across a devastated Germany under endless barrages of Allied bombs. In foregrounding the collaborators—and the Germans—as largely innocent victims of Allied destructiveness, Céline challenged the resistance myth on two fronts. First, his protagonist was no resister but a French collaborator. Moreover, the war's immoral and insane destruction was blamed not on the Nazis and their minions but, at least implicitly, on the Allies and their impersonal agents of destruction. In this fashion, the terms of political good and evil were largely reversed.

Both Aymé and Céline had dubious wartime records, especially Céline, whose virulent anti-Semitism made him an early admirer of Hitler. The authors' collaborationism, moreover, made their denunciations of the resistance myth appear to be thinly disguised efforts at self-justification, which explains why, to a significant degree, the acknowledged dismantling of the Gaullist myth of resistance was left to a younger generation of writers in revolt not only against the complacent misrepresentations of the Gaullist era but, more broadly, against the generation of the fathers as well.

*Revolt*

Although the quintessential work of the revolt phase was Marcel Ophuls's *Le chagrin et la pitié* (The sorrow and the pity), itself imbued, as many commentators have noted, with the "spirit of May," it is important not to overlook Modiano's literary trilogy since, to a very real degree, it set the stage for Ophuls's masterpiece. The first book in the trilogy, *La place de l'Étoile* (1969), enjoyed an immediate *succès de scandale* because it reminded the French reading public—exhaustively and sarcastically—of the long tradition of indigenous French anti-Semitism which (as few wished to remember) dominated the cultural politics of the occupation period. In the second novel, *La ronde de nuit*, Modiano challenged the resistance myth directly by portraying a confused young resistor who oscillates between collaboration and resistance, believes in neither cause, and ultimately betrays his fellow résistants as the novel closes. The third novel in the trilogy painted a largely sympathetic portrait of a father who collaborates and ultimately leads his son to do the same.

In these novels Modiano clearly held nothing sacred, challenging received notions of collaboration and resistance, the ideologies that were supposed to ground them, and even the notion that France was fundamentally different from Germany with regard to anti-Semitism—all this from the perspective of youthful protagonists of a younger generation sullied by the sins of the fathers. There could be no better preparation for *Le chagrin et la pitié* than this.

Originally conceived as a project for French television, *Le chagrin et la pitié* became diverted when the producers, André Harris and Alain de Sédouy, were fired from French television in the wake of May 1968. Ophuls then sought funding from German television and Swiss investors and completed the film in 1969. *Le chagrin et la pitié* was initially released in West Germany, Switzerland, the Netherlands, and the United States. Negotiations with French television to show the film in France were blocked in accordance with what Ophuls called "censorship through inertia." Released in April 1971 in a small movie house in the Latin Quarter, and later in a larger theatre on the Champs Élysées, the film attracted more than 600,000 spectators.

Critical reaction to the film was intense on the left and right. Alfred Fabre-Luce, a former collaborator and one-time apologist for Hitler's New Europe, denounced it in *Le Monde* for its "gimmicks, omissions, and falsifications." He also criticized those, especially Jews, who voiced their hostility to Pétain in the film. For Fabre-Luce, this was the height of ingratitude, since it was Pétain, he claimed, who had saved their lives. Fabre-Luce, like most Pétainists in the postwar years, never missed an opportunity to trot out the thesis that while de Gaulle had been the "sword" fighting France's enemies on the field of battle, Pétain had been the "shield" that had protected the French from the Nazi occupiers. The former résistante Germaine Tillion denounced Fabre-Luce's absurdities but criticized the film herself for offering a "profile of a hideous country." Jean-Paul Sartre observed that *Le chagrin et la pitié* was a "deliberately . . . inaccurate representation" of the occupation. But it was Stanley Hoffmann who perhaps best summed up the film's impact, suggesting that *Le chagrin et la pitié* offered, in effect, a counter myth or counter legend to the Gaullist myth of resistance: the image of a France "united in resistance was supplanted . . . by the image of a France equally united in its cowardice."[20] (Hoffmann would later make the same observation about Malle's *Lacombe Lucien*.)[21]

In what ways did Ophuls's film constitute a thoroughgoing gesture of revolt against the myth of resistance and "break the mirror," to use Rousso's metaphor? While there are heroic résistants in the film, including the peasant Grave brothers, there are also former résistants gone to seed, such as the wartime hero Colonel Gaspar, who now drives a Mercedes and sells television sets to former *collabos* (collaborators). There are also soft-core collabos like the shoe salesman Klein, who took out an ad during the war to announce his Aryan origins to those who did not wish to buy shoes from Jews. There are schoolteacher attentistes who have developed serious cases of amnesia about Jews deported from their school during the war—a very different scenario than the one offered years later in Louis Malle's moving 1987 film, *Au revoir les enfants*, in which the director of a Catholic boarding school attempts to save Jewish children by hiding them at the school under false identities. Most disturbingly perhaps, there are ideologically committed and *idealistic* collaborators, such as the former French volunteer in the Waffen ss Christian de la Mazière, who, if not treated entirely sympathetically in the film, is certainly taken seriously by Ophuls. De la Mazière is not dismissed merely as opportunistic rabble, as were so many collaborators in the postwar years. In his idealism—troubling as it is—he embodies in fact the perfect foil to Jean-Paul Sartre's classic portrait of the vacuous, cynically motivated collaborator in "Qu'est-ce qu'un collaborateur?"[22] Finally, as Rousso notes, the greatest figure of Resistance, de Gaulle himself, is virtually absent from the film, and this omission, more than any others, justifies the claim that *Le chagrin et la pitié* did not reveal the full truth of the Dark Years but rather articulated a counter myth to the one elaborated by de Gaulle, the Gaullists, and, to a large extent, the wartime generation itself.

Like Modiano's early novels and *Le chagrin et la pitié*, Malle's *Lacombe Lucien* challenged all comfortable notions of collaboration and resistance and cast its story in the context of a revolt against the received truths of the older generation. With the notable exception of François Truffaut's 1980 *Le dernier metro*—something of an occupation fairy tale that, according to many critics, attempted to launch a kind of updated version of the Gaullist myth of resistance and paint the lives of the French during the Dark Years as *la vie en rose*—most of the novels and films that followed in the 1980s and 1990s expanded on the portrait of France under Vichy and the Germans offered in the works of the revolt period, added nuance and detail here and there, but offered no radical new interpretations of the Dark Years and their meaning.[23] That said, the films of the 1980s and 1990s did reflect an extraordinary emphasis on Jewish memory. But this shift constituted less a change of focus or an innovation than a narrowing of the aperture.

## Repetitions

Novels dealing with the occupation have been especially numerous since the mid-1980s. They include works by major novelists like Marguerite Duras, whose provocative 1986 novel "memoir" *La douleur* deliberately unsettled any comfortable illusions that might remain concerning the heroism of Gaullism and the resistance. *La douleur* portrayed Gaullists as harsh and domineering members of the upper class, résistants as torturers, albeit sometimes reluctantly, and collaborators as pathetic victims or naive adolescents unaware of the real issues at stake in the war—in other words, a 1980s version of Malle's *Lacombe Lucien*.[24] Other novels dealing with the period by popular writers like Patrick Modiano, Michel del Castillo, Pierre Assouline, and Marc Lambron have offered fictional accounts of the horrors of the period—especially the persecution and deportations of the Jews—or used the Vichy past to develop reflections on the nature and meaning of history and memory. But in many instances these novelists have also clearly chosen the setting of the occupation not in order to rethink it but to help market books dealing with a period that remains scandalous and controversial.

Since the early 1980s there has also been a steady stream of films dealing with the Dark Years made, in the main, by France's most distinguished directors. These include Malle's 1987 *Au revoir les enfants* and Christian de Salonge's grisly film about a real-life doctor, *Docteur Petiot*, who killed Jews by poison injection while claiming to be putting them to sleep temporarily in order to secret them out of the country; their bodies were then burned in an apartment-building incinerator.[25] Other films, however, focused less specifically on the persecution of Jews and dealt with the hardships and injustices suffered by the general population under Vichy. These films include Claude Chabrol's *Une affaire de femmes*, based on another historical episode in which a poor woman performed abortions, at least initially, to help friends in need or others whose health was endangered by the pregnancy. *Une affaire de femmes* concludes (as did the historical episode itself) with the condemnation and execution of the abortionist, a sentence very much in keeping with Vichy's reactionary pronatalist policies and its emphasis on

Legacy of World War II in France   89

family values—Vichy's motto was "Travail, famille, patrie"—which implied the domination of men and the subservience of women.

In keeping with the precedent of excellent documentary films about the realities of the Dark Years established by *Le chagrin et la pitié* in 1971, *Shoah*, Claude Lanzmann's monumental exploration of the Holocaust, was released in 1985. Three years later Marcel Ophuls treated the Holocaust and other issues in his fascinating documentary on what he describes as "the life and times of Klaus Barbie," *Hotel Terminus*. In 1993, with the help of historians Robert Paxton and Jean-Pierre Azéma, Claude Chabrol produced a documentary of the Vichy period constructed entirely from newsreel footage and propaganda films selected to show how Vichy represented itself to the French people and what attitudes and perspectives it sought to instill in them. Foremost among the latter was the view that France brought its 1940 defeat on itself and that it was the leftist Third Republican government—and the Jews—who were responsible for the calamity. The film includes disgusting footage in which Jews are compared to swarms of rats. But the very inclusion of this piece of Vichy propaganda in *L'oeil de Vichy* only confirms the film's indebtedness to *Le chagrin et la pitié*. The very same footage had been included in Ophuls's masterpiece a quarter of a century earlier.

Legal Memory: The Two Purges

The most appropriate model for understanding the legal memory of the Dark Years in postwar France is that of the two purges suggested by Rousso in *Vichy: L'événement, la memoire, l'histoire*. Although the two purges are separated by some forty years, and although the second purge of the 1980s and 1990s had no direct causal link to the postliberation purge, there is no doubt that the common view in the 1980s and 1990s that the initial purge was inadequate and even an abject failure fed the momentum that led to the trials of Klaus Barbie, Paul Touvier, and Maurice Papon, as well as the thwarted efforts to prosecute René Bousquet.

*The First Purge*

From the outset, efforts immediately following the liberation to deal objectively with the Vichy years were undermined by conflicting political passions, ambivalent attitudes, and unforeseen complexities that made a national consensus about the recent past all but impossible. This was especially evident during the *épuration*, or postwar purge of collaborators. The first purge lasted, in effect, from 1944 to 1953, touched all professions and walks of life, and claimed thousands of lives. Of those who died, approximately one sixth were executed after being condemned in accordance with the law.

From the moment of the liberation in 1944 (and in many instances, while the liberation was occurring), the purge of pro-Nazi elements as well as those who had served the Vichy regime was a central concern for resistance groups, the incoming provisional government, and an oppressed population exhausted by war and anxious for retribution against its oppressors. Especially during the liberation itself, acts of summary justice occurred. These included the execution of political collaborators as well as the infamous shaving of heads of women who had slept with the enemy and were therefore guilty of "horizontal collaboration."

The legal basis for the postwar purge trials was initially established in Algeria during the war by the Comité français de libération nationale (CFLN) and later by the Gouvernement provisoire de la République (GPRF). The texts on which prosecutions were based derived from the prewar 1939 penal code, with slight modifications. According to these texts, "only notions of treason or collaboration with the enemy and violations of the constitutional laws of the Republic were considered major crimes."[26] Nothing specific concerning racial persecutions was articulated in these laws because such persecutions were deemed at the time to form part of Vichy's policy of collaboration with the Nazis. The autonomy of Vichy's anti-Jewish statutes of 1940 and 1941, for example, was not recognized as such. In this somewhat skewed (certainly by today's standards) and indeed historically inaccurate context, charges of involvement in the persecution of the Jews were in fact brought against Vichy officials, including Pétain himself, but they were clearly secondary to what were considered to be graver infractions: treason and collaboration with the enemy. Official Vichy anti-Semitism was hardly mentioned in the courtroom during Pétain's trial, and it figured in the verdict only in the context of collaboration with the Nazis and as an example of the État Français's violation of the "rights of man." Ironically, at the same time that Vichy's anti-Semitism was being downplayed and misconstrued in Paris, in London an international agreement creating crimes against humanity was being signed. Crimes against humanity would not be recognized in French law, however, until 1964, an important consideration for understanding both the first and second purges in postwar France.

According to Rousso, the only instance in which racism was explicitly mentioned as a punishable act in French law during the first purge was in the August 1944 law defining the crime of "national indignity." The statute specified that one was guilty of national indignity if one had published "articles, brochures, and books in favor of the enemy, of collaboration with the enemy, of racism, of totalitarianism."[27] Obviously, those most subject to punishment under this law were not government officials who sponsored or carried out Vichy's anti-Semitic policies or, from spring 1942 on, policemen and others involved in the roundup and deportation of Jews in the context of the Final Solution, but writers and journalists. Moreover, among the latter, many of the most important and visible pro-Nazi and collaborationist writers like Robert Brasillach were tried, condemned, and executed on more serious charges. As Alice Kaplan pointed out in her recent study of the trial of Brasillach, Brasillach was accused of treason and tried and convicted in accordance with Article 75 of the penal code, which defined "intelligence with the enemy."[28]

From the moment of its inception, and despite the best efforts of most of those involved to mete out justice fairly and in proportion to the crime committed, the first purge was—and remains—the object of controversy and distortion. Many on the extreme right as well as sympathizers with Vichy and collaborationism have since the war repeatedly blasted the first purge as nothing more than the revenge of the victors. They cite horrible crimes— rape, sadism, torture, even bestiality—which they claim were carried out repeatedly against collaborator-"victims" during and in the immediate aftermath of the liberation. Because of its supposed savagery and brutality, the first purge has been called l'épuration sauvage by its detractors. In his 1986 study Herbert Lottman noted that those hostile to it also compared its victims to victims of the Terror.[29] While in prison awaiting execution, Brasillach likened himself to the poet-martyr of revolutionary terror, André Chenier. Some critics of the first purge even went so far as to compare its "innocent victims" to Captain Dreyfus.[30]

Apologists for Vichy and collaborationism were not the only ones dissatisfied with the first purge. For very different reasons, many were troubled by particular episodes, such as the 1949 trial of René Bousquet, Vichy's chief of police in 1942–43, a participant in the Vel d'Hiv roundups, and the individual responsible for negotiating with German authorities the implementation of the Final Solution throughout France. Because crimes-against-humanity statutes were not on the books until 1964, they were not even at issue in his trial. But even leaving crimes of this magnitude aside, the court's leniency— Bousquet was sentenced to five years in prison, but the sentence was immediately suspended for "acts of Resistance"—still shocked many, and rightly so. A political "insider" before the war (and a postwar friend of François

Mitterrand), Bousquet had clearly benefited from the support of well-placed political allies, some of whom were on the jury. Bousquet was allowed to control the tenor and content of courtroom deliberations and to distort the facts without being challenged. This included discussions of his negotiations with the Germans in 1942 concerning the massive arrests and deportations of the Jews. After the trial, newspapers declared that the verdict flaunted the memory of the resistance, and one newspaper bitterly denounced the verdict as "one minute . . . of national degradation for Bousquet."[31] The true nature and full extent of Bousquet's wartime crimes had in no way been addressed.

While many of the criticisms of the first purge made by Vichy's apologists were based on distortions and exaggerations and were as politically motivated as was, in their view, the first purge itself, the 1949 Bousquet trial revealed real injustices, and the first purge's capacity to sow dissatisfaction among the populace was not simply limited to the wartime losers. Some of the injustices that occurred were, moreover, as much the result of practical considerations as anything else. For instance, those guilty of economic collaboration with the enemy were generally treated much less severely than writers who wrote in favor of collaboration. The same leniency was shown to many mid- and lower-level government officials or *fonctionnaires* like Maurice Papon, who was never charged or tried during the first purge and passed directly from the service of Vichy to that of de Gaulle's provisional government. The reason for the disparity is fairly self-evident: while the economy and the government needed to continue to function without interruption in the postwar period for the sake of national recovery, writers and intellectuals could be—and were—easily replaced by those espousing very different and more "timely" views.

At the time of the first purge, controversy was inevitable because the courts were obliged to deal with extraordinarily complex historical realities, political passions and pressures, and to a certain degree, practical considerations. Moreover, they were forced to work within a patched-together legal framework that was in many ways inadequate to the task. One important result was that, broadly speaking, the first-purge courts failed to make clear in precise terms the nature of the crime committed, including collaboration itself. But, more important, the first purge failed to deal adequately both with the magnitude and destructiveness of Vichy's anti-Semitic policies and with the specificity of Vichy complicity in the Final Solution. Ironically, the 1964 law making crimes against humanity punishable in France was aimed not at rectifying this situation but rather at preventing former Nazis guilty of committing these crimes on French soil from evading prosecution because the statute of limitations on war crimes—twenty years—was about to run out. Nevertheless, the 1964 law did set the stage for the second purge.

## The Second Purge

If one is fully to understand the history and significance of crimes against humanity in France, it is necessary to begin not with the 1990s trials of Frenchmen who served Vichy but rather with the 1987 trial of the Nazi Klaus Barbie. Had Barbie not been tried for crimes against humanity, it would have been impossible to try Touvier and Papon on similar charges in the following decade.

When Klaus Barbie, living under the alias "Klaus Altmann," was arrested in Bolivia and extradited to France in January 1983, the stage was set at last for France to bring to justice and punish one of its most notorious persecutors during the war. Barbie had been Gestapo chief in Lyons during the occupation, had deported Jews, and had tortured and killed resistance fighters, including Jean Moulin. He had been convicted in absentia of war crimes after the liberation, but the National Assembly's 1964 passage of the law governing crimes against humanity—and making them imprescriptable— now made it possible to try Barbie on new charges taking into account all of his crimes.[32]

When the assembly acted on its measure concerning crimes against humanity in 1964, it nevertheless failed to define or spell out the nature of these crimes in the text of the law, contenting itself with simply referring to the Nuremberg statutes. These statutes defined crimes against humanity as consisting of the "murder, extermination, enslavement, deportation, and other inhumane acts committed against any civilian population, . . . or persecutions on political, racial or religious grounds."[33] As the preparations for the Barbie trial got under way, the fly in the ointment quickly became apparent: it would be possible to try Barbie for the persecution and deportation of Jews, specifically the arrest and deportation of Jewish children hidden by the locals in the village of Izieu, but the definition of crimes against humanity as laid out in the Nuremberg statutes did not cover combatants, that is, in Barbie's case, the resistance.

When the situation became clear to former members of the resistance, they protested vehemently. One could not try and convict Barbie and claim that justice had been done on behalf of the French nation if his crimes against the resistance were not included in the charges. Barbie was most notorious, after all, for the torture and murder of Moulin, not for his actions against Jews. Faced with this delicate situation, which risked, in effect, pitting the memory of Nazism's Jewish victims against the memory of its resistance victims, in February 1987 the court of appeals decided to compromise and allow some crimes against resisters to be considered crimes against humanity.

So when Barbie was tried and convicted of crimes against humanity in the late spring and summer of 1987, he was condemned in part for his actions against the resistance, but the conviction also foregrounded the inhumanity of the Nazis' extermination of the Jews. And while the outcome of the trial was generally satisfying to most of the French, it also put pressure on the nation to try *Frenchmen* guilty of similar crimes (although this had not been the intention of the National Assembly in declaring crimes against humanity imprescriptible in 1964). In fact, during the trial of Barbie, defense council Jacques Vergès took pleasure in muddying the historical and legal waters by demanding that those French officials and soldiers linked, for example, to the torture and illegal detention of Algerian freedom fighters during the Algerian War were guilty of crimes against humanity as well, but no one seemed interested in trying them. While Vergès's ploy has never succeeded in bringing Frenchmen to trial for crimes against humanity supposedly committed during decolonization, it did up the ante for bringing the likes of Touvier, Bousquet, and Papon to trial for their crimes during the occupation.

If the Barbie case increased pressure to try Frenchmen accused of similar crimes, unfortunately it did not facilitate the process in legal terms. When the court of appeals modified the law to include Barbie's crimes against resisters, it set a dangerous precedent of modifying the law to suit the political circumstances of the moment. This had particularly explosive consequences in the case against Paul Touvier. From the moment of Touvier's arrest in a monastery in Nice in 1989, his case garnered constant media attention. His release on his own recognizance in 1991—reputedly for reasons of health—provoked massive public outrage: how much sense did it make to release a man like Touvier under these conditions, given that he had spent most of the last forty years fleeing the authorities and eluding justice?

But the scandal surrounding Touvier's 1991 release was nothing compared to controversy provoked by his acquittal by the Paris Court of Appeals in 1992. The court based its decision in part on a second modification written into the definition of crimes against humanity in the context of the Barbie trial in 1985 and in part on its own flawed, not to say outrageously misguided, reading of the history and politics of the Vichy regime. In its 1985 decision in the context of the Barbie case, the court not only allowed re-sistance members to be considered victims of crimes against humanity, it also stipulated that crimes against humanity could only be committed on behalf of a regime "practicing a politics of ideological hegemony." Nazi Germany clearly fit the definition of such a regime, but in its April 1992 decision the Paris Court of Appeals argued that Vichy did not. Whitewash-ing Vichy anti-Semitism for the most part, the court offered a portrait of the regime that was historically inaccurate in the extreme, insisting that the regime was not ideologically monolithic, but was founded instead on a disparate "constellation of good intentions and political animosities."[34]

No matter how inaccurate the court's reading of Vichy, it nevertheless seemed to justify the acquittal of Touvier who, the court argued, had acted solely as an agent of Vichy in carrying out his crimes. In November 1992 the court of appeals decision was partially overturned by the criminal chamber of the Supreme Court, which carefully avoided entering into the debate over the historical and political nature of the Vichy regime itself but did maintain that one of Touvier's crimes, the murder of seven Jewish hostages in the summer of 1944 near the cemetery of Rillieux, was actually carried out at the behest of the Nazis and could therefore be considered a crime against hu-manity. Touvier could therefore stand trial.

Paul Touvier was tried and convicted of crimes against humanity for the Rillieux murders at the Yveline Assizes Court in Versailles in the spring of 1994, but the trial and verdict were far from being entirely satisfactory in historical and legal terms. During the course of the trial it became clear that the Rillieux murders had not been undertaken on German initiatives, de-spite the prosecution's claims to the contrary. Nevertheless, one of the law-yers of the civil plaintiffs, Arno Klarsfeld, son of famed Nazi hunters Serge and Beate Klarsfeld, succeeded in arguing that while the crime was a French crime, due to the subordination of the Milice to the Gestapo (the Milice's leader, Joseph Darnand, had sworn an oath of allegiance to Hitler) the Rillieux murders had been committed under the auspices of Nazism's poli-tics of ideological hegemony.

While Klarsfeld's legal and historical acrobatics made the conviction of Touvier possible, the result was unsatisfactory on at least two scores. First, while a Frenchman had been convicted of crimes against humanity, Vichy's responsibility had been successfully deflected. Moreover, the legal road to Touvier's conviction had witnessed yet another modification of French juris-prudence concerning crimes against humanity, this one inspired not by a desire to serve all the victims of the accused but by jurists apparently in ideological sympathy with Touvier. While the latter fact was disturbing enough, what was even more disturbing to legal specialists was the violence being done to the law itself in the form of expedient changes. Reflecting on the trial in an article published the following summer, Christian Guéry wondered if the definition of crimes against humanity in France had not been stretched to the breaking point. Was it even possible to claim that they even *existed* in the legal sense of the term?[35]

As if these problems were not enough, in *Vichy: An Everpresent Past* Rousso and Éric Conan state that during the entire proceedings at Yvelines, the ghost of René Bousquet hung over the courtroom. Bousquet had been murdered in his apartment the previous summer by a deranged publicity seeker who later claimed that he had "killed a snake." If the murder had not occurred, Bousquet would in fact have stood trial for negotiating with the Germans to implement the Final Solution in France in Spring 1942 and for ordering the Vel d'Hiv roundups.

Given Bousquet's position of power and authority during the occupation, he dwarfed Touvier as a symbol of Vichy's—and France's—iniquity. By comparison, Touvier was mere "political rabble," as François Mitterrand observed, and the magnitude of Bousquet's crimes clearly overshadowed the murders at Rillieux.[36] Moreover, the arrests and deportations ordered by Bousquet were directly linked to Nazi hegemony *and* official Vichy complicity. They were also part of a "concerted plan" being carried out by the ideologically hegemonic Nazis, and thus coincided with yet another amendment to the French definition of crimes against humanity introduced in 1988, which stipulated that such crimes should fit into a "concerted plan" being implemented by the ideologically hegemonic power in question. On this score, as Rousso and Conan point out, the Rillieux murders appeared not to fit the bill.[37] So not only was Touvier's crime—admittedly racist in nature—arguably *not* a crime against humanity when considered in the context of every aspect of the legislation governing crimes against humanity and especially when compared with Bousquet's crimes, but the trial of Touvier was hardly an adequate "symbolic trial" of Vichy complicity with the Nazis' Final Solution, as Bousquet's trial most certainly would have been.

All this, ultimately, lent momentum to efforts to bring Maurice Papon to trial. While admittedly not a government official whose position and role could be compared to Bousquet's, Papon had been secretary-general of the Bordeaux prefecture from 1942 to 1944 and in that capacity was responsible for organizing the arrest, detention, and deportation of Jews in the context of Vichy's complicity in the Final Solution. The deportees were sent to the Drancy detention center in Paris, and most were later deported to Auschwitz.

Papon had also been in the resistance, and he would also cite this in his defense in order to prove that he was innocent of ideological complicity with the Nazis and therefore should not be tried. Besides, as he argued in a 1996 interview in the Parisian daily *Libération*, he was simply a scapegoat being persecuted for bigger fish that got away, namely René Bousquet.[38]

In January 1997 the Court of Cassation ruled, in yet another twist to French statutes governing crimes against humanity, that one could commit crimes against humanity without adhering to the ideologically hegemonic views of the Nazis. This paved the way for a trial which lasted from 8 October 1997 to 2 April 1998, garnered enormous media attention in France and abroad, and ended with a verdict that satisfied very few. Papon was found guilty of crimes against humanity for his actions in the arrest and deportation of his victims, but not of having knowingly sent them to their deaths. He was sentenced to ten years in prison, a remarkably light sentence given that he was guilty of crimes against humanity—by definition, one of the most heinous of crimes—and that such extraordinary efforts had been made to bring him to trial. In fact, Papon's case had dragged through the French courts and legal system, with numerous interruptions, for some fifteen years—a longer period of time than the duration of his sentence.

If the trials of Barbie, Touvier, and Papon, as well as the interrupted prosecution of Bousquet, succeeded in satisfying any national responsibility or obligation—they certainly did not clarify the history of the period to a wider public, nor did they help clarify or make more workable the laws concerning crimes against humanity—these trials did make a good faith effort to satisfy the "duty to memory." Widely discussed and debated in the 1980s and especially the 1990s, the duty to memory—in a judicial context, at least—consisted in the need to do justice to Vichy's Jewish victims, a half century after the fact, by prosecuting those who had been involved in carrying out the Final Solution in France. In this regard, the trials were at least partially successful. And even for the most cynical, who remained skeptical of the value and validity of the trials from start to finish, there was at least the consolation that there were simply no more perpetrators to try.

## The End of the Affair?

In the summer of 1995, in a speech given at the site of the monument dedicated to the victims of the Vel d'Hiv roundups, François Mitterrand's successor Jacques Chirac publicly acknowledged the role of the Vichy regime in backing up the "criminal insanity" of the Nazis in carrying out the Final Solution. Chirac also spoke of a "collective sin" on the part of his countrymen.[39] In *Vichy: An Everpresent Past* Rousso and Conan acknowledge that Chirac's statement marked a sharp break with the attitudes of his predecessors and that his remarks were greeted with satisfaction by the great majority of the public.[40] Combined with the conviction of Maurice Papon after an exhaustive six-month trial, it is possible to argue that by the late 1990s the haunting memory of Vichy was at last being put to rest.

But this is perhaps too optimistic a scenario. In spring 2002 Jean-Marie Le Pen's stunning first-round victory in French presidential elections demonstrated to the nation and the world that xenophobia and racism were very much alive and well in France. For many, this was a painful reminder that the attitudes and prejudices embraced and endorsed by Vichy more than a half century earlier had not been expunged from the national psyche. Moreover, continuing unrest and violence in the Middle East and hostility in many quarters toward Israeli dealings with the Palestinians fueled renewed outbursts of anti-Semitism that continue to this day. Finally, in the fall of 2004, the release of a government commission report on negationism at the University of Lyon III and the denunciations of the commission and its chief investigator, Henry Rousso, by National Front leader Bruno Gollnisch confirm that the denial of the Holocaust is still a sentimental favorite and indeed a rallying cry for many on France's extreme right. Under these circumstances, the ghosts of Vichy and of Nazism itself may not have been entirely banished from France. In the final analysis, only time will tell.

## Notes

1 Lagrou, *The Legacy of Nazi Occupation*, 1.

2 Rousso, *Le Syndrome de Vichy de 1944 à nos jours*. In this essay all citations are from Arthur Goldhammer's excellent translation, *The Vichy Syndrome*.

3 Robert Paxton et al., "Symposium on Mitterrand's Past," 19.

4 Gérard Noiriel, *Le Origines républicaines de Vichy*, 11.

5 I borrow the term "negative myth" from Henry Rousso (see his *Vichy*, 45).

6 Wiell, "Penser le procès Papon," 101–2.

7 For a discussion of the Moulin affair, see Vidal-Naquet, *Le Trait empoisonné*. For a discussion of the Aubrac affair, see Rousso, *The Haunting Past*.

8 Paxton, foreword, xii.

9 Morris, *Collaboration and Resistance Reviewed*, 7–41.

10   Lagrou, *The Legacy of Nazi Occupation*, 39.

11   Ibid., 38.

12   Ibid., 26.

13   Rousso, *The Vichy Syndrome*, 98.

14   Quoted in Rousso, *The Vichy Syndrome*, 123.

15   Ory, "Comme de l'an quarante."

16   Friedländer, *Reflets du nazisme*.

17   Foucault, "Anti-Rétro."

18   *Louis Malle par Louis Malle*, 9.

19   Aymé, *Uranus*, 35–39.

20   Alfred Fabre-Luce, Jean-Paul Sartre, Germaine Tillion, and Stanley Hoffmann's comments about *Le chagrin et la pitié* are all quoted in Rousso, *The Vichy Syndrome*, 106–09.

21   Hoffmann, "Cinquante ans après, quelques conclusions essentielles," 39.

22   Sartre, "Qu'est-ce qu'un collaborateur?"

23   In Antoine de Baecque and Serge Toubiana's 2001 biography, *François Truffaut*, Truffaut is quoted as saying that his memory of the occupation was not that of a constant struggle between French and Germans but of a period that was "much more calm" (689). He also states that he set out to offer this vision of the period in making *Le dernier métro*.

24   Indeed, *La douleur* raised questions as to whether or not, in its vision of the occupation, the French novel has ever moved beyond the Broken Mirror phase and the outlook of the mode rétro. Despite the obvious literary quality of Duras's novel, like many other recent novels—and films—dealing with the Dark Years, *La douleur* offers no new insights into the period itself.

25   Of (perverse) interest, one early account of the real Dr. Petiot was written by the lawyer Jean-Marc Varaut, who would later become Maurice Papon's defense lawyer.

26   Rousso, "Une justice impossible," 748 (my translation).

27   Ibid.

28   Kaplan, *The Collaborator*.

29   Lottman, *The Purge*, 16.

30   Ibid.

31   Newspaper article as quoted in Golsan, *Vichy's Afterlife*, 30–31.

32   There are any number of excellent books on Barbie and the Barbie trial in English, including Erna Paris's *Unhealed Wounds: France and the Klaus Barbie Affair* (1985) and Alain Finkielkraut's *Remembering in Vain: The Klaus Barbie Trial and Crimes against Humanity* (1992). But the most gripping exposition of the Barbie affair is Ophuls's documentary *Hotel Terminus*.

33   Quoted in Reisman and Antoniou, *The Laws of War*, 319.

34   For a full discussion of the legal decisions leading up to the trial of Touvier, see the introduction to my *Memory, the Holocaust, and French Justice*.

35   Guéry, "Une interrogation après le procès Touvier."

36  Mitterrand made this observation in an interview by Olivier Wieviorka, in *Nous entrerons dans la carrière*, 350.

37  Conan and Rousso, *Vichy*, 154–55.

38  The *Libération* interview, along with other documents concerning the Papon trial and interpretive essays by historians and legal experts, is included in my *The Papon Affair*.

39  Chirac as quoted in Conan and Rousso, *Vichy*, 39 and 41.

40  Ibid., 42–43.

WULF KANSTEINER ✳︎

# Losing the War, Winning the Memory Battle

## THE LEGACY OF NAZISM, WORLD WAR II,

## AND THE HOLOCAUST IN THE FEDERAL

## REPUBLIC OF GERMANY

## What Is Vergangenheitsbewältigung?

The phrase *Vergangenheitsbewältigung* (overcoming the past) surfaced in West Germany's public sphere in the late 1950s. At the beginning the term was tinged with irony and used in quotation marks to indicate the authors' dismissal of the latest fad of soul-searching inquiries into Germany's historical responsibility during and after Nazism. The critics who used the phrase in this fashion welcomed honest self-reflection but also emphasized the futility of the exercise and poked fun at its egocentric, self-serving nature.[1] Starting from such humble beginnings the term gradually lost its ironic edge and came to denote all discussions about the appropriate political, social, and moral agendas for the postfascist age and all initiatives designed to implement these alleged historical lessons.[2] Not surprisingly, at any given time the discussions outweighed the practical initiatives.

More than alternative terms such as *Aufarbeitung* (working through) or *Trauerarbeit* (mourning work), the term *Vergangenheitsbewältigung* announced a specific type of public intervention in West Germany's media; it signaled to its audience that they were about to be confronted with some contemporary agenda that sought to derive legitimacy from the German catastrophe. The term represented a plea that left consumers with a range of options. They could dismiss the whole undertaking and reject any link between past and present, an attitude that dominated in the 1950s and gained prominence again in the 1970s and 1990s. Alternatively, the audience could accept the historical logic of this discursive strategy and share the belief that careful reflection about the legacy of the Third Reich would decisively improve the political, social, and economic status quo. Since links between past and present were accepted as a given, the challenge now "merely" consisted of determining the correct paths of exegesis. The question was no longer if but how meaningful connections between Nazism and the Federal Republic were to be constructed.[3]

The history of Vergangenheitsbewältigung (VGB) from the immediate postwar years (*avant la lettre*) to the 1980s represents the triumph of the second attitude over the first. Over the decades it became increasingly unacceptable to question the interpretive continuity between past and present, and rituals of interpretation became ever more deeply engrained in the historical culture of the Federal Republic. Thus, the very origins of the term VGB marked the beginning of a new, self-conscious approach to the Nazi past and this turning point in the late 1950s was at least as important as the ultimate triumph of the paradigm of VGB during the 1980s, when West Germany's elite was most committed to historical self-education.

Beginning in the late 1950s and continuing to this day, VGB flourished in many realms of (West) German culture, often relentlessly pursued by cohorts of memory activists eager to identify yet another remnant of false historical consciousness or another site of memory waiting to be rescued from oblivion. Despite, or perhaps because of, this hectic activity, the practice of VGB has changed significantly since the late 1990s. German mainstream media have not embraced a reactionary, nationalistic agenda, but in response to growing disinterest among some members of the elite and many media consumers, VGB has become an optional, special-interest pursuit. Historical scandals continue to unfold and seemingly unrelated issues—for instance, biotechnology—are still summoned in the court of VGB. But increasingly, even toward the left end of the political spectrum, voices which question the powerful doctrine that any issue in contemporary German life can only be properly understood against the foil of Nazi history have gained strength. After the last reparations deal was struck for the former forced laborers of the Nazi regime, the political elite was convinced that it had paid its dues and was entitled to sever the interpretive continuity between past and present. As in the 1950s and, to a lesser extent, in the 1970s, it had again become possible to split off the Nazi past from contemporary problems.

But in contrast to earlier years, political normalization and Holocaust memory were no longer mutually exclusive. On the sixtieth anniversary of the end of World War II in May 2005, German chancellor Gerhard Schröder participated in the anniversary celebrations in Moscow like many other heads of state. Three days later the president of the German parliament, Wolfgang Thierse, opened a large Holocaust memorial in the center of Berlin. Prominent representations of German guilt and participation in world diplomacy are today dialectically intertwined without forcing German representatives to adopt a special role in international politics, as was the case through the mid-1990s.[4] Past champions of political normalization like former chancellor Helmut Kohl must be pleasantly surprised by this turn of events. Kohl had agreed to build the Holocaust Memorial only under considerable political pressure. During his long tenure from 1982 to 1998 he operated under the assumption that continued emphasis on the Nazi past and the Holocaust would extend indefinitely Germany's diminished influence in world politics. Yet in the first decade of the new millennium, Germany deployed troops in Afghanistan and the former Yugoslavia and has become a key player in world affairs in other respects as well—all of this because of, rather than despite, the extensive, routine display of Holocaust memory in the German media.

Since the mid-1990s scholars in the field of German memory studies have carefully reconstructed interpretations of Nazism that the cultural and political elite of the Federal Republic crafted over the course of six decades. As a result of the focus on elite discourses, the following synthesis is primarily a history of historical culture; it tells us what stories politicians, historians, journalists, novelists, museum designers, and film and television makers told about the Third Reich and how these stories have changed over time. The elite discourses are conceptually and empirically linked to collective memories in three ways. First, they reflect the collective memories of the intellectual and professional communities that produced them. Second, most of the stories about the past which circulated in Germany's public sphere were designed to become successful collective memories; their creators hoped to shape the historical consciousness of their audiences and perhaps even the nation as a whole.[5] Third, and most important, the stories and their creators only rarely attained that position of exceptional influence. In fact, there are good reasons to assume that the products of Germany's historical culture and the elite collective memories that they represent are not identical, perhaps not even compatible with the collective memories of many German families, professions, and mass-media audiences whose members either pay little attention to elite cultural products or use them for identity purposes for which they were not intended. The tensions between different types and levels of collective memory necessitate placing Germany's historical culture within its wider sociological and political context, both nationally and internationally, and paying close attention to collective memories that evolved below the threshold of elite discourses.

## The Discourse of Intellectual Memory

Faced with an overwhelming number of participants and contexts, those who used the discourse of VGB erected clearly visible intellectual signposts, three of which have enjoyed particular popularity through the decades. Since the late 1950s, provocative statements in the works of the philosopher Theodor Adorno have provided important reference points for literary and aesthetic discussions about how to represent Auschwitz. Adorno's dictum "To write poetry after Auschwitz is barbaric" has "provoked and intimidated generations of German intellectuals and artists."[6] Adorno's enigmatic intervention was based on his complex philosophical critique of Western civilization. In his assessment, the self-destructive social, economic, and psychological structures of modern society which had caused the rise of Fascism continued to exist unabated in the postwar era.[7] Many critics on the left wholeheartedly endorsed, albeit in radically simplified form, Adorno's pessimistic warnings about the destructive trajectory of modern German history and forged them into an effective political rhetoric.

The second and single most important signpost derived from the 1967 publication of *The Inability to Mourn*, by Alexander and Margaret Mitscherlich. They explained the shortcomings of West German attempts to come to terms with the past from a psychoanalytical point of view, and their arguments have been used by intellectuals ever since to critique the German achievements in the realm of VGB.[8] As Anson Rabinbach pointed out, it is hardly possible to exaggerate "the Mitscherlichs' extraordinary success in producing the paradigmatic expression of what ultimately became a predominant way of thinking about the burdens of history in Germany in the late 1960s."[9] The Mitscherlichs' diagnosis—that the Germans had reacted to the trauma of the sudden loss of their beloved leader in 1945 by derealizing their past and that this self-protective mechanism had effectively prevented any real processes of mourning for that loss—was quickly summarize/ der the rubric of repression. It has remained the single most popula/ the discourse of VGB. The Mitscherlichs' thesis, like Adorno's, cir/ truncated, simplified versions which directly linked the Germ/

to mourn to a whole range of phenomena—including World War II, the Holocaust, and postwar reconstruction—without taking note of the authors' more elaborate analysis of the German collective psyche.

The third and most recent intellectual marker, representing an anti-VGB stance, derived from a number of essays published in the mid-1980s by the historian and philosopher Hermann Lübbe.[10] His comprehensive defense of the West German record of coming to terms with the past, directed against the Mitscherlichs' position, represented the first intellectual rallying point of the conservative camp. Lübbe argued that the silence about the Nazi past in West Germany in the 1950s resulted from a conscious, tacit agreement between former Nazis and former victims of Nazism, who together decided to focus on the reconstruction of Germany, assure the survival of the nation, and forego self-destructive controversies about the question of guilt. According to Lübbe, that agreement laid the foundation of the postwar democracy and highlighted the radical political discontinuities between the Third Reich and the Federal Republic. Lübbe's critique was directed at the core of the discourse of VGB and justified the silence of the 1950s and 1970s after the fact. A number of scholars who published on questions of German memory in the last two decades have implicitly or explicitly supported Lübbe's perspective.

While in full force, the discursive formation of VGB has only rarely been subject to critical scholarly analysis. Until the early 1990s intellectuals either wholeheartedly participated in the practice of VGB or, from a minority position, somewhat helplessly and polemically attacked its rationale and effects. Publications about the history of German memory reflected primarily political, not academic or aesthetic concerns. But since the mid-1990s Germany's historical culture has become the subject of sustained empirical and theoretical reflection. As a result, the practice of VGB has been relativized and historicized.[11] This process of historicization demonstrates that VGB represented only one of many possible approaches to the past. While any history of the memory of Nazism and World War II in Germany has to give due weight to the success story of VGB, it is equally important to highlight the memory practices which did not unfold within this paradigm and to stress the astonishing diversity within the conceptual and political space of VGB itself. Coming to terms with the past meant different things for different constituencies and generations, which, in the process, created one of the most lively, volatile, and diverse historical cultures in Europe. The historicization of VGB that revealed the limits of the paradigm seems to coincide with the end of an era of exceptionally intense historical reflection and thus marks a significant loss for the political culture of the Federal Republic.

## Rubble Culture: 1945–1948

Immediately after the war the German people, their political representatives, and the Allies focused on concrete and pressing tasks. They tried to repair the apparently formidable damage to the infrastructure and to administer justice and scarce resources with some degree of consistency and fairness.[12] In the process, former bystanders and perpetrators were quickly confronted with their mistakes and their crimes.

Germans had become astute media consumers during the Nazi period. They had enjoyed state-of-the-art entertainment that required sophisticated techniques of interpretation to uncover its factual core.[13] After the liberation of the camps and during the first wave of Allied trials in Nuremberg, they confronted shockingly direct representations of German crimes. Despite occasional attempts to discredit the "victors' propaganda," the new German and Allied news outlets were avidly consumed and generally considered trustworthy. As a result, Nazi crimes became a cornerstone of postwar German identity. Despite other pressing concerns and various attempts at relativization, media representations of German guilt probably left their mark on the psyche of the "survivors" of the Third Reich.[14]

In the years after liberation Germans quickly rebuilt a thriving array of newspapers and journals under the watchful eyes of the Allies. These publications addressed a seemingly insatiable appetite for news. Many journalists, as well as teachers and students, turned to classic authors and religious texts for orientation. In the midst of this cultural renaissance a number of intellectuals also inquired about the causes and the consequences of the German catastrophe. The debates remained controversial and inconclusive, ranging from far-reaching indictments of German history since Luther and Frederick the Great to more detailed analysis of the Nazi movement to far-fetched historical reconstructions that saw a direct link between Nazism and the French Revolution. The question of the precise nature of German guilt provided the explicit or implicit focus of many of these interventions.[15]

The debates reflected fears of Allied denazification efforts that were initially designed to cast a wide net, especially in the U.S. zone. The writers were particularly concerned about the concept of collective guilt, which had briefly surfaced in Allied communications but had quickly been abandoned as impractical and incompatible with Allied interests. In the German debates the concept of collective guilt assumed the role of an intellectual straw man whose moral shortcomings could be easily exposed.[16] In hindsight it is easy to dismiss the limited scope and apologetic tone of many of these interventions, although, undertaken in times of political and existential uncertainty, they remain some of the most straightforward and remarkable contributions to postwar historical culture.[17] In this respect, they differ from the subsequent culture of VGB that was launched from a secure political and economic position at a point in time when the West German experiment had succeeded beyond anybody's expectations.

With the beginning of the Cold War, Allied pressure for German self-examination and reform ended quite suddenly and was replaced by subsidies, lobbying efforts, and self-government. As the denazification apparatus was dismantled, Germans could embrace their most benign memories of the war era with impunity and represent themselves as a nation that had been led astray by a few Nazis and had been more than sufficiently punished by war, expulsion, occupation, and division.[18] But underneath these stories of suffering and sacrifice, which came to dominate all channels of memory, some former citizens of the Third Reich retained memories of the Nazi crimes and recognized that Germans had got off quite lightly.

## Reconstruction, Restoration, and Communicative Silence: The 1950s

Cultural historians of postwar Germany highlight the diversity of the Federal Republic's historical culture during the 1950s.[19] Their interpretations provide a welcome corrective to overly simplistic allegations of German repression in the tradition of Adorno and the Mitscherlichs. Nevertheless, the culture of that decade is still most appropriately characterized as a period of communicative silence about the most troublesome aspects of the burden of the past, a silence that went hand-in-hand with noisy lamentations of German victimhood.[20]

The consequences of war and "war crimes" were acknowledged and addressed by the new political elites in their dealings with their Allied supervisors, but not necessarily in communications with the German population. In the West many of the new political leaders were veterans of moderate Weimar parties who had been disenfranchised after 1933 and returned to the political scene with relatively clean records. They dominated politics throughout the 1950s and pursued a masterful dual strategy vis-à-vis their voters and their Allied supervisors, especially after the founding of the Federal Republic in May 1949. For the benefit of German voters, the new-old political elite expressed its honestly felt concern for the people's survival and well-being, and focused on the social integration of the traumatized population.[21] This task was accomplished with relative ease since reconstruction proved to be a much less daunting challenge than expected and was generously supported by former enemies. In addition, the integration of different social and political groups could be easily concluded on the solid foundation of the Nazi *Volksgemeinschaft*. The mobilization and modernization of German society, both inadvertently and intentionally advanced by the Nazi administration, had effectively neutralized traditional social barriers that were further undermined by the outcome of the war; the delegitimation of the aristocracy through military defeat and expropriation exemplified such unintended egalitarian tendencies.[22] In the end, the functional elite of the Third Reich and the German refugees from Eastern Europe profited most directly from the invention of the postwar community of suffering. The former survived the 1940s without so much as a dent in social status and career development.[23] The latter were generously compensated for their losses and presented as the archetypal German victims of the war era.[24] The policies of national consensus in the West proved far less magnanimous toward the victims of the Nazi regime, especially if these victims were not represented by lobbies influential with Allied leaders, for example, former forced laborers from Eastern Europe who were only recently compensated for their suffering.[25] But even the failed working-class resistance against the Nazis was only selectively acknowledged in the East and West according to the political priorities of the reconstituted socialist and Communist parties.[26]

The West German leaders were much more forthcoming with acknowledgments of past crimes and the need for retribution and reparations in their dealings with the Western Allies. On this second political front, shaped by different expectations than those of the German clientele, German politicians offered their services in the beginning Cold War and actively pursued compensation plans.[27] The victims of choice became the Jewish survivors and the Jewish State, not necessarily because they had suffered the most, which they certainly had, but because they were most effectively represented by a U.S. Jewish leadership that had not aggressively intervened during the war and now grasped the opportunity of belated solidarity.[28]

All political players accepted the effective split between domestic and foreign policies. As long as West German politicians delivered their economic and military contributions to the cause of anti-Communism, the policies of national integration raised no serious objections. Under the circumstances it made perfect sense that the federal government aggressively demanded the release of convicted Nazi war criminals while planning for remilitarization.[29]

The new elite in the East, recruited from political émigrés and a few select surviving resisters, faced similar problems and adopted similar positions but enjoyed less flexibility than their Western counterparts. The Soviet Union insisted on substantial reparations and prevented any public discussions about the expulsion of ethnic Germans from Eastern Europe. Communist leaders made an even more generous peace offering to the German population than their colleagues in the West. By joining the Communist camp, East Germans reinvented themselves as the victims of a capitalist fascist regime. The adoption of a new historical consciousness absolved them from responsibility for many victims of Nazism.[30] The more radical political transformation in the East and the more decisive if not necessarily more precise punishment of Nazi perpetrators lent the East German solution a certain degree of legitimacy.[31] Despite ruthless political repression and the lack of democratic reforms, East German Communism received considerable support from left-leaning intellectuals at home and abroad, who disapproved of the West German restoration and its messy experiment in democratic majority rule. As these intellectuals saw it, the East German approach presented the more ambitious and ideologically coherent response to the Nazi catastrophe.[32] In the early 1950s official East German discourse about Nazism changed in two important respects. Instead of emphasizing the misery that capitalism and authoritarian traditions had caused in Germany and Europe, the East German leadership focused on the positive examples of socialist resistance against Fascism. In the course of that transition and in response to Stalinist anti-Semitism, the suffering of Jews during Nazism was no longer acknowledged in the East German media and Jewish functionaries were expelled from the party.[33]

By 1955 the large majority of German war criminals had been freed from Allied prisons and the last German POWs had returned from the Soviet Union. The latter event, in particular, represented a decisive public-relations victory for the Adenauer government and was enthusiastically celebrated by West Germans. Nobody objected when the press declared the war to be finally over.[34] In the same spirit of closure, federal and state prosecutors abandoned all attempts to bring Nazi perpetrators to justice, and the government sought to settle accounts with the victims as quickly as possible, for instance, through the reparation treaty with Israel.[35] The settlement remained unpopular with the West German voters; in fact, all data indicate that a substantial segment of the population remained ardent anti-Semites.[36]

But selective reconciliation with the victims represented another chapter in the success story of West German recovery that featured more prominently the restoration of national sovereignty, remilitarization, economic success, and a return to international diplomacy. In the decade after the war a national consensus emerged in the West that was time and again reconfirmed in elections and public opinion surveys: West Germans emphasized their own suffering and largely ignored the suffering they had inflicted on others.

All media of memory reflected this consensus. The restructured film industry recycled the stars and aesthetics of the Nazi cinema, brought up-to-date with vague yearnings for Heimat and unapologetic accounts of the courageous struggle of the German army on the Eastern Front.[37] The educational system had dutifully reformed the curricula and issued new textbooks, but for the most part teachers simply opted out of teaching contemporary history; according to them, German history tended to end either in the nineteenth century or at best with the failure of the first German republic.[38] As far as one can tell, the *cordon sanitaire* around Nazi crimes was equally well maintained in the private sphere. For a range of motives, especially unacknowledged guilt and injured pride, Nazi crimes and personal involvement in Nazism remained carefully protected taboo subjects.[39] Adolescents quickly recognized that the topics presented excellent strategic opportunities, but they still lacked the means to use them as leverage and destroy the thin veneer of normality that covered the deep fault lines in the reconstituted patriarchal family.[40]

Since all the signs were so clearly set for amnesia, the question is not why Germans so quickly abandoned self-reflection given the extraordinary opportunities offered them by the Cold War. In fact, such organized forgetfulness corresponds to general patterns of collective memory that appear in other cases of national defeat and ignominy in the twentieth century.[41] The crucial question is why the national consensus broke so quickly, at least in a relative sense, and gave way to an exceptionally ambitious, sustained, and diverse examination of the past, first in the 1960s and then again in the 1980s.

Even in the 1950s there were a number of important dissenting voices, especially in the literary scene of the new republic. A number of authors exposed the repressive and forgetful political climate of the 1950s (Wolfgang Koeppen, for one) and found critical acclaim (if not necessarily readers) for their analysis of their compatriots' communicative silence. Other literary figures, most prominently Heinrich Böll, addressed the bystander syndrome in the Third Reich and espoused a determined pacifism in response to their personal experiences during the war.[42] Such attitudes were shared by a vocal political minority that resisted rearmament in powerful public rallies and later served as the role models of the social movements of the 1970s and 1980s.[43] Occasionally such unpopular positions even received reluctant praise in the mainstream media, whose representatives recognized that the protests and the moral integrity of some of the protesters enhanced the country's democratic legitimacy abroad.

Raising the Specter of the Past: The 1960s

The silence of the 1950s was undermined by a coalition of antifascists of the first generation who had been effectively marginalized in public after 1948 and a new generation of intellectuals who remembered the Nazi era but were too young to have been involved in any crimes. Especially the second cohort, the members of the Hitler Youth-generation, laid the foundation for the self-critical reform of West Germany's historical culture in the 1960s, a cause pursued even more aggressively in subsequent years by the activists of the student movement.

The gradual transformation of West Germany's historical culture was jump-started by a number of coincidental events that exposed the uneasy and unstable compromises at the core of the memory peace of the 1950s.[44] In 1959 the republic was shaken by a wave of anti-Semitic graffiti committed by a few neo-Nazis and (more disturbing) a sizeable number of juvenile copycats across West Germany. The scandals triggered critical interventions from Europe and the United States and prompted reforms of school curricula and teaching practices in several states of the Federal Republic. It became clear that the communicative silence of earlier years had failed to impress the limits of West Germany's political culture on the postwar generation. Whereas the contemporaries of Nazism tended to refrain from *explicit* display of anti-Semitic sentiments, some of their children had not yet recognized that anti-Semitic and neo-Nazi activities represented absolute taboos that could not be transgressed for the purpose of intergenerational provocation.[45]

The educational reforms were quietly and selectively implemented in the 1960s by a new cohort of teachers who began to teach about the Nazi era because this task coincided with their own curiosity about the Germany of their childhood and adolescence. It is difficult to assess the precise impact of these reforms, which progressed fitfully and unevenly within an antagonistic and still largely authoritarian educational infrastructure. But the reforms laid the foundation for more rigorous teachings and might even have raised the historical sensibilities of the student-movement generation. Some topics, however, remained unaddressed in the new educational endeavors: whereas the history of political repression in the Third Reich received some attention, the Holocaust and the crimes of the Wehrmacht did not.[46]

Another scandal of the late 1950s involved an officer in the Einsatzgruppen who sued to regain his former civil-service position. Through a number of coincidences, he was finally put on trial, prompting some media commentators to demand that hidden perpetrators like this ss officer should finally be brought to justice. As a result, the central agency for the research and trial preparation against ns perpetrators was founded in 1958 and managed to launch a number of high-profile public trials in the 1960s that targeted the former ss personnel of the ns concentration and extermination camps.[47] The trials widely publicized the crimes of the Nazi regime and raised awareness of the suffering of the victims. In fact, the most important of the trials—the Auschwitz trial from 1963 to 1965—finally provided a name for the Nazi genocide and exposed it as one of the central characteristics and objectives of the Nazi government. From 1963 to 1979 "Auschwitz" served as the general code word for the Final Solution.[48]

Unlike the Nuremberg and the Eichmann trials, the new West German trials could not be dismissed as victors' or victims' justice based on ex post facto laws. Launched on its own volition by an independent court in a sovereign country and conducted according to the legal code of the Weimar and Nazi era, the Auschwitz trial and its successors retained their legitimacy even in the face of scattered criticism.[49] Nevertheless, the impact of the proceedings on German collective memories should not be overstated. The Eichmann trial had been covered extensively in the West German media, but the majority of West German citizens rejected the way that Eichmann had been captured and found it inappropriate that he was put on trial in Israel. Though the Auschwitz trial received even more attention from journalists, polling data indicate that the population paid less attention to the proceedings in Frankfurt than the previous proceedings in Jerusalem.[50]

In the end, the trials left a lot to be desired from both legal and public-relations perspectives. Since the old legal codes proved ineffective for the punishment of new crimes like genocide, the trials ended with embarrassingly benign sentences and the *Schreibtischtäter* ("desk perpetrators" or bureaucratic perpetrators) were never even indicted. Consequently, the trials inadvertently supported a vision of the Nazi crimes that limited responsibility to a few subordinate ss officers and tended to contain them in a few "remote" geographical settings like the camp of Auschwitz.[51]

The efforts of the courts were supported by the work of historians who provided detailed knowledge about the origins and organization of the Final Solution and confirmed the authenticity of relevant documents. Historical-expert testimony, which had already featured in less prominent trials and compensation litigation, formed the basis for the first historiographical analyses of the history of the Final Solution.[52] According to the needs of the courts, these perpetrator-focused histories unraveled the complicated power structure of the Third Reich and augmented already existing political histories of the regime. Like the progress in the schools, the historiographical advances resulted in part from the work of a young group of scholars who had only known the Third Reich as adolescents. In the 1960s they began their careers as staff members at the Institut für Zeitgeschichte and as postdoctoral students at a number of universities, especially in Cologne. In coming years they revolutionized the study of history and remained a formidable influence on the discipline into the 1990s. But in the early 1960s they faced a historiographical establishment that still embraced conventional methodologies and advocated conservative political positions. Therefore, early scholarship about the Third Reich and the Holocaust, however important as a first step, was not well equipped to approach some of the most challenging questions about the history of Nazism. As yet West German historians had nothing to say about the social history of the Third Reich, and even the first studies of the Final Solution all but ignored the victims.[53] In addition, the studies might have changed the perception of the Nazi era among historical experts, but the new insights had limited impact on the historical culture of the republic. Historians had the greatest influence through their work for the courts and through the selective integration of their findings into school textbooks, although the latter could easily take several decades.

It is quite remarkable that legal experts and academic historians helped reform West Germany's historical culture in the 1960s, since both professions had been severely compromised during the Third Reich and had neither acknowledged their collective failures nor divested themselves of former Nazis in their own ranks. A number of German historians had eagerly provided ideological support to the racist and genocidal measures of the regime and occasionally even supported these efforts as members of the occupational forces. But removed from the centers of power, they were largely prevented from becoming full-scale perpetrators and had "merely" compromised their moral integrity as a result of their passivity and their zealous identification with the Nazi cause.[54] The legal profession, however, had actively shaped and maintained the Nazi terror system in all its manifestations. As a result, the profession as a whole was profoundly compromised, although very few Nazi judges or prosecutors were ever punished for their egregious miscarriages of justice.[55]

The fact that both professions emerged at the forefront of the struggle to reconstitute German collective memory in the 1960s can be attributed to a few restless émigrés, remorseful bystanders, and a small yet active minority among the novices in the professions. Yet these efforts would have been far less successful if the memory dissidents had not been provided with legal tools and an academic infrastructure that could be employed for their revisionist objectives. The reintroduction of the rule of law, first by the Allies and then by the West German State itself, and the expansion and gradual democraticization of the university system gave the active minority the opportunity to revolutionize public representation of the past against the interests of a resentful but effectively silenced majority within their own professions.

The expanding media industry in West Germany contributed to the transformation of the public image of Nazism in the 1960s, although the departure from apologetic representations of the Third Reich occurred even more gradually than in the more specialized environs of the professions. The German film industry had accompanied its audiences through war and occupation, providing reliable entertainment with familiar faces and storylines. In the 1960s this rock of stability fell victim to its U.S. counterpart, the rising medium of television, and the changing viewer preferences that these transformations reflected. The slow death of the *Heimatfilm* indicated that the West German population felt increasingly comfortable with the provisional solution of the Federal Republic. Consumers flocked in growing numbers to the cinemas to watch U.S. productions that, like postwar German films, had little to say about the German past but offered better entertainment than indigenous productions. The few movies that directly addressed the history of World War II confirmed the apologetic representations of the Germany military which had already dominated the German screens. Films like *The Longest Day* went a long way in safeguarding the myth of the chivalrous Wehrmacht and supporting the strategic alignments of the Cold War.[56]

Similar themes and strategies of representation dominated the historical coverage of German public television, which only began to reach mass audiences in the 1960s. Administrators of the new medium were closely supervised by the political elites, who controlled funding and personnel decisions. As a result, television featured the politically correct messages of the day, including a fair amount of philo-Semitic programming that helplessly tried to advance the cause of Christian-Jewish reconciliation after Auschwitz. Television makers did not yet know how to deal with the topic of the Final Solution in any compelling aesthetic fashion, but they provided reliable factual information about the Nazi past through a range of documentaries and television plays. In high-profile programming, such as the ARD series *Das Dritte Reich* and coverage of the Eichmann trial, the crimes of the regime were dutifully noted. In this respect, the television of the decade reflected research advances made in the courts. Yet the historical programming also served a more important and more problematic purpose than simply popularizing the changing perceptions of Nazism among professional interpreters.[57]

According to the programs of the 1960s, the world of the Nazis had been populated by a limited inventory of historical figures. Documentaries and TV shows focused especially on five such stereotypical characters: the dutiful, even courageous, yet helpless German soldier; the heroic but failing resistance fighter; the principled, passive victim; the naïve, coerced, or seduced collaborator; and the vicious Nazi. Most of the figures who occupied center stage were German males who enacted the drama of Nazism in front of an indiscriminate supporting cast of foreign soldiers and civilians, apolitical women, and the occasional Jew. Very few productions disrupted this simple world, and even they generally failed to provide more critical insights into the Nazi era.[58]

The repetitive coverage of the Nazi era during the first decade of German television suggests that the programs were not just intended to inform new generations of East and West Germans about the history of Nazism; they also offered television producers and audiences an opportunity to revisit their messy memories of the Nazi era and reinvent their own lives with the help of the clichés on the screen. Most likely, at the end of this cleansing operation, very few contemporaries of the Third Reich identified with the "vicious Nazi" or the camp guards on trial and preferred less damning role models. Thus, despite ample, accurate historical information available through different venues of West Germany's historical culture, audiences could easily hold the past at bay and avoid painful moral questions about their own personal choices and involvement.

In light of this respectable yet ambivalent media coverage, the literary and theatrical works of the 1960s represent more probing explorations of the moral legacy of Nazism. As in other arenas of West Germany's historical culture, some of the most noteworthy of these explorations were provided by artists who had been confronted with Nazism as adolescents and young adults. When the novelist Günter Grass published his ingenious *The Tin Drum* in 1959, he anticipated the insights of the history of everyday life by more than a decade. Without finding excuses, Grass illustrated how the rise of Fascism and the racist policies of the regime were absorbed and supported by a distracted German citizenry that had many other things on its mind besides politics but still found time to tie its own hopes to the Nazi revolution and take advantage of the new political climate. Grass's brilliant idea to seek for an explanation for Nazism at ground zero in the ordinary lives and failures of its self-occupied activists, reluctant opponents, and detached bystanders contrasted sharply with the dominant explanatory models of the day that focused on the Nazi leadership and its organizational structure.[59]

In a different yet similarly path-breaking work, the dramatist Rolf Hochhuth struck at the heart of the complacent, self-indulgent religious revival of the postwar era when he indicted Pope Pius XII for complicity in the Nazi crimes and caused a controversy that has continued to this very day. Hochhuth's piece of documentary theater, *The Deputy*, which premiered in 1963, corresponded well to concurrent somber and fact-oriented historiography and trial proceedings, but he placed blame where few had dared or cared to look and thus showed clearly that the search for causes and responsibility was only just beginning.[60] Both Grass's *The Tin Drum* and Hochhuth's *The Deputy* illustrate that the reconstruction of West Germany's historical culture in the 1960s resulted in a lively, multifaceted memory culture that was decisively advanced by members of the Hitler Youth generation. But they also show that dominant representations of the time pursued more modest goals.

The 1950s laid the legal and political foundations for seemingly unlikely future confrontations with the past. That framework was subsequently employed, intelligently, by a determined minority in their efforts to uncover and highlight the shameful historical record that most of their contemporaries had chosen to leave unrepresented and unaddressed. As a result, knowledge of Nazism, however selective and limited, permeated West German society and reached its younger members, who had never experienced the Third Reich. The memory culture of the 1960s still avoided the most unsettling questions, but the very process of selective remembrance helped define the memory challenges of the future. The discussions of the 1960s also showed how effectively the burden of the past could be mobilized to generate political strife. By the end of the decade, historical liabilities that had hardly raised eyebrows ten years before were no longer tolerated, and the political scene was opened for players whose antifascist record would have derailed their careers in previous years.

In this context, high-profile opportunists and former perpetrators like Hans Globke and Theodor Oberländer, who had made careers in the Adenauer administration despite their Nazi record, became the target of negative press that was skillfully supported by East German propaganda efforts.[61] Even Chancellor Kiesinger, who took the helm in 1966 as the leader of a coalition between the Christlich Demokratische Union (CDU) and the Sozialdemokratische Partei Deutschlands (SPD), fit the profile of a Nazi opportunist whose past should have disqualified him for public office. Kiesinger had been a member of the Nazi party and a high-level administrator in Goebbels's propaganda ministry, and he was now relentlessly, if unsuccessfully attacked by East Berlin and student activists.[62] At the same time, changing sensibilities permitted former resistance fighters like Willy Brandt to seek and win national office. Brandt was still viciously attacked by the conservative press for having "left his fatherland in times of national crisis" but the campaign did not undermine his candidacy.[63] In fact, during the 1960s the official assessment of the resistance against the Nazi regime was almost completely reversed. The mainstream media still refused to endorse the Communist and Socialist resistance against Hitler, but conservative opponents of the regime, especially the conspirators of 20 July 1944, were no longer vilified as traitors but were instead presented as role models to the soldiers of the Bundeswehr.[64]

When the student movement formed against the seemingly overwhelming power monopoly of the SPD-CDU coalition, many of its political and historical claims were either inaccurate or outdated. The state and federal governments that the students taunted so effectively had already launched a sweeping reform of the university system and once the social-democratic and liberal government took office in 1969, the goals of the government and their radical critics were quite compatible. The agreement between the liberal government and its left-wing critics in questions of VGB became obvious when Brandt kneeled in front of the Warsaw Ghetto Monument in 1970, an event that has remained a defining moment for many members of the postwar generation.[65] But the members of the Brandt administration never found other, similarly compelling gestures of liberal memory work.[66] Moreover, the student movement represented the first serious test for professed democrats in West Germany, and politicians, voters, and the media did not pass the test with flying colors. The students were frequently and inappropriately equated with the thugs of the Nazi Party, and in the course of the escalating crisis, the government passed several pieces of legislation that violated democratic principles.[67]

Student activists insisted that any serious and honest confrontation with the past should begin with a self-critical examination of personal entanglements with the regime and its crimes.[68] That criticism was not rendered invalid by the fact that the critics themselves were conveniently excused from such painful reckoning. But it was surely no coincidence that the specter of the personal was so forcefully raised by a generation that had never been tempted to compromise with the Nazi regime and that had also never watched their own parents enter such compromises. As the first generation with the full privilege of late birth, the student activists redefined the struggle about the past and at the same time secured the moral high ground for themselves. Their strategic interventions improved German collective memory in the long run, but the privilege of late birth also explained the self-satisfied arrogance intrinsic to the culture of Vergangenheitsbewältigung.[69] In this respect, the moral hubris of the first post-Nazi generation is comparable to the defensive, yet indefensible silence of the contemporaries of the Third Reich. The psychological peace of the former rested on the counterfactual assumption that postwar generations would never have joined the Nazi revolution, while the self-delusion of the latter depended on the similarly mistaken belief that having survived the war and rebuilt the country absolved them of further moral responsibility.

The astonishing obsession with the history of the Third Reich originated in a strategic constellation that left few other options for successful intergenerational strife than breaking the functional yet morally corrupt communicative silence of the postwar years. By the end of that process, West German society had turned into a truly democratic society, and VGB had turned into a routine, risk-free, even tedious undertaking that was unceremoniously dismissed by the very same memory activists when they assumed the political leadership of the Federal Republic after unification. This outcome depended on two important factors: the make-believe of a deeply humiliated generation, which professed democratic convictions when it had few other options and was still mired in totalitarian value structures, and the reckless exposure of that illusion by subsequent generations. Together, in an elaborate separation of labor, different age cohorts tried to unlearn anti-Semitism, racism, and other trimmings of fascist culture and invent new traditions and values. Without the make-believe of the postwar years, the post factum antifascists would have been deprived of their marvelous targets and would have been unable to claim as their own a public sphere that was perhaps democratic in name only. But the very fervor of their memory quest attested to the fact that they were not exposing the skeletons in their own closet; they addressed other people's shortcomings on the basis of their secure, suffocatingly stable childhoods in the Adenauer era.[70]

Indifference and Obsession:
The Bifurcation of Collective Memory in the 1970s

Through its Ostpolitik, the Brandt administration changed the perception of Eastern Europe in the West. The coalition between the SPD and the Freie Demokratische Partei (FDP) tried to make West Germans realize that the loss of the territories beyond Oder and Neisse would be permanent and that German division could only be overcome through patient and mutually beneficial diplomacy. At the same time, the East German government significantly changed its politics of history. While the media in the Deutsche Demokratik Republik (GDR) still emphasized the accomplishments of Communist resistance against Nazism, the administration in East Berlin now sought to create an independent GDR national identity as a defense against the West and encouraged the appropriation of many aspects of German history that had not been considered compatible with socialist worldviews.[71] As a result, East and West German media addressed similar historical topics in the 1970s and 1980s, ranging from Luther to Frederick the Great to the history of Nazism (the latter being more pronounced in the West than the East). These parallel explorations of German history followed very different ideological blueprints, and despite the thematic overlap, the East German influence on West Germany's historical culture decreased significantly. The competition between East and West was clearly decided in favor of the latter, and the change in government in Bonn in 1969 eliminated all former Nazis from high profile political positions. As a result, East Berlin could now only intervene indirectly—for instance, by supporting the new social movement ideologically and financially—and these efforts did not make an important qualitative difference in the continuing generational confrontations in the Federal Republic.

The provocations of the students did not quickly transform Germany's historical culture. As the students entered into divisive and circuitous discussions about the nature of Fascism, descended into terrorism, or opted for the long march through the institutions, the Nazi past temporarily disappeared from the media headlines. It seemed that the historical culture of

West Germany reached another equilibrium, as in the 1950s, and that hiatus gave the postwar generation an opportunity to fine-tune their own approach to the burden of the past. The relative indifference toward Nazism in the 1970s was noticeable in all established realms of memory. The second wave of perpetrator trials continued on a relatively low level of intensity and with little public participation. The laborious Majdanek trial, for instance, was conducted in front of empty galleries and concluded with frustratingly lenient sentences, since the judges felt unable to prove the defendants' personal guilt after such a long time.[72] The political elite considered all reparations issues settled and made few attempts to provide support to many Nazi victims who had never been compensated for their suffering.[73] The professional historians of the republic, not unlike their students, engaged in far-ranging abstract discussions about the nature of the Nazi regime but spent little time researching the precise unfolding of the Final Solution, even after pertinent archival collections had been made available to them.[74] Television networks significantly reduced their programs on the Third Reich, especially during prime time, and the few TV shows which did address the topic received much less viewer attention than comparable programs a decade earlier.[75]

The relative indifference about history was perhaps not surprising since the republic faced more pressing concerns, including the oil crisis of 1973 and the climax of terrorism in the fall of 1977. Yet even during the crisis years, the Third Reich remained an important symbolic reference point. The cultural and political elite might have had less inclination to focus on the burden of the past, but public debates about terrorism and the new social movements were laced with more-or-less overt references to Nazism.[76] Moreover, in the cultural space that existed below the radar of the mainstream media—for instance, in the alternative print media of the independent left—the 1970s represented a phase of intense historical reflection which set the stage for the surprising transformation of West Germany's historical culture in the 1980s. Throughout the 1970s, many artists and writers, often sympathetic to the political positions of the student movement, continued an esoteric search for interesting and challenging ways of defining their own subject position vis-à-vis Nazism. Within each subculture, their respective works were avidly discussed but almost completely ignored by established media and therefore had little initial impact beyond a close circle of like-minded individuals.[77]

Among other twists and dead-ends, the liberal discourse of the 1970s gave rise to left-wing anti-Semitism that unfolded according to a peculiar symbolic logic and concerned the general public on at least two occasions. In 1975 and again in 1985 West Germany's mainstream media discussed left-wing anti-Semitism at great length because a Frankfurt theater tried to produce a play, written by the writer and filmmaker Rainer Werner Fassbinder, that contained blatant anti-Semitic stereotypes about Jewish greed and capitalist recklessness. As a result of public protest, especially by Germany's Jewish community, the production was cancelled and the publisher even destroyed the printed copies of the play.[78] The Fassbinder affairs are excellent examples of the radical, iconoclastic energies of the intellectuals of the first postwar generation, who insisted that none of the rules of West Germany's public sphere applied to them. They challenged the pact of silence about Nazi perpetrators as well as the taboos pertaining to the use of Nazi discourse. According to the idiosyncratic logic of the protest culture, the use of anti-Semitic invectives was part didactic provocation, part triumphant expression of historical innocence.

Toward the end of the 1970s, a few academic historians and many more hobby historians turned to the history of everyday life as an alternative, tangible way of approaching the history of Nazism. Using methods of oral history, microhistory, and working class history and following the examples of similar initiatives in other European contries and the United States, a multitude of local history workshops set out to examine everyday life during Fascism and understand what it might have felt like to live in the Third Reich. Many of the workshops focused initially on local resistance during Nazism. They published their findings in exhibits, alternative city tours, and locally printed catalogues. Moreover, they retrieved from oblivion sites of repression and lobbied for the preservation and identification of local camps, Gestapo headquarters, and execution sites. Increasingly, the research also highlighted the fate of the victims and in some communities the workshop activities represented the first attempts to reconstruct the history of local Jewish communities and their destruction by the Nazis.[79]

The history workshops developed as part of the new social movements of the 1970s—including the women's, peace, and ecological movements—and shared the general political outlook of these grassroots initiatives. Many of the leading activists belonged to the first postwar generation, but in a number of cases the research also sparked intergenerational dialogue as high-school students interviewed older citizens about their memories of the Third Reich. Despite these achievements, the activities of the workshop movement had some unfortunate side effects. As a result of misguided local patriotism, some everyday history projects glorified modest resistance efforts. On other occasions, the search for identity and role models led to valorizations of stories and artifacts from the past without providing any critical conceptual framework to explain their significance (or insignificance) for the most important historical events of the period.[80] Nevertheless, the workshop movement attested to an astonishing interest in history, especially the history of the Third Reich, that corresponded to similar initiatives in other areas of the West German society and that later became the focus of a whole range of government, media, and academic initiatives.

As the history activists were digging up the remnants of local history, the Nazi past also interested a much smaller, yet equally diverse and marginal group of people who tried to come to terms with the visual legacy of the Third Reich. What came to be known as the New German Cinema was an assortment of artists who knew what they despised but who otherwise did not agree on any specific political or aesthetic agenda. The young filmmakers were as critical of the Nazi film industry and its postwar derivative as they were disenchanted by the Hollywood paradigm. In their eyes, both the German and the U.S. movie businesses were reactionary in form and content and had stifled aesthetic innovation through their overwhelming economic presence. The filmmakers hoped that the demise of the postwar German cinema would provide an opportunity to regain aesthetic diversity and present the public with engaging films that illustrated the full artistic potential of the medium and not just its mindless contemporary version.[81]

The artists were also unified by their interest in exploring the place of Nazism within the continuity of German history, in determining its influence on German identities, past and present, and in undermining conventional visions of the Third Reich which were still too much informed by the Nazis' masterful and deceitful self-representation. Plans for financial independence never came to fruition because German audiences remained largely uninterested in the awkward, self-reflexive didactics of the New German Cinema. As a result, the fascinating historical inquiries of its directors had limited impact on West Germany's historical culture as a whole. But on the basis of generous government and television subsidies, the filmmakers produced some superb intellectual explorations of the Nazi phenomenon that ranged from neoexpressionist monologues and Brechtian drama to subversive melodrama and ambitious *Alltagsgeschichte* (everyday history).[82]

The astonishing historical creativity of the 1970s also left its mark on more conventional media of representation, including autobiography and the fine arts.[83] In the end, the reinvention of Nazism, which had begun in narrowly circumscribed social locales and subcultures, was taken over by the mainstream media and substantially redefined in the process. As government agencies, television, and major publishing houses reentered the business of history, they did not eliminate the best or the worst elements of the intellectual grassroots initiatives; they edited out the obscure, inconclusive, self-reflexive, and most controversial aspects of the new historical paradigm. In the goal-oriented environment of politics and media the interest in history had to be reconciled with the reproduction of political power and the demands of mass entertainment. But the mainstream institutions of collective memory continued to focus on the tangible and personal aspects of the Nazi past, and retained the emphasis on questions of postwar German identity that had fascinated the memory activists. Also, perhaps more than ever before, the representations of history which came to dominate in the 1980s were closely aligned with historical tastes and expectations in non-German cultures. Because of these competing influences and interests, the collective memory of the Nazi era became a more contentious and overdetermined terrain. Representational taboos were defined and broken, and in the course of over two decades of continuous memory politics, every significant institution and agency felt compelled to enter the arena of history. In the end, even corporate Germany joined the fray although its representatives had fought tooth and nail to avoid being exposed to historical scrutiny.[84]

## The Climax of Vergangenheitsbewältigung in the 1980s

By all accounts the 1980s mark the most active phase of West German memory politics, both in terms of intensity and social depth. Historians, politicians, teachers, and at least some segments of the general public finally concentrated on the Holocaust and competed with one another about ways to acknowledge and contain its legacy.

The U.S. miniseries *Holocaust*, broadcast in West Germany in 1979, accelerated the development of new collective memories like no other event before or after. The miniseries was one of the best-orchestrated media events of all times; provided compelling, attractive, and emotionally engaging television fiction; and showed how effectively history had already been commercialized in the United States. A superb piece of everyday history, *Holocaust* symbolized the rise of the survivor in the international memory of the Final Solution and therefore, more than "Auschwitz," the term "Holocaust" came to represent the suffering of European Jewry. It has been often overlooked, however, that *Holocaust* remained for many years one of very few popular history products that took the question of perpetration seriously and spent as much time relating the suffering of the victims as exploring the everyday life of the perpetrators. The series gave faces and identities to the victims *and* the perpetrators, an achievement that explains its tremendous impact in Germany.

After *Holocaust*, television executives, filmmakers, and historians scrambled to make up for their past sins of omission. Due to intellectual arrogance, misplaced piety, political opportunism, and simple helplessness, they had failed to provide accurate and emotionally engaging representations of Nazi history for mass consumption.[85] Historians now focused more specifically on the Final Solution, but they continued their theoretical deliberations and discussed the concept of the uniqueness of the Holocaust especially during the historians' debate of 1986–87.[86] Although scholars of the Hitler Youth generation had made great advances in exploring the political history of the Nazi regime and in setting social-science history on a solid theoretical foundation, they shrank away from studying the Final Solution in great detail. It was left to non-German experts and another generation of German scholars born after 1945 to unravel the implementation of the Holocaust throughout Europe.

A close look at the production plans of the German film industry indicates that film and television had already launched a wave of new history projects before *Holocaust* hit the screen, but these efforts were massively expanded after the event. Within a few years, the survivor paradigm became one of the staples of German prime time, especially by way of imported productions and expensive television fiction and documentaries. In addition, German television applied the recipe of *Holocaust* and the insights of the hobby historians to other areas of the history of the Third Reich. In the early 1980s hardly a week went by without another prominently featured reenactment of fascist everyday life.[87] For some younger viewers the simulations of history represented their first confrontation with Nazism, because the past had not been a popular subject of family lore and had also been marginalized in formal education. Occasionally, the shows triggered intergenerational discussions with older family members who had personally experienced Nazism.

The reconstruction of German memory in the 1980s precipitated a sharp rise in government policies designed to shape the legacy of the Third Reich directly and proactively. All political leaders of the Federal Republic had to conduct memory politics abroad and at home. Neither Adenauer nor Brandt had the luxury or the desire to ignore the impact of their actions on the perception of Germany and German history among friends and foes.

But in contrast to past administrations, the conservative government of Helmut Kohl assumed that the past was not just a factor to be reckoned with but an opportunity to create a new, positive German historical consciousness. Unlike his predecessors and successors, but like other members of his political generation, Kohl had an enthusiasm (although not necessarily an aptitude) for memory politics. As a trained historian—and with some historians among his advisors—he launched an ambitious campaign for reconciliation and normalization designed to provide Germans with a factually accurate yet positive version of their past. Kohl was convinced that a powerful, conventional national historical identity would enhance political stability and render West Germany more predictable for its citizens, allies, and enemies. He also hoped that his campaign would help put West Germany on an equal political footing with its Western partners.[88]

The results of such ambition were an impressive row of public blunders committed by Kohl and his associates, and a number of expensive cultural initiatives that were intended to define and maintain the official memory of the Nazi past for present and future generations. In addition, the chancellor inadvertently managed to unify his many intellectual critics who were suspicious of the government's endorsement of nationalism and its aggressive attempts at indoctrination. At the same time, the critics were unable to develop compelling alternatives for West Germany's postfascist identity. They rallied around the abstract notion of a postconventional identity that was supposed to be based on the citizens' identification with the democratic principles of their constitution but turned out to be largely illusionary, especially in the context of German unification.[89]

In the past, local and regional authorities had administered German sites of memory according to the principle of the cultural sovereignty of the states. As a result, during the 1960s and 1970s, many former concentration camps had slowly been turned into memorials and museums, and the history-workshop movement added a significant number of historical markers and monuments. These decentralized memory activities accelerated in the 1990s and supplied many German cities and towns with more-or-less obtrusive reminders of German crimes.[90] But the Kohl initiatives were on a different scale both in terms of size and focus. With the Museum of the Federal Republic, the Museum of German History, a central national memorial site for the nation's war dead, and a reluctantly supported Holocaust memorial, the government planned to have all memory bases covered and determine the interpretation of the past for decades to come.

During Kohl's long reign from 1982 to 1998, the many debates about each new initiative and each public-relations disaster followed the same ritual and blend into each other in hindsight. From Jerusalem to Bitburg and Verdun, and from one historical commission report to the next, Kohl and his associates were lambasted for their lack of sensitivity and sophistication. Yet the government, sometimes defended by sympathetic conservative intellectuals, simply followed its memory agenda unperturbed.[91] With one exception—the resignation of the president of parliament, Philipp Jenninger, in 1987—the attacks seemed to be of little consequence other than helping to establish an extraordinarily lively memory culture.[92] In the end, Kohl's historical program has been very successful. While the public rituals of reconciliation, especially in Bitburg, were indeed often quite embarrassing for Kohl and his guests, the museums and memorials never turned out to be as revisionistic and nationalistic as the critics had imagined.

Three institutions in particular illustrate this pattern: the National Memorial for the Victims of War and Terror in Berlin, the Museum of the Federal Republic in Bonn, and the Museum of German History in Berlin. The National Memorial, for which Kohl selected the Zeughaus in Berlin, is the least compelling of the three institutions; it had to be amended at the last minute because the Association of German Jewry demanded more explicit acknowledgments of the Holocaust.[93] Yet precisely because of its internal contradictions, the memorial did not emerge as a site of nationalistic propaganda. The Museum of the Federal Republic in Bonn certainly focuses on the success story of West German consumerism, but it also contains explicit references to the Final Solution.[94] The Museum of German History in Berlin deals as much with German as with European history and does not appear to be a likely future source for right-wing ideologies.[95] While these three institutions of cultural memory do not offer readings of German history as reactionary as the critics had expected, they nevertheless embody one key aspect of Kohl's historicization agenda: all three sites integrate Nazism into the continuity of German and European history such that the Third Reich appears to be a significant but short interlude which is not representative of its larger historical context.

As far as one can tell, the institutions of cultural memory championed by Kohl have been accepted by their audiences. Their success might have been enhanced by the fact that German unification, which Kohl orchestrated with such skill and speed once the surprising chance offered itself, retroactively and unforeseeably validated Kohl's memory agenda. It certainly helped Kohl's objectives that the postconventional identity theories of the left neither explained unification nor seemed helpful for finding solutions to the problems the unified country faced. Therefore, after 1989, many outspoken critics of the government felt compelled to rethink the concepts of national identity and national history that they had so summarily dismissed.[96]

The historicization strategies that inform the museums and memorial in Bonn and Berlin coexist with the new Holocaust memorial close to the Brandenburg Gate.[97] The fact that the memorial came into existence in the first place, after seventeen years of deliberation and debate, illustrates the increasing influence of the German Jewish community on the historical culture of the Federal Republic. For the first decades after World War II, German Jews remembered the victims of the Holocaust among themselves, although the Jewish communities were already subject to substantial philo-Semitic curiosity, especially during the annual weeks of brotherhood organized by the societies for Jewish-Christian cooperation.[98] Since the mid-1970s, as a result of generational turn-over within the Jewish community, the democratization of German society, and the rise of Holocaust memory, Jews increasingly intervened in public debates, and government representatives paid closer attention to Jewish rituals of mourning, especially on the anniversaries of the November pogrom. In the Kohl era the conservative administration and the Association of German Jewry entered into a particularly intense symbiotic relationship. In exchange for lending legitimacy to Kohl's memory agenda, West Germany's Jews became one of very few groups outside the government that had any real say in the design of the museums and memorials in Bonn and Berlin. Kohl even championed the Memorial to the Murdered Jews of Europe which was initially not part of his political plans. But critics of the close cooperation between the government and the Jewish community pointed out that the privilege of access came at a substantial price, since German Jews were now subject to the roles and expectations that their powerful allies defined for them.[99]

In the weeks and months after the memorial opened on 12 May 2005, it quickly became apparent that the large site, with its 2700 steles, could serve many different purposes. As expected, international dignitaries flocked to the site, neo-Nazis applied unappetizing graffiti, and the small exhibit on the premises attracted an impressive number of visitors.[100] But the memorial also appeals to urban dwellers with very little interest in history. To the consternation of some commentators and, presumably, the furtive satisfaction of the memorial's two full-time guards, children and adolescents play hide-and-seek and jump from stele to stele while some adults appreciate the memorial as a great rendezvous and picnic site.[101] The memorial's multiple-use value illustrates how well it fits into Berlin's modernist urban landscape.

Its success might also indicate that German Holocaust memory has entered a phase of self-confident, permissive remembrance; authorities appear to be very comfortable with Peter Eisenman's open design and the ways in which it has been appropriated by Berliners and their guests. Most important, however, the reception of the memorial highlights one key ingredient of successful VGB that informed all venues of Germany's historical culture. Stories about the Nazi past that became collective memories had educational and artistic merits and at least the appearance of moral integrity. But successful strategies of historical interpretation offered additional benefits, for instance, entertainment value or strategic political advantages. In this respect, the kind of pleasure experienced by the children who jumped across Eisenman's symbolic graveyard for the murdered Jews of Europe highlights a key ingredient of the culture of Vergangenheitsbewältigung.

Routinization, Professionalization, and Fragmentation:
Historical Culture since the 1990s

The liberal government that succeeded Kohl in 1998 has been far less proactive in memory matters. Its leaders, most prominently Chancellor Gerhard Schröder and Foreign Minister Joschka Fischer, were themselves part of the social movements of the 1970s. But once in power, the former activists turned career politicians entered the arena of memory politics only when disagreements about the Nazi legacy infringed on the economic and political well-being of unified Germany. In order to bring to a successful conclusion the unfinished memory business of the prior administration, they sponsored a compromise regarding the endless disputes about Berlin's Holocaust Memorial, and convinced German business executives to contribute to a reparation fund for former slave laborers. But Schröder and Fischer have also made clear that they consider the question of compensation closed and see no need for new federal initiatives to shape the Nazi legacy.[102] According to the foreign minister, the Nazi past simply provides extra incentives for determined opposition, including military opposition, against policies of genocide and ethnic cleansing.

The German government's relaxed and relatively self-confident stance about the burden of the past has been supported by many European politicians. Since the international celebrations of the fiftieth anniversary of the end of World War II in 1995, European political leaders have transformed the divisive memory of Nazi aggression and occupation into a shared, self-critical memory of an era of European human-rights abuses that unites former victims, perpetrators, and bystanders, and lends legitimacy to the European Union.[103] The new memory consensus was an integral part of the decision for military intervention in former Yugoslavia, especially with regard to the remilitarization of German foreign policy.[104] The agreement among Europe's political elite explains why rituals of memory that were originally designed to recall the struggle and triumph over Nazi Germany are now staged with enthusiastic German participation. In the summer of 2004 Schröder became the first German chancellor to be invited to the D-Day festivities in Normandy which marked the sixtieth anniversary of the Allied assault on occupied France. Schröder's speech on that occasion nicely illustrated the subtle shift of interpretation entailed in the transition from national to European memory: drawing applause from the assembled dignitaries, Schröder declared the Allied campaign a victory for Europe and Germany, and thus retroactively integrated Germany into the antifascist community of Western nations.[105] Schröder reiterated the same themes in his public statement on the sixtieth anniversary of the end of World War II in May 2005.[106]

The lack of concern about the Nazi past among Germany's new political elite corresponds to recent achievements of professional historians. Trained in the methods of social history, everyday history, and political history, a new generation of scholars has turned empirical Holocaust studies into a thriving field in unified Germany. Based on long-established archival collections in the Federal Republic, as well as newly opened archives in Eastern Europe, their studies illustrate how the midlevel leadership of the ss and the Wehrmacht organized the Final Solution with a wide range of motives and objectives in mind.[107] The recent wave of scholarship attests to the normalization, professionalization, and routinization of elite discourses about Nazism that is also evident on the political scene. The Third Reich is now studied with the same self-confidence and inventory of methods that historians bring to bear on other research topics. There is no indication that younger generations of scholars encounter the psychological and moral dilemmas which their predecessors had to deal with in the study of Nazism and which frequently triggered intense public debate. The new findings represent remarkable scholarly achievements, but because they are presented in complex, technical language and are relatively uncontroversial, they will not find their way into more widely consumed publications. Even historians who have attempted to summarize and make accessible the complex historiography of the Final Solution have produced reference works that tend to deter the general readership.[108]

The structural incompatibilities and resulting communication barriers between elite and popular levels of Germany's historical culture might explain why significant segments of the media audience have not reached the same degree of normalization and routinization in memory matters that characterizes professional discourses about the past. Different layers of memory were clearly at odds with each other during the unfolding of the key memory events of the 1990s. For scholarly and intellectual observers the memory scandals of the 1990s brought few new historical facts to light and followed predictable discursive patterns, that is, intense discussions of the respective memory event by the memory pundits of the national press (for the first time also covered by national television), succeeded by a number of edited volumes that documented the debates for memory experts at home and abroad. But audiences with less experience in the consumption and analysis of history products were drawn to the specific books, exhibits, or speeches in question precisely because they represented for them a new, intense, and unexpected encounter with the German criminal past and problems of guilt and continuity. In the 1990s a sizeable minority of the German population—relatively well educated, intellectually curious, and predominantly but not exclusively members of postwar generations—focused first on perpetrators of the Nazi era and then on German victims of the war.[109]

The memory controversies of the 1990s included the unlikely case of a scholarly bestseller, Daniel Goldhagen's *Hitler's Willing Executioners*. Goldhagen was immediately stripped of his scholarly credentials by his colleagues in Germany and abroad because his emphasis on the ideological motives of Nazi perpetrators contradicted the current consensus in the discipline that NS perpetrators were motivated by a whole range of causes including "normal" motives like peer pressure and careerism.[110] Goldhagen's success with the general educated public in public readings and television broadcasts illustrated that different spheres of Germany's historical culture could be seriously out of tune at any given point in time.[111] While all of German culture seemed to focus on the perpetrators of the Holocaust, historical experts endorsed very different explanatory models than other constituencies. Scholars effectively undermined the anthropological distance between themselves and the Nazis; they assumed that the latter were ordinary people and that human beings could be relatively easily turned into perpetrators given the right circumstances. In contrast, the public that cheered Goldhagen was very satisfied to hear about the extraordinary ideological impetus behind the Holocaust and pleased to learn that today's ordinary Germans have little in common with their relentless forefathers.

Another example for disjointed perpetrator memories was the belated public deconstruction of the myth of the courageous and chivalrous Wehrmacht which survived through the late 1990s. Although scholars had exposed the involvement of the military in genocide and ethnic cleansing in academic publications dating back to the late 1970s, their voices had not penetrated the public sphere.[112] Therefore, the facts only became common knowledge through the traveling exhibition *Verbrechen der Wehrmacht* that the Hamburg Institute of Social Research organized on the occasion of the fiftieth anniversary of the end of World War II. The exhibition was ultimately disassembled and reorganized, because the institute's overzealous staff had incorrectly linked the Wehrmacht to a number of photos representing postwar crimes committed by Eastern European militias. Despite such shortcomings, the "damage" had been done, since many Germans, including former Wehrmacht soldiers, began to reconsider the role of the German military during the war.[113]

The belated public interest in the perpetrators of the Holocaust, illustrated by the reception of Goldhagen's work and the Wehrmacht exhibit, was also noticeable in German television programming of the 1990s. After the Goldhagen debate, a number of documentaries depicted the Nazi leadership's precise involvement in the unfolding of the Final Solution and occasionally tried to determine the specific responsibility of lower-level Nazi personnel and German bystanders. The documentaries did not reflect the new historiographical insights into the topic, but instead emphasized traditionally held beliefs about the ideological origins of genocide. In addition, the most visible and influential of these programs, produced under the leadership of Guido Knopp at Zweite Deutsche Fernsehen (ZDF), provided ambivalent visions of the Nazi past. On the one hand, Knopp and his collaborators crafted accurate and sensitive Holocaust documentaries that carefully integrated victim and perpetrator testimony. On the other hand, the ZDF team released a much more extensive string of programs about Hitler and World War II that contained politically correct messages about the evils of Nazism but, at the same time, presented suspenseful, well-edited, fast-paced visual narratives that paid tribute to the extraordinary nature of Nazi power.[114]

The programming efforts of the 1990s were limited in their potential impact since they took place in a new television environment. Commercial television had been introduced into the Federal Republic in 1984, and by the beginning of the next decade numerous commercial and public networks were vying for the attention of the viewers. The public television stations

ARD and ZDF, which had sustained the history wave of the 1980s, could no longer afford the same amount of historical coverage and lost a large share of their audience. Historical programming dropped during prime time, and documentaries about perpetrator history, while quite successful, reached a smaller segment of the German public than had the historical fiction of the 1980s.[115] This fragmentation of the German media market contributed to an increased diversity of collective memories in post-unification Germany.

Like the developments in the 1960s, interest in perpetrator history in the 1990s was preceded by a significant shift in educational practice. A new generation of teachers, who had joined the profession in the 1970s and 1980s, actively pursued teaching contemporary history in German high schools. A few of the teachers had themselves undertaken the long march through the institutions and many others shared their peers' memory politics, although they might not have been actively involved in the social movements of their student days. As a result, for the last twenty years, West German high-school graduates have encountered detailed and graphic accounts of the Holocaust and the Third Reich, often accompanied by the liberal political outlook which informed their teachers' interpretation of this history. The educational reforms reflected shifts in historical consciousness indicated by media events like *Holocaust*, but a number of critics objected to the politics and didactics of historical education that, from their perspective, reduced the teaching of German history to mass screenings of *Schindler's List*. Consequently, for the first time in postwar history, there are serious concerns that Holocaust education in Germany might have reached a point of saturation and caused a number of counterproductive and undesirable side effects as students seek to distance themselves from the overwhelmingly negative representations of "their" history.[116]

These concerns correlate to similar misgivings in other institutional and cultural settings and suggest that the enlarged Federal Republic experienced a temporary backlash against the successful Holocaust culture of the 1980s. The novelist Martin Walser effectively focused the critique of VGB in October 1998, when he admonished the political instrumentalization and repetitive, excessive, and repressive nature of public Holocaust memory in Germany. The public debate triggered by Walser's remarks disproved some of his allegations: the wide spectrum of supportive, as well as critical, comments indicated that Germany did not suffer from a monolithic, repressive memory culture that blocked out alternative perceptions of German history. To the contrary, the open discussion following Walser's speech spoke to the relative maturity of Germany's democratic public sphere.[117] At the same time, the strange coalition of discouraged students and their disaffected parents, self-conscious and media savvy intellectuals like Walser, liberal politicians who found that their own past memory politics interfered with their current realpolitik, and professional historians who attested to the normal disposition of the perpetrators indicated that World War II and the Holocaust may be gradually stripped of its exceptional status and integrated within histories of modern warfare and genocide.

In the most recent chapter of memory politics, perhaps as a result of Walser's programmatic critique, the theme of German suffering during and after World War II has returned to the front pages. The fate of German refugees and expellees from Eastern Europe and the victims of Allied bombings had been acknowledged in the 1950s but became a politically incorrect topic in subsequent, more self-critical phases of VGB. The majority of actors in the arena of memory politics conveniently forgot about their suffering because they did not want to give the impression that they intended to equate the Jewish victims of the Holocaust with the German victims of war and expulsion. In 2002 a coalition of young authors and established novelists, most prominently Günter Grass, made it their business to remember German victimization and add yet another facet to the Federal Republic's extraordinarily diverse historical culture.[118]

The current countermemories are nothing extraordinary in the history of VGB. Similar attitudes have informed other contributions, including, for instance, Edgar Reitz's ambitious television blockbuster *Heimat* of 1984, which he crafted in response to *Holocaust*.[119] As in the past, with the exception of the 1950s, these voices will fail to dominate public discourse because more critical positions are at least equally well represented. Although the Nazi past will continue to lend itself for instrumentalizations of all kinds—which explains the rise of Germany's extraordinary memory culture in the first place—a growing "honest" indifference about the past reflected in the marginalization of the topic in mainstream media indicates that the historicization of the Third Reich and the professionalization of VGB are well under way.

## Conclusion: Generations of Memory

On the basis of the narrative above it is possible to offer a rough periodization of the process of coming to terms with the past as it is reflected in intellectual and cultural developments from 1945 to the present. The following model stresses the generational factor in dealing with Nazism, which has been emphasized by many scholars.[120]

Following a short period of lively discussion about Nazism and the problem of German guilt in the immediate postwar years, West Germans reached a temporary understanding of how to deal with the past. During the 1950s the contemporaries of Nazism settled on a number of widely shared, mostly self-defensive and apologetic strategies to deal with Nazism, including the demonization of Hitler and his entourage, and an exculpatory antitotalitarian equation of Nazism and Stalinism. West Germans found this consensus because psychological-emotional dispositions and political-strategic interests converged. The former citizens of the Third Reich were culturally and psychologically ill-prepared to work through trauma, guilt, and shame. Therefore, for the most part, they avoided any rigorous inquiries into their own responsibility for the Nazi catastrophe. But they also adopted a self-centered victim identity for very pragmatic reasons: it helped them come to terms with Germany's division, large-scale destruction, and foreign occupation. The West German elite, in particular, took advantage of any loophole offered to them by their new allies and wholeheartedly embraced Cold War antitotalitarianism.

The first substantial changes in the interpretations of Nazism occurred in the late 1950s and early 1960s. These changes were initiated and carried out by a small group of memory dissenters in the ranks of the war generations and a more sizeable group of critics who belonged to the Hitler Youth generation and had been socialized during the Nazi period, yet were too young to have been involved in any crimes. The professionals and intellectuals of this generation advanced the theoretical, systematic study of Nazism which is expressed by their important contribution to the historiography of the Nazi period, their efforts to reform the educational system, their participation in the second phase of the prosecution of Nazi criminals, and in some of the artistic achievements of the period: the highly self-reflexive, detached prose of Günter Grass, Martin Walser, and Uwe Johnson; the documentary theater of Peter Weiss and Heiner Kipphardt; and the elaborate film collages of Alexander Kluge, to name a few. Those intellectuals' desire to self-reflexively examine and self-critically objectify the past may be closely linked to their own deeply ambivalent relationship to Nazism. Naturally, not all intellectuals of that generation followed the same innovative path, and they therefore often clashed in their interpretations of the Third Reich. Some of the most important historiographical debates in West Germany have been conducted among members of that generation, and events as recent as the Goldhagen debate have been influenced by that generation's interpretive preferences.

The next set of important revisions in the representation of Nazism was undertaken by intellectuals belonging to the *Kriegs- und Trümmerkinder* (the children of war and ruins) cohort, who were born during or immediately after the war and who are generally referred to as the student-movement generation. They inherited and destroyed the systematic interpretive paradigms of their predecessors, as, for instance, during obsessive debates about theories of Fascism conducted during the 1970s. But more important, as the first generation without personal memories of Nazism, they introduced a subjective factor into representations of the past, further politicized the debates about the meaning and appropriate response to Nazism, and highlighted personal, social, and institutional continuities which tied the Federal Republic to the Nazi era. The paradigm of everyday history, the wave of autobiographical writings in the late 1970s exemplified by Bernhard Vesper's *Die Reise*, the political discussions about Nazism and personal guilt raised by the student activists, the founding of educational centers at the sites of the Nazi crimes, and many films of the New German Cinema by directors like Rainer Werner Fassbinder, Werner Herzog, or Margarete von Trotta provided tangible, subjective, and emotional encounters with Nazism which had not been offered in the works of intellectuals of the older generations. Members of the first postwar generation made use of visual media such as film, television, and exhibitions, whereas their predecessors had preferred more traditional, discursive modes of representation.

While the critical intellectuals of the first postwar generation dominated the cultural sphere from the late 1970s to the mid-1990s, they have more recently encountered opposition from members of the second postwar generation, who are currently in their thirties and forties. These scholars and intellectuals have reinterpreted Nazism and its postwar legacy in a seemingly detached and objective fashion that differs markedly from the self-critical approach of the Hitler Youth generation and especially from the *Betroffenheitskultur*, the culture of emotional involvement and commitment, in which they grew up.[121] It is still too early to provide a final assessment of this generation's contribution to the process of coming to terms with Nazism. But some members of this generation interpret the history of the Third Reich from the perspective of conventional large-scale research paradigms—modernity or nationalism, for instance—or with the help of new theoretical approaches like the transnational human-rights discourse. All these strategies of interpretation historicize Nazism by turning it into a prime example of a class of events much larger than the short history of the Third Reich. The process of semantic integration and normalization is also noticeable on the level of form, since many arenas of Germany's historical culture have returned to conventional genres and narrative formats for the representation of Nazism that had been considered problematic in previous decades.

This schematic outline of different phases in the treatment of the Nazi legacy in the Federal Republic of Germany should be more accurately conceptualized as a successive development of new perspectives on the past which existed side by side and which produced increasingly complex layers of interpretation and representation. In addition, the generational model should not be carried too far: in each case only a small minority of intellectuals have been involved in the development of the new interpretive paradigms, and while different approaches to the burden of the past can be linked to specific generational interests and perspectives, they have never reflected the political and intellectual endeavors of whole generations. But the generational model does clearly illustrate that the process of coming to terms with the past is based on a complex separation of labor between different age groups. While adult contemporaries of Nazism contributed fairly little to the *intellectual* working through of the past they did, perhaps inadvertently, provide the essential preconditions by rebuilding West Germany in the image of the Western Allies. On this basis, subsequent generations have concentrated first on the cognitive and then on the emotional challenges and problems which Nazism represents for all Germans.

Even with hindsight it is difficult to determine to what extent Germany's remarkably self-critical historical culture reflected the historical consciousness of its population. Available quantitative and qualitative data suggest that the culture of vGB influenced the knowledge and feelings of many citizens, although not necessarily in the way that producers of the vGB discourse intended. The one-sided communication between politicians, educators, novelists, historians, filmmakers, TV producers, and their audiences sustained a wide range of memories as consumers integrated bits and pieces of cultural memory with private stories and interpretations of the Nazi past. The resulting collages illustrate that Germans have proven quite adept at turning a bleak historical record into emotionally satisfying collective memories.[122] But research about German historical consciousness also demonstrates the impressive degree of miscommunication between champions of vGB in positions of power and significant segments of the population. Perhaps the best example of such miscommunication is the persistence of anti-

Semitism and right-wing extremism which are reproduced in social contexts that operate outside the mainstream media.[123]

While elite and subcultural memories reveal little overlap in terms of content, they share the same utilitarian bend. The intellectual concept of VGB was crafted in pursuit of a wide range of political objectives, including the salutary interest in fostering self-critical memories of Nazism and the more pragmatic goal of displacing political rivals and political generations from power. When the postwar generations finally took over political power in the Federal Republic in the late 1990s, VGB lost its usefulness as a political weapon and will have to be substantially revised to fit the strategic needs of future generations.

In a sense, VGB has become a victim of its own success. The globalization, fragmentation, and commercialization of modern memory, especially with regard to the Holocaust, challenges the cohesion of local and national interpretive communities that constructed the memory of the Shoah in the first place, even in such unlikely places as Germany. After the end of the Cold War, Holocaust memory plays a vital role in the transnational human-rights discourse that has been codified in international law and enshrined in popular culture, and is frequently invoked to scandalize human-rights violations in different parts of the world. This global, commercial Holocaust memory interacts with local and national collective memories but is increasingly reproduced independently of local and national contexts in its own institutions of remembrance. The very success and independence of transnational Holocaust memory has made it easier for local and national communities to abandon the kind of self-reflexive memory politics that thrived in Germany in the 1980s. Across Europe right-wing political identities that never subscribed to the values of Holocaust memory or are crafted in explicit opposition to the demands of Holocaust culture have gained strength. Moreover, and more important, concrete policies of many Western governments have become less, rather than more self-reflexive about the use of power, while the same governments pay lip-service to transnational Holocaust memory and the institutions that sustain it. The lack of self-reflexivity is particularly noticeable in the foreign policy of the United States, but it had already influenced the remilitarization of German foreign policy in the 1990s. From immigration policies to the use of military force, Western governments have adopted measures under the cover of Holocaust memory that are not compatible with the humanitarian demands that that Holocaust memory allegedly imposes on the international community. This process demonstrates what is at stake when the national and local communities, which helped construct Holocaust memory in the first place, divest themselves of its obligations and project those obligations on international political and cultural institutions. These institutions are powerful enough to reproduce themselves discursively—for instance, by keeping alive the memory of the Holocaust—but most certainly lack the power to implement their own ethical rules in concrete political terms.[124] That contradiction is well illustrated by the fact that in January 2005 the United Nations for the first time marked the anniversary of the liberation of Auschwitz by a special session of the general assembly. The featured speakers were, among others, the United Nations secretary Kofi Annan, the Holocaust survivor Elie Wiesel, the Israeli foreign minister Silvan Schalom, and his German colleague Joschka Fischer.[125] The sixtieth anniversary ceremony showed clearly that Germany is now considered one of the key sites of Holocaust memory, but it also, inadvertently, underlined the impotence of the United Nations. As the self-congratulatory celebrations took place in New York, the genocide in Sudan continued unabated.

## Notes

1    Wenke, " 'Bewältigte Vergangenheit' und 'Aufgearbeitete Geschichte' "; Gerhard Schoenbrenner, "Was heisst Bewältigung der Vergangenheit?" *Die Zeit*, 8 September 1963.

2    Klingenstein, "Über Herkunft und Verwendung des Wortes 'Vergangenheitsbewältigung' "; Kittel, *Die Legende von der "Zweiten Schuld,"* 21–28.

3    Among many problematic statements this is one of the interesting critical insights of Armin Mohler's *Der Nasenring*; see also Plack, *Hitlers langer Schatten.*

4    Stefan Reinecke, "Ein Skandal, der gefällt," *Die Tageszeitung*, 10 May 2005.

5    Müller, *Memory and Power in Post-War Europe*, 1–35.

6    Theodor Adorno, *Prisms*, 34. Adorno continued, "And this corrodes even the knowledge of why it has become impossible to write poetry today." In most references to and discussions of that quote the second half of the sentence is conveniently omitted, thus radically simplifying Adorno's negative dialectic. Laermann, "Nach Auschwitz ein Gedicht zu schreiben, ist barbarisch," 11.

7    Adorno, *Erziehung zur Mündigkeit*, 93. Adorno's critique of Western civilization, which cannot be discussed here in greater detail, is developed in three of his major works: *Negative Dialectics*; *Minima Moralia*; and, written with Max Horkheimer, *Dialectic of Enlightenment.*

8    Mitscherlich and Mitscherlich, *The Inability to Mourn*. See also Mitscherlich, *Erinnerungsarbeit: Zur Psychoanalyse der Unfähigkeit zu trauern*; Mitscherlich, "Die Unfähigkeit zu trauern in Ost- und Westdeutschland."

9    Rabinbach, "Response to Karen Brecht," 317.

10  Lübbe, "Der Nationalsozialismus im deutschen Nachkriegsbewusstsein";
Lübbe, "Verdrängung?"

11  Schaal and Wöll, *Vergangenheitsbewältigung*; König, Kohlstruck, and Wöll,
*Vergangenheitsbewältigung am Ende des zwanzigsten Jahrhunderts*; Herz and Schwab-
Trapp, *Umkämpfte Vergangenheit*.

12  These challenges are well summarized in Hughes, *Shouldering the Burdens of
Defeat*, 5–21; see also Förster and Beck, "Post-Traumatic Stress Disorder and World
War II."

13  See, for example, Rentschler, *The Ministry of Illusion*.

14  Brink, *Ikonen der Vernichtung*; Knoch, *Die Tat als Bild*.

15  Wolgast, *Die Wahrnehmung des Dritten Reiches in der unmittelbaren Nachkriegszeit*; Eberan, *Wer war an Hitler schuld?*; Koebner, "Die Schuldfrage"; and
Schivelbusch, *In a Cold Crater*. The most explicit contemporary acknowledgment of
German culpability was the Protestant Church's famous declaration of guilt in October 1945 (see Greschat, ed., *Im Zeichen der Schuld*).

16  N. Frei, "Von deutscher Erfindungskraft."

17  That applies in particular to Jaspers, *Die Schuldfrage*. On Jaspers's text and the
German guilt discourse, see Diner, *Beyond the Conceivable*, 218–30. One of the most
self-reflexive voices during the postwar years was that of the first president of the
Federal Republic, Theodor Heuss (see Baumgärtner, *Reden nach Hitler*).

18  On denazification, see especially Niethammer, *Die Mitläuferfabrik*; Klaus-
Dietmar Henke, "Die Trennung von Nationalsozialismus"; Baumgärtner, *Reden nach
Hitler*.

19  Moeller, *War Stories*; Naumann, ed., *Nachkrieg in Deutschland*.

20  Among many publications that share this assessment, see Assmann and Frevert, *Geschichtsvergessenheit/Geschichtsversessenheit*.

21  The politics of memory of the 1950s are one of the best-researched chapters of
Germany's historical culture. See especially N. Frei, *Vergangenheitspolitik*; Herf, *Divided Memory*; Brochhagen, *Nach Nürnberg*; Rogers, *Politics after Hitler*.

22  Prinz and Zitelmann, *Nationalsozialismus und Modernisierung*.

23  Roth and Rusinek, *Verwandlungspolitik*; N. Frei, *Karrieren im Zwielicht*.

24  Hughes, *Shouldering the Burden of Defeat*; Ahonen, *After the Expulsion*; Schillinger, "Der Lastenausgleich."

25  Goschler, *Schuld und Schulden*, 450–75.

26  See the contributions in Danyel, *Die geteilte Vergangenheit*.

27  Goschler, *Schuld and Schulden*, 159–75.

28  Ne'man Arad, *America, Its Jews, and the Rise of Nazism*; Shafir, *The American
Jewish Community and Germany since 1945*.

29  Manig, *Die Politik der Ehre*, 197–233; Herf, *Divided Memory*, 267. N. Frei,
*Vergangenheitspolitik*, 195.

30  Kattago, *Ambiguous Memory*.

31  Meyer-Seitz, *Die Verfolgung von NS-Straftaten in der Sowjetischen Besatzungs-*

zone; Zeidler, *Stalinjustiz contra NS-Verbrechen*; Weinke, *Die Verfolgung von NS-Tätern im geteilten Deutschland.*

32  Sabrow, *Verwaltete Vergangenheit*; Fox, *Stated Memory*; Herf, *Divided Memory.*

33  Herf, *Divided Memory*; Kattago, *Ambiguous Memory.*

34  Moeller, *War Stories*, 88.

35  Rückerl, *NS-Verbrechen vor Gericht*, 116. Weinke, *Verfolgung von NS-Tätern*; Goschler, *Schuld und Schulden*, 215–17.

36  Herf, *Divided Memory*, 267; Stern, *The Whitewashing of the Yellow Badge*, 347. For a succinct overview of German reparations from 1945 to the present, see Doehring, Fehn, and Hockerts, *Jahrhudertschuld, Jahrhundertsühne.*

37  Reichel, *Erfundene Erinnerung*; Becker and Schöll, *In jenen Tagen.* See also a more positive assessment in Fehrenbach, *Cinema in Democratizing Germany.*

38  Dudek, *"Der Rückblick auf die Vergangenheit wird sich nicht vermeiden lassen."*

39  Leonhard, *Politik- und Geschichtsbewusstsein im Wandel*, 297–302. See also Müller-Hohagen, *Verleugnet, verdrängt, verschwiegen*; Schwan, *Politik und Schuld.*

40  Preuss-Lausitz, *Kriegskinder, Konsumkinder, Krisenkinder.*

41  Giesen and Schneider, *Tätertrauma*; König, Kohlstruck, and Wöll, *Vergangenheitsbewältigung am Ende des zwanzigsten Jahrhunderts*; Bock and Wolfrum, *Umkämpfte Vergangenheit*; Knigge and Frei, *Verbrechen erinnern.*

42  Braese, *Deutsche Nachkriegsliteratur und der Holocaust*; Schlant, *The Language of Silence*; Heulenkamp, *Deutsche Erinnerung.*

43  Otto, *Vom Ostermarsch zur Apo.*

44  Schörken, *Jugend 1945*; Bude, *Deutsche Karrieren.*

45  Bergmann, *Antisemitismus in öffentlichern Konflikten*, 235.

46  Herbst, *Didaktik des Geschichtsunterrichts zwischen Traditionalismus und Reformismus.*

47  Von Miquel, *Ahnden oder Amnestieren?* 146–85; Rückerl, *NS-Verbrechen vor Gericht*, 140; Weinke, *Verfolgung von NS-Tätern.* See also the contributions in Weber and Steinbach, *Vergangenheitsbewältigung durch Strafverfahren*; Frei, van Laak, and Stolleis, *Geschichte vor Gericht.*

48  N. Frei, "Auschwitz und Holocaust."

49  Werle and Wandres, *Auschwitz vor Gericht*; Schneider, *Auschwitz.*

50  Wilke, Schenk, Cohen, and Zemach, *Holocaust und NS-Prozesse.*

51  For critique of the trials, see especially Friedrich, *Die kalte Amnestie*; Giordano, *Die zweite Schuld oder von der Last Deutscher zu sein*; and Lichtenstein, *Im Namen des Volkes.*

52  N. Frei, "Der Frankfurter Auschwitz-Prozess und die deutsche Zeitgeschichtsforschung."

53  Herbert, "Vernichtungspolitik"; Lorenz, "Border-Crossings." See also the interviews with historians of the Hitler Youth generation included in Hohls and Jarausch, *Versäumte Fragen*; Kansteiner, "The Rise and Fall of Metaphor."

54  Schöttler, *Geschichtsschreibung als Legitimationswissensschaft*; Aly, *Macht,*

*Geist, Wahn*; Fahlbusch, *Wissenschaft im Dienst der nationalsozialistischen Politik?*; Schulze and Oexle, *Deutsche Historiker im Nationalsozialismus*.

55 Perels, *Das juristische Erbe des "Dritten Reiches"*; I. Müller, *Hitler's Justice*.

56 Hoffmann and Schober, *Zwischen Gestern und Morgen*; Becker and Schöll, *"In jenen Tagen"*; Reichel, *Erfundene Erinnerung*.

57 ARD is the abbreviation for Arbeitsgemeinschaft der öffentlichen-rechtlichen Rundfunkanstalten der Bundesrepublik Deutschland. Classen, *Bilder der Vergangenheit*; Fritsche, *Vergangenheitsbewältigung im Fernsehen*; Hicketheir, "Der zweite Weltkrieg und der Holocaust im Fernsehen der fünfziger und frühen sechziger Jahre."

58 Geisler, "The Disposal of Memory;" Kansteiner, "Nazis, Viewers, and Statistics."

59 Schlant, *The Language of Silence*; and Richter, *Günter Grass*; Preece, *The Life and Work of Günter Grass*.

60 Raddatz, *Summa Inuiria oder Durfte der Papst schweigen*; Berg, *Hochhuths "Stellvertreter" und die "Stellvertreter"-Debatte*; Feinberg, *Wiedergutmachung im Programm*.

61 Wachs, *Der Fall Theodor Oberländer (1905–1998)*; Jacobs, "Der Streit um Dr. Hans Globke in der öffentlichen Meinung der Bundesrepublik Deutschland 1949–1973"; Schwabb-Trapp, *Konflikt, Kultur und Interpretation*, 100–129; Teschke, *Hitler's Legacy*.

62 The most famous attack on Kiesinger occurred in November 1968 when the political activist Beate Klarsfeld, yelling "Kiesinger, Nazi," slapped Kiesinger during a CDU party congress (see Kraushaar, *1968*, 282–84).

63 Merseburger, *Willy Brandt 1913–1992*, 578.

64 Holler, *20. Juli 1944*; Büchel, *Der deutsche Widerstand im Spiegel von Fachliteratur und Publizistik seit 1945*.

65 Schneider, "Der Warschauer Kniefall"; Rother, "Willy Brandt."

66 Wolfrum, *Geschichtspolitik in der Bundesrepublik Deutschland*. See also Kansteiner, *In Pursuit of German Memory*.

67 That applies especially to the decision to remove alleged political radicals from the civil service (see Histor, *Willy Brandts vergessene Opfer*).

68 Haug, *Vom hilflosen Antifaschismus zur Gnade der späten Geburt*; Bude, *Das Altern einer Generation*; Bude and Kohli, *Radikalisierte Aufklärung*; Schneider, "Den Kopf verkehrt aufgesetzt."

69 Voigt, *Aktivismus und moralischer Rigorismus*; Fels, *Der Aufruhr der 68er*; and compare to Baier, *Die Früchte der Revolte*.

70 Preuss-Lausitz, *Kriegskinder, Konsumkinder, Krisenkinder*.

71 Herf, *Divided Memory*; Kattago, *Ambiguous Memory*.

72 Lichtenstein, *Majdanek*.

73 Goschler, *Schuld und Schulden*, 357.

74 Herbert, "Neue Antworten und Fragen."

75  Kansteiner, "Nazis, Viewers, and Statistics."

76  Dubiel, *Niemand ist frei von der Geschichte*, 139–60; Varon, *Bringing the War Home*.

77  One of the alternative print media that focused on the exploration of Fascism, as well as many other concerns of the new social movements, was the radical neo-Marxist journal *Das Argument* (see, for example, Behrens, *Faschismus und Ideologie*).

78  Reichel, *Erfundene Erinnerung*, 143–48. See also Bodek, *Die Fassbinder-Kontroversen*.

79  On the intellectual origins and the development of Alltagsgeschichte, see Eley, "Labor History, Social History, Alltagsgeschichte"; Lüdke, "Einleitung"; Schulze, *Sozialgeschichte, Alltagsgeschichte, Mikro-Historie*; Iggers, *Geschichtswissenschaft im 20. Jahrhundert*, 73–87.

80  See the critiques of Alltagsgeschichte in Institut für Zeitgeschichte, *Alltagsgeschichte der NS-Zeit*; Brüggemeier and Kocka, "*Geschichte von unten, Geschichte von innen*."

81  Elsaesser, *New German Cinema*; Rentschler, *West German Filmmakers on Film*.

82  Kaes, *From Hitler to Heimat*; Wenzel, *Gedächnisraum Film*.

83  Vogt, *Erinnerung ist unsere Aufgabe*; Satzman and Kiefer, *Anselm Kiefer and Art after Auschwitz*.

84  On the elegant avoidance of responsibility by Germany's economic elite after World War II, see Wiesen, *West German Industry and the Challenge of the Nazi Past*.

85  On the media event *Holocaust*, see Märtesheimer and Frenzel, *Im Kreuzfeuer*; Ahren et al., *Das Lehrstück "Holocaust"*; Thiele, *Publizistisch Kontroversen über den Holocaust im Film*, 298–338; and the self-critical remarks by Hans Mommsen in "Holocaust und die Deutsche Geschichtswissenschaft."

86  The debate is documented in Augstein et al., *Historikerstreit*. For a contextualization of the debate, see Kansteiner "Between Politics and Memory."

87  Kansteiner, "Nazis, Viewers, and Statistics."

88  Quite sympathetic to Kohl's memory agenda is Seuthe, "*Geistig-moralische Wende*"? More critical are Moller, *Die Entkonkretisierung der NS-Herrschaft in der Ära Kohl*; Reichel, *Politik mit der Erinnerung*. See also Kattago, *Ambiguous Memory*.

89  For Habermas's concept of postnational identity, see Habermas, "Historical Consciousness and Post-Traditional Identity; Habermas, "Grenzen des Neohistorismus." For the philosophical underpinnings of the concept, see Wolin, introduction to *The New Conservatism*; Matustik, *Postnational Identity*, especially 3–28.

90  The representation of Nazism in West German architecture and memorials is one of the best-researched subfields of German memory studies. See, for example, Schafft and Zeidler, *Die KZ-Mahn- und Gedenkstätten in Deutschland*; Reichel, *Politik mit der Erinnerung*; Koshar, *From Monuments to Traces*; and the complete inventory of all memorials in Puvogel and Stankowski, *Gedenkstätten für die Opfer des Nationalsozialismus*; Endlich et al., *Gedenkstätten für die Opfer des Nationalsozialismus*.

91 See, for example, Hartman, *Bitburg in Moral and Political Perspective.*

92 Linn, *"Noch heute ein Faszinosum"*; Domansky, "'Kristallnacht,' the Holocaust and German Unity."

93 Thoma, *Vergangenheitsbewältigung am Beispiel der Auseinandersetzungen um die Neue Wache*; Schmidt, Mittig, and Böhm, *Nationaler Totenkult*; Reichel, *Politik mit der Erinnerung*, 131–246.

94 Benedikt Erenz, "Geschenk an die Jugend, Jahrmarkt mit Peinlichkeiten: In Bonn wurde das Haus der Geschichte der Bundesrepublik Deutschland eröffnet," *Die Zeit*, 24 June 1994. See also Seuthe, *NS-Vergangenheit in der Ära Kohl*, 180–81.

95 Seuthe, *NS-Vergangenheit in der Ära Kohl*, 222.

96 S. Berger, *The Search for Normality*; J.-W. Müller, *Another Country.*

97 The long discussions that preceded the decisions to build the memorial are documented in Kirsch, *Nationaler Mythos oder historische Trauer?*; Stavginski, *Das Holocaust-Denkmal*; Quack, *Auf dem Weg zur Realisierung.*

98 Stern, *The Whitewashing of the Yellow Badge*; Baumgärtner, *Reden nach Hitler*, 209–32.

99 See especially Bodemann, *Gedächnistheater*; Bodemann, *In den Wogen der Erinnerung.*

100 Philipp Grassmann, "Versteckspiele im Stelenwald," *Süddeutsche Zeitung*, 16 May 2005; and "Hakenkreuze am Holocaust-Mahnmal," *Spiegel Online*, 1 June 2005, http://www.spiegel.de.

101 Bettina Schneuer, "'Mama, das ist doch kein Grab,'" *Stern*, 19 May 2005; Miguel Sanches, "Ein Mahnmal als Spielplatz," *Westfälische Rundschau*, 21 May 2005; Jörg Lau, "Stelenhüpfen: Der Alltag und das Holocaust-Mahnmal," *Die Zeit*, 25 May 2005.

102 Regarding the Berlin Holocaust Memorial, see Brumlik, Funke, and Rensmann, *Umkämpftes Vergessen* and note 97 above. The reparations settlement is precisely summarized in Saathoff, "Entschädigung für Zwangsarbeiter?" and Goschler, *Schuld und Schulden*, 450–75. See also the critiques in Matthias Arning, *Späte Abrechnung*; Zumbansen, *Zwangsrbeit im Dritten Reich*. Compare to Spiliotis, *Verantwortung und Rechtsfrieden.*

103 Seuthe, *NS-Vergangenheit in der Ära Kohl*, 103–46; Niven, *Facing the Nazi Past*, 108–18; Kirsch, *"Wir haben aus der Geschichte gelernt,"* 151–200. The new European Holocaust memory was celebrated by Europe's political elite during the 2000 Stockholm Holocaust conference (see Michael Jeismann, *Auf Wiedersehen Gestern*, 139–51; Levy and Sznaider, *Erinnerung im globalen Zeitalter*, 210–16).

104 Michael Schwabb-Trapp, *Kriegsdiskurse.*

105 "Schröders Rede im Wortlaut," *Die Welt*, 6 June 2004; Malte Lehming, "Der Westen findet sich," *Der Tagesspiegel*, 7 June 2004.

106 Gerhard Schröder, "'Wir stehen erst am Ende einer langen Nachkriegszeit,'" *Süddeutsche Zeitung*, 7 May 2005. Note the contradictory title of Schröder's article. Like many of his predecessors, Schröder wanted to make clear that Germans had reached the end of the postwar period. At the same time, he did not want to be

perceived as an opponent of ongoing VGB efforts and therefore conceded that it had been an especially long postwar period and that Germans were only just reaching its end. It will be interesting to see how German and other European elites rephrase their enthusiasm for European unity in light of the extensive popular resentment of the European Union's bureaucracy and its lack of democratic legitimacy.

107 See especially the publications of the scholars who contributed to Herbert, *National-Socialist Extermination Policies*.

108 See, for example, the synthesis by Peter Longerich in *Politik der Vernichtung*.

109 See the profiles of different types of German historical consciousness developed by Felix Philipp Lutz in *Das Geschichtsbewusstsein der Deutschen*.

110 Schoeps, *Ein Volk von Mördern?*; Finkelstein and Birn, *A Nation of Trial*; Shandley, *Unwilling Germans?*

111 Heil and Erb, *Geschichtswissenschaft und Öffentlichkeit*.

112 See especially Streit, *Keine Kameraden*.

113 The catalog of the exhibition was published by Hannes Heer and Klaus Naumann (*Vernichtungskrieg*). See also Heer, *War of Extermination*; Niven, *Nazi Past*, 143–74. For discussions of the mistakes made by the organizers, see the contributions in Greven and Wrochem, *Der Krieg in der Nachkriegszeit*. For reactions of visitors of the exhibit, see especially Bernd, *Besucher einer Ausstellung*.

114 Kinkel, "Viele Taten, wenig Täter"; Keilbach, "Fernsehbilder der Geschichte"; Kansteiner, "The Radicalization of German Memory in the Age of Its Commercial Reproduction."

115 Kansteiner, "Nazis, Viewers, and Statistics"; Kansteiner, "Entertaining Catastrophe."

116 Gutte and Huisken, *Alles bewältigt, nichts begriffen!*

117 Walser made his remarks in his acceptance speech of the prestigious peace prize awarded by the German publishers' association (Friedenspreis des Deutschen Buchhandels). The subsequent debate is documented in Schirrmacher, *Die Walser-Bubis-Debatte*.

118 Noack, "Die Deutschen als Opfer," *Der Spiegel*, 25 March 2002; Hage, "Autoren unter Generalverdacht," *Der Spiegel*, 8 April 2002.

119 Kaes, *From Hitler to Heimat*; and the special issue on *Heimat* of the *New German Critique* 36 (1985).

120 The generational model is based on suggestions in Bude, *Bilanz der Nachfolge* and Norbert Frei, *1945 und wir*. See also Bude, *Deutsche Karrieren*; Bude, *Das Altern einer Generation*; Kohlstruck, *Zwischen Erinnerung und Geschichte*; Marcuse, *Legacies of Dachau*. Many of these scholars follow Mannheim, "Das Problem der Generationen."

121 For a critique of Betroffenheitskultur, see Stephan, *Der Betroffenheitskult*.

122 Welzer, Moller, and Tschuggnall, "*Opa war kein Nazi.*" See also Lutz, *Geschichtsbewusstsein*; Leonhard, *Politik- und Geschichtsbewusstsein*.

123 For an analysis of contemporary German right-wing and anti-Semitic discourses, see, for example, Grumke and Wagner, *Handbuch Rechtsradikalismus*; and Rensmann, *Demokratic und Judenbild*.

124  In this respect Daniel Levy and Natan Sznaider are much too optimistic when they expect that cosmopolitan collective memories that come into existence as a result of globalization in the second modernity are intrinsically linked to increased political self-reflexivity (see Levy and Sznaider, *Erinnerung im globalen Zeitalter*).

125  Stefan Ulrich, "60 Jahre Auschwitz-Befreiung: Die UN gedenken erstmals offiziell des Holocausts," *Süddeutsche Zeitung*, 24 January 2005.

CLAUDIO FOGU ❋

# *Italiani brava gente*

## THE LEGACY OF FASCIST HISTORICAL CULTURE

## ON ITALIAN POLITICS OF MEMORY

Italians seem to want to be freed from the war, Fascism, and themselves.
—An Allied officer in July 1945

Statements concerning the difficulty encountered by Allied officers in finding a single "fascist" among the liberated Italians have penetrated in Italian
popular folklore more widely and deeply than any fascist claim to a "Great
Italy" produced in the *ventennio nero* (the two "black" decades of fascist
regime between 1922 and 1943).[1] The mental image they hark back to is one
that Italians and philo-Italian public opinion have learned to love: from
Roberto Rossellini's *Open City* (1945) to Roberto Benigni's *Life Is Beautiful*
(1999) representations of the fascist Italian past have consolidated an image
of Italians as *brava gente* (good folks).[2] In their own eyes and in those of their
liberators, Italians possessed a fundamental banality of goodness that had
prevented them from perpetrating inhuman and criminal acts. If anything,
they had been victims of *nazifascismo* (Nazi Fascism) and bore no sense of
collective responsibility for their fascist past.[3] Even in the memory of their
own victims, fascist wars of aggression were motivated by the desire to *fare
bella figura* (make a good impression) rather than by anti-Semitic, racist, or
imperialist designs.[4]

The brava gente image of Italians can be traced across so many media
(from professional historiography to film and television) and postwar generations (from the oral memories of the Turin working class collected by
Luisa Passerini in 1984 to the teenagers interviewed by Daniele Mezzana
fifteen years later) that it could be easily mistaken as the quintessential
expression of a truly collective memory—that is, as "a set of recollections
attributable to some overarching group mind that could recall past events in

the (admittedly poorly understood) ways in which we believe that individuals recall the past."[5] Yet, to study the Italian memorialization of the war and Nazi Fascism means primarily to probe the subtle negotiations between the politics governing the institutionalization of memory events and the poetics that absorb them into metahistorical narratives; it also means, in the process, to expose the continuities between fascist and postfascist historical imaginaries.[6]

Benito Mussolini and the fascist movement came to power on 28 October 1922, instituting a dictatorial authoritarian regime that lasted until 25 July 1943, a few days after the landing of the Allies in Sicily. On that latter date, the fascist Grand Council voted Mussolini out of power and the king had him arrested, entrusting the government to an army general, Pietro Badoglio, who proceeded to disband the fascist party but used the armed forces to repress any attempt at popular insurrection. For the next forty-five days Italians were liberated from Fascism but still fought next to the Germans against the Allied invader.

On 8 September 1943 Badoglio finally announced the signing of an armistice with the Allies. Yet, Italian soldiers were given no instruction on how to interpret the armistice, so in the days that followed, the Italian military and state apparatus dissolved in utter chaos. The king and Badoglio's government left Rome, putting themselves under the protection of the Allies in the south of Italy, while German forces rescued Mussolini from his captivity and led him to the northern city of Salò to set up the Repubblica Sociale Italiana (Italian Social Republic [RSI]). There, Mussolini, joined by several old-guard fascists, instituted a republican form of fascist regime that extended its authority from north of Milan to just south of Rome but was itself under close Nazi scrutiny and control. Italian soldiers, left to their own devices in Italy and abroad, were either arrested and deported to concentration camps —approximately 600,000 soldiers suffered this fate—or took to the mountains to organize the armed "resistance" to Nazi Fascism. Over the next two years, dozens of partisan bands sprang up all over northern Italy to help the Allies advance by sabotaging and killing German soldiers and officers. This partisan movement reached a maximum membership of 250,000 women and men, a majority of whom were Communists, and was slowly unified in the National Liberation Committee, which represented all antifascist forces: Communists, Catholics, and Liberals. After two years of bitter fighting, on 25 April 1945 a combined Allied offensive and resistance-led insurrection drove the Germans out of Italy, brought the RSI to an end, and resulted in Mussolini's death and ritual desecration in Milan.

Although public memorialization-historicization of Fascism and the war underwent several phases in the postwar era, three general characteristics of this process remained constant and in remarkable tension in relation to each other. First, the Italian experience of the war years could not but yield a "divided memory" along both geographical and political lines.[7] For twenty months, between September 1943 and April 1945, the Italian peninsula was divided into a Nazi-occupied and fascist-administered center-north, and an Allied-liberated south under the formal authority of the Italian monarchy; the resistance movement and the Nazi-fascist repression of civilians were therefore an almost exclusively northern phenomena. In the south the long-lasting Allied liberation rapidly overshadowed the memory of the brief German occupation. In this respect, postwar identification of the Italian war experience with the partisan resistance marginalized the memory of southern Italians as well as the countermemories of the many communities who had suffered and survived the atrocities perpetrated by the Wehrmacht and Nazi-fascist military units in retaliation or as preemptive strikes against partisan military operations.[8] At the same time, the equation of the resistance with anti-Fascism tout court provided the new political forces of the young Italian republic with a founding myth for their democratic constitution and with a lasting bone of symbolic contention for the legitimization of their political struggles.[9] In particular, the claim of continuity with the resistance *as* the political heir of anti-Fascism constituted for several decades a key discursive strategy adopted by the Italian Communist Party to establish its national-democratic credentials and gather consensus.[10]

Second, the identification of the resistance with anti-Fascism can be considered the hinge on which the memorialization-historicization of Nazi Fascism has turned in postwar Italy, until very recently. The second hinge is the fact that, with the monumentalization of the *biennio* (the two years between the fall of Mussolini on 25 July 1943 and the insurrection of 25 April 1945), the fascist ventennio was effectively marginalized in the memory of those who lived under the regime and virtually obliterated from the official history of the Italian postwar republic. In the immediate aftermath of the war and for at least the next four decades, the double image of Fascism as a parenthesis in Italian history and an external virus that had penetrated its healthy historical body—famously elaborated by the liberal philosopher Benedetto Croce—sustained and legitimized both public amnesia regarding the ventennio and the historicization of the biennio as the true face of Italian national identity.[11] For example, while the mass media and ritual commemorations succeeded in nationalizing the memory of the resistance even in southern Italy, the teaching of history at all scholastic levels for decades terminated at World War I.[12] And, as the scholar Mirco Dondi recently remarked, even academic "historiography has surprisingly failed to cope with the issue of cultural continuity in Italy and thus with the question of the survival of the fascist mentality in the Republic."[13] As a result, the first postwar generations of Italians never even acquired an "official" image of Fascism. On the contrary, beginning with the immediate aftermath of the war, a very active process of forgetting has invested all areas of the regime related to aggressive foreign policy, anti-Semitism, and racism: the brutal invasion of Ethiopia in 1935–1936; the anti-Semitic laws passed in 1938; the aggressive war fought by the Italian fascist army in the Balkans between 1940 and 1943; and the deportation of foreign and Italian Jews initiated in October 1943.[14]

To a great extent, then, the lasting image of Italians as brava gente has been the result of active efforts to purge Fascism of "perpetrator" traits. Yet—and here is the third characteristic of the Italian memorialization-historicization process—the replacement of the biennio for the ventennio in public memory took place in forms that were absorbed and transfigured from fascist historical culture itself. Contrary to Croce's influential image, Fascism was not a parenthesis either in the history of Italy or in the historical consciousness of Italians who lived under the regime. On the contrary, the elaboration of a fascist form of historical imagination was one of the most distinguishing traits of the twenty-year-long Mussolinian dictatorship. In its two decades of power, the fascist regime produced scores of rituals connected to the memorialization of the Italian national past from the Risorgimento to the Great War and undertook an impressive effort to give visual form to a specifically fascist historic imaginary, in other words, a self-image of Fascism as a history-making agent.[15] This image was institutionalized at all levels of fascist discourse and mass culture celebrating Fascism as both the historical fulfillment of the Italian Risorgimento, with a capital R (the process of independence and unification of the Italian nation between 1848 and 1860) and of a *risorgimento* (literally, a resurrection or resurgence in the making— that is, the Latin-Catholic response to the Marxist concept of revolution).[16] If Italians in the postwar era were successful at reinventing themselves as antifascist, it was not only by forgetting that they (or a majority of them) *ever were* fascist but also by transfiguring the historical imaginary they had absorbed under the regime. With regard to the process of negotiation with fascist historical culture, one can identify four mental images corresponding to four phases in the development of a "postfascist" Italian imaginary: (1) *Il secondo Risorgimento* (The Second Risorgimento), 1945–1960; (2) *La Rivoluzione mancata* (The missed revolution), 1960–1975; (3) *La guerra civile* (The civil war), 1975–1990; and (4) *La morte della patria* (The death of the fatherland), 1990–present.[17]

## Il Secondo Risorgimento, 1946–1960

On 25 April 1946 Italy celebrated the first *festa della liberazione* (liberation day) as "the day of our Second Risorgimento."[18] For the following decade and a half, the annual 25 April celebration would remain the sole ritual *lieu de mémoire* (site of memory) dedicated by the state to the war years, and the image of a Second Risorgimento the sole official paradigm for the historicization of the resistance. From the beginning, then, the resistance was identified as an expression of the anti-Fascism of all Italians and, eviscerated of its social and insurrectional traits, was enshrined as the sign of an harmonious national identity. Changes in this ritual commemoration would eventually signal rapid shifts in the phases of memorialization, but the very fact that 25 April, rather than 25 July (the day Mussolini was arrested) or 8 September (the day Italy signed the armistice with the Allies), was selected and maintained as the founding date of the republic cannot be underestimated.

With the commemoration of the insurrectional date, Italians were invited to celebrate the encounter between a militant antifascist minority and the silent popular majority that had endured or supported the RSI, rather than be forced to remember the fascist ventennio or the fascist war itself. Furthermore, with the dehistoricized reference to a "second" risorgimento, the new Italy officially founded itself on the rejection of the fascist claim to have fulfilled the Risorgimento, as well as on the obliteration of the period of national history (1860–1945) between the first and second risorgimentos.[19] A Catholic paradigm of commemoration was thus extracted from fascist claims to "risorgimental" agency—which had resurrected the fatherland— and drafted onto the memorialization of the resistance as the Second Risorgimento. Whether in the official celebrations of 25 April, or in the monuments to "the fallen of all wars" inaugurated between 1945 and 1949 throughout the northern territory, or in works of neorealist cinema such as Rossellini's *Open City* (1945), the partisans were represented and celebrated as martyrs—rather than victors or heroes—and the Italian fascists were obliterated under the demonic image of the Nazi occupation.[20] In addition, the decriminalization of Fascism was sustained by the very limited and purely symbolic purges of fascist collaborators which took place between 1946 and 1948.

Only the crimes committed during the bienno were persecuted and, by and large, only the most recognizable *gerarchi*—those who had been in the newsreels—and, more often, their girlfriends were punished. In order to shield the monarchy, which was still in power until the referendum of 1946, defascistization laws did not entail any reworking of the state, and where they did, they were not applied.[21] Most of the administrative, judicial, and even police apparatus of the fascist state and party was left untouched and effortlessly integrated into the new republican order.[22] Finally, an active policy of censorship and suppression of information concerning the fascist wars of aggression ensured the removal of the most troubling fascist past from memory.[23] In 1953, for example, the journalists Guido Renzi and Guido Aristarco were accused of "insult to the armed forces," put before a military tribunal, and sentenced to some months of prison because they had been preparing a film on the disastrous military campaign in Greece.[24] Postwar Italians were allowed to remember only the partisan war fought against the Nazi "invader" from September 1943 to April 1945 and to actively forget the one they had joined as allies of the Nazis in June 1940. Thus constructed, the historic image of the resistance as Second Risorgimento reappropriated the Catholic trope of "resurgence" from fascist use in order to allow the postfascist Italian State to present itself simultaneously as an epochal break and the realization of a submerged national continuity (Risorgimento–postwar Republic). In fact, it would not be long before Catholic form would transform itself into political content.

In April 1948 the Christian Democrats won the first republican elections, defeating the Italian Communist Party (PCI) and, with it, the idea of the resistance as a unified antifascist front. From that year onward and throughout the Cold War decades, the Christian Democrats held power in the name of anti-Communism. The PCI, however, remained the strongest Communist party in the Western hemisphere. As a result, from the 1950s onward, Italy was a privileged battlefield for Cold War politics, and on this battlefield the commemoration of 25 April served as a symbolic thermometer with which to measure the political temperature in the ideological conflict between Catholicism and Communism. From 1948 to 1953 the uninterrupted electoral success of the Christian Democrats allowed the center-right coalition to exclude partisan associations from the commemoration and to completely transfigure the insurrectional referent of 25 April into an official occasion for celebrating the Italian armed forces. Thus Catholicized, the official commemoration of 25 April dissolved the resistance martyrs into the Christian community of those fallen for the fatherland; yet, it did not prevent the development of a parallel and antithetical culture of commemoration.

The PCI used the very same commemorative occasions to organize counter-demonstrations of partisan associations in order to reaffirm its national-democratic credentials on the one hand and, on the other, to remind both its adversaries and its allies on the left of the primary role that Communist partisans had played in the Second Risorgimento. Thus, beginning with the first drop in Christian Democratic votes in the elections of 1953, the Communists' claims to legitimacy began to defeat the censorship and ostracism of the right-wing faction controlling the centrist government. In 1955, on the solemn occasion of the commemoration of the *decennale* (tenth anniversary) of the resistance, the Christian Democrats were forced to make a number of concessions. For the first time, armed forces and partisan leaders, state representatives and Communist senators found themselves on the same podium, in Milan, to celebrate a symbolic compromise that seemed to open a new political season. Yet, the symbolic legitimization won by the Communists in 1955 was not translated into either a change of government or a leftward turn in the Christian Democratic monopoly of power. On the contrary, with the gradual waning of their electoral majority the Christian Democrats began relying more and more on the external support of the right-wing parties, including the Movimento Sociale Italiano (MSI)—a legally reconstituted neofascist formation. This policy backfired, however, demonstrating the sensitive relationship that existed between the political and commemorative barometers in the 1950s.[25] It was, in fact, the military mobilization of the partisans themselves against the MSI in July 1960 that would lead to a dramatic opening of the Christian Democrats to the non-Communist left and to a new phase in the memorialization-historicization of Fascism, the war years, and the resistance.

## La rivoluzione mancata, 1960–1975

In March 1960 the Christian Democrat Ferdinando Tambroni was elected premier with the external support of monarchists and neofascists. Returning the favor, Tambroni in July gave the MSI permission to hold its national congress in the "red" city of Genoa. Receiving this as an unacceptable provocation, the partisan associations of Genoa reconstituted themselves as armed bands demanding and obtaining the repeal of the decree, as well as the dismissal of Tambroni. The insurrectional threat of the so-called July Days was serious enough to occasion the end of the informal center-right coalition that had ruled since 1953. With the removal of Tambroni, the left wing of the Christian Democrats came to power by convincing the Italian Socialist Party to participate in a center-left coalition, which lasted throughout the 1960s and into the 1970s, thanks in part to the external support of the PCI. Suddenly, the "red" resistance was lifted out of the dustbin to become the object of both official and cultural memorialization. To begin with, gold medals were awarded with ever greater frequency to individuals, villages, and cities that had distinguished themselves in the partisan war. Second, after more than a decade of inactivity, a spectacular second wave of monuments was inaugurated throughout the northern territory between 1963 and 1975. In contrast to the earlier monuments to the "fallen of all wars," these monuments emphasized the antifascist value of the partisans' choice and sacrifice.[26] In addition, concentration camps, such as the Risiera di San Sabba in Trieste, established by Nazi occupying forces in late 1943 and featuring cremation ovens, were finally acknowledged and turned into "national monuments."[27]

The new political climate also allowed a complete lifting of the veil on the public representation of Fascism itself. On the big screen, a new wave of talented directors such as Federico Fellini, Lina Wertmuller, Bernardo Bertolucci, and Pier Paolo Pasolini confronted themselves—and their Italian audiences—with the fascist past. Breaking with both the neorealist aesthetics of the previous decade, films such as *The Conformist* (Bertolucci, 1970), *The Night Porter* (Cavani, 1973), *Amarcord* (Fellini, 1973), *Salò* (Pasolini, 1975), *Seven Beauties* (Wertmuller, 1975) and *Novecento* (Bertolucci, 1976) mixed memory and history by introducing several layers of complexity in the representation of Fascism and the fight against it, as well as in the representation of the relationship between fascist past and postfascist present.[28] Finally, from 1962 onward the historic dates of the resistance (25 July, 8 September, and 25 April) became the occasion for "historical colossals"—hybrid documentary-style programs mixing commentary on newsreel footage with interviews of protagonists, witnesses, and historians—which were produced and aired by the Italian state-broadcasting system (RAI). Programmed during prime time and broadcast over several continuous evenings, the historical colossals of the 1960s and 1970s constituted not only a primary means for the transmission of antifascist images to the postwar generations but also for their historicization as a result of the firsthand involvement of witnesses, journalists, and historians. The masterpiece of the genre was Sergio Zavoli's 1972 six-part documentary *Nascita di una dittatura*

(Birth of a dictatorship), realized with the help of Marxist, liberal, and Catholic historians, and containing the "scoop" interview with Rachele Mussolini, the aging wife of Il Duce.[29]

From the perspective of the 1990s, the 1960s have been viewed as (and accused of) "officializing" the equation between the "red" resistance and anti-Fascism, thereby allowing a Marxist vision of the recent Italian past to become culturally dominant in order to support a "historic compromise" between Christian democrats and Communists.[30] This affirmation has a lot more to do with the revisionist atmosphere of the 1990s than the supposed Marxist orthodoxy of the 1960s. Neither the television colossals of the late 1960s, nor Bertolucci's award-winning *Novecento*, nor the celebration of the *ventennale* (twentieth anniversary) of the resistance directly challenged the nationalizing image of the resistance as Second Risorgimento. The "false" recollection that a Marxist vision of history had come to dominate the official memory of the resistance in the 1960s records instead the intensity of the attack that the youth of the " '68 generation" brought to the officialized image of a "red" resistance sponsored by the PCI.[31]

It was not so much that all teachers and fathers were accused of having been fascists by the young, self-declared revolutionaries who occupied Italian universities and factories from late 1967 through the summer of 1968. Most of these youth knew and openly recognized that their fathers had been genuine partisans, but, for that very reason, they accused them of having betrayed the resistance as both experience and memory.[32] By presenting the resistance as the endpoint of political anti-Fascism and as the Second Risorgimento, the traditional Marxist left had purged the resistance of its status as a genuinely insurrectional and revolutionary phenomenon. Instead, for the '68 generation the resistance was "red" in the sense of Mao's little book, not Garibaldi's shirt. While this revolutionary image of the resistance came on the heels of its official revaluation in the mass media, literature, and celebrations of the 1960s, it nevertheless led to the coalescence of a new historical imaginary. The *cattocomunista* (Catholic Communist) image of the resistance as Second Risorgimento was now accompanied and confronted by that of the rivoluzione mancata (missed revolutionary opportunity)—an image ironically derived from the writings on the (first) Risorgimento that the PCI's founder, Antonio Gramsci, had composed while imprisoned by the fascist regime.[33]

Contrary to the image of the Second Risorgimento, that of the missed revolution highlighted not only the political-institutional continuities between fascist and republican Italy but also the attitudes carried over by the prewar generations into the postwar era. The student movement forcefully denounced the stereotyped image of the Second Risorgimento not only for its traits of Catholic conciliation but also for its blindness to the *antifascismo esistenziale* (existentialist)—rather than merely *resistenziale* (resistentialist)—of the partisans.[34] Appreciating the spontaneous, anarchical character of the armed resistance above its political lineage, the '68 generation saw itself as aligned with a mental type of anti-Fascism found in those who had opposed the authoritarian and virilist traits of the fascist regime—regardless of whether or not they had joined the partisan formations. Naturally, when we say '68 generation we speak of that minority of militant activists who joined the student-workers movement of protest from the late 1960s through the mid-1970s. Yet, this minority movement certainly functioned as the catalyst for a legitimacy crisis in the conciliatory image of the Second Risorgimento.

The image of the rivoluzione mancata was rejected by all political forces, including the PCI and the protagonists themselves. All partisan formations denounced it because, on the one hand, it conjured up what they had all agreed to cover up—that is, the memory of armed resistance as an often spontaneous choice that only rarely was the point of arrival of a political anti-Fascism demonstrated throughout the ventennio—and, on the other, because it elided all distinctions between the fascist past and the democratic present they had contributed to building. Yet, precisely for these reasons, the image of the missed revolution was endorsed, radicalized, and literally embodied by some of the terrorist groups—the Red Brigades, in particular—who dominated the "years of lead" (1970s) and projected themselves as *resistenti ad oltranza* (permanent partisans).[35] Thus, although all democratic parties—the PCI, above all—were united in rejecting all forms of terrorism, the conciliatory memorialization-historicization process that had held sway since 1960 was seriously disrupted. The image of the resistance-missed revolution rendered justice to the aspect that had been most successfully purged from the memorialization of the resistance *as* Second Risorgimento: violence.

Suddenly, the violence that had characterized the "civil war" between partisans and fascists, with all its tragic consequences for the civil population, began emerging from the private realm of memories to bear on the construction of a new historical imaginary—or the deconstruction of an old one. After the silence of the 1950s and the sudden officialization of the resistance in the 1960s, a truly divided memory began to emerge, breaking the ice of consensus thinned by the internal debate on the left.[36] In particular, the official-national celebration of the partisans as the martyrs of the republic began to be confronted by the private-local resentment against the partisans, who were held to be responsible for having directed the homicidal fury of the Nazi army onto the civil population. Stimulated by the explicit goal of the terrorists to provoke civil war, the emergence of this divided memory was powerful enough to begin devaluating the symbolic capital attached to anti-Fascism as the least common denominator holding together the whole republican parliamentary spectrum. In the mid-1970s all representational fields took hold of the image of the resistance; this time, however, the process started from the revision of Fascism itself, and it sought to highlight other dimensions of the war experience, *other*, that is, than the resistance.

## Guerra civile, 1975–1990

Beginning in the late 1960s, with the progressive demise of the Cold War climate of the previous decades and the firm denunciation of the Soviet invasion of Czechoslovakia by prominent European Communists, anti-Communism was generally attenuated everywhere in Europe. In Italy the PCI's firm rejection of terrorist or insurrectional tactics contributed to its democratic legitimization far more effectively than its monopoly over the partisan legacy had done in the early 1960s. Yet, the unsuccessful attempts of prominent political leaders on both sides to integrate the Communists—and the labor movement along with them—into the sociopolitical fabric of post-1968 Italy was, at least in part, the result of a subtle erosion of anti-Fascism itself as the founding ideology of the republic. Many political and generational factors contributed to this erosion, including, notably, the formidable impact of television on the formation of mass trends and changes in public discourse. From the mid-1970s television began affirming itself as the primary agent for the consolidation and transformation of the historical imaginary of the postwar generations of Italians.[37]

From all quantitative and qualitative points of view, the panorama offered by the RAI between 1975 and 1990 differed dramatically from the ritualistic officialization of the resistance in the 1960s and the silence of the 1950s. First, during this period, the percentage of programs on the resistance period (1943–1945) dropped dramatically from 40 percent to 15 percent of all historical programs dedicated to the period 1922–1945. Second, within this 15 percent, programs about other aspects of the Italian war experience outnumbered those dedicated specifically to the resistance and were more evenly distributed across time and programming space, as opposed to being clustered around commemorative dates.[38] Third, and most important, several documentaries on the war years exposed the nation to the lingering popular memory of a "civil war" fought between fascist and antifascists, the price of which had been mostly paid by civilians due to the ferocious retaliation of the German army.[39]

Whether intended or not, in programs such as 1981's *Finchè dura la memoria* (Until memory lasts) the heroic image of the partisan began to be tainted with the blood of thousands of civilians.[40] And although historiographically the debate on the resistance as civil war would have to await the publication of Claudio Pavone's *Una guerra civile* in 1991, the shift from the antifascist images of the Second Risorgimento to the theme of the missed revolution was well under way at the level of popular imaginary in the early 1980s.[41] Symptomatic of this shift were the many television documentaries that began to focus on the tragic or heroic fate of the *internati*, the 600,000 Italian soldiers who had been captured by the Germans after September 8th and were deported to concentration camps for refusing to collaborate. The importance of these programs was not so much in their audience share, but in their frequency and their ability to solicit political responses and raise public discussions in the print media. Through these public debates even the ultra-leftist image of the "existential" resistance was completely transfigured. In the public imaginary, the internato began slowly to accompany and even displace the *partigiano* (resistance fighter) as the icon of an existential anti-Fascism that most Italians could identify with.

The devaluation of the resistance as the pivot on which all processes of memorialization-historicization of the war years had rotated for three decades was accompanied by an equally dramatic increase in the percentage and absolute number of television programs dedicated to the fascist ventennio. Beginning with the famous televised debate between historians Denis Mack Smith and Renzo De Felice in 1976, the programs broadcast by RAI and privately owned television channels from the late 1970s through the late 1980s began to render visible how "politically" polarized the memory of Fascism itself remained.[42] De Felice had authored a multivolume biography of Mussolini which utilized fascist archival documents and memoirs, almost to the exclusion of antifascist sources.[43] The topic and methodology of his monumental book had rapidly characterized him as the leading proponent of a non-antifascist historiographical perspective, soon to be regarded by his detractors as anti-antifascist and "revisionist."[44] Until the mid-1970s, however, the debate on De Felice's scholarship and on Fascism as a whole had remained mostly limited to professional historiographical circles.[45] The televised debate, therefore, brought anti-Fascism *and* revisionism simultaneously to the attention of a much larger public audience. Fascism was suddenly brought out of the representational closet and in such a way that the Crocean image of a fascist parenthesis in Italian history was thoroughly delegitimized. During this period television producers and directors began to take full advantage of archived but never-before-utilized footage of the ventennio, especially newsreels that documented "normal" life in 1920s and 1930s—rather than "fascist"—Italy. The innovative everyday-history approach was therefore the first perspective on the regime that postwar generations of Italians experienced at the level of mass media. Yet, unlike in Germany, this approach did not offer a critical tool for the study of bystanders and perpetrators.[46] In the hands of the Italian mass media everyday history was used to highlight the private and the anecdotal over the political face of Fascism. As a result, overall mass-media production in the 1980s tended to successfully "normalize" Fascism under the apolitical trope of *come eravamo* (the way we were), thereby undermining the antifascist paradigm which had allowed the process of memorialization-historicization of the war years to hide the black ventennio below the glorious carpet of the red biennio.[47] Therefore, it was at the level of the representation of life under Fascism that the fateful shift from the officialization of the resistance to the ideological delegitimation of anti-Fascism began to take place.

Particularly representative of this anti-antifascist trend were documentaries such as Nicola Caracciolo's *Tutti gli uomini del duce* (The Duce's henchmen) that focused entirely on the personality of Mussolini, his family, and close collaborators. If Sergio Zavoli's *Nascita di una dittatura* (Birth of a dictatorship)—realized in 1972 with the help of historians representing all ideological positions on Fascism—exemplifies the antifascist paradigm sustaining the representation of Fascism from the 1950s through the mid-1970s, *Tutti gli uomini del duce* opened up a revisionist phase dominated by the spectacularization of private memory and the privatization of history.[48] From the fictional reconstruction of the life of Mussolini's lover in *Claretta* (1984), to Alberto Negrin's *Io e il duce* (The Duce and I [1985]), to the war docudramas *C'ero anch'io* (I was there, too [1983]) and *La mia guerra* (My war [1985]), the history of Fascism was offered to Italians in the form of biography throughout the 1980s.

These documentaries were openly inspired by the revisionist trend in the historiography of Fascism attributed to De Felice and his school. Yet, the mass-media deconstruction of the antifascist paradigm was no mere revisionist ploy, as some critics contended. The revision opened a window onto aspects of both antifascist and fascist experiences which had never found official avenues of representation, but were firmly ingrained in popular memory.[49] In particular, the television programs of the 1980s highlighted a fundamental aspect of the experience and memory of Fascism that had remained submerged under the symbolic weight of anti-Fascism from the 1950s onward: namely, the constitutive tension between *mussolinismo* (the cult of Mussolini) and *fascismo* proper.

Since its inception Fascism presented and organized itself as a political religion. At the same time, the fascist sacralization of politics always oscillated between two poles: a cult of Fascism, organized by the party and transmitted through ritual politics, and a largely spontaneous cult of Mussolini, dependent instead on the imaginary relationship that Mussolini cultivated with the Italian masses.[50] The mutual interdependence between the latter and their demigod, Il Duce, was neither a byproduct of their fascist faith, nor was it of the same nature as the Führer cult in Nazi Germany. It was marked by the imaginary construction of Mussolini as offering to Italians both a refuge from the menace of modernity and the opportunity to acquire collective *distinction* in the eyes of the world, rather than mere national *identity*.[51]

At first, the cult of Fascism and the cult of Mussolini developed side by side, but in time mussolinismo overtook and undermined its institutionalized rival. The millions of postcards sent to Mussolini by ordinary Italians throughout the ventennio, just as much as the many mottoes and jokes that separated Mussolini from his henchmen, spoke the popular-cultural language of a simultaneously saintly and heretical sort of veneration. Similarly, in the desecration of Mussolini's dead body—which was exposed in Piazzale Loreto in Milan, first arranged as a dead king holding a scepter, then hanged upside down—one recognizes the ancient scene of a divinity profaned for having failed to protect his adorers and maintain his promises of glory. Finally, the puzzling fact that the large majority of Italians who had not taken up arms either against or in defense of the Nazi-fascist regime could transform itself overnight into an antifascist mass may have had a lot to do with their psychological ability to remember themselves as Mussolinians rather than as fascists. In fact, there are good reasons to assume that the Italians' imaginary investment in and their emotional attachment to Mussolini survived well beyond the fall of Fascism.

After having been exposed to the macabre anger of the Milanese crowds, Mussolini's body was kidnapped in 1946 by neofascists and after more than a decade entombed in his birth town of Predappio in 1957, where it was allowed to become the object of pilgrimages and veneration.[52] Yet, the interest in ensuring the symbolic survival of mussolinismo in the collective imaginary of postfascist Italians cannot be restricted to either political or popular expressions of neo-Fascism. On the contrary, as early as 1947 and 1948, the popular magazines *Gente* and *Epoca* published exclusive interviews with the wife and daughter of Mussolini, respectively. Similarly, polemics concerning the modality, location, and responsibilities for the arrest and killing of Mussolini surfaced with regularity in the popular press and have not yet subsided. In fact, as demonstrated by Luisa Passerini's study of working-class memory in Turin, the imaginary separation between Mussolini and Fascism survived as one of the fundamental elements that guaranteed whatever consensus the regime obtained from workers.[53]

The Cold War climate first and then the monumentalization of the antifascist paradigm completely obliterated the memory of this imaginary separation. By contrast, the historiographical impact of De Felice's multivolume biography of Mussolini in the mid-1970s may have had a lot more to do with its implicit reflection of the lingering cult of Mussolini than with the explicitly anti-Marxist tone of his revisionist theses concerning the interclassist composition and appeal of Fascism. By the same token, the very popularity of the personalizing and privatizing television programs of the 1980s reflected and stimulated much more plausibly the (re-)emergence of mussolinismo from collective oblivion than any public agreement on the "objectivist" claims of De Felice against his "ideological" adversaries. The most glaring sign of the interconnection between the definitive demise of the antifascist paradigm and the legitimization of Mussolinism found folkloristic expression in the image of *Italia-cocomero* (Italy-watermelon) and a political reflection in the popularity of socialist premier Bettino Craxi. Popularized in left-wing circles, the image of postwar Italy as a watermelon—only the red (Communism) was good, the white (Christian Democrats) was indigestible, and the black seeds (the neofascists) needed to be spit out—demonstrated that irony had undermined even left-wing representations of the resistance. On the other front, the openly anti-Communist and self-proclaimed modernizer Craxi never reacted to being caricaturized as a Second Mussolini—his public image recalling that of the "man of providence," which had been embodied by the original Duce.


La morte della patria, 1990–Present

With the exception of Germany, the most direct impact of the fall of the Berlin Wall and the end of Communism in the West was recorded in the systemic crisis of the Italian political system in the first half of the 1990s.

This crisis involved three separate but concurrent processes. First, the PCI underwent a dramatic transformation from a mass-Communist party to the social-democratic Partito della Sinistra Democratica (Democratic Party of the Left), which was firmly determined to leave behind any ideological trait that kept it out of power. Second, a wave of judicial inquiries into the pervasive corruption that had characterized the five decades of anti-Communist power-sharing led to the unexpected and sudden demise of all government parties: the Christian Democrats, the Socialists, the Republicans and the Liberals. Finally, a challenge to the very unity of the nation was issued by a separatist movement in the Italian northeast led by a new political formation, the Lega Nord (Northern League). As a result of these intersecting processes, between 1990 and 1995 two generations of political leaders who had dominated the political scene for five decades were abruptly— though only temporarily—swept out of power, and with them appeared to go the politics of memory that had rotated around the main lieux de mémoire of the Republican nation-state: the *Resistenza-liberazione*.

With the suggestive image of an auto-da-fé of memory, an acute commentator, Mario Isnenghi, recently highlighted the swiftness and nonchalance with which the intellectual and political leadership of the post-Communist Italian left tended to accept the definitive separation of the resistance *as* civil war from anti-Fascism, and the complete inversion of its political charge.[54] To remember the resistance as a civil war meant that *partigiani* (resistance fighters) and *repubblichini* (RSI adherents) could no longer be neatly distinguished on the moral grounds of good-heroic (the former) versus evil-cowardly (the latter). And, in the wake of the popular denunciation of the *partitocrazia* (the power of political parties) that had supposedly ruled the "First Republic," this moral relativization of the resistance was rapidly translated into a political attack on anti-Fascism itself.[55] Entrenched for five decades at the constitutional heart of the (first) republic, the connection between political anti-Fascism and armed resistance was now openly held to be responsible for the formation of the "Republic of parties."[56]

Symptoms of this last shift in the Italian memorialization-historicization of the war and Fascism are scattered everywhere in the commemorations of the 1990s as well as in public discourse. Once again, however, they are most visible in the media, where the moral and political relativization of the resistance and anti-Fascism initiated in the 1980s found full-blown expression in television programs that naturalized history by historicizing memory. Since the early 1990s references to the resistance, anti-Fascism, and Fascism have become ubiquitous in every kind of television program, from game shows to soap operas to host shows. No longer clustered around historic dates or wrapped in the docudramatic forms that had contained them in previous decades, memory *schegge* ("splinters," a term derived from the title of the most innovative television program of the 1990s) began to be distributed throughout the palimpsest of both private and state-controlled broadcasting stations. Several RAI programs, too, began to self-reflexively focus on how Italians remembered the war years during the five postwar decades, in particular the way in which and the extent to which television itself has shaped the "national memory" of Nazi-fascism.[57] Furthermore, while continuing the personalization and spectacularization of history typical of the 1980s, several productions of the early 1990s have also been more bluntly revisionist.

Between 1990 and 1994, De Felice himself was a primary consultant in at least five RAI productions, and several additional ones were inspired by his anti-antifascist historiography.[58] Among these, the documentary *Combat Film*, broadcast in April 1994, marked a turning point in the representation of the war years. On the surface, the film presented footage, taken by the advancing U.S. Army, that showed not only scenes of partisan resistance but also of life under American and the Nazi-fascist occupation. Yet, the very "foreign" nature of the footage, its "selective" montage, and, above all, the "neutralistic," on-the-air comments of the host and invited guests contributed to the widespread perception that a key representational taboo had been broken. Never before had the dead of the resistance and of the fascist Republic of Salò been officially commemorated as equals—and this under the sign of the come eravamo. Even more significant, never before had such a program been shown on an occasion as solemn as the forty-ninth anniversary of the "liberation." In fact, if one considers the disproportionate public debate that followed this broadcast in the light of the actual celebrations of 25 April 1994, one finds clues to a new phase of memory that differed from all preceding phases.[59]

In March 1994, for the first time in thirty-four years, a center-right coalition was elected to power. Led by the Italian media mogul Silvio Berlusconi, this coalition included the separatist Northern League and the self-proclaimed "postfascist" party, Alleanza Nazionale, a formation ostensibly born of the dissolution of the neofascist MSI and the explicit renunciation of its historical affiliation to the RSI. Within a month, the celebration of 25 April brought 300,000 people into the squares of Milan to protest the new "fascist" government. For the first time since the mid-1960s the commemoration of the liberation had reverted to being a largely spontaneous event with the participation of thousands of young people. Some veteran-partisans declared it the most beautiful celebration since 1946, because, for the first time, young people participated in greater numbers than aging partisans. Yet, among the participants in Milan was also Umberto Bossi, leader of the Northern League, who, despite the threats and insults he received during the celebration, insisted on his right to participate. And in Rome, Gianfranco Fini, leader of Alleanza Nazionale, celebrated the historic date with a "postfascist" mass of conciliation for antifascists and ex-fascists. Berlusconi prudently kept away from both scenes, following the celebrations through the images diffused by his private networks.[60]

What does this paradoxical celebration suggest about the most recent trends in the Italian memorialization-historicization of the war and Nazi Fascism? The participation of many young people confirms that, notwithstanding the virtual absence of Fascism and the war in school curricula—an absence remedied by law only in 1997—the memory of the resistance as the founding event of the republic has been successfully transmitted to the younger generations. According to a recent study, all of the strategies of memorialization-historicization discussed above have circulated on both a national and an intergenerational scale. At the same time, the younger generations seem to be the least affected by the latest shifts in the Italian historical imaginary: 70 percent of them explicitly reject the image of the resistance *as* civil war.[61] For the older generations, the process of transfiguring the resistance from Second Risorgimento to missed revolution to civil war seems to have gradually defused the composite date-event "Resistance-Liberation-25 April" of much of its historic charge.

No longer subject either to symbolic repression or monopolization, the "normalized" resistance must be celebrated as a national patrimony of memory even by its political adversaries on the right (Fini and Bossi) or be observed (watched on TV) as a national spectacle (Berlusconi). On the other side of the political spectrum, the repeated displays of indignation—such as those following *Combat Film*—reveal the lucid awareness of the new post-Communist left that the transfigurations of the Italian historical imaginary in the postwar period have come full cycle to undermine their historic fulcrum. That is to say, the image of the resistance qua civil war has not merely superceded those of the resistance qua missed revolution and resistance qua Second Risorgimento but eroded the symbolic centrality of April 25 as the historic event around which all processes of memorialization-historicization rotated from 1945 onward. During the last decade the original connection between the historic date April 25 and the Second Risorgimento has begun to be replaced by the association of September 8th with the so-called Second Republic—the new political system that emerged from the crises of 1990–91.

In 1996 the influential political scientist Ernesto Galli della Loggia published a small book in which he accused the antifascist memorialization of the resistance of having covered up the fundamental trauma of September 8th with the glorification of 25 April. Galli della Loggia posited instead that the majority of Italians experienced the shock of seeing their king and government flee Rome, of being left without military-political direction, of having their country invaded by two foreign armies and then ravaged by civil war as a proper morte della patria (death of the fatherland). The 8 September date, therefore, caused a break in the feeling of national identity for most Italians, which was only deepened by the memorialization-historicization of the resistance in the postwar period. Accordingly, for Galli della Loggia, the extreme ideologization of political struggle during the first "Republic of the parties" was not only founded on the Marxist-inspired monumentalization of 25 April-resistance but also, and above all, on a more collective denial of the "death of the fatherland."[62]

Following on the interrelated images of the Second Risorgimento, the missed revolution, and the civil war, the image of the death of the fatherland is the first to replace the historic event of the resistance with that of the dishonoring armistice. Endorsed by De Felice and his revisionist school—as well as the new center-right coalition—it has captured the attention of public intellectuals, media, and politicians alike, rapidly and deeply modifying the historical imaginary of the Second Republic. Yet, this image is neither the symptom of the repressed memory of the nonpartisan majority resurfacing after more than five decades of suppression nor the mere result of the delegitimization of anti-Fascism pursued by right-wing forces and the mass media since the early 1980s.[63] As with each of the preceding three images-phases, that of the death of the fatherland authorizes certain public discourses about the past and delegitimizes others; it centers political debate around certain dichotomies rather than others.

For example, the memory of the "civilian" victims of both Nazi Fascism and the resistance has left the realm of the private, the local, and the counter-memorial to enter that of the official, the national, and the historically significant. In the 1990s a series of well-publicized trials brought the most well-known sites of Nazi massacres—Marzabotto and the Fosse Ardeatine—into the public eye. Quite aside from their resolutions, these trials highlighted unsuspected lacunae in both antifascist historiography and the historical imaginary of Italians generally. On the one hand, there still exist no "scientific reconstructions" of either massacre; on the other, as several commentators have remarked, the officialized and ritualized memories of both massacres kept other equally traumatic but more politically complex massacres confined to local memory for decades.[64] The recent rise to national prominence of local massacres—such as those of Civitella Val di Chiana, Padule di Fucecchio, and Sant'Anna di Stazzema—helped definitively lift the memory divide from its ideological polarization of left (Communist) versus right (Catholic) and insert it into a national-identity spectrum.[65]

Most representative of this new trend is the case of the *foibe*. Until the late 1980s the term *foibe* was probably unknown to most Italians or else understood simply in its geographical sense, as referring to the deep cracks in the mountainous terrain that extends between the northern region of Friuli Venezia Giulia and the former Yugoslavian territory of Istria (now in Slovenia). Today, most Italians would understand *foibe* to refer to accusations, levied by the local Italian population, that Communist partisans allied themselves with their Slav counterparts in an "ethnic cleansing" operation during which an undetermined number of nonfascist (and non-Communist) Italians were killed and dropped into the foibe. The national notoriety assumed by the foibe in recent years is part of the return of the right to legitimacy and power in Italy. In 1993 President Oscar Luigi Scalfaro raised a memorial to the victims of the foibe, which had been privately erected by a local right-wing association in the village of Basovizza, near Trieste, in 1954, to the status of national monument, and in 1995, Alleanza Nazionale requested that the foibe "be treated as a special theme in Italian classrooms."[66] Yet, public polemics about the foibe, from both left and right, have also revealed how evocations of the Slav "other" served as a primary backdrop not only in fascist and neofascist definitions of Italianness but in all postwar (re-)negotiations of Italian national identity. The fascist theme of the Slav threat is equally traceable in the 1965 decision by the center-left government to make the Risiera di San Sabba's concentration camp a national monument, as well as in the more recent one to give the Basovizza foibe the same honor. In the first case, the monumentalization of a "Nazi" camp covered up the extensive collaboration of the local Italian population in the ethnic persecution of Jews and Slavs in the area; in the second, the "post-fascist call to reconciliation" found its most effective expression in "remembering a shared Slav enemy."[67]

The image of the death of the fatherland and its direct connection to the issue of "national identity" has underlined all processes of memorialization and institutionalization in the last decade. That the public polemics on the foibe have taken place within the context of a resurgence of (Yugo)slavo-phobia in the West also marks the importance of these new processes to the wider (re-)negotiations between national and supranational forms of identity. The correct ways to conjugate the rebirth of a "national" identity with the necessities of forming and sustaining a feeling of Europeanness among Italians assumed center stage in the political debate of the 1990s—so much so that even the principal heirs of the Italian Communist Party, the Democratici di Sinistra, endorsed right-wing calls to national reconciliation between ex-partisans and ex-fascists. Nobody, however, seemed to have noticed the irony in the fact that the image of the "death of the fatherland," currently attached to the supposed crisis of postwar Italian national identity, was first formulated in 1979 by the psychoanalyst and ethnographer Elivio Fachinelli to refer to the formation of the "fascist mentality" itself in the immediate aftermath of World War I.[68]

According to Fachinelli's thesis, the ideological compound of Fascism had coalesced in response to a combined traumatic event: the contemporaneous Soviet revolution and the defeat of the Italian army at Caporetto in October 1917, which threatened the value-figure of the "nation-fatherland" for which so many Italians had fought, suffered, and sacrificed their lives.[69] To this double threat, Fascism had responded by elevating the value-figure of "the state" to a level of symbolic importance entirely unknown until then. The fascist sacralization of the state rested therefore on the perceived death of the fatherland in October 1917.[70] Analogously, the image of the death of the fatherland resurged before the double demise of the institutionalized October Revolution (USSR) and the First Italian Republic. By contrast, the contemporary image of the death of the fatherland refers to a distant event in time (8 September 1943) and is being agitated in order to build an ambivalent politics of patriotism and de-statalization. The uncanny analogy between the postfascist image of the death of the fatherland and the founding image of the fascist historic imaginary does not suggest any underlining similarity between the two historical moments or actors, but reveals instead a unique and remarkable continuity in the Italian *Vergangenheitsbewälti-gung* (coming to terms with the past).

Unlike in Germany, the Italian "coming to terms" seems not to have been with the past in particular, but primarily with the rhetorical tropes inherited from fascist historical culture. With the image of the death of the fatherland, Italians may have finally worked through this process to reach the point of origin of their historical imaginaries. In a not-so-distant future a more "critical" (in Nietzsche's sense of generationally antagonistic) politics of memory may at last develop with Italians of younger generations and join or even replace the monumental (antifascist paradigm) and antiquarian (revisionist paradigm) approaches to the memorialization-historicization of the fascist past.[71] And there are signs that younger Italians are beginning to confront the legacies of fascist historical culture directly.

A first indication of this trend can be found in the self-conscious connection that young people establish between the "myth" of the resistance and the democratic, constitutional foundations of the Italian Republican State.[72] Equally significant is their explicit recognition that the national fascination with strong media personalities might have more to do with submerged and never fully acknowledged mussolinismo, rather than with any belated or neofascist attempt to rebuild their national identity.[73] As with Craxi's popularity in the 1980s, the popularity of Italy's farcical premier, Silvio Berlusconi—who shares with his tragic predecessor, Mussolini, a career in the media—cannot be separated from the fact that all of these figures give Italians style and offer them a feeling of distinction. On the other hand, the enthusiasm of younger Italians for Roberto Benigni's *Life Is Beautiful* may have had much more to do with its presentation of an antifascist paradigm of masculinity than with a specific need to exonerate themselves from any responsibility in the Final Solution. Benigni's character, Guido, is not only Jewish but also represents the caring father, that is, the antithesis of the composite fascist ideal of phallic but mother-dominated manhood.[74] Despite its questionable paradigm of victimhood, *Life Is Beautiful* seems to have contributed to pulling down—rather than reinforcing—the wall of oblivion that for decades surrounded the memory and history of Italian-fascist anti-Semitism and its relationship to the Shoah.[75]

The politics of memory related to the fate of Italian and foreign Jews under Fascism do not follow the periodization described above but are nonetheless key to understanding the establishment, longevity, and recent demise of the "resistential" paradigm of memory in postwar Italy. Several historically undisputed facts and events bear on the memorialization of this aspect of the Nazi-fascist past in Italy. In November 1938 Mussolini's regime issued a series of laws for the defense of the Italian race, commonly known as anti-Semitic laws. These led to a racial (not religious) definition of belonging to the Jewish race, the prohibition of marriages between Jews and Italians, and the progressive disenfranchisement and persecution of foreign and Italian Jews via expulsion from schools and civil-service sectors between late 1938 and September 1943. The anti-Semitic laws affected 58,412 Jews, 11,756 of whom were converts to Catholicism but still Jewish according to fascist law and four-fifths of whom were Italian citizens. However, as citizens of a Nazi ally, Italian Jews and foreign Jews dwelling in lands under Italian-fascist occupation were not subject to deportation to extermination camps until quite late, that is, until Italy signed the armistice with the Allies on 8 September 1943. At that time, 40,157 Jews still remained under Nazi-fascist control on the Italian territory and in lands of Italian occupation. Their systematic deportation to Auschwitz began on 16 September 1943 and lasted until 24 February 1945 and affected only 8,566 of them. Of these 83 percent survived.[76]

These numbers are sufficiently eloquent to explain the great success of the myth of the *bravo italiano*. The myth attributed to Italians an innate humanism that had supposedly prevented them from actively participating in the Final Solution and it gained extraordinary credibility through the fact that most Jews under Italian jurisdiction survived the Holocaust.[77] Add to these favorable numbers the countless stories and rumors of meritorious behavior by non-Jewish Italians, Catholic priests, and even fascist officials who protected Jews from deportation, and one can easily understand why some Italian-Jewish survivors were among the first and loudest supporters of the myth.[78] A primary characteristic of the establishment of Italian-Jewish politics of memory may thus have been the active forgetting of the anti-Semitic measures passed by the fascist regime in 1938 in favor of the affirmation of a "parenthetical" vision of anti-Semitism as epiphenomenal to Italian Fascism and extraneous to the humanist body of the Italian people.[79]

Several scholars have tied the codification of this exculpatory paradigm and the lack of coming to terms with the deep cultural roots of Italian-fascist anti-Semitism to the strategic efforts made by Italian-Jewish community leaders to establish the best possible relations with the new Italian State and the Vatican.[80] Particularly telling in this respect is the uncanny gratitude expressed by prominent Jewish and Israeli leaders to Pope Pius XII in the aftermath of the war. That numerous Catholic priests and even bishops had done much to protect Jews from harm was visible to the whole world, but so was the official silence of the Vatican before the passage of the anti-Semitic laws in 1938, as well as the deportation of Jews in 1943–1945.[81] Yet, political expediency alone—on the part of Jewish leaders just as much as the Vatican —cannot explain the longevity of the silence and the depth of institutional repression of memory with regard to the connection between the fascist persecution of Jews (1938–1943) and their deportation and extermination in 1943–1945.

The protracted silence of Jewish-Italian survivors about their camp experiences played an important role, but it was neither as absolute as commonly assumed nor did it last in Italy much longer than in other countries. From the immediate aftermath of the war to the late 1950s, fourteen memoirs of survivors and persecuted Jews were published (mostly by small publishers). In 1958 one of Italy's premier publishers, Einaudi, published Primo Levi's *Se questo è un uomo* (If this is a man).[82] Levi's first memoir, along with his other books, opened the doors of major publishers to many others. The number of memoirs published in the 1960s more than doubled that of the previous decade, and with each decade the number grew: thirty-three in the 1970s, forty-six in the 1980s, twenty-two in the first half of the 1990s.[83] Yet, despite this numerical and qualitative increase, and the international recognition bestowed on Primo Levi as one of the most morally sophisticated voices of Jewish memory, most Italian institutions and much of society have responded to the memory of Italian anti-Semitism with consistent indifference for over four decades. Jews, for example, were never even included in the category of those "politically persecuted" by Fascism, and not until 1987 were the last remnants of anti-Semitic legislation definitively abrogated by the Italian Republic. And when this was done, rather than apologize for the absurd delay, the prime minister and historian Giovanni Spadolini used the occasion to declare that "Italy had now paid its debt to the Jews in full."[84] Adding insult to injury, some prominent Italian intellectuals went so far as to invoke the "unspeakability" of the experience of the camps to justify the supposed silence of Italian Jews on their sufferings.[85]

As Anna Bravo suggests, the bravo italiano paradigm seems to have embraced and sustained the pretense of innocence for the time before the persecution and the deportation of Italian Jews, just as much as the pretense of innocence for the decades of institutional silence of memory about the legacy of Italian anti-Semitism. But what sustained the longevity of the bravo italiano icon itself was more than the political expediency of metonymic substitution: the meritorious behavior of few between 1943 and 1945 for the indifference of all from 1938. However unintentional, the key factor in maintaining the institutional silence of memory on Italian-fascist racism and anti-Semitism was the centrality assumed by the resistance in Italian politics of memory as a whole. The memorialization of the biennio successfully suppressed the memory of the ventennio for over four decades. In this respect the bravo italiano myth functioned as positive corollary to this repression, and their symbiotic relationship was further reinforced by the founding image of the Second Risorgimento.

This image was predicated on the projection of Fascism as anti-Risorgimento, that is, as a betrayal of the "liberal tradition" that had led to the formation of the nation and the emancipations of Jews. Anti-Semitism, therefore, could be seen as the proof that Fascism was anti-Italian, precisely as Croce had suggested.[86] Conversely, the successive transfigurations of the Risorgimental trope concerned only the memory of the resistance and therefore did not disturb institutional silence on Italian racism and anti-Semitism. The centrality of the resistance in Italian politics of memory in fact contributed to the repression of the memory of the deportations of Jews by also suppressing that of Italian deportees. On the one hand, a paradigm of common victimhood uniting Italian soldiers and Jews deported to the camps after 8 September 1943 helped dilute the memory of the specificity of the crimes perpetrated against the "most ancient of Italian minorities" in the aftermath of the war.[87] On the other, the equation of anti-Fascism and the resistance condemned both internati (Italian POWs in Nazi camps) and deportati (deported Jews) to a common fate of oblivion.[88]

It is not by chance, therefore, that the reevaluation of the suffering and existential resistance of the internati, which started in the mid-1980s, also opened the door for the memory of anti-Semitism to emerge in the public sphere. In no other field of memorialization-historicization has the generational divide between the "Mussolini youth" and the postwar generations been as clearly observable as in the abrupt passage from the direct oblivion, exculpatory explanations, and mellowing memories cultivated by the parents and grandparents for over four decades to the thematization of Italian-fascist anti-Semitism and the wholesale denunciation of all the politics of memory that had allowed this oblivion, operated by the sons and daughters over the last two decades.[89] Along these lines, Life Is Beautiful brought the plight of Italian Jews to the big screen for the first time at the same moment as the first wave of studies on the relationship between the "persecution of the rights" (1938–1943) and the "persecution of the lives" of Italian Jews (1943–1945) began to appear in Italy.[90] For the first time, therefore, Italians were being exposed to images, studies, and, more recently, solemn commemorations linking the "anti-Semitic laws" of 1938 and the substantial apathy with which they were accepted by the majority of Italians to the deportation of thousands of Italian Jews to extermination camps.

On 27 January 2002, the first Day of Memory was celebrated throughout Europe to commemorate the fiftieth anniversary of the liberation of Auschwitz. In Italy, notwithstanding the center-right coalition in power, the ceremonies were as solemn as anywhere in Europe, and the participation of young people surpassed all expectations.[91] By the same token, the election of a German cardinal, Joseph Ratzinger, to become Pope Benedict XVI in April 2005 raised surprisingly little clamor on the left side of the Italian political spectrum, despite the well-known fact that Ratzinger had belonged to the Hitler Youth during the war. Although the pope was immediately nick-named "the German Shepherd" by the Italian press, political figures on the left have clamored against any off-color exploitation of this image that might characterize the new pope as a Nazi sympathizer. The pope's public condemn-nation of the Nazi crimes against humanity a month after his election was given equal space by both the right- and left-wing press. It could be said, albeit tentatively, that Italian politics of memory are slowly becoming more "European" and less politically polarized. It might then be that, via the image of the death of the (fascist) fatherland, the youngest generations of Italians will be the first to identify Fascism as a phenomenon of Euro-pean dimensions grounded in the rejection and suppression of the internal (political-racial) other. And, along these lines, it might be possible that the last and most resilient taboo concerning the racist war crimes perpetrated by the Italian-fascist military apparatus in Ethiopia and the Balkans will soon be lifted.[92] The day might therefore not be too far off in which the historic date of 25 July 1943, when most Italians spontaneously expressed their libera-tion from Fascism by destroying images of Mussolini, will replace both 8 September and 25 April, and be commemorated as the founding date of a truly postfascist and equally post-Mussolinian identity.

## Notes

1   On the popular memory of Fascism in Italy, see Passerini, *Fascism in Popular Memory*.

2   Bidussa, *Il mito del bravo italiano*.

3   The awkward terms *nazifascismo* and *nazifascisti* were coined during the war to refer to the supporters of the Italian Social Republic (RSI), the puppet state set up by Mussolini in Nazi-occupied central-northern Italy from September 1943 to April 1945. Those terms, however, have become metonymic for the whole fascist ventennio, thereby allowing the externalization of violence and criminal activity onto the Nazi, or the "Germans" as a whole. I use this term throughout the essay to amplify and problematize, rather than cover up or exploit, its exculpatory resonances.

4   Doumanis, "The Italian Empire and *brava gente*."

5   Passerini, *Fascism in Popular Memory*; Mezzana, *La memoria storica della Re-sistenza nelle nuove generazioni*. The definition of collective memory is taken from K. L. Klein, "On the Emergence of *Memory* in Historical Discourse," 135. The concept of collective memory was theorized in the 1930s by French sociologist Maurice

Halbwachs, whose writings are now collected in Halbwachs, *On Collective Memory*, but its fortunes have all to do with its reconceptualization in Pierre Nora's monumental oeuvre on French sites of memory (see Nora, *The State*; Nora, "Between Memory and History").

6   In contrast to the polarization between memory and history characteristics of the notion and discourse on collective memory, I take as my point of departure Friedrich Nietzsche's discussion of history as the prevalent form that memory takes in Western cultures (see Nietzsche, "On the Advantages and Disadvantages of History for Life"). For a critique of the notion of collective memory, see Klein, "On the Emergence of *Memory* in Historical Discourse." To compare the approach pursued in this essay to a more orthodox collective-memory approach to the study of Italian *lieux de mémoire* (sites of memory), see Isnenghi, "Memoria pubblica della Resistenza"; Isnenghi, *I luoghi della memoria*. Although my essay is written from a different methodological perspective, the monumental work of Isnenghi and his collaborators, *I luoghi della memoria*, has been invaluable to my synthesis, particularly the following essays: del Boca, "L'impero"; di Cori, "Le leggi razziali"; Dondi, "Piazzale Loreto"; Baioni, "Predappio"; Ranzato, "La guerra di Spagna"; Rochat, "La guerra di Grecia"; Bellone, "La Resistenza"; Isnenghi, "Conclusione"; Franzielli, "25 luglio"; Franzielli, "L'8 settembre"; Tranfaglia, "La repubblica"; de Luna, "I fatti di luglio 1960"; Luisa Passerini, "Il '68."

7   Contini, *La memoria divisa*.

8   Absalom, "Peasant Memory and the Italian Resistance, 1943–1945."

9   On the political uses of the past in postwar Italy, see Zunino, *La Repubblica e il suo passato*.

10   Paggi, "La repubblica senza Pantheon."

11   Benedetto Croce, "Chi è fascista?" *Il Giornale di Napoli*, 29 October 1944, p. 3.

12   Although in 1960 the center-left government passed a law that prescribed teaching history up to World War II and including lessons about Fascism in high schools, the law was never applied. Hence, in 1997 a new law was drafted to require that teachings about the twentieth-century take priority over all other topics in the last year of high-school education (see Mezzana, *La memoria storica della Resistenza nelle nuove generazioni*, 23–24.

13   Dondi, "The Fascist Mentality after Fascism."

14   On the active process of forgetting, see Renate Siebert's insightful comments in "Don't Forget."

15   I discuss the history and theory of fascist historic imaginary in my *The Historic Imaginary* and, more synthetically, in my "'To Make History.'"

16   This image of Fascism as "permanent resurgence" was elaborated by the regime's prime philosopher, Giovanni Gentile. See Dainotto, "'Tramonto' and 'Risorgimento.'"

17   Although the term *postfascist* has become quite fashionable to describe a host of revisionist phenomena and to characterize the demise of the "antifascist" paradigm of Italian politics of memory in the last decade, I use the term here in direct

analogy with the Lyotardian conception of the circular relationship between *modern* and *postmodern*. According to Lyotard, "The postmodern is always part of the modern," so that, conversely, "postmodernism is not modernism at its end but in the nascent state, and this state is constant" (*The Postmodern Condition*, 44). From this perspective I contend that many forms of thought and politics that have been traditionally associated with anti-Fascism, may be more fruitfully understood as post-fascist precisely because they find their origins in the semiotic overproduction typical of fascist political culture. For an analysis of continuities between prominent anti-fascist cultural phenomena, such as cinematic neorealism, and fascist literary culture, see Ben-Ghiat, *Fascist Modernities*.

18  Cenci, "Rituale e memoria," 335. For a more general perspective on national commemorations, see Ridolfi, *Le feste nazionali*.

19  Pavone, "Le idee della Resistenza."

20  On the monumentalization of the resistance, see Dogliani, "Constructing Memory and Anti-Memory." On early cinematic representations of Fascism and the resistance, see Ben-Ghiat, "Liberation."

21  Domenico, *Italian Fascists on Trial, 1943–1948*.

22  Dondi, "The Fascist Mentality after Fascism."

23  Crainz, "The Representation of Fascism and the Resistance in the Documentaries of Italian State Television"; Bosworth, "Film Memories of Fascism."

24  The two journalists were not required to serve their sentence, but they were not allowed to make their film either (Bosworth, "Film Memories of Fascism," 109).

25  Cenci, "Rituale e memoria," 361.

26  Dogliani, "Constructing Memory and Anti-Memory," 24–27.

27  Sluga, "Italian National Memory, National Identity, and Fascism," 182–83.

28  Bosworth, "Film Memories of Fascism," 111–17; Forgacs, "Days of Sodom." For an insightful discussion of the contribution made by 1970s Italian filmmakers to complicating memorialization-historicization processes, see Ravetto, *The Unmaking of Fascist Aesthetics*.

29  Although there are no measures of audience share or satisfaction for this program, critics consider its impact comparable to that of the television series *Holocaust* in Germany (Farassino, "Mediologia della Resistenza, radio e televisione").

30  See De Felice, *Rosso e nero*. From the opposite perspective, see Tranfaglia, *Un passato scomodo*.

31  De Luna and Revelli, *Fascismo, antifascismo*.

32  Ibid., 141–48.

33  Gramsci, *Prison Notebooks*, 107.

34  De Luna and Revelli, *Fascismo, antifascismo*, 84.

35  Ibid., 148–55.

36  Paggi, "Storia di una memoria anti-partigiana."

37  Gallerano, "I programmi," 67–69.

38  Winterhalter, "L'immagine della Resistenza nella radio e nella televisione."

39  Klinkhammer, "La politica di repressione della Wehrmacht in Italia."

40  Gallerano, "I programmi," 77.

41  Pavone, *Una guerra civile*; Pavone, "La resistenza in Italia."

42  Crainz, "The Representation of Fascism and the Resistance in the Documentaries of Italian State Television," 133.

43  See De Felice, *Interpretations of Fascism*.

44  Dogliani, "The Debate on the Historiography of Fascism"; Bosworth and Dogliani, *Italian Fascism*.

45  On the role of historians in Italian politics of memory, see Di Rienzo, *Un dopoguerra storiografico*.

46  See Wulf Kansteiner's essay in this volume.

47  Farassino, "Mediologia della Resistenza, radio e televisione," 107–14.

48  Gallerano, "I programmi," 78–79.

49  Tranfaglia, "Fascismo e mass media."

50  Gentile, *The Sacralization of Politics in Fascist Italy*.

51  Passerini, *Mussolini immaginario*.

52  On the history of Mussolini's body, see Luzzatto, *Il corpo del duce*; Dondi, "Piazzale Loreto"; Baioni, "Predappio."

53  Passerini, *Fascism in Popular Memory*.

54  Mario Isnenghi, "Conclusione," in *I luoghi della memoria*, 430.

55  On the crisis of anti-Fascism, see Luzzatto, *La crisi dell'antifascsmo*; Santomassimo, *Antifascismo e dintorni*.

56  Pavone, "L'eredità della guerra civile e il nuovo quadro istituzionale," 15.

57  Farassino, "Mediologia della Resistenza, radio e televisione," 114–24.

58  Gallerano, "I programmi," 81.

59  All commentators agree that the debate that *Combat Film* spurred in newspapers and magazines for months after its broadcast, was excessively long and disproportionately polemical compared to both the audience-share of the program and its not-so-incendiary content. However, most commentaries simply explain this excess away by referring it to the political context I discuss below. The excessive discourse produced around *Combat Film* is symptomatic of a deeper restructuring of the historical imaginary of Italians in the last decade (see Crainz, "The Representation of Fascism and the Resistance in the Documentaries of Italian State Television," 136–37).

60  Cenci, "Rituale e memoria," 375–78.

61  Mezzana, *La memoria storica della Resistenza nelle nuove generazioni*, 77–88.

62  Galli della Loggia, *La morte della patria*.

63  Compare to Bosworth, "The Italian 'Second Republic' and the History of Fascism."

64  Klinkhammer, "La politica di repressione della Wehrmacht in Italia," 85.

65  Pezzino, "Guerra ai civili. Le stragi tra storia e memoria"; Franzinelli, *Le stragi nascoste*.

66  Sluga, "Italian National Memory, National Identity, and Fascism," 185.

67  Ibid., 186.

68  Facchinelli, "Il fenomeno fascista."

69  Fogu, *The Historic Imaginary*, 62–64.

70  According to Fachinelli and several studies of the Italian response to the Great War trauma, the military-moral disarray of both war- and home-front in the aftermath of the defeat of Caporetto was symptomatic of a very ambiguous mixture of desire and fear for the death of the value-figure (the fatherland) they had fought for.

71  I am referring the critical, monumental, and antiquarian historical senses described by Nietzsche in "On the Advantages and Disadvantages of History for Life."

72  Mezzana, *La memoria storica*, 112–34.

73  Ibid., 143.

74  I develop this argument in "Fascismo-Stile."

75  Ruth Ben Ghiat, "The Secret Histories of Roberto Benigni's *Life Is Beautiful*."

76  On the persecution and deportation of Jews under Fascism, see the pioneering 1961 study of Renzo De Felice, now available in English under the title *The Jews in Fascist Italy*. The definitive study of the Italian-Jewish Shoah is Forgion, *Il libro della memoria*.

77  Beside Bidussa's *Il mito del bravo Italiano*, see, in English, Poliakov and Sabille, *The Jews under the Italian Occupation*; Steinberg, *All or Nothing*; Carpi, *Between Mussolini and Hitler*; Caracciolo, *Uncertain Refuge*.

78  A full historical account of these stories is in Zuccotti, *The Italians and the Holocaust*. For a more anecdotal but more complex view, see Stille, *Benevolence and Betrayal*.

79  Bravo, "Gli scritti di memoria della deportazione dall'Italia (1944–1993)."

80  Schwarz, "Gli ebrei italiani e la memoria della persecuzione fascista (1945–1955)."

81  Zuccotti, *Under His Very Windows*.

82  Bravo, "Gli scritti di memoria della deportazione dall'Italia (1944–1993)," 67.

83  Ibid., 69.

84  Ben-Ghiat, "The Secret Histories of Roberto Benigni's *Life Is Beautiful*," 269.

85  Bravo, "Gli scritti di memoria della deportazione dall'Italia (1944–1993)," 73.

86  Schwarz, "Gli ebrei italiani e la memoria della persecuzione fascista (1945–1955)," 111.

87  Pugliese, *The Most Ancient of Minorities*.

88  di Cori, "Le leggi raziali," 464.

89  Ibid., 464–65. In homage to the popular label "Hitler-Youth generation," I use "Mussolini generation" to refer to those who were old enough to have memories of the ventennio and/or the war years. To the postwar generations belong those born after the war or too young to have any firsthand memory of Fascism or the war.

90  See the studies cited in notes 76 to 88 and Baldissara and Pezzino, *Crimini e memorie di Guerra*.

91  See http://www.repubblica.it.

92  So predicts James Walston in "History and Memory of the Italian Concentration Camps."

ANNAMARIA ORLA-BUKOWSKA ✳

# New Threads on an Old Loom

## NATIONAL MEMORY AND SOCIAL IDENTITY IN POSTWAR
## AND POST-COMMUNIST POLAND

There is a difference between history and memory,
especially group memory: between what happened and the way we
frame our perceptions of what happened and turn it into a
story that explains us to ourselves.
Jonathan Sacks, *Studies in Renewal*

Over a half-century later and seeping into the next millennium, it is still World War II which weighs heaviest on and delineates Polish national memory.[1] Cities in whose postwar reconstruction the entire nation's population personally participated, physically and financially, broadcast their war experience. In central Warsaw hardly a step can be taken without encountering histories of original edifices on their contemporary replicas, or roll calls of tortured and executed innocents outside prisons, or poignant pre- and postwar photographs in church vestibules. At any given time, candles and flowers rest beside plaques, memorials, and tombstones; almost every day is an anniversary, and the capital continues, in a sense, to mourn its war dead.[2]

In Poland, *lieux de mémoire* abound not only in the metropolis but also in the smallest hamlet through which one could pass. Crosses, steles, plaques, and monuments dot the physical and spiritual landscape of the country. They designate which war experiences should be remembered and how, and shape the historical awareness of the nation's most horrific tragedy. Poland is a country which has had to regularly update editions of an encyclopedic guide to include the increasing number of World War II memorial sites—all denoting death at the hands of Germans.[3]

For decades, the German occupation was the exclusive focal point of official national memory. The Soviet occupation could not be, since Poland was made part of the Communist bloc. Moreover, when the Allies agreed with Stalin to push Poland's borders westward, they inadvertently guaranteed that the vast majority of sites associated with terror under the USSR would forever lie outside Polish territory while concurrently placing more German sites inside it.[4]

The trauma of World War II and its immediate consequences necessitated not only the incorporation of the war into Polish memory but also a reorientation of Polish identity. Yet, although the political system had turned the country 180 degrees—to face East, not West—the Poles, for the most part, did not follow. A bifurcation of discourse occurred, segregating (though in some areas they would overlap) the official and public from the unofficial and private spheres.[5] Nonetheless, both spheres needed to react—via amnesia or total recall or something in between—to the Polish-German, Polish-Russian, and Polish-Jewish aspects of the war.[6] The way these components figured in the national memory shaped postwar social identity, then directed its adaptations after June 1989. Much later, however, the image in which the Poles had invested and rooted their sense of self would turn out not to reflect the image the outside world held, a confrontation that aroused—and still is arousing—both intellectual and popular debates about history and identity in Poland.

Old Threads on an Old Loom

Even the most radical new political system cannot completely sever but must tie into the threads, colors, and patterns of the tapestry delineating the national persona. From a broad palette of equivocal elements, individuals and groups continually choose the new fibers which best fit the warp threads of the past while working most effectively in the present, with its amended group definitions. Conversely, "It is precisely group identity which makes the past something real and capable of living in the present . . . someone's vision of history, filtered through collective memory and rooted in it, useful for the concept of group identity of those existing in a given time."[7] "There is no single memory. Each memory remembers something else and remembers differently."[8] An event will live on only because of and only in the way that it serves the group. Some victories and defeats, dates and persons will be selected for remembrance, others for forgetting.

Yet, the defining trauma, which has marked Polish collective memory in modernity and postmodernity, came nearly a century and a half prior to World War II. Just four years after passing Europe's first constitution (3 May

1791), the vast kingdom of Poland was partitioned and devoured whole in 1795 by the Prussian, Russian, and Austro-Hungarian Empires.[9] Poland's sovereignty, its Golden Age, and its democracy came to a definitive close: Poles were plunged into feudal rule under three different autocrats for over six generations.[10] Thus, Polish identity in the nineteenth century developed along ethnocultural and bloodlines instead of along civic and territorial lines. Instead of separation of church and state, religion was the sole consistent carrier of the national ethos for the divided people, who thereafter fought with the church against the state.[11] Finally, instead of a modern, liberal Christianity, believers reverted to magical and mystical beliefs associated with sacrifice. Poles came to view their past, present, and future as conscious martyrdom not only for the cause of Polska but—crucially significant for Polish identity—of Europa. Fighting "for our freedom and yours," in places near and far, the Polish people were destined to quixotically rebel and resurrect—for longer or briefer periods of modernity—phoenix-like from the ashes.[12] Polish history came to be understood as a series of sacrificial uprisings and battles against any power that would conquer her people or conquer Europe.

The general framework for war memory comprised two roles (in most countries, with obvious exceptions and necessary variations): as victim and, foremost, as resistance hero. Poland did not vary from this schema of self-representation as the country followed the old patterns on the loom. The underlying, incontestable assumptions were that (1) Poles were the war's first official victims; (2) laid on the altar to be slaughtered, they fought against two totalitarianisms; (3) they were the purest and noblest of heroes, the only nation on the continent which neither collaborated with (via open alliance, facilitated annexation, or unengaged neutrality) nor formally surrendered to the Third Reich; and (4) though sacrificed to Soviet totalitarianism, Poland had saved Europe from German Fascism and contributed to peace on the continent.[13]

After World War II, what Polish political and social leaders, historians, teachers, and the society as a whole would pull from the materials of this latest tribulation had to be strands and beads which could be sewn into the construct painstakingly fashioned over the course of centuries. On the one hand, the archetypal images providing the warp threads of continuity were the national memory of Poland in her Golden Age, from the sixteenth to the eighteenth centuries, as a noble Camelot—increasingly democratic and parliamentary, and tolerant toward its numerous and multifarious minorities— and of Poland in her demise as the "Christ of Nations"—forever a martyr (though, unlike the Redeemer, not pacifistic). On the other, the new skeins woven in would be Poland's latest sacrifice in order to save Europe from being devoured, the German-USSR partition of 1939, the highest per-capita economic damages and death rates (in particular, the murder of half of its elites under the two occupations), the Soviet presence from September 1939 until even after June 1989, and the Holocaust perpetrated on its occupied territory.[14] The tension between these last two elements, however, has most recently stressed the loom and required reworking parts of the tapestry of Polish collective memory.

Weaving World War II and the Holocaust In and Out

In the twentieth century the ultimate failed litmus test for Western civilization was not only the fact of a second world war within a generation of the first but, above all, the Shoah. As a result, concurrent and often dichotomous factors have needed to be addressed: the tragedy of all citizens of a country and the tragedy of its Jewish citizens, the tragedy of each nation-state and the tragedy of the Jewish nation. Postwar collective memory has further had to address the role and actions of the nation vis-à-vis the designated enemy of Fascism and, subsequently, vis-à-vis the Holocaust itself—all in a manner befitting the existing collective identity.

In Poland the Jewish factor was uniquely weighted. Due to its long and relatively open, multicultural past, pre–World War II Poland encompassed the largest Jewish community in Europe.[15] It was also the first country to be fully occupied. Ultimately, it was also determined to be demographically, economically, and politically more feasible to transport the smaller numbers of Jewish citizens from other countries to labor, concentration, and death camps on occupied territory than to transfer Poland's 3.5 million elsewhere. Furthermore, since Poles never surrendered to or sided with Germany, any possible doors to negotiation for the lives of citizens, whatever their ethnicity, were effectively closed. Hence, in reconciling postwar memory and identity, Poland, like most nations, has not only had to confront the Shoah but also, unlike other countries, had to come to terms with the fact that its citizens witnessed more of the horror. Moreover, since 1945, Poles have been cemetery-keepers not only for their own Jews but also for Jews from nearly every other state in Europe.[16]

Nonetheless, for various psychological and political reasons, while World War II as a whole soon figured centrally in national historical memories, its most traumatic specific experiences—most notably the Shoah—did not.[17] Saul Friedländer commented:

> The fifteen or twenty years of "latency" that followed the war in regard to talking or writing about the Shoah, particularly in the United States, should not be equated with massive repression exclusively. . . . Against this background, the more sustained silence of the intellectuals, and particularly the historians, must be mentioned. The most renowned Jewish historians of the post-war period did not allude to the Shoah during the 1940s and 1950s, or for that matter at any time later on.[18]

In every nation certain aspects of the war trauma would be consigned to a form of oblivion. In the Communist bloc there were additional reasons for a void in certain areas. In Poland the onset of amnesia was not immediate, nor was it ever total. With the passage of time, at least four specifically Polish phases—governing especially the bifurcation of official and unofficial memory—can be roughly identified: 1945–1950, when emotional, living memory of direct and shared experiences dominated most discourse; 1950–1980, when official discourse dominated publicly, propagating half-truths and creating *biate plamy* (literally, "white stains," or "blank pages" of history), while unofficial discourse dominated privately, reverting progressively to an absolute faith in alternative, underground sources of information; 1980–1989, when the lining between public and private discourse became worn and permeable; and 1989 to the present, with varying private and group memories being incorporated into the public collective memory.[19]

## 1945–1950: Unspun Fibers

Apart from the private exchange of war experiences among the reunited, the initial half-decade in postwar Poland was replete with the public discourse of the press, poetry and prose (some penned during the conflagration itself), photojournalism, newsreels and feature films, testimony and other documentation, and war-crimes trials. All this persisted despite ongoing civil war, more overtly against the Ukrainian Uprising Army in the southeast, more covertly between the Polish government-in-exile in England and the Soviet-backed one being installed on the continent. This began even while the vast majority of the population was either moving from a newer home to a former one or vice versa—often, distressingly, uprooted from the distant eastern borderlands now made part of the USSR to the far corners of the western and northeastern territories assigned as compensation from Germany.[20]

In first order it was the government's war-crimes trials which carded the wool, thereby setting the foundations for official discourse. During the war itself, the Home Army and other underground military formations had in fact "tried" and carried out summary executions of persons collaborating with either of the two enemies; later, however, the focus was only on one of those enemies. To the victor belongs the judging, and Poland was not among the victorious, so it could not dictate what constituted a war crime against its citizens, neither before international tribunals, nor at home. Here Soviet ideology was decisive.

Extradition of Rudolf Höss and other German war criminals was granted in order to put them on trial *in situ*: Höss was hung on a scaffold beside the first crematorium and a stone's throw from his former offices at Auschwitz. Poles accused of German collaboration were rapidly tried and sentenced, including those who had taken part in massacres such as those at Jedwabne or Kielce, whether they had taken place in wartime or in the war's wake.[21] Still, the early criminal-justice process laid blame on the weakness of traitorous individuals—exceptions proving the rule—and did not affect the collective memory of heroic resistance.

Yet for Poles, betrayed at Yalta and slipping into the grasp of the USSR, the final blows dealt them by the Allies were the omissions and concealments of the Molotov-Ribbentrop Pact; the mass deportations, arrests, and imprisonments in Soviet jails and camps; and the par excellence Polish symbol of mass murder: the Katyń Forest massacre of some 5,000 Polish reserve officers which the Soviet Union actually tried to place on the Nuremberg list of German crimes.[22] As Nils Christie commented, "And then the gulags. Of course they could not be discussed in Nuremberg with a prominent Russian among the judges. But while they decided on death in Nuremberg, the gulags bulged."[23] Particularly for those millions of Poles who had actually suffered the Soviet occupation, the obvious exclusion of their story led to heightened remembrance in the private national memory.

The rapid establishment of a feigned rule of law, organized under the auspices and direction of the Soviet Union, was intended to confirm the new order's superiority. By twisted logic, the absolute condemnation, via fascist Germany, of the Western ideological system provided legal grounds for another crime: "treason" against the USSR during the war and against the new regime after the war. Postwar trials purged predominantly anti-Communist (fewer and fewer anti-Jewish or pro-German) Poles. Among others, distinguished officers of the highly respected Armia Krajowa (Home Army) were summarily executed after one-day mock trials. The torture, persecution, imprisonment, and executions of persons perceived by society as wartime heroes gave rise to and firmly rooted an unofficial discourse of continued occupation, or "Fourth Partition" as it came to be known in the unofficial vernacular. The postwar Soviet army bases located in Poland only served to reinforce this view.

Yet individual memories were uncombed and unrefined; official directives could not always fully rein in or tame them. Before the yarn was spun and discourse synthesized, the first five years brought fictional and cinematic pieces dealing with all manner of World War II experience. Though these were primarily by Polish non-Jewish authors and artists, not only the war in general but certain aspects of the Shoah also appeared therein. In literature the Nobel laureate Czesław Miłosz's now-famous *Biedny chrześcijanin patrzy na getto* (The poor Christian looks at the ghetto) and *Campo di Fiori* were among works actually written during the war. Zofia Nałkowska's *Medaliony* (Medallions) and Jerzy Andrzejewski's *Wielki Tydzień* (Holy week) were published in 1946, followed shortly thereafter by Tadeusz Borowski's *Tędy do gazu panie i panowie* (This way to the gas, ladies and gentleman), an autobiographical work based on the author's imprisonment in Auschwitz.[24]

Although the country was still very much in ruins in those first postwar years, it was important to begin weaving a broader collective memory from the raw devastation. Cinema could reach the masses more easily than literature, so filmmaking was reinitiated in astoundingly short order with the help of state resources. To this day, Ludwik Starski's 1946 *Zakazane piosenki* (Forbidden songs), the very first postwar production and a fitting illustration of the discourse of the first period, is often televised on 1 September, the anniversary of the war's outbreak.[25]

During *Zakazane piosenki*'s opening scene, which is set in a Warsaw apartment, various survivors (including a woman) begin recounting their wartime experiences to a Polish soldier who has returned from serving with the (unmentioned) Allied forces in the West. Along with the soldier, the viewer is introduced to a list of concentration and death camps as well as of underground army formations such as the officially "approved" Gwardia Ludowa (People's Guard) and the "unapproved" Armia Krajowa, mention of which was soon to be banned and service in which was likely to land a person in prison. While the film emphasizes that no Polish family was unscathed by the war, the crux of the film is a demonstration of how one and all had fulfilled their patriotic duty to resist: men, women, and children had, for example, publicly sung anti-German songs in blatant civil disobedience. Cruel Germans are shown shooting women and children in particular for this offense.

Though unmistakably propagandistic, this film, to its credit, depicts an elderly, cowardly soul (mocked by the young heroine), as well as outright collaborators (though they are inevitably and summarily executed at the hands of honorable Poles). Additionally, there is a Polish Jew in hiding, who inadvertently betrays himself when he cannot resist coming to the window while a courtyard chanteuse sings a melancholic Jewish melody.

Notably, except for a command in Russian toward the end, the Soviet Army is invisible; firsthand memories were no doubt too fresh and the regime too new to be able to inculcate a pro-USSR line. Nonetheless, shortly after its premiere in January 1947, the film was removed from cinemas with the precise intent of reworking the role of the Red Army in the fight against Fascism.[26] In both versions the overall cant underlines the enemy role of the ruthless and brutal Germans and bleaches that of the Russians, who are thus "whitewashed" of any wrongdoing.

Another key element in this first phase of memory-weaving was billing the victorious forces not as the "Allies" but as the "antifascist bloc" in accord with the internationalist message heralded by the Soviet Union. This ideology met no resistance from the ethnic Poles who felt they had shared the same fate as Polish Jews and all other citizens under the occupation. Ethnicity was thus mentioned only to exemplify crosscultural camaraderie, alliance, and solidarity in the resistance. In the first Polish film about Auschwitz, *Ostatni etap* (The final stage [1948]), the director Wanda Jakubowska, on whose personal experience the work is based, portrayed her German Communist, Russian POW, and Polish Jewish heroines as true peers. In turn, *Ulica graniczna* (Border street [1947]) made by the Polish Jewish director Aleksander Ford, had Polish Jews and non-Jews fighting side by side in the Warsaw Ghetto Uprising.

A more permanent and formal means of taming even the most horrific fibers of the war were the death-camp museums. The Auschwitz-Birkenau, Majdanek, and Treblinka camps illustrated, above all, joint resistance against Nazi Germany. The camp at Auschwitz-Birkenau entered the collective memory very quickly. As Andrew Charlesworth pointed out, "Auschwitz was chosen in 1947 by a Polish Parliament by then dominated by a Stalinist, Moscow-led Communist Party whose leadership's main task was to suppress Polish national sentiment and stress solidarity between Poland and the Soviet Union."[27] That the Red Army had liberated the camp was emphasized, especially through a staged propaganda film, the footage or the whole of which is still shown at the Auschwitz-Birkenau Museum and even worldwide. Certainly Auschwitz-Birkenau was well-suited for this propaganda purpose since, unlike Majdanek for example, Auschwitz had not been used for postwar incarceration of Home Army members, nor was it near Lublin, the 1944 seat of the puppet government. Nor was it so close to the Bug River that it would serve as a reminder of the lost Kresy.[28]

Gradually all countries whose citizens had been imprisoned at Auschwitz-Birkenau were given space in which to design and organize their own exhibit. Yet more crucial, "By emphasizing its international character and ignoring the fact the victims were Jewish, the Communists linked Poland through the memorialisation of Auschwitz to the other Warsaw Pact countries, both as past and potential victims of German aggression and as present beneficiaries of their liberation by the Red Army and of their continuing defense by the Soviet Union."[29]

On the one hand, the USSR pavilion at Auschwitz, plus a sign in Block 11 informing the reader that Zyklon B had first been applied against Soviet POWs held there, and the originally inflated figure of four-million Auschwitz dead, which thus made room for more Russian casualties, all planted the Soviet Union decidedly on the side of the "victims" and "heroes." In any case, anti-Semitism was defined as a fascist aberration, which the declassed and de-ethnicized brotherhood of Communism precluded.

On the other hand, and despite separate national exhibitions, the victims of Auschwitz-Birkenau were generally deprived of identities other than as "citizens" of their respective states. Indeed, many Polish non-Jews had been confined at Auschwitz-Birkenau, and this gradually became the basis of a national Polish memory of this site.[30] As Deborah Dwork and Robert van Pelt stated, "Auschwitz had been established as the Nazis' instrument to subjugate the Poles into serfdom—an enslavement the Poles rightly interpreted as the initial steps towards a 'Final Solution' of a 'Polish problem.' Auschwitz was a tremendously significant site in Polish history, and it made sense that a *Państwowe Muzeum* [national museum] would concentrate the nation's meager resources on it."[31]

Intriguingly enough, and in blatant incongruity with the progressive homogenization, Jews would actually be the only minority group ever identified separately. Historic Jewish quarters included (and often still do) a Jewish Street (*ulica Żydowska*), as well as one named after Berek Joselewicz, a Polish Jewish officer who fought in the 1863 uprising. Moreover, a postwar Ghetto Heroes Square (*plac Bohaterów Getta*) appeared in several larger cities.[32] Still another inconsistency was the Ghetto Heroes Monument in Warsaw, already standing in 1948 for the fifth anniversary of the ghetto uprising.[33]

When a community restructures its identity after traumatic experiences, the simplest way is to organize the new identity around specific symbolic axes, such as time and space, and via heroes, museums, monuments, and the like. A significant and usually obvious warp thread around which collective memory is woven is the cyclical commemoration of events, particularly tying new dates to old ones. Yet, though other Soviet-bloc states introduced 9 May as a federal holiday, postwar Poland lost dates, including the official erasure of two key post–World War I holidays: 3 May, the anniversary of the 1791 Polish constitution, and 11 November, the anniversary of Poland's twentieth-century resurrection. The socialist workers holiday of 1 May replaced the former, but nothing ever replaced the latter: no national holiday was ever created to mark World War II.[34] Polish Armed Forces Day on 12 October, which commemorated the Battle of Lenino, was as close as it came. Officially, that battle was a victory for the Soviets and Polish troops organized under their command; unofficially, the battle involved sending Poles to the frontlines as cannon fodder. September 1st, which could have safely been memorialized because it marked the German, not Soviet, invasion, was nevertheless only discreetly recognized by wreath-laying at monuments and somber television programming. The anniversary of the May 1945 peace treaty was ignored publicly and privately—better not to broadcast a date which many associated with another political enslavement.

1950–1980: The Double-Sided Tapestry

The first five years had been filled with voices, unofficial as well as official. But as the new political system and its messages came to dominate, particularly with the onset of the worst years of Stalinism, "unspeaking" set in. The totalitarian regime—in the interests of redirecting identity toward Communism—limited the pool of historical "truths." Many facts were ignored, the in-depth examination of others was avoided, and an official memory of the war was institutionalized. In some cases (and best for the ruling elite) explicit and unambiguous interpretations were forced into the public discourse; in other cases (and somewhat better for society) the implicit "white stains" were unofficially filled in by private discourse among trusted family and friends.

Between 1945 and 1956, those who served as unwanted reminders or tried to steer national memory in an undesired direction were arrested and/or executed.[35] With time, more insidious means were employed. Censorship reigned over textbooks, literature (foreign as well as autochthonous), theater and film scripts and productions, the limited TV programming, and, above all, the press. Socialist-realism propaganda posters and slogans—on paper and monumentally muraled across whole walls—warned of the evils of imperialism and hailed the good work of building socialism. Especially expressive in the early years were posters depicting officially disapproved groups as arch-capitalists, ugly dwarves, or insects.[36]

World War II was everywhere: the country was (and continues to be) "littered" with ubiquitous monuments and plaques. Reinforcing the ever-lasting anti-German thread, the nationwide, official symbol for World War II sites became the "Grunwald swords," referring to Poland's fifteenth-century victory over the Teutonic knights.[37] Shifting attention away from the sins of the Soviets—and away from the anti-Russian warp—the World War II sites suggested a friendly and cooperative coalition with the USSR without whose assistance Poland could not have defeated the *hitlerowcy*—the personified Nazis. Schoolbooks referred to the antifascist bloc in which the Soviet Union had purportedly played the greatest role. Public memory of Soviet occupation of Poland evaporated; eventually, young children came to recite patriotic poems about armies of Polish soldiers gathering from all corners of the Soviet Union, never questioning how it was that these men had found themselves there.

Falsification in the form of substitution was introduced: the Battle of Lenino was honored, not Monte Cassino; the People's Guard was honored, not the Home Army; Communist generals were honored, not those who had served with the Allies. The official model for identity was loathing of Western capitalism and imperialism in general, and of the traditional Polish, non-Russian foes—Germans and Jews—in the form of West Germany and Zionist Israel in specific.[38] On the other side of the tapestry, the opposite image was privately formed.

In the long run, however, both public and private discourse tied collective memory of World War II securely to the warp thread of all previous heroic struggles, sacrifices, and martyrdom in the name of Poland's and Europe's liberty. The guidebook to Polish lieux de mémoire reminded its readers, "Here present and future generations will find a description of the material symbols of our nation's tradition of freedom fighting, . . . which we are accustomed to calling sites of national memory. They are of priceless ideological-patriotic and historical value."[39]

In the aftermath of any great struggle, official memory will accent the intrepidness of its citizens and raise some of them into the pantheon of national heroes. Yet, the public honoring of those who had fought against the Germans risked evoking private homage to those who had fought against the Russians. In any case, the new socialist identity required its own champions. Cityscapes came to be dominated by massive socialist-realism statues of protagonists in the proactive rebuilding of the country and creation of the new system of government. Still, the paradigm of the muscular socialist worker symbolizing physical strength and labor did not take root for long: its rather rapid and dishonorable discharge was openly documented in such films as Andrzej Wajda's *Człowiek z marmuru* (Man of marble [1977; script written in 1963]).

Although Polish artists later gained a reputation for dissidence, their works in the first postwar decade or two were more apt to carry the threads of the public and less the private discourse about the war. Among films still shown to mark 1 September are those on the 1944 capital city uprising—Wajda's *Kanał* (Canal [1956]) or Janusz Morgenstern's *Godzina "W"* (The "W" hour [1979, based on a story published in 1956]). Both these films had to wait a long time for production approval because they referred to the taboo subject of the 1944 Warsaw Uprising, a noble but doomed effort to free the capital from the German occupation before the Soviets arrived.[40] In fact, *Kanał* was actually part of a 1954–1958 trilogy dealing with the resistance in Warsaw; although the director himself had been born and spent the war years in Warsaw, the films depict it in surprisingly bleak and grim light.

Since Poland had been resurrected for only a few decades, her citizens had had relatively recent experience in sustaining an unofficial discourse at odds with the official one—creating a double-sided tapestry as it were. In private discourse the Home Army dominated, with the People's Guard, Independent Armed Forces, and other "pro-USSR" units omitted almost completely (in correspondence with their overemphasis in public discourse).

If officially all evil came from the West, then unofficially it came from the East. The more the public discourse highlighted ties to the East, the more the private one accented historical, especially wartime, ties to the West. Despite jammed airwaves and the risk of punishment for listeners, Radio Free Europe and Voice of America increasingly guided the weaving in of alternative strands. The West was seen in this instance not as "rotting imperialism" but as a source of "truth," which encompassed almost anything that stood opposed to the official discourse, never mind that such stands, too, were subject to distortions. The Western orientation in the private sphere was such that by 1980 even a weather report that mentioned a cold Eastern wind could produce knowing looks and chuckles.

Paradoxically, after World War II, the Europe Adolf Hitler wanted to create—*judenrein* and ethnically monocultural—was realized to a great degree in Central and Eastern Europe. Most of the Jews had been murdered, while many of the remaining took off for the West or for newly created Israel; other peoples had been evicted from their homes and sent to their ethnic homelands. Socialism did permit a "politically correct" (that is, Communist-oriented) patriotism of the dominant culture but strictly controlled it. It suppressed reminders of minority cultures; all World War II memorials and monuments therefore accented the murder of "Poles" and "Polish citizens," without identifying them as Polish Jews, Roma, Ukrainians, and so on. This pattern, however, worked well on both sides of the tapestry—both the public and private discourses preferred to present the history of the majority.

A shattered national identity required uncluttered concentration around the core national memory, but that memory was politically Polish Communist on the one hand and socially Polish Roman Catholic on the other. The regime officially hooked into the warp threads that depicted Poles perennially fighting for the just cause, while society highlighted those threads that connected to the image of a Christlike, sacrificial offering to the Allied peace and, concurrently, to the image of the rebel who continued to fight for his freedom and to regain his Camelot. Again, the anti-Germanism emphasized and enforced by postwar regimes in the public sphere led to a proportionately enhanced resistance to Communism in the private sphere. This worked twofold against Jewish interpretations of war memory on the private side of the tapestry: the Shoah was part and parcel of the German, not Soviet occupation; persons of Jewish descent were overrepresented in the official apparatus of the socialist system.

Nonetheless, by the 1960s and 1970s the principle "the enemy of my enemy is my friend" steered the opposition. Growing progressively more inclusive of and siding with anyone whom the socialist regime officially disclaimed, the opposition maintained surreptitious contacts with and wrote in favor of the West, of Germans and Germany, and of Jews. With regard to Germany, the Polish Roman Catholic episcopate opened the door with a 1965 letter addressed to their fellow German bishops. Although the Polish regime was initially aghast and strongly disapproved, this unofficial move led to government-level talks that culminated in 1970 with West German recognition of the Oder-Neisse border and with the Helsinki agreements, which facilitated reunions of families split by the war or its aftermath. Polish-

German relationships before, during, and after the war could then be more visibly and increasingly woven into the private and public discourse.

With regard to Poles of Jewish ancestry, progressive disenchantment with Marxism in general and with political purges and social attacks in specific (in the wake of strikes and protests in 1956 and again in 1968) contributed to developing inclusion of and participation by the "enemy's enemy" in the political counterculture. For instance, not only did some of the most important Catholic opposition leaders side with the Polish Jewish population during the anti-Zionist purge in 1968, but non-Jewish students also attended the Jewish "flying university" of the 1970s. Unofficial, grassroots-organized Jewish-culture weeks, under the auspices of the Warsaw branch of the liberal Catholic and democratic Klub Inteligencji Katolickiej (Catholic Intelligentsia Club), furthered contact and thus more open discussion of Polish Jewish relations. Finally, a book directly dealing with the Shoah was published in 1977: Hanna Krall's *Sheltering the Flame*, an interview with Marek Edelman (the last surviving fighter of the Warsaw Ghetto and Warsaw Uprisings). By the end of the decade Jewish strands were being spun and interwoven into private discourse with ever-increasing speed.[41]

Thus on the private and the public side of the tapestry, Poles were imagined as heroes in solidarity with other victims, altruists in their sacrifice, and brave in their fight and defiance against any and all perpetrators. Such was the Polish self-image during the partitions: "If, however, our sacrifice is to be like Christ's sacrifice (not as great or sacred, but just as innocent), and Poland is the righteous among ruffians, nailed to the cross in order to save not so much itself as the entire world, then the entire fault lies with the assailants, satanic charlatans such as Fredrick and Katherine."[42] And such was the self-portrait woven after World War II. Among other things, the high number of Poles who have been awarded the Yad Vashem "Righteous among the Nations of the World" certificate for saving Jews is then taken as proof of its veracity.[43]

Postwar Polish Jewry constructed a similar image of themselves (though presented variously by Bundists, Zionists, Communists, and so on). "A martyrological vision of the fate of one's nation was a natural need among the surviving Jews. The rebuilding of their identity anew would provide an escape from a feeling of a deep humiliation, the loss of their individual and group dignity."[44] The erection of the Ghetto Heroes Monument in 1948 and then commemorations of successive anniversaries became occasions to recall a "stereotypically Polish" hopeless but valiant fight, as well as civil, unarmed resistance by Polish Jews. Just as with all battles by Poles, this Jewish resistance, too, came to be anchored in religion and messianism.[45]

As a result, as time passed and protests increased in frequency and scale, more and more Polish Jews found themselves working with the ethnic Polish and liberal Roman Catholic elites rebelling against totalitarianism.[46] Poles reverted to ideals carried by the warp threads and—after major strikes and protests in 1956, 1968, 1970, 1976, and 1980—relearned old lessons. Joining forces, the intelligentsia and the workers, Warsaw and Kraków, Jewish Poles and non-Jewish Poles alike began to unite and see themselves as heroes of freedom.[47] The tapestry of their unofficial discourses became of one design as well.


## 1980–1989: Unraveling and Tearing

The Poles were reliving their 1795–1920 history: after failed uprisings came victory against the Soviet Union. The first ceremonial surrender of the government—the signing of the Gdańsk agreements in August 1980—was broadcast on radio, TV, and newsreels while photographs of Lech Wałęsa with his oversized pen were splayed across newspaper pages. Amazed at how much had been won but wary because freedom had often been short-lived, authors quickly printed literature they had written *do szuflady* (into the drawer), publishers issued blacklisted authors (Czesław Miłosz, for example, who had escaped to the West in the 1950s), documentary and commercial films were unshelved and premiered, scholars printed the results of "unapproved" research, and the Solidarity press published articles on taboo topics.[48] Among the key issues raised were the Soviet occupation and the Shoah. The former was and continues to be a solely Polish issue; the latter surfaced in conjunction with a worldwide awakening of Holocaust remembrance.

The sixteen months of Solidarity thus allowed the in-weaving of all manner of previously dropped threads, from the Katyń Forest to the Kielce pogrom. During this period, Poles were able to and did openly question the official versions of their wartime history, with the subject of the Soviet occupation, in particular, dominating public discourse—perhaps to spite the public discourse theretofore. Jewish and the Holocaust strands were highlighted, too. Martial law, declared on 13 December 1981, hampered but could not halt this process.

In keeping with the warp threads of its collective memory, each setback— longer or briefer, more grave or less—called for a tie-in to the warp thread of lost Polish nationhood. The very first martial-law issue of *Tygodnik Powszechny* (on 23 May 1982, after a five-month interruption) carried a front-page article whose title boldly proclaimed, "Poland Is a Fatherland." This article in the liberal Roman Catholic weekly, the most public voice of private discourse, carried portentous and potent hidden messages (the Poles had learned to read well and deeply between the lines). Its author, Father Józef Tischner, a highly respected and renowned priest and Jagiellonian University philosophy professor, was the epitome of an opposition figure. The article itself opened and was liberally sown with quotes by the Polish romantic poet Cyprian Norwid; the first quote asserted, "No one can effect the annihilation of a nation without the participation of the citizens of that nation."[49] These words reaffirmed that nothing—not even a military junta—would ever vanquish the Poles.

If the Polish state continued to avoid observing dates, then Polish society was now determined to overcommemorate time and to do so in symbolic spaces. Especially in the 1980s, the missing May and November dates of remembrance were marked privately in a public but very legal manner: via en masse participation in Roman Catholic church services. Just as Poles had done during the partitions, they attended evening church services on 3 May and 11 November; in Kraków, these masses at the Royal Cathedral on Wawel Castle Hill resulted in regular postservice marches and clashes with the *milicja*, the combination police and national-guard force. In other parishes, patriotic masses became popular, often marking dates crucial to the unofficial discourse, for example, the 13th of December or even the 13th of every month. At St. Stanisław Kostka Church in Warsaw, Father Jerzy Popiełuszko's monthly "mass for the Fatherland" was held on the last Sunday of each month, until his political murder in October 1984. Finally, crosses of flowers laid out at various significant sites in Warsaw and other cities—either on an everyday basis such as in Warsaw near the Tomb of the Unknown Soldier, or only on anniversary dates at the Solidarity monuments in Gdańsk and Poznań—also constituted unofficial creations of lieux de mémoire. All of these dates, along with newly sacrificed saints such as Father Popiełuszko, were woven around the warp threads of Polish martyrology.[50]

Still, even while socialism was going bankrupt economically and politically throughout the Warsaw Pact states, it continued to relay its own versions of World War II socially. The 1988 preface to *Przewodnik po upamiętnionych miejscach walk i męczeństwa lata wojny* (Guide to remembered sites of battle and martyrdom) emphasized the contribution of the Russians to the liberation of Poland: 600,000 Red Army soldiers had given their lives, and an additional 800,000 were tortured and murdered as prisoners of war on Polish soil.[51] Amazingly, the preface stated that only about 230,000 "citizens" of other European states had died in German camps in occupied Poland. Yet a connection to the warp threads of national identity had to be made, along with at least an indirect one to the new strand of the Holocaust: the World War II monuments "immortalize the places consecrated by the suffering and death of the citizens of our country, [and] which have become synonyms for genocide."[52]

Once signs of this strand on the private side of the tapestry surfaced on the gradually more threadbare public side, they could not be ignored. In spite of martial law, Monika Krajewska's *Czas kamieni* (Time of Stones), a photo album of Jewish cemeteries in Poland, was officially published by one of the major government presses in 1982. Next, quite daringly, the editors of the Kraków-based Catholic monthly, *Znak*—who were members, too, of the Klub Inteligencji Katolickiej—requested and received government permission for a double issue on Judaism, Jews, Polish Jewish history, and the Holocaust in memory of the fortieth anniversary of the Warsaw Ghetto Uprising.[53] The regime, in turn, eager to be seen in a more positive light by the country and the world—not only because of the political crisis but also due to an incredible Western debt—seized the opportunity. The February–March 1983 issue of *Znak* was a turning point: an official commemoration of the insurrection was held (thus stymieing any Solidarity plans for its own ceremony), and Polish Jewish themes became permanently evident on both sides of the tapestry.

In 1987, four years after martial law had been suspended, Hannah Arendt's *Eichmann in Jerusalem* was officially published; more surreptitiously, Alexander Hertz's *The Jews in Polish Culture* and Alina Cała's *Image of the Jew in Polish Folk Culture* were distributed through churches and other unofficial channels. Hannah Krall's contemporary works of fiction were accompanied by the reappearance of those by Isaac Bashevis Singer, Julian Stryjkowski, and Bruno Szulc. The first anthology of Polish Holocaust literature came out in 1988.[54]

The documentary filmmaker Marcel Łoziński, inspired by a Warsaw historian's 1981 Solidarity newspaper article on the July 1946 Kielce incident, decided to make *Świadkowie* (Witnesses) in remembrance of the incident's fortieth anniversary. Still, it was private, unofficial weavers—including the bishop of Kielce and the Klub Inteligencji Katolickiej—who facilitated the film's production as well as its premiere. What ultimately brought the "Jewish Question" to the forefront were the 1986 eruption of the Carmelite-convent controversy at Auschwitz (though the debates became more open and public in 1989–1990) and the showing of Claude Lanzmann's nine-hour *Shoah* in its entirety in some cinemas and in part on prime-time television (even while Łoziński's film could not debut officially).[55]

The following year, in 1987, *Tygodnik Powszechny* printed an essay by a Jagiellonian University literary critic and professor, Jan Błoński. In the essay Błoński, referring to Czesław Miłosz's Warsaw Ghetto Uprising–inspired poems, raised the issue of Polish co-responsibility as witnesses to the Shoah who were sometimes helpless, but often pitiless. Responses and letters to the editor began to appear immediately, and a debate ensued between Błoński and Władysław Siła-Nowicki, a lawyer with impeccable wartime and post-war credentials. Some of the reactions were published that same year, the remainder subsequently printed in the early, post-Communist 1990s.[56] This discourse on Polish memory and identity vis-à-vis the war, the Holocaust, the Germans, and the Jews, which began on the private side of the tapestry— worked in by the intellectual elite of the opposition—bled through to the public side in larger and larger patterns, affecting more and more average Poles. This progression straddled the 1989 transformation and continues to date.

Significant, however, is that this issue was made visible to broader circles of Polish society only after the introduction of imported fibers, that is, via the extraterritorial discussions on the convent crisis and Lanzmann's film. Both issues presented the general public with external opinions regarding the commission of the Shoah on occupied Polish land.[57] Perhaps more to the point, it meant that Poland's role in the Shoah was dealt with at the very moment when internal opinions were being formed. Thenceforth, Poles became increasingly aware of how they were characterized by the outside world and knew that they would be addressing Polish-Jewish and Polish-Shoah relations under the persevering eye of the West.[58]

In Poland's eyes West Germany very quickly became a "friend," while the Soviet Union and the Soviet bloc—especially after the construction of the Berlin Wall, the embodiment of Churchill's Iron Curtain—became the "foe." West Germany became a member of NATO and of the European Union, allying itself militarily, politically, and economically with the very states which had been its adversaries during the war. In the meantime, the countries further east were members of the Warsaw Pact forcibly aligned with the USSR. It was a shock to the Poles to discover that, as a consequence, their war record with the Allies had been bleached out while a Cold War animosity toward all things associated with the East had stained their identity quite black. Holes appeared in the fabric—ultimately, it tore.

## 1989: Reweaving

The onset of a break in the silence on World War II traumas and the subsequent emergence of globalized memory of those traumas appeared concurrently with the increasingly evident decay of Communism and a rise in recalcitrance in Poland. Come June 1989 and Poland, yet again in its modern history, had resisted and rebelled successfully.[59] Not without meaning for Poles was that they had sacrificed to overthrow an occupying power and freed others in the process—this time leading to the restoration to Europa's fold of the remaining nation-states which had been under Communism. Not only did the Fourth Partition come to an end, but also the totalitarian tradition could be unraveled and the liberal-democratic tradition rewoven.

Threads of the old design had to be symbolically restored to the loom. Not until Lech Wałęsa was sworn into office in late 1990 as the first freely elected president of the Third Republic of Poland did the Polish government-in-exile (representing the Second Republic) in London cease its functioning, passing on the insignia of the office which had been held outside Poland since September 1939. Continuity between the Second Republic (1918–1939) and the Third was then established.

Such replacement of strands linking back to the past included, too, the rechristening of streets bearing names of the since discredited. Thoroughfares adorned with the names of Communist leaders, the dates of a town's "liberation" by the Red Army, and the like now reverted to their 1939 appellations. Contemporary roads honor postwar heroes such as Home Army generals and Pope John Paul II.[60]

Both 3 May and 11 November were almost immediately reinstated as national holidays (without the deduction of 1 May, however). A relatively unnoticed but meaningful shift was the post-Communist government's reassignment of Polish Army Day to 15 August. With one stroke it came to commemorate the crucial 1920 "Miracle on the Vistula" against the Soviets, which, in being tied to the Feast of the Assumption, became a holy event.[61] On the same day when pilgrimages from all across the country culminate at the shrine of the Black Madonna in Częstochowa, the Polish president participates in ceremonies at the Tomb of the Unknown Soldier in Warsaw.

A post-1989 edition of the *Guide to Remembered Sites of Battle and Martyr-dom*, which would describe the new monuments commemorating the Polish martyrs of the Soviet occupation and system, has yet to be issued. These testimonials have been erected mostly in Warsaw and will always resonate with a different timbre since actual sites (e.g., camps, mass graves, etc.) are located within various former–Soviet Union republics. In the meantime, while the Tomb of the Unknown Polish Soldier is prominent to this day in Warsaw, the Tomb of the Soviet Soldiers in Kraków—under constant surveillance by the milicja for fear of vandalism and other attacks—was finally dismantled and moved to the local military cemetery. In all major cities, statues of Communist "heroes" were removed demonstratively in broad daylight (nearly causing an international incident when Warsaw's statue of Feliks Dzierżyński was decapitated in the process) or stealthily in the dead of night (as with Nowa Huta's statue of Lenin). Statues of other heroes were never erected: children play on a barren foundation deprived in 1989 of its nearly completed statue honoring the Red Army general who took Kraków from the Germans.

Yet while the new official public discourse began to increasingly tie into the old, as well as to the previously unofficial and private discourse, many artists, filmmakers, and writers felt lost for a while: their political context of opposition had vanished and the tapestry was being woven on one side again. A decade into post-Communism, however, the films of Andrzej Wajda reflected the designs of current national identity and memory work. Weaving in new Shoah threads as well as restoring the old warp, the director's films included *Korczak* (1990), about the Warsaw ghetto teacher, doctor, and author of children's literature; *Wielki Tydzień* (Holy week [1995]), a film version of Jerzy Andrzejewski's 1943 tale of a Jewish woman in hiding; as well as—highly significant for Poles but nearly unknown in the West—the grand classics *Pan Tadeusz* (1998) and *Zemsta* (2002).[62]

The post-millennium, post-Communist cinematic return to the classics (not only by Wajda) assuages fears and affirms the continued presence of the oldest of warp threads. Ethnic Polish Roman Catholics feel themselves to be still in the process of reclaiming their own cultural landscape, which had been lost to them for over half a century. Poland's World War II memory now recalls and accents—privately and publicly—the dual occupation for the duration of the war. Nonetheless, just when Poles could finally speak about and investigate the Polish–Soviet Russian aspects of the war, the world has been pressuring them to return again to the Polish-German aspects, albeit now with a stronger emphasis on the history of Polish-Jewish relations.[63] Not unjustly perhaps, many Poles feel that the world is still ignoring their war wounds and their betrayal by the Allies; more nationalistic Poles specifically resent dictates from the West as to the proper focus of work on postwar memory and identity. With many Poles unable to cope with the new, confusing, and radically changed situation, the will to define national identity has become a "mobilizing force."[64]

In time, however, the Holocaust strand was gradually taken up not only by the liberal Roman Catholic elites of the previously private and unofficial tapestry but by the public and the official post-Communist political elites. Recurring formal apologies during various ceremonies and ceremonial occasions—by President Wałęsa in the Knesset, by the Polish minister of foreign affairs in Kielce on the fiftieth anniversary of the Holocaust, by President Kwaśniewski in Jedwabne on the sixtieth anniversary—have seriously snagged the heroic martyr thread of Polish historical memory.

Shifting the emphasis precisely to Poland's role in the Shoah, Jan Tomasz Gross's *Sąsiedzi* (Neighbors, a detailed account of the Jedwabne Massacre [2000]) served as the latest turning point. If discourse regarding collaboration, complicity, or co-responsibility had already filled in the design, then *Neighbors* forced Poles to elaborate further. Though the Shoah had begun to enter the weave in the previous decade, it was still easier to think of a few aberrant individuals than to consider responsibility, or even guilt, as a wider, if not widespread, phenomenon. In Jedwabne (as in Kielce) Poles were neither victims nor heroes nor innocent bystanders, but perpetrators. Poles began to debate the book's contents in very heated but also very open discussions in the mass media, in all manner of discourse, and in deeper analyses regarding the moral issues of direct and indirect Polish collusion. The on-site commemoration in July 2001 was attended by dignitaries, the president and prime minister, and the then Israeli Ambassador to Poland (Shevach Weiss, himself rescued from the Holocaust by Christian Poles); a public apology affirmed by the president marked the zenith of the ceremony, but not the end of the discourse.[65]

Indeed, television, radio, and the press keep all manner of Polish Jewish issues in the foreground. But they give voice to a wide range of opinions and discourses: from the narrowly nationalistic, which stresses the warp thread of heroic martyrdom, to the more liberal, which also sees the woof threads woven by Polish minorities.[66] In addition, given the full palette of fibers in post-Communist Poland, museums and memorials are being rethought and reworked. Recently, the Roma massacred in Szczurowa have been identified on their monument, a permanent exhibition barrack has been assigned at

Auschwitz I, and the overnight liquidation of the former "Gypsy Camp" at Auschwitz II-Birkenau is commemorated annually on 2 August. The fate of German military graves (World War I and World War II) is also being discussed.

However, the increasing interest in Jewish history and culture has been ironically accompanied by a series of conflicts associated with the Auschwitz-Birkenau Museum. The appearance of crosses at various locations in and around the two camps, the canonization of Sister Teresa Benedict of the Cross (Edith Stein), and the 1996 supermarket and 2001 discotheque controversies have served as flashpoints for discussions—within and outside Poland's borders—about the Polish Roman Catholic as a not just dominant but dominating national identity.[67] Recognizing the need for the imported as well as homespun threads, Poland in 1989 established an international advisory council whose members were Jews and non-Jews from Poland and beyond. This body now makes decisions about Auschwitz-Birkenau and all the death-camp sites.

Nonetheless, with normalization begun in the 1960s, post-reunification financial, military, and other considerations have built solid foundations for reworking Polish and German histories and identities vis-à-vis each other. With regards to Polish Jewish history, the fact of ongoing progress for about two decades also bodes well for the processing of war memory and postwar identity.[68] A Jewish Museum project is being realized, and the establishment of commemorative sites such as Umschlagplatz and the Warsaw Ghetto Martyrology Route, as well as the restoration of Jewish cemeteries, synagogues, and the like demonstrate continual work in this area. Physical alterations in the landscape and the appearance of new lieux de memoire (not to mention the large number of German and Israeli tourists) influence the way the average Pole perceives these threads. Contributing to this are official agreements between ministries of education (Poland-Germany, Poland-Israel, Poland-Lithuania, and so on) to create joint commissions for the rewriting of history textbooks—if not, as it were, history itself.

In contrast, the post-Communist relationship between Poland and Russia, a nation heir to the collective identity of the USSR, has not been one of consistent and constructive progression. Late USSR and early Federation of Russia leaders (from Mikhail Gorbachev to Boris Yeltsin to Vladimir Putin) have refused and rebuffed attempts by Polish leaders (regardless of post-Solidarity affiliation, as Lech Wałęsa had, or post-Communist affiliation, as Aleksander Kwaśniewski had) to cooperate in addressing Polish-USSR wartime and postwar history. Not only has Russia refused to admit to and apologize for any aspect of the Soviet occupation from 1939–1945, but it has even denied access to sixty-year-old documents regarding the assassination of approximately 20,000 Polish reserve officers in April 1940. Polish president Aleksander Kwaśniewski's assistance in resolving the 2005 Ukrainian election crisis that led to the success of the "Orange Revolution" was highly and openly criticized by Russian President Vladimir Putin. Later, the Russian presence as evidenced in the names of the Soviet victims of Auschwitz-Birkenau was emphasized during the sixtieth anniversary of that camp's liberation by the Red Army, whereas the Polish leader's subsequent participation in Moscow's sixtieth anniversary of the "Great Fatherland War" was much subdued.

The confrontations between mythology and history—between the warp and the weft—led to unremitting examinations of the many "truths" regarding World War II. While the opposition had been inclusive of "all enemies of my enemy," it had, indeed, centered on a "nationalism" equated with patriotism to the cause of the "real" Poland. Thus, whereas in the days of Solidarity the opposition was understood to comprise all who were against the government for whatever reason, in the post-Communist period various visions for the tapestry across the political spectrum of society have been revealed.

This is not to imply that the majority of Poles readily accept the need to undertake the task of reworking the fabric. Fervent nationalists and others for whom the warp has been the sole remaining constant amid the tumult of the twentieth century are averse to foreign fibers being introduced into the filling, preferring an even more threadbare or plain tapestry. The oral histories regarding wartime acts gathered in a recent sociological study, *Biography and National Identity*, reveal only tales of aid and assistance, rarely noting cowardice, demoralized behavior, or egoism. If mentioned at all, such behavior is usually marginalized.[69] Nevertheless, in 2003 a doctoral dissertation on Jagiellonian University scholars employed by a German wartime institute established in Kraków briefly provoked outrage while opening a new field for discourse: the Polish intelligentsia as heroes or collaborators.[70] The breadth of the work is continually being stretched.

## Conclusions

"One can say that a wave of memory has spilled out of the depths and over, across the world—everywhere connecting a faithfulness to the real or imagined past very closely to a feeling of belonging, the collective consciousness to the individual self-awareness, memory to identity."[71] It is against this backdrop that one can analyze how Polish historical memory connects with its social identity. As noted in the introduction to one periodical in the midst of the Jedwabne debates, "The subject [of discussion] is memory, but the goal is a determination regarding social identity."[72]

With World War II, a social world and spiritual community fell apart catastrophically; a symbolic universe—the Polish army, government, and historical landmarks and monuments—had been ripped asunder, figuratively and literally.[73] Afterward, the Polish loom, the Polish sense of self was badly damaged. Warp threads needed to be repaired and restrung, then new threads of the weft had to be knotted, more or less neatly, to the previous. Mythology, history, identity, the defeat and destruction, the negative and pessimistic individual and collective experiences of World War II had to be transformed into positive and optimistic ones; they had to be defined as proactive (albeit martyrological) choices consciously made by the Poles, even if officially other elements had to be acknowledged.

"Every nation mythologizes its past. The average man on the street does not delve into historical research. What he needs is a simplified version of the past."[74] More precisely, what the average man needs is a sense of continuity, a sense of connectedness, and a sense that the distant past is of one thread with the recent past and will carry him into the future. After the "Communist" phases of 1945–1950 (a tangled ball of war memories expressed rather freely), 1950–1980 (amnesia and silence politically imposed and enforced), and the post-Solidarity 1980–1989 (a bleeding-through of the unofficial discourse), Poland is in the post-Communist, post-1989 phase when all can and is being discussed, although not always unreservedly. Polish society is in the process of yet another social transformation. Repairing and restringing are again a priority.

The political and economic shifts have come as suddenly as before. Polish society has found itself again suffering post-traumatic shock. The subsequent social anomie has begotten both apathy and fear. The Poles' frustration and disappointment at not finding Camelot awaiting them with Poland's return to democracy and capitalism, their panic at having to suddenly shoulder responsibility after a half century of having everything either decided or limited by a totalitarian government, all this has created a situation in which some persons and groups feel that "justice for all" has not brought social justice to most. Uncertainty has led to a psychological need for clear-cut distinctions, us-them divisions, and Manichaeanism.

"Thus, it comes as no surprise that the post-Communist countries are facing the re-activation of national identities. The nation is replacing the Communist state as the main institution providing people with a sense of stability and togetherness."[75] In Poland history rears its ugly head when the national majority and one of its minorities clash over varying collective memories. This plays out in all combinations—Polish-Jewish, Polish-Ukrainian, Polish-German, Polish-Lithuanian, and others: "What is most noticeable is the feeling of 'the excess of history' of both parties. . . . History in the disputes was considered as still not finished and continuing . . . ; it was perceived as repeating or bringing back the past harm and victims (memory-repetition), which made it difficult to understand the arguments of the other party. Above all, there was no critical approach to history and no attempt to close it and treat [it] as a finished event—a recollection (memory-recollection)."[76]

In his milestone 1987 essay, Jan Błoński expressed the crux of the dilemma: "Because what will others think of us? What will we think of ourselves? . . . This concern about one's 'good name' is incessantly present in private—and even more so in public statements."[77] Reworking Polish national memory as grounds for a new postwar but also now post-Communist identity after limits and restraints have been lifted means judicious selection from among all the fibers, textures, and colors. It means an informed patriotism: "In developing my own sense of dignity and taking pride in that which is praiseworthy, I am not allowed to close my eyes to that which in my tradition was stupid or ignominious. Therefore I must continuously re-perform a reckoning of conscience. Being a nation appears to be a sort of ethical undertaking; one is a nation for a reason."[78]

This current phase of reopened investigations into World War II history, new trials, and unrestricted public debates on all (but particularly the ethnic and nationalist) aspects of that trauma is bringing Poles back to the very framework of their identity. It is forcing them to question and deconstruct most parts of the postwar identity, to push the envelope to include all of the roles ethnic Poles played during World War II, particularly during the Shoah, and to incorporate the war memories of non-ethnic Poles into an inclusive Polish identity.[79]

For much of today's youth, however, not only is World War II a foreign country, but the generation now coming of age is too young to have even experienced Solidarity and martial law or to really remember 1989. They focus nearly exclusively on their future, which they see as part of Western civilization. Yet the world will not allow them the luxury of shutting out their national past in the move from totalitarian (Nazi-Soviet) Europe to

Brussels Europe. Global politics and an international raison d'être intervene in Poland's work on national memory and its new social identity.

Although democratization is not a foreign concept in Poland—it is, in fact, something which Poland feels it nearly brought to Europe in the eighteenth century—Poles, especially Polish elites, are nevertheless aware that the society needs to prove itself in order to participate in Western structures such as NATO and the European Union. But whereas those guiding the shuttle on the loom in the pre-1989 period were, on the one hand, the party principals and, on the other, the liberal Roman Catholic dissident intelligentsia, with each subsequent decade the number of weavers has grown larger. In the past the patterns were designed by the two elites and passed down to the masses. Now a free press and uncomplicated access to the Internet mean that any discourse quickly spreads to all levels at once. In fact, if there is something both guiding and facilitating the weave, it is the mass media—on- and offline—that invites the general public to join in the work on Polish memory and identity.

"We perceive selectively, we remember selectively, we recall selectively. We construct. We are human beings."[80] The loom has been braced, and a newer weft, one of varied fibers and textures, is being woven over and under the old warp. What new tale of its past Poland will eventually compose—and what new self is cut from this fabric—depends on the interwoven threads of minority and majority history, individual and collective memory, both in public and private discourse. Social transformations are said to require some forty years, or two generations, to complete. Poles have had just over a decade, so this is a work in progress.[81] The new national memory they build and the new social identity they shape around it will be known only in a few decades.

## Notes

1   Perhaps still too fresh to need to be marked, or perhaps because it was a victory for the country while a traumatic shift for individuals, the new caesura—the fall of the Soviet empire—has not reached this level of significance: Poles remain ambivalent about 1989.

2   This was made unmistakably clear again in 2004 with a sixty-three-day commemoration of the sixtieth anniversary of the 1944 Warsaw Uprising. Not only was a new museum opened in the capital city, and not only was each day marked with the lighting of a candle (all symbolically extinguished on the final day), but the entire country participated as readers of the newly published *Rising '44: The Battle for*

*Warsaw*, by Norman Davies, and as viewers of nationwide television programming that broadcast official ceremonies, films, panel discussions, interviews, and the like. Of note was a documentary specifically on Polish Jewish combatants—survivors of the previous year's Warsaw Ghetto Uprising—fighting in a second rebellion against the Germans.

3  See Rada Ochrony Pomników Walki i Męczeństwa, *Przewodnik po upamiętnionych miejscach walk i męczeństwa lata wojny 1939–1945*. The "author" is the Council for the Preservation of Monuments to Battle and Martyrdom, and the title translates as a *Guide to Remembered Sites of Battle and Martyrdom*. After the first edition in 1964, expanded ones were issued in 1966, 1980, and 1988. The first included two thousand descriptions, while the last had ten thousand, though noting that over twenty thousand sites existed, with more being discovered each month (9–10).

4  For instance, the synagogues in Opole, Wrocław, and other cities in today's western Poland were destroyed before the war; in Germany they were destroyed in November 1938, during Kristallnacht.

5  For an in-depth analysis of the messages relayed by these two spheres, especially in the last two decades of the Polish People's Republic, see Kubik, *The Power of Symbols against the Symbols of Power* (chap. 2 in particular).

6  In Polish history, Germany and Russia, in their various incarnations, have always been the quintessential foes, with the latter consistently viewed as the crueler. The USSR, from a Polish perspective, was a carry-over of the Russian Empire; Poles continued to use "Moscow" and "Russians" as reference metonyms. As Ryszard Kapuściński noted, "From the middle of the eighteenth century, throughout the entire nineteenth, and then even into the twentieth, hundreds of thousands—in the end, millions—of Poles were sent to Siberia and to the labor camps; they were deported, persecuted, imprisoned, and often murdered, shot. No one will ever experience to the same degree the level, the long duration, and the systematicness of that extermination. Hence stems the understandable Polish resentment and apprehension" (*Lapidaria*, 285; my translation).

7  Sławomir Kapralski, "Oświęcim," 142.

8  Kapuściński, *Lapidaria*, 338.

9  It should be noted, however, that—per the long-standing views mentioned in note 6—the Prussian and Russian partitions are continually defamed. Austrian Galicia, by contrast, is even romantically mythologized.

10  From 1795 until the present, Poland has been a sovereign state only for the two decades of the interwar years and for the fifteen-plus years since 1989.

11  Limited space and a different focus does not allow me to go into the role of the Roman Catholic Church in Polish history. However, for anyone familiar with its role in carrying and preserving "Polishness" during the partitions, it is not surprising that this institution—or more accurately—various circles of believers and/or clergy again undertook this task when Poland found itself under the "Fourth Partition" of socialist rule. Among other works explicating the intricate connection between Polish history, Polish Roman Catholicism, and Polish identity see Davies, *God's Playground*.

12    This saying has been quoted two ways: "for our freedom and yours" and "for your freedom and ours." The Warsaw Ghetto Uprising leaders referred to this phrase in April 1943, monuments very frequently bear it, and many foreign politicians (including U.S. presidents Bill Clinton and George H. W. Bush) have included it in speeches made on Polish soil. "Places near and far" included, for instance, the participation of Generals Tadeusz Kościuszko and Kazimierz Pułaski in the American War of Independence.

13    The Polish government-in-exile was first established in France, then reformed in London; no puppet state was instituted within occupied Poland. Meanwhile, the Polish underground was the most extensive on the continent.

14    Among earlier battles in which Poles saw themselves symbolically rescuing Europe were the Battle of Vienna in 1683, when Polish forces routed the Turks, and the "Miracle on the Vistula" in 1920 when they routed the Red Army. In both cases, the Polish interpretation is that Poland—the bastion of Latin Christian European civilization—prevented invasion by non-European, "infidel" forces. With regard to the Soviet presence, the last Red Army soldiers did not leave bases in Poland until 1993, well after the USSR had ceased to exist.

15    This community was at the time surpassed in size only by the American Jewish community, which numbered 4 million but represented only 3 percent of the U.S. population. In 1930s Poland over 3.5 million Jews comprised the country's second-largest minority and some 10 percent of the general population.

16    For my other works that deal specifically and in-depth with these issues see Orla-Bukowska, "Representing the Shoah in Poland and Poland in the Shoah"; Orla-Bukowska, "Presenting and Representing the Shoah in the Post-Communist World."

17    See Christie "Answers to Atrocities." Christie notes subsequent phases in response to a traumatic act of violence: a period of amnesia and silence, followed by remembrance, truth-seeking and/or legal trials, subsequently by punishment and retribution, and/or by amnesty.

18    Friedländer, "Trauma, Memory, and Transference," 259.

19    Terminology similar to *białe plamy* was used to describe this phenomenon throughout the socialist bloc.

20    By war's end, two-thirds of the population (over 20 million) found itself in a different place than it had inhabited in 1939. Postwar "repatriation"—from not only the Kresy, the eastern borderlands of prewar Poland but from all the corners of the Soviet Union into that land which occupation had tossed to the Poles—lasted well into the 1950s. Kresy hometowns subsequently ceased to exist, even as tourist destinations; only in the late 1980s did it become possible to gain a visa, for example, to visit family graves on All Saints Day.

21    On 10 July 1941, Jedwabne, a small town in northeastern Poland, was the site of a massacre of up to 1,600 Polish Jews who were burned in a barn; on 4 July 1946, in Kielce, a city in south central Poland, a blood-libel accusation led to the death of forty-two survivors of the Holocaust. Like the name "Auschwitz" is to all death camps, these two place names have become the symbols for all events of simi-

lar caliber. Additional war-crimes investigations were conducted by the Centralny Komitet Żydów w Polsce (Central Committee of Jews in Poland), established in 1944. Its legal department gathered evidence in cases of Polish non-Jewish perpetrators of war crimes against Jews (files referred to the new Public Security Bureau) but also directly tried, even posthumously, those it considered Polish Jewish war criminals.

22 The number of officers killed in April 1940 totaled over 15,000; the burial sites of the remaining 10,000 or so reserve officers were located in two other forests after the fall of the USSR. No one has been tried for these mass murders. Among the 4,421 victims at Katyń were about 200 Polish Jewish officers, including the chief rabbi of the Polish Army, Major Baruch Steinberg.

When German troops discovered the bodies in April 1943, the official Soviet—and consequently Allied—line was that the massacre had been a Nazi provocation. As Norman Davies disclosed, "The situation was summarized in confidential SOE files: 'The official line in the UK has been to pretend that the whole affair was a fake. . . . Any other view would have been distasteful to the public, since it could be inferred that we were allied to a power guilty of the same sort of atrocities as the Germans.' . . . Decades later, in 1990–1, when Soviet responsibility was confirmed by President Gorbachev in part, and then by President Yeltsin in full, the British War Crimes Act was carefully designed to exclude Allied criminals from its purview" (*Europe*, 1004–5).

23 Christie, "Answers to Atrocities," 342.

24 Borowski (b. 1922) was a member of the "tragic generation," those born in the first years of Poland's Second Republic but whose coming of age coincided with its defeat. That same generation was also called "Kolumbowie" after Roman Bratny's 1957 novel, *Kolumbowie: Rocznik 20*, which conveyed their plight.

25 Significantly, it has reached a transgenerational audience. From 1952 to 1989 the film was shown to a captive audience on the single nationwide Polish television channel. Since 1989 it has been broadcast on one of the two existing national channels (*Gazeta Wyborcza-Gazeta Telewizyjna*, 27 July–2 August 2001, pp. 31, 33).

26 *Gazeta Wyborcza-Gazeta Telewizyjna*, 27 July–2 August 2001, p. 33.

27 Charlesworth, "Contesting Places of Memory," 580.

28 Ibid., 582–83.

29 Ibid., 583.

30 About 150,000 Polish non-Jews were confined at Auschwitz-Birkenau, approximately half of whom perished.

31 Dwork and van Pelt, "Reclaiming Auschwitz," 241. For more on the role of the Auschwitz-Birkenau Museum in official memory see Huener, *Auschwitz, Poland, and the Politics of Commemoration, 1945–1979*.

32 The "heroic martyr" status typical of Polish memory and identity was thus conferred on Polish Jews. Noteworthy, too, were the Polish military orders (in the form of crosses, as in most of Europe) awarded posthumously to Polish Jews, for example, to Mordechai Anielewicz and other Warsaw Ghetto Uprising heroes, as well as to all victims of Auschwitz II-Birkenau.

**33**  No monument to those who had perished under the Soviet occupation was erected until after 1989.

**34**  The Soviet October Revolution—though not a holiday per se—was observed with shop displays, flags, and the like.

**35**  For example, about forty Home Army officers were tried and convicted in the early 1950s; half of these men were executed (Zblewski, *Leksykon PRLu*, 118–19). The Primate of Poland, Archbishop Cardinal Stefan Wyszyński, was himself imprisoned between 1953 and 1956.

**36**  Compare Zblewski *Leksykon PRLu*; Kuroń and Żakowski, *PRL dla początkujących*.

**37**  Legend recounts that in 1410, as the Polish King Jagiełło was waging war against them, the German Grand Master sent an emissary to the Polish camp, sardonically offering the monarch two swords with which to better equip his army. The offer was refused, the knights were beaten, and the Battle of Grunwald became an icon of victory over Germanic occupation.

**38**  Paralleling this, the hotter the Cold War got, the more the West taught similar lessons about the "Iron Curtain" countries.

**39**  Paszkowski, "Przedmowa do czwartego wydania," 6.

**40**  The uprising—now woven into the history of Polish rebellion and sacrifice—began on 1 August 1944 and lasted sixty-three days. At the end, human losses numbered 18,000 soldiers and over 150,000 civilians. (See Davies, *Rising '44*).

**41**  For various cultural and political reasons—unique to each group—only a handful of Ukrainian or Roma intellectuals have been involved and included in Polish Roman Catholic dialogues with minorities.

**42**  Prokop, *Universum polskie*, 53.

**43**  As of January 2005, of the 20,757 non-Jews who have received this award, 5,874 are Polish.

**44**  Cała, "Kształtowanie się polskiej i żydowskiej wizji martyrologicznej po II wojnie światowej," 176.

**45**  Ibid., 177.

**46**  Key here is that a member of that elite, the archbishop of Kraków, Cardinal Karol Wojtyła, was elected Pope John Paul II in October 1978; his first homeland pilgrimage came the following year. Most persons agree that Solidarity would not have happened without this psychological edge, which the "Polish Pope" lent his compatriots.

**47**  Although there can be no doubt that the 1968 generation, especially students at Warsaw University, was vital to the protests of that year, the fight to free Poland from Soviet shackles transcended and overrode age-group differences. However, the true significance of that generation is clear today when looking at the founders of *Gazeta Wyborcza*, as well as leading politicians, journalists, and social activists.

**48**  The tendency of the Communists to permit the making of documentaries but not their release dates to the beginning of the postwar period. Such works came to be called *półkowniki*, which derived not only from the Polish word *półka* (referring to the shelves where the films sat) but also from *pułkowniki* (literally, "colonels," refer-ring to the military regime of the 1980s). A 1946 film, for instance, was shown after the thaw in 1957, a 1977 film debuted in 1981, and martial-law films premiered between 1984 and 1989.

49  Żakowski, *Pół wieku pod włos*, 145.

50  Not only Father Popiełuszko but also, for instance, Solidarity activists such as Grażyna Kuroń, who was the wife of the recently deceased Jacek Kuroń and who became minister of labor in the first post-Communist government. The anniversary of her 1982 death is still annually memorialized.

51  Paszkowski, "Przedmowa do czwartego wydania," 5. In fact, about 10,000 Soviet soldiers were held as POWs at Auschwitz-Birkenau alone; nearly all perished there, including 850 on whom Zyklon B was tested, via primitive methods, as a means of mass execution.

52  Ibid., 6.

53  The Kraków-based *Tygodnik Powszechny* and *Znak* (a monthly magazine as well as general publishing house) were rather elite periodicals but, being among the rare non-Communist media, were very widely read. Today, though readership shares are likely down, both publications continue to facilitate sophisticated discussions of controversial issues beyond narrow circles of intelligentsia.

54  See Maciejewska, *Męczeństwo i zagłada Żydów w zapisach literatury polskiej*.

55  During and after martial-law period, the Roman Catholic Church in Poland was given unutilized state property in order to prevent new churches from being erected; one building adjacent to the Auschwitz-Birkenau Museum was assigned to the Carmelite order. Although there has been a Carmelite convent at Dachau since the 1960s, this one aroused a tempest of protest. For more detail see Bartoszewski, *The Convent at Auschwitz*; E. Klein, *The Battle of Auschwitz*; Webber, *The Future of Auschwitz*.

56  Much has been written on the discussions evoked by Błoński's essay. For a more scholarly overview see Polonsky, *My Brother's Keeper*.

57  One postwar stereotype about which the Poles learned—the phrase "Polish death camps," which implied such camps were not German—was expressed by such ·respected publications as the *New York Times* and the *Boston Globe*. In 2003 the Simon Wiesenthal Center was moved to print a retraction after doing likewise in a press release.

58  For analysis of the confrontations between how Polish society and Western societies perceive the role of Poland and Poles in the Shoah see Orla-Bukowska, "Representing the Shoah in Poland and Poland in the Shoah"; Orla-Bukowska, "Presenting and Representing the Shoah in the Post-Communist World"; Weinbaum, *The Struggle for Memory in Poland*.

59  Though 1956 in the Eastern bloc is associated with October in Hungary, and 1968 with June in Prague, unrest began with protests in Poland in the months of June and March respectively. Again, awareness that they had been the forerunners in all rebellions and ultimately triumphant in bringing down Communism strength-

ened the conviction among Poles that Poland had consistently been the resurrecting Christ-figure, as well as the boldest of heroes.

**60** This included such oddities as, for instance, ulica Bohaterów Stalingradu (Stalingrad Heroes Street), which existed in Kraków long after its Soviet reference had vanished from maps.

**61** A newly reconstituted Polish military faced the Red Army standing on the east side of the Vistula (the country's key north-south artery and the river of its poetry and music). Field Marshal Piłsudski astoundingly routed the Soviets, sending them in retreat toward Mińsk and, in Polish eyes, rescuing Europa from Communism.

**62** It was not until 2002 that Roman Polanski, himself a Polish Jewish Shoah survivor, presented his Oscar-winning *The Pianist*.

**63** The Instytut Pamięci Narodowej (Institute of National Memory)—the Polish equivalent of the Gauck Commission established in 2000 just months after Jan Gross's book was published—was forced to devote nearly all its first-year efforts to a Jedwabne white paper, rather than begin with cases which had never seen the light of a courtroom day, such as the Katyń Forest executions.

**64** Bajt, "Invisible Nationalism," 199.

**65** For more on the discussions see Borkowicz et al., *Thou Shalt Not Kill*; Polonsky, ed., *My Brother's Keeper*; Weinbaum, *The Struggle for Memory in Poland*; Orla-Bukowska, "Representing the Shoah in Poland and Poland in the Shoah"; and Machcewicz and Persak, *Wokół Jedwabnego*, the official, two-volume Instytut Pamięci Narodowej white paper.

**66** The monocultural policies of the socialist system were unsuccessful in erasing Poland's minorities. Although these minorities now constitute only about 5 percent of the population (as opposed to 33 percent in 1939), traditional ethnoreligious minorities such as the Tatar Muslims and Ukrainian Byzantine Catholics are joined by new ones such as Vietnamese or Armenian economic immigrants.

**67** While the long canonization process was brought to its conclusion under Pope John Paul II in 1998, it had actually been opened by German bishops in 1962. Each crisis provoked many articles, and even sometimes whole books, in various languages, illustrating various perspectives. Description and analysis of these are beyond the purview of this article.

**68** A low-level, rather nonviolent anti-Semitism—more politically incorrect talk than action—persists, but its nature has changed markedly since World War II (see Krzemiński, *Antysemitizm w Polsce i na Ukrainie*; Krzemiński, *Czy Polacy są antysemitami?*).

**69** For more on this phenomenon see Rokuszewska-Pawełek, "Pożoga wojenna," for Polish responses; Welzer, Moller, Tschuggnall, *Opa war kein Nazi*, for the German.

**70** See Rybicka, *Instytut Niemieckiej Pracy Wschodniej*. Some of the professors are still alive; several protested innocence, producing evidence of double agency: while working in the German institute, they continued, for example, to illegally teach underground university classes. Among other works see *Tygodnik Powszechny* issues from 8 June through 31 August of 2003.

71 Nora, "Czas pamięci," 37.

72 Marcin Król, "Pamięć i historia," 5.

73 Rokuszewska-Pawełek, "Pożoga wojenna," 63.

74 Davies, "O historii prawdziwej," 42.

75 Bajt, 199.

76 Łodziński, " 'Battles for Monuments and Memory,' " 208.

77 Błoński, "Biedni Polacy patrzą na getto," *Tygodnik Powszechny*, 11 January 1987.

78 Prokop, *Universum polskie*, 8.

79 The most obvious have been Polish-Jewish issues recurrently revisited since the beginning of the 1980s. In each case—whether instigated, for example, by Lanzmann's film, by Błoński's essay, or Gross's book—responses have been both strongly defensive and deeply reflective. The very recent debates on Rybicka's dissertation—this time connected with Polish-German wartime relations—ran likewise. As mentioned earlier, the Katyń and other Soviet-era issues remain relatively ignored, weighing heavily on Polish-Russian relations. However, each successive heated discussion has led to an increased readiness by more persons to undertake this reweaving task more fully and openly.

80 Christie, "Answers to Atrocities," 338.

81 The topic of "Pamięć i Historia" (Memory and History) to which two issues of *Res Publica Nowa* were devoted in 2001, was subsequently revisited in the form of an ongoing polemic in *Tygodnik Powszechny*. It began with "Niepamięć zbiorowa" (Collective non-memory) by Jan Tomasz Gross; several well-respected figures—historians, philosophers, politicians, journalists—participated (see *Tygodnik Powszechny*, issues from 8 August through 7 November 2004). The title of Konstanty Gebert's essay—published 10 October 2004 under his pseudonym, David Warszawski—exemplified what Sławomir Łodziński and others see as the core of Poland's memory and identity work: "Wojny pamięci" (Wars of memory).

REGULA LUDI ✣

# What Is So Special about Switzerland?

WARTIME MEMORY AS A NATIONAL IDEOLOGY

IN THE COLD WAR ERA

On 25 July 1940 Henri Guisan, the wartime commander of the Swiss army, held a meeting of several hundred high-ranking officers on the Rütli, a meadow in the mountainous area of central Switzerland. The general addressed the officer assembly as follows: "We are at a turning point of our history. What is at stake now is the very existence of Switzerland. At this place, we, the soldiers of 1940, shall be inspired by the lessons and the spirit of the past to face the present and the future of this country with resolution and to hear the mystic call originating from this meadow."[1] The speech had a lasting effect on the participants of the meeting, some of whom burst into tears on hearing Guisan's words. Its message was spread through similar appeals in the media. In people's recollections, this manifestation of resistance merged with the simultaneous announcement of a strategic decision controversial among Swiss military leaders: the plan to withdraw troops from the most densely populated areas of Switzerland and concentrate them in the Alps, a move that became known by its French term *Réduit national.*

The event of the Rütli gathering was diligently prepared; the location, deliberately chosen, was Switzerland's most prominent *lieu de mémoire*; and the moment, just weeks after the defeat of France, was one of the most critical in the country's wartime history.[2] Switzerland, at that point, was almost entirely encircled by the Axis powers. Witnessing the breathtaking and devastating victories of the Wehrmacht in Western Europe and the chaotic disintegration of the French defense in the spring and early summer of 1940 had left the Swiss public demoralized. Thousands fled from the border regions to the central parts of the country, fearing a German invasion. A portion of the Swiss establishment urged a rapprochement with Nazi Germany and, to mollify the Nazi leadership, insisted on political concessions, including drastic restrictions of the freedom of speech. Such demands seemed to resonate with a disoriented government. Following the armistice in France, Marcel Pilet-Golaz, the head of the Federal Council, appealed via radio for a return to normalcy, which by many was understood as a sign of the authorities' accommodation to the new circumstances.[3]

In this atmosphere of anxious confusion, the general's resolve was a convincing alternative to the political leadership's apparent wavering. In choosing the Rütli as the location for his proclamation, Guisan skillfully linked the present situation to popular Swiss mythology of freedom and independence. The risky decision to hold the meeting on an open field, where the top military leadership was an easy target for an enemy's air strike, reinforced the impression of the general's bravery. His forceful rhetoric of national resistance succeeded in uniting the public and placing the army in central opposition to Nazi Germany.

The Rütli gathering soon claimed a prominent position in popular representations of wartime history. In conjunction with the Réduit national, it became the symbol of national defiance and glory, the heart of all narratives explaining how the country survived World War II, unscathed, through the deterrent power of military defense. To some extent this was the outcome of the general's own memory politics.[4] Guisan was not only a true master of historical ceremony who in the most desperate situations evoked the past as a compelling metaphor for contemporary events; he was also a skillful architect of a wartime remembrance that celebrated military achievements in a nearly religious way and inflated his own merits as the savior of the nation.

For over four decades, these accounts, omnipresent in everyday life, dominated the interpretation of Switzerland's history during the Nazi era and played a vital role in fashioning Switzerland's political culture of the Cold War era. At once bundling men's diverging wartime experience and conveying deeper meaning of historical events, this memory construction helped produce a lasting consensus on the country's role and mission in the world.[5] Borrowing a phrase introduced by Pieter Lagrou, I deem such narratives "patriotic wartime memory."[6]

Reflecting a common European pattern, these narratives communicated an often simplified image of the past that typically obscured controversial aspects while emphasizing resistance at the cost of collaboration or adaptation. A canonical version of national martyrdom condensed the diverging histories of victimization and blurred the distinctions between different victim categories.[7] Patriotic memories denied domestic involvement in anti-Semitic policies as well as the fact that the Nazis could only carry out the expropriation and deportation of the Jews with the help of local bureaucracies.[8]

These narratives could prevail because remembrance was predominantly inspired by the needs of the immediate postwar period. A climate of revenge and conflicts between different memory camps made measures of domestic pacification necessary in most war-torn countries. This pacification favored images of the past that helped bridge the gaps and reintegrate compromised elites. In the years that followed, the Cold War froze distorted representations and transformed them into metaphors for the challenges of the present.[9]

Switzerland's memory construction was in line with these general patterns. Wartime remembrance produced its own myth of national resistance. It glorified the sacrifices of "veterans" and conveyed the impression that they had saved the nation.[10] It obscured instances of economic collaborations with and political concessions to the Nazis, and it transformed humanitarian failures into a narrative of achievements and generosity toward refugees. When accused of wartime accommodation, the authorities quickly turned the tables and came up with a version of national victimization not unlike the Austrian "victim myth" to minimize culpability and deny political responsibility.[11]

And yet, notwithstanding these common features, Swiss narratives constantly referred to a core element of self-definition inextricably linked to the wartime past: the *Sonderfall Schweiz*. This catchphrase captured the idea that Switzerland was a special case, incomparable to any European nation, because of its neutrality, its long tradition of democratic institutions, its lobbying for freedom and independence, its multilingual nature, its numerous constitutional peculiarities—an amalgamation of shared values and convictions that merged to form a "national identity."[12] Special-case rhetoric did not entirely lack a foundation. Switzerland in 1945 indeed was in a different situation than its European neighbors. It was spared the experience of Nazi occupation, its territorial integrity remained untouched, and it suffered neither a significant loss of civilians nor the destruction of its infrastructure and cities. But in the decades that followed, the trope mainly served to justify many national oddities: for example, the country's absence from international organizations, the subordination of human-rights guarantees to the sovereignty of the people, and the persistent disenfranchisement of female citizens, all of which were somehow linked to the identity-forming role of the wartime experience.

The omnipresence of wartime remembrance and the bizarre convergence of and striking similarities between the Swiss special-case rhetoric and memory constructions in belligerent and formerly occupied nations raise a number of questions as to the functions of collective memories in Switzerland. For what reasons did wartime remembrance become so vital in a country that was spared an involvement in the armed conflict? Why did wartime remembrance—institutional memories as well as individual recollections—exclusively focus on military aspects, while countermemories were largely absent in public discourse? Why and for which political purposes did wartime remembrance become the main source of national self-definition in the postwar era? And finally, was Swiss wartime behavior as distinctive as the aforementioned representations suggest, or does it instead have more features in common with other European countries than conventionally assumed?

Representations of the past generally depend on a frame of reference informed by present needs, concerns, and values. Over decades, political constellations furthered the forging of national myths that ex post facto turned whole populations into fervent antifascists. In recent years, however, major shifts in the comprehension and assessment of the Nazi era have occurred, as a global trend. As a result, the Holocaust has moved from the fringes of historical consciousness to become one of the most crucial and challenging subjects of research and public debate, an event deemed "a rupture in civilization."[13] Nowadays it is regarded as the event casting the longest shadow on Europe's recent history, a period replete with atrocities and state-committed crimes.[14] As a consequence, the Holocaust more and more frequently is being referred to as a universalized moral symbol whose memory fashions responses to current humanitarian crises.[15] The pivotal change in its meaning tends to stress common characteristics rather than distinctions among European nations and their history during the Nazi era.

The appearance, after the fall of Communism, of unresolved restitution issues has further popularized knowledge about the Nazi extermination policies while raising awareness of their moral and political implications. The scandals of the late 1990s over Holocaust-era assets have forced European governments and numerous multinational corporations to reexamine their Nazi-era past. A far more multifaceted version of recent history—one of interdependence, economic involvement, political accommodation, and instances of individual resistance—has since been uncovered. Such reassessment compelled states and economic agents to acknowledge responsibility for condoning the Nazi genocidal policy and failing its victims.[16] Thus, narratives of national resistance have become less and less reconcilable with this growing body of research.

In the course of the recent reparation scandal, Switzerland was the first state to be shamed and to face political consequences for its reluctance to take adequate action. But in contrast to other societies that in previous years had been confronted with international outrage over disclosures of their wartime past—Austria in response to the Waldheim affair, France with its contentious legacy of collaboration—Switzerland up to that point had successfully preserved the image of a country that survived the Nazi era politically and morally unscathed.[17] The discrepancy could not have been bigger in the mid-1990s between its officially endorsed image as the paragon of virtue—the cradle of the Red Cross and humanitarian law—and charges that painted the country as a Holocaust bystander ruthlessly profiteering from other people's misery. In the eyes of observers from abroad, the Swiss appeared totally oblivious of their wartime past.[18]

This has given rise to the mistaken impression that the Swiss have been silent about their history of the Nazi-era past. Official memory politics indeed suppressed unfavorable facts and thwarted the emergence of debates, and this furthered biased narratives. Yet given the prevalence of wartime remembrance and national self-reflection, disclosures of previously unknown facts regularly caused domestic irritation and stirred up opposing views.

Still, as long as the framework of collective memories remained unchallenged by external events, none of these incidents led to dramatic questioning of received images of the past. This only happened with the collapse of the bipolar world order. When the scandal over Holocaust-era assets escalated, Switzerland found itself in the middle of a soul-searching process often deemed an "identity crisis" by the media and epitomized, in a tongue-in-cheek manner, by the slogan "La Suiza non existe," which headed the country's self-presentation at the Sevilla World Fair of 1992. Confronting the past in the late 1990s thus sparked highly emotional debates and produced a juxtaposition of memory and history: the veteran generation claimed unmitigated access to the past while professional historiography, vested with unprecedented research privileges, shattered the remaining foundations of wartime myths.[19]

The heat of these debates revealed how deeply ingrained received representations were and testified to the function of wartime memory as a framework of the ongoing quest for a national identity. At the same time, however, the Swiss case and its successful resolution became the model for restitution claims raised against other European agents.[20] These events generalized the moral and political criticism initially aimed solely at Switzerland and eased the Swiss efforts at "normalizing" their wartime history.[21]

When looked at in terms of their political functions, wartime remembrance and special-case rhetoric were Switzerland's response to its particular situation in the Cold War era as a neutral, though determined anti-Communist, country. Therefore, I will concentrate on this period of postwar history when addressing the aforementioned questions. But to begin, I will embed Swiss memory constructions in a lineage of national heritage through which the wartime experience was framed. The heritage's emphasis on a martial past privileged the military aspects of the wartime experience and produced a particular relevance hierarchy to be inscribed on identity constructions.

The parts to follow focus on selected aspects of Swiss self-definitions and on the question of how they determined political choices: on the linkage between patriotic wartime memory and neutrality conceptions, on the "Helvetic malaise" as an early expression of discomfort with national stereotypes, and finally on the humanitarian myth that was by far the major obstacle to a reconceptualization of Switzerland's role as a Holocaust bystander.

### Inventing Continuity: National Heritage and the Wartime Experience

At the time of World War II, a mythical vision of the past played a vital role as a metaphor for the impending dangers of the present. The compelling message of its lieux de mémoire helped make sense of disturbing events and convey meaning in a daunting situation, as the Rütli gathering and its circumstances illustrated. Yet reverence for national heritage had a long tradition in Switzerland, and its symbols and legends—mostly of a martial past— were household icons often referred to in political discourse.[22]

The Rütli in particular captured various strains of common beliefs and convictions, but also diverging interpretations.[23] Deemed the cradle of the Swiss nation, it is said to be the place where in 1291 representatives of three Alpine communities founded the first federation in an act of resistance to feudal lords.[24] It stands, together with the William Tell saga, which originated in the same area, for independence, self-defense, and democratic rule. Similar values are expressed by medieval tales about peasant-warriors who triumphed over well-armed troops of knights, thwarted imperial ambitions of feudal lords, and preferred to fall in combat than live under foreign rule. This heritage—often the only bond uniting the members of the loose Swiss federation through centuries of internal strife and religious division—kept alive a memory of self-government to be revived by the Enlightenment's enthusiasm for freedom.[25]

In the nineteenth century Switzerland experienced intensified efforts at the "invention of tradition," deemed an "imagologic bricolage" by students of Swiss national identity. Its symbols were popularized by the era's mass media by means of compulsory education, the military, popular festivities, and folkloristic drama.[26] This cult of history served two vital needs of the fledgling nation-state. First, it promoted the integration of rural and conservative opponents to modern democracy by investing political innovations with the glory of a heroic past, as illustrated by a pilgrimage to the Rütli that was one of the first ceremonial acts to be performed by the authorities of the Helvetic republic. Ruling by Napoleon's grace after the breakdown of the old order in 1798, the new men in charge felt compelled to demonstrate continuity by embracing national heritage while redefining its lineage in accordance with the ideals of the French revolution.[27] In addition, Friedrich Schiller's stylish interpretation of the William Tell saga, first performed as a drama in 1804, provided the Swiss liberals with a forceful countermemory to European monarchism, one of freedom and resistance to foreign rule.[28]

Second, reference to the past was Switzerland's response to thriving nationalism in neighboring states. With the doctrine of the *Willensnation Schweiz* (a nation created by the people's will), which was substantiated by a mythological past, the history cult compensated for the country's lack of a common language, ethnicity, or culture as foundations of a modern nationhood.[29] Invoking the past also justified political institutions when Switzerland, as one of the few states left with a liberal constitution after 1848, was regarded with suspicion by Europe's monarchic governments. Swiss authorities often invoked tradition to defend political decisions; they did so, for example, when facing allegations of furthering insurgence with an asylum policy that tolerated the political activity of exiled revolutionaries from all over Europe.[30]

With the rise of Fascism, a revival of national heritage seemed an appropriate answer both to Italian and German jingoism that jeopardized domestic coherence and to authoritarian tendencies that questioned democratic institutions. Concerted efforts in the 1930s by Swiss intellectuals and the authorities coalesced in a national revival dubbed *Geistige Landesverteidigung* (spiritual national defense).[31] An amalgamation of liberal traditions and conservative ideology, it consisted of two main components: a canonization of the medieval past and an idealization of the Alps as the melting pot of European cultures. In blending history and nature, it centered on the Gotthard region—not only the area where the Rütli is located but traditionally a region of major strategic significance.

The Gotthard Pass and its railway tunnel is one of Europe's vital routes through the Alps. Therefore, it had been the subject of frequent conflicts since the first pass road had been built in the Middle Ages, some of which comprise the historically documented foundations of the Swiss founding myths. In emphasizing the forming influence of geography, however, the national revival of the 1930s also responded to race theories that denied the existence of a Swiss ethnicity and instead claimed that over time the mountains had formed a Swiss people that existed in its own right, regardless of obvious diversity in language and culture.[32]

Such manifestations of national unity had an ambiguous impact. On the one hand, they helped forge a broad antifascist coalition to defend democracy and liberal freedom rights. On the other hand, with its veneration of old customs, the national revival was suspicious of modernism and furthered a narrow idea of "Swiss identity" unreceptive to any external influence. The medieval lieux de mémoire thus represented a nostalgic counter-image to the highly industrialized class-society of Switzerland, one of self-sufficient peasants and pastorals who revered tradition and proximity to nature. This was expressed most explicitly by the norms and ideas of the gender regime projected onto the old legends. They propagated a strict sexual division that denied the facts of women's integration in the labor market and participation in public life.[33]

The first to suffer from Switzerland's increasingly self-centered vision were the growing number of refugees who sought asylum after Hitler's rise to power. They met hostility resulting from a xenophobic discourse emerging in response to the country's transformation into an immigrant society by the turn of the century. This discourse was a byproduct of intensified efforts at identity construction in the interwar era.[34]

In sum, the lieu de mémoire General Guisan chose for his Rütli gathering enshrined various traditions with often contradictory connotations. Yet the national revival of the 1930s ascribed a socially conservative meaning to national heritage. This became the lens through which the experience of World War II was being framed. The Rütli gathering and similar invocations of history paralleled wartime events with a martial past that allowed the soldiers to identify with its larger-than-life heroes. It helped construct a notion of continuity that absorbed the threat of Nazism and embedded the outcome of World War II in a line of successful armed resistances to tyranny and foreign rule. Thus, Nazi Germany just seemed the most recent, though the most existential, in a long series of national ordeals. This perception resulted in a collective memory of peril and redemption, an interpretation that seemingly confirmed Switzerland's vigor and military prowess and transformed the survival of World War II into a reward for special merits and achievements, if not an act of heavenly providence.

Inventing Perpetuity:
Wartime Memory and Everlasting Neutrality

Notwithstanding the feeling of relief and gratitude expressed by many Swiss immediately after the war, there was something startling to them about the fact of being spared a Nazi occupation. "Why did the Germans spare us, since they attacked nearly every other European country?" was the question that absorbed public attention and guided historians' research in the decades to come. And with the aforementioned framing of the wartime experience, the answer seemed obvious: national survival was owed to the Swiss determination to defend freedom and independence at any cost. Only a handful of dissenters dared express what appeared more plausible, given the obvious imbalance of power and German military supremacy: that a neutral and well-functioning Switzerland might have been of better use to the Nazis than a conquered territory with a demolished infrastructure and that only the Allied liberation of Europe prevented Switzerland from eventually becoming incorporated into the Third Reich.[35]

But neutrality, increasingly identified with a defiance of Nazi impositions that was apparently tested by the outcome of World War II, emerged as Switzerland's political religion of the postwar era. It became a "national myth with nearly religious sanctification," as one historian put it in 1943, and furthermore a political virtue deemed everlasting and hence dehistoricized and surrounded by many taboos.[36] Such idealization filled an initially void concept with moral values quite contrary to its actual history, or at least difficult to substantiate by hard evidence. Moreover, patriotic images of the past and neutrality were but two mutually reinforcing strains of one discourse that basically fulfilled two primary purposes: the defense of wartime behavior and the construction of constraints that made political choices of the Cold War era appear necessary and compelling.

In reality, neutrality has long been a guideline of Switzerland's foreign policy, but rarely a strictly observed norm. As a binding principle of international law it was imposed in 1815 on the Swiss confederation by the Vienna

Congress. The big powers then conceived it as a precondition of the country's sovereignty, primarily to keep adversarial camps in Switzerland from meddling in external affairs and endangering international stability by provoking foreign interventions. In a legal sense, neutrality merely implied Switzerland's absence from supranational defense alliances and banned Swiss political interference in foreign affairs.[37] The Hague Conventions of 1907 codified these older customary-law principles and spelled out the rights and duties of neutrals and belligerents in armed conflicts. But imperial Germany's disrespect in 1914 of Belgian neutrality was the first sign of the disintegration of international law's classical doctrine. Neutrality eventually lost its justification with the appearance of a collective security system.

In the nineteenth and early twentieth centuries, the Swiss had fared well with their foreign policy. Given the fragile and often changing power balance in Europe, neutrality protected Switzerland from being drawn into the conflicts caused by revolutionary wars, national unification movements, and the competition for global supremacy. At the same time, it allowed the Swiss to establish free-trade relations and vastly expand their export industry unhindered by any loyalties owed to allies. Treated as a flexible instrument, neutrality did not prevent the country from becoming a member of the League of Nations. Only when Hitler and Mussolini's flagrant defiance of international law exposed the weakness of the collective security system did Switzerland consider it advisable to retreat to a narrow definition of neutrality. In reality, however, this step pleased the German and Italian governments and eased relations with the country's immediate neighbors. Based on the grounds of neutrality, the Swiss government refused to observe sanctions against Italy after its attack on Ethiopia, and it was one of the first states to recognize the Nazi annexation of Austria.[38]

After the beginning of World War II, Switzerland upheld trade relations with all belligerents, including the export of weapons and technical devices used for warfare production.[39] Though neutral in a literal sense, business activity after the fall of France almost exclusively favored the Axis powers, who by then controlled commercial activity across the Swiss borders. To secure the country's supply of coal, steel, and food, the Swiss government in several trade agreements fulfilled a number of the Nazis' economic demands, including the unhindered use of the Swiss railway system and substantial export credits (paying for German purchases of war-relevant products from Switzerland) that added up to more than one billion Swiss francs by the end of the war.[40] The terms of this agreement were negotiated while preparations for the Réduit were in full swing and on the home front a rhetoric of national resistance to Nazi Germany prevailed. Their basic results, though confidential, were an open secret in Switzerland, as expressed by the popular saying "Six days of the week we work for Germany, and on Sunday we pray for the Allied victory."[41]

The authorities' primary motivation to make such concessions was their determination to guarantee social peace. They feared a repetition of the World War I experience, when unemployment and soaring prices caused domestic unrest and fueled revolutionary activities. Similar deliberations influenced strategic planning: military and business leaders held that political stability and a smoothly working Swiss economy would convince the Nazi regime of the advantages an unoccupied Switzerland offered. Therefore, two-thirds of the troops were demobilized after the armistice in France. This decision was part of the Réduit plan, which not only meant the fortification of the Alps but also carried the implication of leaving densely populated and industrial areas exposed to an attack—a controversial decision that provoked dissenting officers to mock the idea of defending glaciers and uninhabitable mountains instead of protecting the civilian population.[42] Yet the Réduit capitalized on the idealization of the Gotthard region and therefore easily merged with a popular cult of resistance.

So, economic—and, to a larger extent, financial—services rendered to Germany were part of Swiss efforts to demonstrate to the Nazis the usefulness of their neutrality. In particular, the gold transactions carried out by the Swiss National Bank during most of the war enabled the Nazi regime to make use of looted property, both monetary reserves as well as victims' assets. It gave them access to the freely convertible Swiss currency they needed to purchase important raw materials from other neutrals that refused to accept German gold due to its dubious origins.[43] As part of a larger national-security strategy, Swiss business activity, therefore, cannot easily be dismissed as an explanation of the country's survival, although documentary evidence for the role it played in German strategic planning is sparse.[44]

In terms of neutrality law, many Swiss financial and economic decisions meant sailing close to the wind.[45] The export credits to Nazi Germany, the warfare supplies, and the gold transactions in particular flouted moral principles associated with a neutral stance; legally, they were difficult to substantiate. By the end of the war, neutrality policy thus represented a diplomatic calamity for the Swiss authorities, above all because they had failed to pay attention to Allied warnings of Nazi looting first issued in December of 1942 and repeated on several occasions after this date, and refused to cut economic ties to Nazi Germany even when the latter no longer represented an immediate military threat.[46] As a result, Stalin scorned Switzerland for its "pro-fascist" wartime behavior and snubbed the Swiss request to reestablish diplomatic relations that had been broken off after the October Revolution.[47] The United States and Great Britain, in turn, declined to lift the embargo against Swiss corporations that were engaged in business with Nazi Germany and suspected of obstructing safe-haven measures. The Western Allies also required as a condition for normalization of diplomatic relations that the Swiss government participate in reparation programs and return a portion of the Nazi gold, claims that implied the idea of a shared Swiss responsibility fiercely refuted by the Swiss authorities.[48]

These controversies exposed clashing conceptions of neutrality and opposing interpretations of its meaning during World War II. For the victorious powers, wartime neutrality policy at the very least represented a flagrant misperception of what had been at stake: the rescue of Western civilization through Germany's unconditional surrender. In the worst case, it stood for a barely veiled accommodation of the Nazis and for war profiteering. The neutrals' reluctance to comply with the goal of bringing the Nazi war economy to its knees was a motive for the Allies to accuse neutral countries of prolonging the war.[49] In Switzerland, on the other hand, such criticism entrenched sentiments of national defiance, reviving the wartime discourse of resistance. When confronted with Allied restitution claims, the top diplomat Walter Stucki compared U.S. pressure with Hitler's disrespect for small states.[50] This remark expressed the prevailing understanding of Switzerland's role in World War II and its aftermath: of a country constantly bullied by the big powers that only survived because of its determination to remain independent at any cost. So, criticism of neutrality, which by the Swiss was considered a legitimate instrument to secure national survival, met a knee-jerk reaction aimed at fending off presumed victimization.

Apart from that, such responses reflected some deeply ingrained assumptions that were a lasting legacy of the wartime control of public opinion.[51] At the time of the war, the Swiss federal authorities suppressed the dissemination of knowledge on trade relations, financial services, export of war material, and other key issues likely to cause controversy. Their silence on the most disturbing events deepened the general confusion about the reliability of information and furthered distorted perceptions. On the pretext that it was unreliable hearsay and could easily lead to questions about Switzerland's neutrality in the eyes of the belligerents, army censorship banned the publication of information on the Holocaust. On the same grounds, the federal government systematically obstructed protests against Nazi mass crimes.[52]

Standing for national security, neutrality thus became a forceful argument to silence political opposition and prevent an open debate.[53] This was an excruciating experience for critics of Swiss wartime policy who warned of the morally corrupting impact of neutrality, in particular when conceived as a "neutrality of conviction" that was binding for all individual citizens. The theologian Karl Barth, for instance, anticipated a decay in democratic culture to be a lasting legacy of wartime policy, one that risked eroding respect for human dignity and advanced indifference toward the rest of the world.[54]

By the end of the Second World War, a portion of the public actually was willing to abandon a strict and narrow interpretation of neutrality, as an opinion poll carried out in the spring of 1946 showed, and some insisted that their survival of the war engendered obligations toward the international community and the victims of the conflagration.[55] Up until 1946—albeit while moving toward the neutrality-cult stance—the authorities did not entirely dismiss Swiss participation in the evolving collective security system. Vested interests, however, raised strong opposition to United Nations (UN) membership because they feared international obligations would impose restrictions on the Swiss business community and thus diminish obvious national advantages, for instance, with regard to banking legislation.[56] The country's diplomatic difficulties in the immediate postwar years made it easier for the vested interests to find public approval as foreign criticism boosted resistance to international demands. The swift disintegration of the war coalition and the rapid deterioration of East-West relations seemingly confirmed this vision.[57]

With the beginning of the Cold War, Swiss policymakers drew a simple lesson from the wartime experience: history apparently proved that the "Alpine dwarf could resist the northern giant," which suggested that Switzerland was not doomed as long as it was willing to endorse "armed neutrality" and defend its independence.[58] Therefore, the construction of patriotic wartime memories underlined political choices that were not consensual or obvious from the very beginning, in particular the absence of international cooperation. At the same time, neutrality permitted Switzerland to maintain the fiction of impartiality, although undeniably adhering to the West (and even making secret concessions to NATO with respect to the ban on technology exports to Communist countries).[59] The Swiss public widely endorsed this foreign policy. Its approval of a strict neutrality, implying nonparticipation in most international organizations, remained high for the entire Cold War era.[60] Tentative attempts in the late 1970s and 1980s by the authorities to revise foreign policy principles thus failed to find public support; almost 75 percent of the voters declined UN membership in a 1986 referendum.

According to the Swiss doctrine, armed neutrality, with its emphasis on an independent defense policy, implied a constant military preparedness. By the end of the Cold War, Switzerland surpassed all Western European nations in terms of weapons, mobilized soldiers, and per capita expenditures for civil defense.[61] But such sacrifices were hardly justifiable without the existence of tangible threats or a concept of the enemy at hand. Given the strong anti-Bolshevist tradition in Switzerland and a simplified understanding of totalitarianism that identified Nazism with Communism, the real threat of Nazi Germany was easily replaced by the imagined one of Soviet Russia. The prevalence of resistance memories provided a compelling analogy for this shift and sustained a climate of national alert that prolonged the illusion of being under attack.[62] The historian and political analyst Jean-Rodolphe von Salis, who had become famous for his weekly radio comments on international events during World War II, exposed this phantasm with a sardonic remark in 1961, stating that Switzerland seemed to be in the midst of an armed conflict with the Soviet Union, gauged by the martial language prevailing in the media.[63]

"The saying 'Switzerland does not have an army, but it is an army' describes a reality that frequently draws admiration abroad," a government report proudly declared as late as 1988.[64] Epitomized by a fortress mentality, the conflation of military and civic life was the result of blending wartime memory with anti-Communism—carried to the extremes by the identification of the army and the nation. Its institutional foundations lay with a definition of citizenship that linked democratic rights to military service. Universal conscription, the militia system, and the regular military training of virtually all men allowed male citizens to hold business and professional leadership positions while accomplishing political and officer careers, thus creating a civic militarism. The popular, though increasingly ritualized, habit of commemorating the wartime past was the symbolic expression of this civic militarism. Remembrance came to life whenever soldiers of the same unit met, privately or during their military service, often under the auspices of General Guisan's portrait, which could be found in many pubs.

A Swiss author of the 1960s testified to the omnipresence of living memory in civil life, in particular its military aspects, and also pointed at its mechanisms of integration and exclusion: "Women of all walks of society complain that whenever friends meet there is a risk that men start debating military issues and exchange recollections of their service in the army. Once such a conversation gets going, there is no way to stop it."[65] Sharing recollections united the age groups that had served during the war—virtually all male citizens born before the mid-1920s—but also integrated younger men who frequently represented the audience of such conversations. The result of this everyday practice was an idealized vision of the past, one that glossed over existing social and cultural differences among the soldiers. It helped bridge class antagonism and eased the political integration of the socialists, creating a stable party coalition that included virtually all political forces (and absorbed opposition for most of the Cold War era).[66]

Given its integrating and identity-forming nature, the military experience of World War II came to represent for all walks of (male) society a period of individual and collective accomplishments. This forged a political community among men based on the assertion of saving the nation in its most urgent ordeal and resulted in an interpretation of the wartime era that disqualified women's (and other civilians') experiences as irrelevant to the polity's existence. The veterans' monopolizing of wartime remembrance, furthermore, invigorated the prevailing rhetoric of separate spheres. It reinforced sexual division, particularly in the 1950s and early 1960s, as the determining principle of the postwar gender regime, a strictly hierarchical arrangement that became the major obstacle to women's enfranchisement (which was only achieved in 1971).[67]

The impression of continuous external threats was what held together the oxymoronic fusion of neutrality and anti-Communism. The Red Scare conveyed a sense of national alert, fuelled by a paranoid obsession with psychological warfare and Soviet subversion and often sponsored by former members of secret wartime-resistance organizations.[68] Anti-Communist activities since the late 1950s revived the "spiritual national defence" activity of the 1930s, which became the flagship of private and public intelligence services that collected data on suspected "state enemies" and "moles of the Soviet Union." A shocked public eventually learned after the fall of the Berlin Wall that almost every sixth resident in Swiss territory, citizens as well as aliens, had been subject to secret surveillance during the Cold War era, and that numerous surveillance practices were similar to those applied by Stasi agents in East Germany. Most of those observed turned out to be harmless citizens with dissenting political opinions, ranging from Christian pacifists, environmentalists, and feminists to the moderate and radical left.[69]

One explanation for the paradox of why precisely in Switzerland patriotic wartime memory played such an important role, therefore, lies in its blending of neutrality and resistance—an amalgamation first promoted as the official response to Allied criticism of wartime behavior—that became the most important metaphor for the present. Wartime remembrance, embedded in a line of national heritage determining its deeper meaning and smoothing out the Nazi rupture in civilization, served as a new founding myth whose political lessons seemed to be confirmed by the East-West conflict. Far from being seen in Switzerland as an "imaginary war,"[70] the latter perpetuated the sentiments of alert existing at the time of World War II and maintained the need for national unity, thus forging a widespread consensus both justifying the suppression of political dissent and bolstering civic militarism. Many contemporaries thus experienced an unbroken continuity that began in the late 1930s and reached into the present—or, as a historian expressed it in 1957, Switzerland's history of World War II could not yet be written because this epoch was still going on.[71]

## The "Helvetic Malaise": Questioning National Stereotypes

The manifold functions patriotic memory fulfilled gave rise to canonized narratives that underlined its stereotypical nature and led to an ossification of the ideas it embodied. As early as the 1950s, this engendered uneasiness among intellectuals. Although a public debate only came to life periodically and with regard to isolated issues, writers repeatedly questioned the message of wartime memories. Until the 1970s, however, their objections rarely resonated with the larger public. Nonetheless, they birthed more widely shared feelings of discomfort—later to be deemed the "Helvetic malaise."[72]

Max Frisch was not the only writer to take on stereotyped self-perceptions, but he did it in a blunt language and a straightforward way that often invited harsh reactions. His novel *I'm Not Stiller*, first published in 1954, centers on the problem of ascribed and chosen identities. It is about the main figure's reluctance to accept his identity as the Swiss citizen Anatol Stiller. Pretending to be an alien allows Stiller to analyze Swiss culture from an uninvolved and distant viewpoint and to criticize Switzerland's dealing with the legacies of the recent past. In an argument with his attorney, a devout patriot, Stiller develops his own interpretation of wartime behavior. He tells the lawyer, " 'You were lucky, Herr Doktor, that Hitler threatened your sovereignty and hence your trade; that stopped you from developing towards Fascism yourselves. But surely you don't believe that the Swiss bourgeoisie, alone in the world, would show no tendency towards Fascism if it happened to be good for trade instead of harmful?' "[73]

This interpretation, obviously inspired by Marxist theories of Fascism, was blasphemy for most Swiss readers. The novel was badly received in Switzerland, and Frisch, though celebrated as a talented author, was increasingly marginalized as a politically aware citizen. Swiss critics deemed his reckoning immature, and some even accused him of sympathizing with Communism. It was only in later years that a younger generation, more critically engaged with recent history, came to appreciate Frisch's questioning of Swiss myths, in particular the revision in the 1970s of his own wartime recollections.[74] In a critical reflection on Switzerland's behavior and his own shared responsibility as a citizen and soldier, Frisch expressed skepticism about his own enthusiastic assessment of military resistance as a young man. He found that Swiss war preparations had been futile in the face of the Nazis' military supremacy. Also, he reminded his readers of fascist sympathies among conservative officers and a portion of the Swiss establishment, and destroyed the illusion that the military transcended class society. By many of his generation, this was seen as an open attack on the army's merits, and they found their own achievements demeaned.[75]

In the course of the 1960s and 1970s, it came into fashion among intellectuals to characterize Switzerland's conservative mentality by the term *geistiges Réduit* (mental redoubt), insinuating that their contemporaries failed to transcend the self-inflicted constrictions of the wartime era. These were the first symptoms of a generational conflict, though in the beginning it was mostly becoming manifest in a growing nervousness among the political establishment. Consumerism and the easing of international tensions in the aftermath of the Cuban missile crisis gradually undermined the implicitness of received values and choices. Saving, self-restraint, duties, and sacrifices for the sake of the nation—all virtues ascribed to patriotic wartime memory—were losing their justification. As a result, the national consensus blending wartime memory with the Red Scare and national isolationism was unraveling. Sexual liberation, growing unrest among the young, and women's complaints about their persisting political exclusion appeared in the eyes of the wartime generations as the signs of society's disintegration.[76] The paradoxes of the previous two decades resurfaced: the odd mélange of rapid economic growth, technological modernization, and mass consumption in conjunction with political conservatism and a retrospective cultural orientation.[77]

Still, traditional mechanisms of marginalizing protest continued to guarantee a relative conformity. The educational system handed the transfigured representations of the wartime era down to younger generations, while the military still proved to be very effective in reproducing and transmitting its memories in everyday practice.[78] Breaking taboos thus came at a high price, as the painful experience of Swiss writers associated with the 1968 generation illustrated. The most tragic example was Walter Matthias Diggelmann. He openly attacked a number of Swiss myths and stereotypes in his fiction. A novel with the telling title *Die Hinterlassenschaft* (The legacy) was his most controversial text. Partly a documentary account of real events, it parallels domestic anti-Semitism of the 1930s with an anti-Communist witch hunt of the 1950s. Its public reception was devastating: ugly defamations, some of which wrongly accused Diggelmann of joining the ss as a voluntary conscript (in reality, he had been imprisoned in Nazi Germany after fleeing to Italy from Switzerland in 1944 to avoid an arrest for a minor property offense), diverted attention away from the novel and its message.[79] Diggelmann died in 1979, mentally ruined and mostly forgotten as a writer.

### Resistance or Adaptation? Challenging Received Representations, Confirming the Dominant Framework

In the 1960s, events that revived international debates on the Nazi-era past and inspired a more sincere dealing with its political and juridical legacies— for instance, the Eichmann and Auschwitz trials—failed to have similar effects in Switzerland. The country's own vision of being politically disconnected from the rest of the world continued to shelter representations of the past from changes that happened elsewhere. While attempted national soul-searching met public hostility, official strategies in turn fostered ongoing myth production.

What motivated the authorities and the public to address selected issues of wartime history were mostly homegrown memory crises, albeit often triggered by the publication of foreign documents. The manner of their overcoming rarely advanced the reevaluation of the past, but instead contributed to the invigoration of received representations. The handling of disclosures on wartime-neutrality policy is a telling example of how official memory politics set the terms of interpretation, even for academic research, and influenced debates for decades to follow.

The prevalence of a resistance myth had produced a tendency to frame wartime history through the binary opposition of "adaptation or resistance" and interpret it from a purely national viewpoint that emphasized the significance of "armed neutrality."[80] This vision, however, seemed seriously challenged when in 1961 the existence of a secret agreement between the Swiss general Henri Guisan and French army leaders came to light. The documents, dating back to the early phase of World War II, included the French army leaders' pledge of assistance in the case of a German attack on Switzerland. This could be understood as a violation of neutrality law, one that entailed the risk of serious consequences: it could have served the Nazi leadership as a pretext for an invasion after the Wehrmacht confiscated the documents in 1940 together with other French military records.[81]

Its revelation created an embarrassing situation for the authorities. Once the basic facts were known, debates could no longer be suppressed. But official containment strategies successfully suspended a grappling with wartime history. The federal government commissioned the renowned historian Edgar Bonjour to investigate the history of neutrality and vested him with privileged access to classified documents. Public attention to the subject cooled down, which allowed the authorities to keep back the results. When finally released in 1970, Bonjour's voluminous account failed to initiate a reevaluation of neutrality, nor was it followed by a major debate, not least due to the author's conclusions. Apart from critical remarks on the treatment of refugees, Bonjour conformed to the adaptation-or-resistance paradigm and for the most part justified neutrality policy.[82]

Knowledge of economic and financial relations, albeit gradually more available, remained confined to an academic and intellectual milieu. The gap was nonetheless widening between official memory and popular remembrance on the one hand and critical research on the other. Younger historians increasingly stressed the ambiguous meaning of icons of wartime resistance, highlighting for instance that the Rütli meeting had coincided with the German-Swiss trade negotiations and various economic concessions or that the Réduit, accompanied by a partial demobilization, could also be seen as an act of compliance with the Nazis' "New Europe."[83] Research in the 1970s and 1980s also produced a long list of reasons considered more important to Switzerland's safety than its military defense: the substantial export credits granted to Nazi Germany; the wartime access to undamaged railway connections; the freely convertible Swiss currency and the gold transactions; an intact economy capable of producing warfare supplies; and, finally, numerous diplomatic and humanitarian services that benefited all belligerents. When looked at in this light, even the spirit of resistance seemed an element that eased accommodation for keeping up the morale and upholding social peace.[84]

In their effort to uncover the denied darker side of history, often within a framework informed by neo-Marxist theorizing, younger historians and writers in the 1970s and 1980s cast doubt on the allegedly tough stance of the establishment and revealed fascist sympathies that had existed among a portion of the Swiss elite. In emerging countermemories the left discovered their own heroes of underdog resistance.[85] Yet they also brought new myths into being and came forward with an idealized view of wartime resistance that left little room for ambiguity and paradox, and on a structural level, confirmed the persisting adaptation-or-resistance paradigm. Their criticism of neutrality policy even advanced the tendency to inoculate neutrality with positive connotations. This anchored the concept even deeper in political culture and produced a leftist neutrality cult of its own kind.[86]

Given the significance of wartime memory for national ideology, the iconoclastic impetus of these younger writers and scholars was primarily aimed at contemporary taboos. Their targets were the army and its role in Swiss society. Since the 1970s the rigid treatment of conscientious objectors and high defense spending have become the battlefield of disagreements over military issues. In the eyes of the establishment and many of the wartime generation this obvious link between the World War II historiography and political dissent overall tainted the new findings. The older generation scorned the young authors for "fouling their own nest," as the following example illustrates. In 1970 the periodical *Neutralität* (founded in 1963 by writers who critically engaged political culture, foreign policy, and wartime history) published an article by the young writer Christoph Geiser. The text questioned the army's capability to defend the country if attacked by Nazi Germany, deemed the Rütli gathering an act of capitulation, and suggested that the establishment would have smoothly complied with the aggressor's demands. It provoked an equally outraged and condescending response in the military press which deemed Geiser's claims "frivolous," a "prankster's trick," but also an insult to the "veterans of the active military service."[87]

The conflict over the military escalated when in the 1980s the radical left launched a petition to abolish the army through a constitutional amendment. Headed by the battle cry "to slaughter the holy cow," the pacifist proposal was aimed at—and perceived by most of the public as—the desecration of a national icon and therefore a primarily symbolic proposal. The controversies that followed revealed the deep alienation of different mentalities and attitudes, occasionally deemed a belated generational conflict, though it also triggered new criticism among members of the wartime generation.[88] In the eyes of many veterans, disdain for the military was a sign of disrespect for proven traditions and their own lifetime achievements. For the younger generation, in turn, the army and its cult of wartime resistance stood for an encrusted political culture located in an imagined past and no longer able to deal with present-day challenges.

The petitioners' intent to provoke debate largely succeeded because of the authorities' misapprehension and inept responses, which triggered a major memory crisis in 1989. On fairly short notice, the government prepared a commemoration on the occasion of the fiftieth anniversary of the beginning of World War II. It was to take place in September 1989, just weeks before the referendum on the army was scheduled. Officially it was to honor the war-time generation's achievements, though women were only integrated after women's protests. But its hidden purpose—to mobilize elderly and more conservative voters in favor of an impressive plebiscite for the army—was too obvious. So, instead of generating unity, it further polarized the public and cast doubt on official memory politics in general. Immediately, the leftist opposition raised the allegation that the establishment self-righteously glorified the past and took pride in events that represented a disaster for most of Europe.[89]

Eventually, the referendum failed. But given the importance of the military to civic life and citizenship conceptions, a surprising 35 percent of the voters approved the proposition and gave evidence of a widespread dissatisfaction with defense policy. For the government, the result was disastrous. It exposed both the failure of official memory politics and a loss of confidence in the ruling four-party coalition. The referendum's coincidence with the fall of the Berlin Wall further deepened the crisis. While international events unfolded at an unforeseen tempo, the framework of political orientation in Switzerland disintegrated within months, precipitated by scandals over disclosures of secret surveillance activities and cronyism among the establishment. The pace of domestic developments merely reflected the acceleration of time triggered by the collapse of the postwar world order.[90] With the sudden disappearance of the Communist threat, the country plunged into a crisis of political orientation that left neither the establishment nor the leftist opposition unaffected. Upcoming debates centered on the quest for a new national identity, with neutrality and its implicit assumptions becoming meaningless after the end of the East-West conflict and in the face of the accelerated European integration.[91]

In hindsight, the 1989 memory crisis appears to have marked the beginning of a paradigm shift in interpretations of the past. But its immediate outcome was a clash of diverging worldviews. One was embodied by recollections that were exposed as a nostalgic tribute to a perishing world and which relied on the fiction of an unbroken continuity that apparently began with World War II and lasted for half a century, until the demise of Communism. The other one was driven by an iconoclastic impetus aimed at overcoming Switzerland's conservative and increasingly blocked political culture; but it was similarly captivated by stereotyped perceptions and surprised by international events and so only gradually developed more concrete visions for the future.

So, the controversy of 1989 marked the first public confrontation with distorted representations of the past, but failed to produce new collective memories that more adequately fit the challenges of the present. In its self-centered reckoning with the past it once more confirmed the conventional framework of interpretation. The bill for this failure to acknowledge ongoing shifts in the assessment of the Nazi era past was eventually presented to Switzerland in the late 1990s.

### How to Conceive of the Role as a Holocaust Bystander?

On 27 November 1945 a New York City audience warmly received the release of *The Last Chance*. The picture on Swiss asylum policy—the fictional story of a group of refugees who crossed the snow-covered Alps after the German occupation of northern Italy to find asylum in Switzerland—was highly decorated and internationally approved, one of the most successful films in the history of Swiss movie production. Its director, Leopold Lindtberg, an Austrian who survived the war in Swiss exile, meant to draw a critical picture of the Swiss asylum policy. But contrary to his intentions and the authorities' concerns, public reception turned the film into a cornerstone of Switzerland's humanitarian myth. It advanced the illusion, domestically and internationally, that upholding the values of humanitarianism was the chief merit of Swiss neutrality policy and helped promote the impression that Switzerland had been particularly sympathetic to the victims' plight.[92]

Ironically, fifty years later the fiercest attacks as yet on the image of humanitarian Switzerland originated from the very place where this myth first found international resonance. In the mid-1990s Jewish organizations based in the United States resumed their claim to restitution for Holocaust victim assets in Swiss banks. Their demands dated back to the resolution of reparation issues through the Washington Accord of 1946. In this agreement with the Western Allies, Switzerland made the commitment to identify heirless assets of Holocaust victims and transfer the receipts to Jewish reconstruction organizations, an obligation the Swiss authorities subsequently failed to fulfill. The powerful Swiss Bankers Association thwarted all efforts to identify victims' accounts. The first federal legislation to deal with heirless assets, a bill of 1962, was a toothless instrument that left the banks many loopholes to evade their obligations. A lack of international awareness further helped convey to the Swiss the impression of closure, and thus the issue was settled in silence.[93]

In the 1990s, however, the circumstances dramatically changed. Globalization was producing a favorable climate for international business activity, and the booming U.S. economy attracted foreign investment. Swiss financial institutes, traditionally strongly engaged on the international market, desired to expand their overseas activity. At the same time, two major Swiss banks were preparing one of the world's largest mergers. This exposed the banking industry to political pressure of all sorts. To the victim organizations it represented a unique chance, and with the assistance of U.S. politicians and officials of the Clinton administration, representatives of Jewish organizations and attorneys who had filed class-action suits for Holocaust survivors launched a political and media campaign to obtain restitution. It resulted in 1998 in a settlement between the major Swiss banks and the victims' lawyers.

The campaign received broad international media coverage and was accompanied by intensive research, mostly in U.S. and British archives. These investigations unearthed many of the mostly forgotten charges from the immediate postwar era.[94] And for the first time, the role of Holocaust bystanders became an issue of international concern. It was at the heart of many accusations that targeted Switzerland and other neutrals in the course of the 1990s.

In Switzerland the restitution campaign—domestically dubbed the "dormant accounts scandal"—precipitated a political and diplomatic crisis. As in the immediate postwar years, Switzerland was internationally under fire. Unlike those years, however, national survival could no longer pass as a legitimate excuse for wartime mistakes and even less so for postwar omissions regarding restitution and heirless assets. The concerted attacks from abroad not only challenged popularly held beliefs about wartime behavior but also damaged the country's international image and had diplomatic ramifications. Suddenly, Switzerland's moral geography was totally confused, an aspect echoed by a federal councilor's public musing in 1996 over the question of whether Auschwitz was located in Switzerland, considering the gravity and bitterness of the foreign accusations.[95]

Popular reflexes and the authorities' initial responses revealed a complete misapprehension of what was at stake and a flagrant ignorance regarding shifts in the understanding of the Holocaust. In Switzerland the threat of Nazism was still predominantly viewed from a national perspective bequeathed by the debates of the 1980s.[96] But international allegations raised numerous issues of wartime behavior, exposing that national paradigm as entirely inadequate, ranging from financial transfers to business activities that had directly benefited from the "Aryanization" of Jewish property and the Nazi extermination policy. All testified to an intensive economic, financial, and political entanglement between Switzerland and Nazi Germany.[97] Suddenly, the national borders, long considered impermeable territorially as well as mentally—a *cordon sanitaire* that had shielded Switzerland from the encroachment of Nazism—were exposed as a chimera.

There had always been one important exception, though: to the thousands of refugees who were refused entrance, the borders had indeed been insurmountable. Thus none of the revelations caused as much irritation and anger as the charges of anti-Semitism in asylum policy, compliance with Nazi race theories, and inhumane treatment of refugees. More than anything else, they affected deeply felt convictions regarding Switzerland's special merits as the protector of the weak.

For nearly five decades, the Swiss had cultivated a belief in their humanitarian achievements and were convinced of the neutral's special mission as the guardian of humanitarian law. These assumptions impeded open confrontation of the treatment of Nazi victims before, during, and after World War II. They fed on individual recollections and deliberate memory politics as well. Official accounts of asylum policy, for instance, stressed that Switzerland had hosted 300,000 refugees at the time of the war. But they omitted that the majority were war fugitives who only stayed for a brief period of time or military internees whom Switzerland was legally obligated to accept according to the Hague Conventions. And above all, these representations almost systematically omitted that the official asylum policy had failed those who were most in need of being saved: the Jews.[98]

The transfiguration of humanitarian achievements largely stemmed from responses to Allied criticism in the last phase of the war. The Swiss authorities then revised asylum policy, though at a very late moment, and enhanced efforts to compensate for the deplorable record of the previous years. In July 1944, for instance, they opened the border to Jews, who before had not been considered "political refugees" entitled to enter the country and apply for asylum. Some months later, they agreed to accept convoys of concentration-camp survivors and encouraged private initiatives to support European reconstruction. The memory of these activities quickly superseded less-favorable facts: for instance, recollections of expulsions, of official anti-Semitism, or of abuses in refugee camps. And they successfully silenced criticism from abroad, as neighboring states were in deep need of immediate relief efforts and investments to help economic recovery.[99]

International priorities, in particular the beginning of the Cold War, soon reduced Allied pressure on Switzerland. Being shielded from external criticism that could fuel domestic questioning allowed the Swiss authorities to gloss over sensitive issues, which resulted in highly selective memories. In 1951, for instance, they considered the publication of an internal report on refugee policy unnecessary, if not detrimental, because it would have drawn attention to the subject even though it whitewashed wartime behavior. Since scandalous facts were withheld from public knowledge, almost every Swiss in turn had some positive recollections of helping refugees—either hosting children from war-torn countries or having encounters with military internees, who were often placed as cheap hands with farmers. These individual memories bolstered the creation of the humanitarian myth as the public ignored certain facts, namely, that Swiss authorities had excluded Jewish children from popular relief programs after the Nazis started rounding up Jews in occupied territories, and police officers had secretly issued restrictive orders despite their promise to accept more refugees in response to the protests that followed the closing of the border in August 1942.[100]

Similarly, official remembrance, in its attempt to conceal failures and lay an exclusive claim to humanitarian achievements, distorted the ideas of humanitarianism. It condemned to oblivion individuals who rescued Nazi victims and were punished because they broke regulations and disregarded orders to save lives. The officials and diplomats who issued visas without authorization, the helpers who smuggled refugees over the border, and all those who refused to comply with neutrality policy and openly condemned Nazi atrocities found the memory of their deeds either obliterated or denigrated. Many were ostracized long after the end of the war and faced disadvantages in their professional careers.

The most striking example is Paul Grüninger, the St. Gallen police commander who, according to estimates, rescued several hundred, if not more than a thousand, refugees. He let them enter the country when the borders were closed after the annexation of Austria in 1938, and he turned a blind eye to illegal border trafficking. In some cases he even falsified official documents to prevent refugees from being expelled. When his rescue activities were discovered, Grüninger lost his position and was indicted for abuse of official power. Unproved rumors charging him with corruption damaged his reputation, and he remained barred from public service for the rest of his life. Although he was internationally honored for his rescue activity, the local authorities repeatedly denied his rehabilitation; it happened only in 1995, long after he had died.[101]

Continuities in administrative personnel and legal practices explain such distortions and denials which are characteristic of postwar politics. The end of World War II was not seen as a turn of the tide in Switzerland. Thus the establishment did not undergo any major changes, let alone purges. Many condemnable practices, despite their similarity to Nazi race policies, were not considered human-rights violations and continued after 1945, for example, the removal of Gypsy children from their families and the forced sterilization of welfare clients and patients of mental institutions, both carried out until the early 1970s.[102]

Moreover, those responsible for refugee policy stayed in office well into the 1950s, going to great lengths to forestall accountability. The conservative Philipp Etter, on his resignation in 1959, had served for more than two decades as federal councilor and head of the Department of the Interior. In this function he had been one of the main architects of the national revival and adopted a cultural policy that capitalized on xenophobic anxieties. In the fall of 1942 he was the driving force behind the obstruction of a public appeal prepared by the International Committee of the Red Cross to condemn the Nazi genocidal policy. His colleague Eduard von Steiger, who deemed Switzerland an "overcrowded life boat" when closing the border for Jewish refugees in August of 1942, stayed in office until 1951. Heinrich Rothmund, the head of the federal police, retired in 1954. He was known for his obsessions with *Überfremdung* (inundation by foreigners) and with what he called an impending "Jewification of Switzerland."[103]

But official efforts to cover up humanitarian failures were successful only as long as the Swiss authorities had exclusive control over access to documentary evidence. This was no longer possible when in 1954 documents were published from the German foreign ministry of the 1930s that shed light on the introduction of the infamous "J" stamp. Until then the Swiss public held that its existence was another example of vicious Nazi anti-Semitism, a belief shattered by the newly uncovered evidence, which exposed the pathetic role Swiss diplomats had played in the process leading to the introduction of the "J" stamp. Worried about the increasing number of Jewish refugees from Austria, Swiss authorities in the summer of 1938 had urged the Nazi leadership to restrict Jewish emigration to Switzerland. This demand obviously contradicted the Nazi goal of rendering the Third Reich "judenfrei" by expelling all Jews living on German and formerly Austrian territory. Still, the bilateral negotiations that followed resulted in the German proposal to mark the passports of the Jews, though only after the Swiss had threatened to reintroduce the entry visa for all German citizens. This measure eventually allowed the Swiss government to discriminate against German Jews exclusively through the visa requirement issued in the fall of 1938.[104]

More than just revealing the entanglement of Swiss officials in anti-Semitic measures, the disclosures refuted the general conviction that Switzerland had been immune from racial anti-Semitism. It showed instead how little it had taken for the political leadership at that time to sacrifice the principle of equal treatment. Yet this shock was quickly contained. A scapegoat was easily found in the person of Heinrich Rothmund, notorious for his anti-Semitism and xenophobic attitudes, to whom the whole responsibility could be shunted.[105] Ironically, however, Rothmund had been one of the few to express reservations about the "J" stamp in 1938, fearing that the Nazis would insist on reciprocity, a measure that would hardly have been approved by most of the Swiss public. But singling him out as the sole culprit provided a ready excuse for many who were involved in anti-Semitic measures and bore responsibility as his superiors, the Federal Council and the revered general Guisan included.

Giving rise to rumors and suspicions of all sorts, the "J"-stamp affair nevertheless called for a sincere investigation. The federal government commissioned the legal scholar Carl Ludwig, himself a former magistrate, to examine refugee policy. Against all odds, his report turned out to be a diligently examined and sobering account. But it failed to stir a debate when published in 1957. Only a few speakers, during a parliamentary session of 1958, expressed feelings of guilt and shame or even acknowledged that Switzerland could have saved more lives without putting national independence at risk. Instead, most considered the past a closed chapter and justified the government's actions.[106] Only when Ludwig's findings were spread through popularly written books and films did a larger public slowly take notice that wartime asylum policy had not only saved lives but had also had fatal consequences for many Jewish refugees.[107]

But in the short run the "J"-stamp affair had little lasting impact. Its only immediate result was the authorities' growing nervousness about unresolved legacies of the Nazi era. Suddenly, the delayed resolution came to embody the risk of further scandals, and in the aftermath of the Ludwig report the federal government tackled a number of long-neglected issues, such as the heirless assets in Swiss banks and the compensation claims of Swiss victims of Nazi persecution. But legislation was aimed at a swift closure, and the federal government went to any length to prevent public grappling with the Nazi-era past and to evade the question of official accountability.[108]

With its strategy of covering up failures, commissioning investigations when facts could no longer be denied, and, in the face of looming scandals, rushing the resolution of issues that had been dragged out over years, the authorities successfully preserved Switzerland's humanitarian image, bene-fiting from the public's reluctance to give up dear beliefs. Yet stressing humanitarianism as a core national value both raised expectations and risked idealists feeling deceived once the discrepancy between myths and actual achievements was exposed. This finally happened when research in the wake of the Holocaust-era asset scandal uncovered the full extent of wartime failures in refugee policy.

The findings of the international historian commission, appointed in 1996 to examine the history of the Nazi-era past, shattered the remaining foundations of popular assumptions. Its reports on gold transactions and refugees in particular, published in 1998 and 1999 respectively, showed that all agents—officials as well as the business community—were well aware of the consequences of their actions and much better informed about Nazi atrocities than they had made believe. The commission thus arrived at the conclusion that the Swiss authorities, with their restrictive asylum policy that discriminated against Jewish refugees, had helped the Nazi regime achieve its genocidal goals.[109]

For the first time, Switzerland's role as a Holocaust bystander was officially framed through a paradigm based on the state's duty to protect human rights and dignity. Research has also shown that in the shadow of neutrality doctrine and the humanitarian myth a business-as-usual attitude prevailed during and after the Nazi era. This mentality desensitized both political and business leaders to the moral consequences of their entanglement with Nazi policies and in the postwar era similarly made many turn a blind eye on ongoing human-rights violations abroad. A striking example of such continuities was the Swiss engagement in South Africa. Swiss corporations refused to withdraw their investments, some even taking advantage of the new opportunities created by the international sanctions after the UN had issued economic sanctions against the apartheid regime. The authorities, furthermore, justified their reluctance to ban business activity in South Africa—and other countries with deplorable human-rights records—with an interpretation of neutrality that drew an artificial line between politics and business.[110]

The realization that legacies of the past reemerge—that they can haunt both states and private bodies and tend to come with a price tag attached—is a relatively new phenomenon in Switzerland's business community. In combination with globalization and increasing international interdependency, the Holocaust-era asset scandal has advanced the awareness of moral questions in business relations. It also has (temporarily) changed attitudes toward neutrality. In the late 1990s a growing portion of the public abandoned transfigured and morally inflated ideas of neutrality that were no longer considered intrinsic to Switzerland's national identity.[111] In a 2002 referendum a small majority of voters approved UN membership, eventually abolishing one of the remaining Swiss oddities.

But domestic responses to international criticism also entrenched nationalistic reflexes, particularly among the wartime generation. Defying international criticism and the new findings of historical research for many became an act of defending a national honor supposedly tainted by the recognition of wartime failures.[112] The frustration resulting from public soul-searching was easily exploited by the national-conservative right who fused their xenophobic platform with a revival of the Cold War neutrality doctrine in an aggressively nationalistic propaganda. In depicting Switzerland as a victim of the German aggressor, right-wing discourse interpreted the economic concessions (that could no longer be denied) as a shrewd policy to secure national independence. One of their prominent exponents, the historian and Cold War politician Walther Hofer, in 1997 declared that Switzerland was a "victim of trends in world history," referring both to the Nazi era and the ongoing international restitution campaign.[113] And the right drew the conclusion that keeping aloof from international participation was the only way for small states to preserve their sovereignty and identity.

The outcome of the recent memory crisis, therefore, is ambiguous. It removed a corset of ideological constraints and made room for new political options. But it has polarized the public and led to a juxtaposition of "memory"—the wartime generation's claim to have a direct access to the past—and "history," as an academic discipline, being increasingly accused of moralizing and producing biased assessments.[114] The destruction of dear beliefs, furthermore, alienated many citizens from the political establishment who has largely endorsed the new interpretations. Widespread frustration eventually benefited the national-conservative right, with the

Schweizerische Volkspartei (People's Party) becoming the strongest force on the federal level.

## Can Switzerland Remain on the "Balcony Over Europe"?

So, what is so special about Switzerland? Does it really differ from other nations in its dealing with the past? The answer is yes and no. In some respects, Switzerland has followed general trends. Its political grappling with Nazi legacies in the Cold War era was far from unique. Instead, it was in line with the prevailing trends among Western nations, which since the early 1950s have subordinated victims' claims and restitution issues to other political and financial priorities, as reflected by the London Debt Conference of 1953, when the governments of the West endorsed the postponement of further German reparation payments to a final peace treaty and thus deprived many Nazi victims of the opportunity to claim compensation.[115] Similarly, the reemergence of restitution issues after the fall of Communism represents a tidal change on an international scale: political transformation in Eastern Europe gave rise to property issues that often became catalysts in the process of confronting the past.[116] Not unlike many other European societies, Switzerland addressed Holocaust legacies only under international pressure resulting from these developments.

Moreover, new research drawing a morally and politically complex picture tends to nullify clear distinctions between the behavior of occupied and unoccupied countries. Given the emphasis on both structural interdependencies and the agents' room to maneuver, a clear-cut assessment of the past is ever more difficult. As a result, representations of the Nazi era reflect many paradoxes that deprive memory constructions of their metaphoric functions. The Nazi era and its legacies have thus become a thorn in the flesh of all European societies, with no closure in sight. Moreover, with the passing away of the wartime generations, issues are being depersonalized and generalized, at once promoting more abstract and subtler approaches. This suggests a paradoxical outcome of the recent grappling with history: on the one hand, concrete accounts that highlight the broad variety of behavior and actions; on the other, ever more universalized moral lessons as expressed by those drawn from Holocaust memory.

These common features notwithstanding, there are some obvious distinctions in the Swiss case. In no other country was patriotic wartime memory so pervasive, lasting, widely endorsed, and instilled with positive connotations as in Switzerland. Controversies that briefly flared up between 1944 and 1946 did not reemerge before the mid-1950s. The first postwar decade thus appears as an era of eloquent silence. Even in the years that followed, when controversial issues indeed resurfaced, their impact was easily contained and critical voices soon silenced. Patriotic wartime memory thus could evolve as the founding myth of modern Switzerland, alone in the fact that the country was spared an involvement in combat. This allowed the Swiss to take pride in presumed military achievements and remember the wartime era in a triumphant manner.

Two factors explain the distinctiveness of Swiss memory constructions, one being a structural continuity in representing the past, the other one referring to the functions of collective memory in the Cold War era. A cult of national heritage was crucial for modern Swiss identity constructions, given that Switzerland as a multilingual and multireligious country became an oddity in the age of nationalism. The bricolage of a mythical heritage compensated for these deficits. But national unity was never fully achieved before the Nazis' rise to power, as the World War I experience demonstrated. Cultural frictions—the French- and German-speaking populations each identified with opposed belligerents—and intensified class conflicts questioned national coherence between 1914 and 1918. World War II eventually became the event that bound the Swiss together in the face of the external threat. The framing of its experience through medieval legends facilitated this outcome; its conflation with national heritage allowed attention to be diverted from existing domestic conflicts and was a powerful bracket in the decades of the Cold War era that followed.

The second factor was the construction of a wartime memory that allowed the establishment to drive questionable wartime decisions under the carpet and to secure the considerable profits reaped from business with Nazi Germany. But more important, patriotic wartime memory also bolstered a political constellation that was extremely beneficial for a large portion of the Swiss society. Neutrality conceptions that allegedly hindered Switzerland from participating in international organizations and complying with their norms actually created foreign-investment opportunities that contributed to postwar prosperity. To the larger public neutrality conveyed the inaccurate impression of self-sufficiency. It veiled the extent of international interdependency and its controversial consequences, and thus immunized the corporate world from public scrutiny, with lasting legacies. As of today, conventional wisdom holds that export industry and foreign investment are rather insignificant for the Swiss economy, although the country ranks among the most globalized economies.[117]

The lessons drawn from patriotic wartime memory, finally, ensured the dominance of military values, fostering mechanisms of male bonding and resulting in a close-knit establishment with a strong leaning toward cronyism. This helped preserve a backward-oriented gender regime by impeding access to institutional power for women.

So, choosing the seat on "the balcony over Europe" as supposedly uninvolved spectators of world history was indeed profitable for many Swiss.[118] But as the European house continues to grow, Switzerland is losing its sunny spot. Economically and politically, this has become manifest in a lingering economic, political, and identity crisis that has lasted since the early 1990s. The rapidly changing global environment requires new references of orientation and a redefinition of national values, which entails a process of reassessing the past. This process started to unfold in the late 1980s. But of late, as the forces trying to roll back the clock have picked up steam, Swiss society seems to be stuck halfway.

## Notes

1   For accounts of the speech (of which no official transcripts exist) see Gautschi, *General Henri Guisan*, 273 (my translation, from the German). On its reception see ibid., 281–93; Bonjour, *Geschichte der schweizerischen Neutralität*, 4:155–68.

2   For the concept of "lieux de mémoire," see Nora, "Between Memory and History," 7–25.

3   Jost, *Politik und Wirtschaft im Krieg*, 63–98; Wylie, "Pilet-Golaz and the Making of Swiss Foreign Policy," 158–70; Bucher, *Zwischen Bundesrat und General*, 509–98.

4   Van Dongen, *La Suisse face à la Seconde Guerre mondiale 1945–1948*.

5   Research on collective memory in Switzerland is fragmentary and mostly focused on institutional memory. For general reflections, see Picard, "Eine Politik der Erinnerung"; Tanner, "Die Krise der Gedächtnisorte und die Havarie der Erinnerungspolitik."

6   Lagrou, *The Legacy of Nazi Occupation*.

7   A. Wieviorka, *Déportation et génocide*; Lagrou, "The Victims of Genocide and National Memory."

8   Only recent research has stressed the involvement of local bureaucracies and the greater public in anti-Semitic measures, in particular the expropriation of the Jews. See the exemplary study by Frank Bajohr, *"Aryanisation" in Hamburg*. For a survey of recent research in various European countries, see Goschler and Ther, *Raub und Restitution*, 225–37.

9   See the contributions in Deák et al., *The Politics of Retribution in Europe*; J.-W. Müller, *Memory and Power in Post-War Europe*.

10   I use the term *veteran*, although incorrect, as a surrogate for the untranslat-

able German *Aktivdienstgeneration* and French *génération de la Mob*, both referring to the military's mobilization of 1939 to 1945. *Veteran*, however, comes closest to the wartime generation's self-perception and the stereotyped use of the aforementioned terms in Swiss discourse.

11 See Independent Commission of Experts Switzerland–Second World War, *Switzerland, National Socialism and the Second World War*, 423–92.

12 The concept of "national identity" has become central to conservative and right-wing discourse. Because of this political connotation that tends to deny cultural and social diversity, its use as an analytical category is problematic. (See Niethammer, *Kollektive Identität*.) In Switzerland, the construction of collective identities is mostly characterized by cross-cutting loyalties based on a shifting endorsement of regional, confessional, lingual, and political interests (see Steinberg, *Why Switzerland?*). On the construction of national identities, see Marchal and Mattioli, *Erfundene Schweiz*; Kreis, *Die Schweiz unterwegs*.

13 See Diner, *Zivilisationsbruch*; Friedländer, *Memory, History, and the Extermination of the Jews in Europe*; Marrus, "Reflections on the Historiography of the Holocaust"; G. Koch, *Bruchlinien*.

14 Mazower, *Dark Continent*; Torpey, " 'Making Whole What Has Been Smashed.' "

15 Alexander, "On the Social Construction of Moral Universals"; Levy and Sznaider, *Erinnerung im globalen Zeitalter*.

16 Barkan, *The Guilt of Nations*; Bazyler, *Holocaust Justice*.

17 On France and Austria, see the chapters in this volume by Richard J. Golsan and Heidemarie Uhl.

18 See Rickman, *Swiss Banks and Jewish Souls*.

19 In 1996 the Swiss government installed an international historian commission, Independent Commission of Experts Switzerland–Second World War (ICE), which was also called the "Bergier Commission" after its president, the Swiss medievalist Jean-François Bergier. The purpose of the commission was to investigate political, financial, and economic relations between Switzerland and Nazi Germany, humanitarian issues, and postwar restitution policies. It was granted privileged access to archives, including private corporations (i.e., the bank secrecy was lifted for this special investigation). The ICE published several intermediary and final reports (in four languages and accessible on the Internet) and twenty-five volumes on specialized subjects. See ICE, *Final Report* and http://www.uek.ch.

20 See Authers and Wolffe, *The Victim's Fortune*; Eizenstat, *Imperfect Justice*.

21 In the Swiss context normalizing the past signifies the demise of special-case rhetoric and thus has an entirely different meaning than it did in the German Historikerstreit, where it stood for the apologetic attempt to banalize the Holocaust (see Augstein et al., "*Historikerstreit*"; Diner, *Ist der Nationalsozialismus Geschichte?*).

22 Hettling, "Geschichtlichkeit."

23 As a national icon, the Rütli of today is increasingly claimed by the radical

right. But in the nineteenth century its legacy also stood for liberal ideas, as was evident in the name of the first socialist association: "Grütli-Verein."

24 The founding year of 1291 was canonized in the late nineteenth century. Hettling, "Geschichtlichkeit," 123–24; D. Frei, *Die Förderung des schweizerischen Nationalbewusstseins nach dem Zusammenbruch der Alten Eidgenossenschaft 1798.*

25 Marchal, "Die 'Alten Eidgenossen' im Wandel der Zeiten"; Im Hof, *Mythos Schweiz*; Weishaupt, *Bauern, Hirten und "frume edle puren."*

26 Marchal and Mattioli, *Erfundene Schweiz*; Bendix, "National Sentiment in the Enactment and Discourse of Swiss Political Ritual"; Hettling, "Das Fähnlein der Treffsicheren." See also Hobsbawm and Ranger, *The Invention of Tradition.*

27 Böning, Der Traum von Freiheit und Gleichheit, 207–13.

28 Bergier, *Guillaume Tell*. It is telling that Bergier (who became the president of the ICE in 1996) dedicated his research on the Tell myth, first published in 1988, to the people of Poland and Afghanistan, universalizing the independence message of the Tell saga.

29 On the construction of national identities, see Anderson, *Imagined Communities*; Smith, *National Identity.*

30 "Asyl in der Schweiz nach den Revolutionen von 1848."

31 Mooser, "'Spiritual National Defence' in the 1930s"; Zimmer, "'A Unique Fusion of the Natural and the Man-made.'"

32 Kreis, "'Der 'homo alpinus helveticus.'"

33 See the contributions in Dejung and Stämpfli, *Armee, Staat und Geschlecht.*

34 Gast, *Von der Kontrolle zur Abwehr*; Mächler, "Kampf gegen das Chaos."

35 See, for instance, Barth, *Eine Schweizer Stimme 1938–1945.*

36 Bonjour, *Die schweizerische Neutralität*, 5. For a critical account of neutrality doctrine, see Gabriel, *Sackgasse Neutralität*; on its metaphorical use, see Picard, "Switzerland as a 'Bystander' of History."

37 Suter, "Neutralität."

38 Jost, *Politik und Wirtschaft im Krieg*, 31–37.

39 Hug, *Schweizer Rüstungsindustrie und Kriegsmaterialhandel zur Zeit des Nationalsozialismus.*

40 Bourgeois, *Le Troisième Reich et la Suisse, 1933–1941*; Bourgeois, *Business helvétique et Troisième Reich*; Meier et al., *Schweizerische Aussenwirtschaftspolitik 1930–1948.*

41 On information available at the time of the war, see Imhof et al., *Die Flüchtlings- und Aussenwirtschaftspolitik der Schweiz im Kontext der öffentlichen politischen Kommunikation 1938–1950.*

42 On the Réduit preparations and the criticism of dissenting officers, see Gautschi, *General Henri Guisan*, 304–28. On the economic rationale, see Tanner, *Bundeshaushalt, Währung und Kriegswirtschaft*; Tanner, "'Réduit national' und Aussenwirtschaft"; Independent Commission of Experts Switzerland–Second World War, *Final Report*, 82–84.

43  Independent Commission of Experts Switzerland–Second World War, *Switzerland and Gold Transactions in the Second World War.*

44  The question of what reasons kept Hitler from invading Switzerland caused controversies between opposing camps of historians, one insisting on the predominance of military reasons, the other one stressing the importance of economic and financial arguments. Recent research has contributed to a more differentiated and balanced interpretation that integrates both points of view (see Urner, *"Let's Swallow Switzerland"*). For a general assessment, see Independent Commission of Experts Switzerland–Second World War, *Final Report,* 86–88.

45  Urner, "Die schweizerische Aussenhandelspolitik 1939–1945"; Schindler, "Fragen des Neutralitätsrechts im Zweiten Weltkrieg."

46  For an account of Allied criticism, see U.S. Department of State, *U.S. and Allied Efforts to Recover and Restore Gold and Other Assets Stolen or Hidden by Germany during World War II.*

47  Gehrig-Straube, *Beziehungslose Zeiten.*

48  Durrer, *Die schweizerisch-amerikanischen Finanzbeziehungen im Zweiten Weltkrieg.*

49  U.S. Department of State (ed.), *U.S. and Allied Efforts to Recover and Restore Gold and Other Assets Stolen or Hidden by Germany during World War II,* iii–xii, 24–25. For a response to these charges, see Independent Commission of Experts Switzerland–Second World War, *Final Report,* 518–19.

50  Tanner and Weigel, "Gedächtnis, Geld und Gesetz in der Politik mit der Vergangenheit," 10.

51  On numerous occasions, the federal authorities prevented the publication of documents, thwarted historians' attempts to examine subjects of wartime history, and commissioned handpicked scholars to prepare reports on sensitive issues (see Zala, "Gebändigte Geschichte").

52  Haas, *"Wenn man gewusst hätte, was sich drüben im Reich abspielte" 1941–1943.*

53  The most outspoken critics of neutrality doctrine faced criminal investigations for disregarding military censorship (see Bonjour, *Geschichte der Schweizerischen Neutralität,* 6:176).

54  Barth, *Eine Schweizer Stimme 1938–1945,* 201–32, 334–70.

55  Verein Volksumfrage, *Die Schweiz hält durch.*

56  Möckli, "Neutralität, Solidarität, Sonderfall; Hug, "Verhinderte oder verpasste Chancen?" Vested interests in Switzerland traditionally have a strong influence on foreign-policy decisions (see Hug and Kloter, *Aufstieg und Niedergang des Bilateralismus*).

57  Kunz, *Aufbruchstimmung und Sonderfall-Rhetorik.*

58  Statement by the historian and politician Peter Dürrenmatt in 1949 (cited in Kreis, "Introduction," 1).

59  Montavi, *Schweizerische Sicherheitspolitik im Kalten Krieg 1947–1963*; Hug, "Vom Neutralismus zur Westintegration."

60 Haltiner, Bertossa, and Spillmann, "Sicherheit '97."

61 Tanner, "Militär und Gesellschaft in der Schweiz."

62 See, for instance, Hofer, *Neutralität als Maxime der schweizerischen Aussenpolitik.*

63 Von Salis, "Die Schweiz im Kalten Krieg."

64 "Botschaft des Bundesrates vom 25. Mai 1988," 975 (my translation, from the German).

65 Guggenbühl, *Die Schweizer sind anders*, 96 (my translation, from the German).

66 In 1959 the Socialist Party entered the ruling coalition according to its representation in parliament. A socialist was elected federal councilor for the first time in 1943. (See Degen, *Sozialdemokratie.*) The uniting experience of the wartime situation was also praised by professional historians (see Dürrenmatt, *Schweizer Geschichte*, 856.

67 See my essay "Gendering Citizenship and the State in Switzerland after 1945."

68 Imhof, "Wiedergeburt der geistigen Landesverteidigung"; Bretscher-Spindler, *Vom heissen zum Kalten Krieg.*

69 Vorkommnisse im EJPD; Komitee Schluss mit dem Schnüffelstaat, *Schnüffelstaat Schweiz*; Kreis, *Staatsschutz in der Schweiz.*

70 Kaldor, *The Imaginary War.*

71 Dürrenmatt, *Schweizer Geschichte*, 821.

72 Imboden, *Helvetisches Malaise.*

73 Frisch, *I'm Not Stiller*, 171. The German original *Stiller* was published in 1954.

74 Rüegg, "Ich hasse nicht die Schweiz, sondern die Verlogenheit."

75 Frisch, *Blätter aus dem Brotsack*; Frisch, *Dienstbüchlein.* For examples of an unfavorable reception, see Ernst Leisi, "Die Kunst der Insinuation: Bemerkungen zu Max Frischs 'Dienstbüchlein,'" *Neue Zürcher Zeitung*, 20 September 1974; Lüthi, *Max Frisch*, 132–42.

76 Expressed, for instance, in parliamentary debates on foreign policy issues and national defense (see Raissig, *Geistige Landesverteidigung*; "Amtliches Stenographisches Bulletin der Bundesversammlung" [7 October 1965]).

77 Tanner, "Die Schweiz in den 1950er Jahren."

78 Imhof, Kleger, and Romano, *Vom Kalten Krieg zur Kulturrevolution*; König et al., *Dynamisierung und Umbau.*

79 Diggelmann, *Die Hinterlassenschaft.*

80 Meyer, *Anpassung oder Widerstand.*

81 Gautschi, *General Henri Guisan*, 368–82; Zala, "Governmental Malaise with History: From the White Paper to the Bonjour Report."

82 Bonjour, *Geschichte der schweizerischen Neutralität*, 6:409. One of the few to question Bonjour's interpretation was Meienberg, "Bonsoir, Herr Bonjour" (first published in 1971).

83 The first to stress these aspects in the 1970s and 1980s were Bourgeois, *Le Troisième Reich et la Suisse*; Tanner, *Bundeshaushalt, Währung und Kriegswirtschaft.*

The gold transactions were first covered by Werner Rings's popular book, *Raubgold aus Deutschland*.

84  For a popularly written survey of the research and new interpretations of the 1970s and 1980s, see Heiniger, *Dreizehn Gründe warum die Schweiz im Zweiten Weltkrieg nicht erobert wurde*.

85  Most pronounced in the texts by the talented writer Niklaus Meienberg, whose influential research contributed to the demise of wartime myths (see Meienberg, *Reportagen aus der Schweiz*; Meienberg, *Die Erschiessung des Landesverräters Ernst S.*).

86  The left opposition to EU membership, which contributed to the failure of a 1992 referendum, testified to a leftist-version special-case rhetoric.

87  Geiser, "Der Schweizer Soldat," 8. Geiser's article was reprinted in the following issue with the editor's comment that the Swiss were lucky to live in a country where dissenters could publish such texts without facing serious consequences.

88  See contributions by Max Frisch, Friedrich Dürrenmatt, and others in Pestalozzi, *Rettet die Schweiz*; Brodmann, et al., *Unterweg zu einer Schweiz ohne Armee*.

89  Chiquet, "Der Anfang der Auseinandersetzung." For a survey of arguments, see the parliamentary debates "Amtliches Bulletin der Bundesversammlung" (1988), 1710–67; "Amtliches Bulletin der Bundesversammlung" (1989), 779–817.

90  The film *Beresina oder die letzten Tage der Schweiz* (1999), directed by Daniel Schmid, is a parody of the events that followed the referendum of 1989. It tells the fictive story of a Russian call girl who unwittingly triggers a coup d'état by a secret resistance organization of wartime veterans who were her customers.

91  Niggli and Frischknecht, Rechte Seilschaften.

92  The authorities delayed the release of the film because they disapproved of its presumably critical message (see Dumont, *Leopold Lindtberg und der Schweizer Film 1935–1953*, 94–114).

93  On the Washington Accord of 1946, see Independent Commission of Experts Switzerland–Second World War, *Switzerland and Gold Transactions in the Second World War*, 185–90. On heirless assets, see Hug and Perrenoud, "In der Schweiz liegende Vermögenswerte von Nazi-Opfern und Entschädigungsabkommen mit Oststaaten"; Bonhage, Lussy, and Perrenoud, *Nachrichtenlose Vermögen bei Schweizer Banken*.

94  In particular the research carried out since the mid-1990s under the auspices of the U.S. Department of State and the U.K. Foreign and Common Wealth Office and the discussions at the London Conference on Nazi Gold, December 1997, and the Washington Conference on Holocaust Era Assets, December 1998 (for the conference proceedings, see http://www.state.gov/www/regions/eur/holocaust/heac.html). Since 1996 a number of popularly written books have presented the results of older research and new findings to an international public, often in conjunction with harsh criticism aimed at Swiss banks, financial institutes, and authorities for their handling of looted property and their neglect of restitution obligations (see, for instance, Bower, *The Blood Money*; P. F. Koch, *Geheim-Depot Schweiz*).

95  Federal Councilor Jean-Pascal Delamuraz made these statements, in combination with charges of extortion raised against Jewish organizations, in an interview on 31 December 1996 when leaving office as the head of the government. For critical responses, see Muschg, *Wenn Auschwitz in der Schweiz liegt.*

96  Exceptions are the research by Jacques Picard (*Die Schweiz und die Juden, 1933–1945*) and Jean-Claude Favez (*The Red Cross and the Holocaust*, first published in French in 1988).

97  Well-researched examples can be found in Balzli, *Treuhänder des Reichs.*

98  Until the early 1990s high-school textbooks conveyed this impression ("Popularisierung, Ablehnung, Gleichgültigkeit: Wie die Bergier-Berichte aufgenommen wurden," *Neue Zürcher Zeitung*, 24 February 2003, 9). On numbers and categories of refugees, see Independent Commission of Experts Switzerland–Second World War, *Switzerland and Refugees in the Nazi Era*, 19–25. To date the most accurate estimate of the number of refugees who were not accepted runs to 25,000; the percentage of Jews is unknown (see Koller, "Entscheidungen über Leben und Tod").

99  Independent Commission of Experts Switzerland–Second World War, *Switzerland and Refugees in the Nazi Era*, 235–57; J.-C. Favez, "Le Don Suisse et la politique étrangère."

100  Independent Commission of Experts Switzerland–Second World War, *Switzerland and Refugees in the Nazi Era*, 16, 101–74. On relief programs for children, see Schmidlin, *Eine andere Schweiz.*

101  Keller, *Grüningers Fall.* On rescue activity of Swiss diplomats, see Tschuy, *Dangerous Diplomacy*; Independent Commission of Experts Switzerland–Second World War, *Switzerland and Refugees in the Nazi Era*, 111–27. In 2002 the federal parliament enacted legislation to lift the sentences against refugee helpers who were punished for smuggling people over the border.

102  Leimgruber, Meier, and Sablonier, *Das Hilfswerk für die Kinder der Landstrasse*; Huonker, *Anstaltseinweisungen, Kindswegnahmen, Eheverbote, Sterilisationen, Kastrationen.*

103  On Philipp Etter, see J. Favez, *The Red Cross and the Holocaust*; Kreis, "Philipp Etter." On Eduard von Steiger and Heinrich Rothmund, see Mächler, "Kampf gegen das Chaos"; Independent Commission of Experts Switzerland–Second World War, *Switzerland and Refugees in the Nazi Era*, 94–96.

104  Independent Commission of Experts Switzerland–Second World War, *Switzerland and Refugees in the Nazi Era*, 73–85.

105  Kreis, *Die Rückkehr des J-Stempels.*

106  "Amtliches Stenographisches Bulletin der Bundesversammlung" (30 January 1958), 16–39.

107  Landmarks were Alfred A. Häsler's popular book *The Lifeboat Is Full: Switzerland and the Refugees, 1933–1945*, first published in 1967, and Max Imhof's film *Das Boot ist voll* (1981). See also the critical memoirs by the former refugee Max Brusto (*Im schweizerischen Rettungsboot*) and by the aid-organization founder Regina Kägi-Fuchsmann (*Das gute Herz genügt nicht: Mein Leben und meine Arbeit*).

108 On Swiss Nazi victims, see Ludi and Speck, "Swiss Victims of National Social-ism: An Example of How Switzerland Came to Terms with the Past"; Ludi, "Die Parzellierung der Vergangenheit."

109 Independent Commission of Experts Switzerland–Second World War, *Switzerland and Refugees in the Nazi Era*, 271; Independent Commission of Experts Switzerland–Second World War, *Final Report*.

110 The South Africa engagement became the subject of closer scrutiny in the wake of the Holocaust-era asset scandal, but in contrast to the examinations of the Nazi-era past, research on South Africa business faced considerable political obsta-cles. Its results have not yet been published. For a survey, see http://www.snf.ch. On human rights and foreign investment, see Schläppi and Kälin, *Schweizerische Aussen-wirtschaftshilfe und Menschenrechtspolitik*.

111 See the annual reports *Sicherheit: Aussen-, sicherheits- und verteidigungspoli-tische Meinungsbildung im Trend* (1999–2003) by the Zürcher Forschungsstelle für Sicherheitspolitik und Konfliktanalyse (available online at http://www.ssn.ethz.ch).

112 Since 1997, many revisionist publications were aimed at the defense of na-tional honor (see, for instance, Leisi, *Freispruch für die Schweiz*; Stamm, *Kniefall der Schweiz*; Lambelet, *Le mobbing d'un petit pays*; Arbeitskreis Gelebte Geschichte, *Erpresste Schweiz*.

113 Cited by Tanner and Weigel, "Gedächtnis, Geld und Gesetz in der Politik mit der Vergangenheit," 9.

114 See Bundesarchiv, dossier no. 11, *Erinnerung und Geschichte 1939–1999*, "... *denn es ist alles wahr*" (1990). A video project in the late 1990s tried to bridge the gap and documented several hundred oral history interviews with members of the wartime generation (see http://www.archimob.ch).

115 Fisch, *Reparationen nach dem Zweiten Weltkrieg*; Herbert, "Nicht entschädi-gungsfähig?"

116 On reprivatization, restitution, and memory constructions in Eastern Eu-rope, see Pogany, *Righting Wrongs in Eastern Europe*.

117 According to the Foreign Policy Globalization Index, Switzerland in 2003 ranked second after Ireland (see http://www.foreignpolicy.com).

118 "The Balcony over Europe" was the title of a book on Swiss wartime history (see Béguin, *Le balcon sur l'Europe*).

THOMAS C. WOLFE ⁎

# Past as Present, Myth, or History?

DISCOURSES OF TIME AND THE

GREAT FATHERLAND WAR

With the exception of Germany, no European society was as thoroughly marked—demographically, culturally, and, politically—by the catastrophic years of invasion, occupation, and, ultimately, victory, as was the Soviet Union. The basic historical outline is familiar: in June 1941 the Soviet Union experienced a three-pronged invasion of its western regions, and within six months three of its major cities—Leningrad in the north, Moscow in the center, Stalingrad in the south—appeared near surrender. And yet against all apparent odds these cities resisted capture, and by the summer of 1943 the Soviet Red Army had begun to take back those western territories that had been so easily invaded and occupied. In April 1945 Soviet forces finally destroyed the remnants of Hitler's army in the bombed-out streets and alleys of Berlin, setting the stage for a Soviet photographer to capture on film a Soviet soldier fixing the Red Army flag to the top of the Reichstag, an image that became an icon portraying the heroism, courage, and victory of the Soviet people. This war, known in the Soviet Union as the Great Fatherland War (Great Patriotic War), surpassed all previous wars in its scope, ferocity, and destructiveness: one accounting of the toll it took on the Soviet populace asserted that 700 towns and 70,000 villages were razed, 25 million people made homeless, and 31,000 industrial enterprises and 65,000 kilometers of railroad track destroyed.[1] The number of Soviet citizens killed in the war has been the subject of endless debate, but most appraisals put the figure near 20 million. The war was an upheaval with immense significance for Soviet and world history.

Fit within a larger task of analyzing how the memory of the war shaped processes of political democratization in its individual, institutional, and collective modes, the Soviet case appears stubbornly anomalous. Not until the late 1980s did the political framework erected in the 1920s begin to change, and only in December 1991 did Russia's new leaders openly identify their state with liberal market democracies that only several years before had been the Soviet Union's political and military opponents. Before 1990 the Communist Party held a monopoly on political agency and activity in the Soviet Union, supervising a vast network of mass media whose contents were painstakingly scrutinized for their ideological correctness and political appropriateness. The Soviet Union possessed no public sphere crisscrossed with the presences and silences of historical interpretation, no public consciousness struggling with the meaning and memory of the war, no political system contested through the institutional channels of civil society. If the politics of memory in the West was a function of the stakes all elites had in supposing 1945 a significant break in national histories, the postwar government of the Soviet Union was instead fully continuous with that of the prewar era, with Stalin being the only leader of a major power who led his society in both the prewar and postwar eras. After 1945 in the Soviet Union there was no new government or new set of elites compelled to renounce, reconfigure, or reimagine the past to suit their own specific ends.[2] There were none of the complex negotiations over memory between political parties and their corresponding social and cultural constituencies, corporate and state media, generational cohorts, and diverse institutions of state and local power that were apparent in the West.

These historical particulars help explain why post-Soviet Russia has not seen the kind of Vergangenheitsbewältigung, or effort at coming to grips with the past, that has been a vital issue in other European states.[3] Russia produced no sensational trials of war criminals, no blockbuster works of history like *Le Syndrome de Vichy* that almost single-handedly transformed the terms of France's politics of memory, no Historikerstreit that renewed, recalled, and challenged memories of the war via the mass media. The reburial of Tsar Nicholas II in St. Petersburg's Peter and Paul Cathedral in 1998 set off no cathartic national exploration of guilt and responsibility. The Soviet Union had both a different experience of war and a different experience of politics and these special circumstances make any analysis of the country's politics of memory particularly challenging.

The absence of a truthful accounting is one that troubles many observers, who for a variety of reasons—from a deeply felt concern for Russia's twentieth-century sufferings to a desire to consolidate a dominant narrative around the failings of socialism—believe that something will remain faulty about Russian society until this void is filled. In a 1998 essay Alain Besançon, a respected historian of Russia and the Soviet Union, lamented historians' relative lack of interest in Russia about its own twentieth-century past.

However painful the memory of the past—or just because it is so painful—young Russian historians tend to avert their gaze from the Communist period, and thereby to consign it to oblivion. Meanwhile, the Russian state is again closing the relevant archives. As for the circle of dissidents, who did preserve a lucid memory of Communism, it rapidly broke down after 1991 and has not found a place for itself in the new order of things. An entity that means to perpetuate memory must attain a certain critical mass in society, whether by dint of numbers, political strength, or cultural influence. This the dissidents have not done—and neither, for that matter, have the spokesmen for the Armenians, the Ukrainians, the Kazakhs, the Chechens, or the Tibetans, not to mention many other victims of Communist terror.[4]

Between the lines of Besançon's passage, one can identify yet another problem for a Soviet/Russian politics of memory: which events, exactly, should be examined as a basis for the collective therapeutic project of acknowledging the crimes of the past? Germans have the Nazi crimes and the Holocaust to grapple with, and the other European powers have the burden of wartime collaboration to confront, but what is it that contemporary Russian citizens should concern themselves with? Besançon, along with many other historians, philosophers, and thinkers, implies that the entire Communist period requires attention and that those who once considered themselves Communist need to renounce their former beliefs and seek apologies from their fellow citizens who were victimized by the system. Thus a Russian Vergangenheitsbewältigung should reach back far earlier than the outbreak of war: it should begin with the founding of the Bolshevik regime.

Faced with such a lack, historians in a sense have two choices. Either they can borrow (again!) the example of the West against which to measure where and how Russia is not yet developed enough to experience a suitable kind of memory work, or they can discard external models of (healthy) development and grapple with the complexity and contradictoriness of what is present. The latter involves considering all the ways in which the past is encoded in the present. It means, for example, not stopping with the fact that there was no special place for Jewish sufferings in official Russian history, that there was no public Jewish reckoning with Stalin's crimes, but proceeding by attending to the complex histories of works of literature like Yevgeni Yevtushenko's poem "Babi Yar," which described a 1943 massacre outside of Kiev.

The movement, survival, and disappearance of memory in the Soviet Union is to be sought and pursued in essential processes where time is defined and manipulated. Historical memory is a part of the networks of discourse that constitute a culture, and any description of the situation of historical memory must acknowledge the basic structures and events that have shaped these networks. Thus, the very reason that some scholars use to justify their demand for an explanation of the Soviet lack of truthful accounting—that is, the breadth of the violence and suffering—in fact suggests that one should approach these questions from a respectful distance and with prudent caution. For example, Catherine Merridale's study of, in the words of her subtitle, "Death and memory in twentieth-century Russia," is a marvelous examination of this kind of cultural embeddedness.[5] She does not present "death and memory" as isolated objects, but rather in their connections to landscapes, mementos, relationships between men and women, poetry, medicine, and religion. Historical memory certainly cannot be conceptualized apart from these other spheres.

Hopefully complementing Merridale's broad and brilliant sweep, I will argue here for the importance of two historical objects in any attempt to describe the discursive networks that grappled with the memory of the Great Fatherland War. The first is what one might call the war's generational transmission, the different ways in which the war existed in everyday life as a topic of conversations and silences, as the basis of pride, envy, or resentment, and as part of the general burden of the past that gets transferred to and translated from one generation to the next. The implication that each generation has a language for its engagement with the past is deliberate, if slightly too poetic: in the Soviet Union, as in all countries, the war was (and remains) an object that generations put into their own idioms of feeling, understanding, and representation, idioms that posed problems for succeeding generations. Therefore, I will suggest ways to grasp the very different languages used by the three postwar generations to express their ongoing relationship to the war. Then there is the State's side of things. The uniqueness of the Soviet case derives in great measure from the particular ways the Soviet political system responded to the war, which begs an analysis of how the past was rendered thinkable within the discourses of Soviet Marxism. Though all-too-often ignored in recent scholarly and journalistic writing about the Soviet past, the significance of socialism—understood as the compendium of governmental strategies that *intended* a society to be marked by equality and justice—must be taken into consideration in "understanding" the Soviet Union.

Read together with the postwar experiences of other European states, the Soviet case helps illuminate one crucial dimension of the cultural gulf that constituted the gap between the Soviet Union and the rest of Europe, including perhaps its own allies, during the Cold War. The politics of memory in the West confirmed the existence of Western societies as historical cultures; in the Soviet Union, by contrast, there was no dominant cultural understanding that time was an abstract grid of empty space uniting the past with the future in a seamless field. Postwar discussions about identity and responsibility in Western European societies strengthened commitment to a concept of a historical record whose ambiguities and blank spaces did not undermine general faith in that record's existence, while in the Soviet Union the sense of the past was a function of the different possibilities for defining the meaning and significance of time within Marxist revolutionary discourse.

By attending simultaneously to the cultural mechanics of postwar memory and to the possibilities and limits inherent in the Soviet State's grasp of the war, one can construct a better foundation from which to compare the Soviet case to other national case studies. At the same time, however, one must keep in mind how these two processes interacted, for the party's interests evolved along with, and not despite, the potentials and demands it recognized in Soviet society. Thus emerges the superimposition of two schemas of evolution.

## Three Generations of Postwar Memory

World War II provided postwar Europeans a point of reference around which political and social identities were constructed. The concept of a generation is one way to approach the question of the evolution of these constructions in time, even though as many students of collective memory have pointed out, a "generation" is hardly an unproblematic concept. For example, to whom exactly does it refer? To everyone with birthdays between two dates? The obvious danger with the term is that it imposes an artificial kind of unity on what must inevitably be a diverse set of experiences, personalities, and understandings. The term can be defended, however, on the grounds that it refers to discourse rather than to something "real" and countable. In this sense, "generation" can refer to individuals' recognitions that they share a common identity because they have all been marked— psychologically, emotionally, sometimes bodily—by a specific and temporally bounded common experience.[6] From this perspective, the concept of a "war generation" is particularly salient in the Soviet context because of the scope and scale of catastrophe brought about by the Nazi invasion.[7] While hardly "provable" with the conventional tools of social science, that such wrenching experiences of deprivation, violence, hunger, and suffering would leave those who survived them with a sense of shared identity nevertheless makes profound intuitive sense. The war generated untold numbers of stories of suffering, courage, and sacrifice, none more powerful, perhaps, than those around the siege of Leningrad. The survival of the city's inhabitants for over 900 days, through siege, blockade, and two harsh winters, became a kind of archetype for the entire country's suffering and will to survive. Indeed, the observer has the formidable task of imagining the meanings of victory for those Soviet citizens who endured the five long years of war and whose lives acquired a sense of focus and purpose from their involvement in the struggle against the Germans.[8] The emotive and affective power of suffering, coupled with the Communist Party's understanding of the war as continuous with the revolutionary heritage of 1917, enabled the conviction that Soviet citizens had together "experienced" the war.

World War II was one of the most intense generational experiences of the twentieth century, and thus it was inevitable that the social and cultural processes of postwar society would be so dominated by the unfolding dynamics between the generation who had known war and the two subsequent ones that did not. The best way to understand this dynamics, perhaps, is to consider how postwar generations responded to the party's demand that the war be viewed as a foundational event for Soviet identity. It is essential to recognize how profoundly the first postwar generation was marked by the war's transformation into forms of mediation. This was the first generation for whom the war was largely imaginary, condemned to being reenacted and restaged on the pages of novels and on the stages and screens of theaters. This was the generation that in the 1950s and 1960s took seriously the Communist Party's claim that the war was an integral part of the revolutionary legacy of 1917, as well as its assertion that both to produce and consume these stories affirmed one's Soviet identity. This generation approached works of art and entertainment as if they were authentic documents attesting to real experience, and they understood these representations as expressions of national purpose. The second postwar generation, by contrast, was marked by a certain estrangement from the meaningfulness of the war's representation. For this generation, born after 1960 and coming of age in the late 1970s and 1980s, the war was "twice removed," existing "beneath" and "within" the enigmatic presences of grandfathers and grandmothers, and in the often all-too-predictable plot lines of novels, films, and plays. And they perceived their parents' readings of these media representations as more or less naive, refusing to acknowledge the party's interests in claiming that the military victory was the victory of the party and the socialist system.

Having given these rough definitions of the relevant generations of memory in the postwar Soviet Union, I should quickly add that these, of course, were not static discourses, but had their own complex and dynamic tendencies. One can hypothesize, for example, that the war generation grew accustomed to seeing itself portrayed in the products of the Soviet mass media and that these portrayals created a certain dissonance with, if not displaced altogether, the memories people had of their wartime lives. One can imagine the satisfaction and enjoyment engendered by their association with victory and national salvation, as well as their confusion at the appearance of a generation that was not always willing or able to accept that the war was viewed as the crucible of their identities as well. One can imagine, too, a latent conservatism in the wartime generation, as the society that they believed they had preserved from destruction became the object of criticisms articulated by those who had never experienced the dismemberment of the national body. The first postwar generation's connection to the fashioning of the war into cultural objects, by contrast, involved a more complex mix of emotions. Perhaps there was some measure of impatience and frustration at being so directly tied to the war, at feeling the obligation and compulsion to reenact the war so many times. This generation felt the guilty recognition that all these works of art, literature, and drama that attested to the heroic victory of the Soviet people were often excruciatingly stilted and boring. The second postwar generation's predicaments were in some ways the most complicated, since neither history nor culture offered themselves as avenues for the forging of their own relationship to the war. As long as representations of the war remained the object of the party's control, it remained closed to any kind of personal or independent historical investigation.

Time and the Problem of Soviet Identity

Stephen Hanson's *Time and Revolution: Marxism and the Design of Soviet Institutions* analyzes the dilemma around time that, Hanson argues, lies at the heart of both Marx's philosophy and Lenin's politics, and that provided the boundaries within which Soviet political and economic developments would take place after 1917. Hanson's book is a work of Weberian historical sociology whose aim is to describe how a nation or society's development can be understood both as an expression of and as limited by the worldview of the society's dominant groups. In this case, the ideas are those of Marxism, and the history is that of the Soviet Union, whose end in 1991 occurred not so much because of geopolitics or economic problems, but because of the exhaustion of this system of ideas, its inability to be sufficiently flexible to explain and respond to the social and political conditions of the USSR in the last decade of the twentieth century.

The Weberian framework has its critics, who argue that it is ultimately a species of idealism that relies on a kind of methodological determinism: because events are ultimately "determined" by ideas, the task is to match an event with its idea and then to fit it into its rightful place in the overall logic and structure of a worldview. Furthermore, the Weberian method leaves little or no room for contingency and accident in history, and encourages a schematic understanding of the past in place of an examination of the nuts and bolts of its contrasts and contradictions. But while the Weberian method can, like every social-science method, produce simplistic accounts, it can also produce finely grained descriptions of how social actions emerge from a conceptual universe and how individuals translate into practice concepts, ideas, and arguments; it is most useful not in providing a simple key to understand the past but in providing a sense of the movement of ideas through different terrains of social practice, thus undermining static visions of ideology and culture. Indeed, one of Hanson's most valuable contributions has been to convey a sense of the durability of the movement of Marxism across languages, cultures, and social epochs.

Hanson believes that at the heart of European Marxist practice and theory of socialism was the problem of time, and that at the heart of Communism as a revolutionary ideology was the problem of how individuals can live a new relationship to time, how time can be "transcended" by redefining its place in social reproduction. Such transcendence was the goal of the charismatic approach to revolution as it was articulated originally by Marx, and later by Lenin, an approach famously referenced in *The German Ideology* when Marx and Engels write of doing "one thing today and another tomorrow, to hunt in the morning, fish in the afternoon, rear cattle in the evening, criticize in the evening, just as I have a mind."[9] In this image of Communism what is evoked is not only a new arrangement of political and economic power but also a new organization of human experience, in which time ceases to be something feared, wasted, or mastered. At the same time, Hanson notes, there is another understanding of time in Marx, one that stresses the rational domination of time in modern methods of production wherein time exists in an empty, abstract grid. These two strands of charismatic and rational approaches to time comprise for Hanson the double helix of European Marxism, two blueprints, as it were, that would generate various iterations of these positions in different historical moments and under different national conditions. The history of revolutionary politics therefore can be read in terms of a series of solutions to the problem of the tensions between these two strands that arose in the nineteenth and early twentieth centuries. The basic pattern is that of a left-charismatic approach or impulse opposed by a right-rational attitude, both of which criticize and are criticized by a center-orthodox position whose chief aim is to consolidate the gains already achieved and not to risk new, untried policies of left or right.

Hanson's book is so valuable because it helps with the connection between political events and the specific, evolving framework of Marxist socialist ideas. He provides a sense of the cultural and discursive meanings of the terms *left*, *right*, and *center* as they appeared and reappeared throughout Soviet history. To think of *left* as oriented toward time transcendence and *right* as oriented toward time acceptance, if not the embrace of abstract, clock time, gives an entirely different sense of the choices made by specific leaders in specific circumstances. It also provides a sense of unity to the entire period of Soviet history, subverting one's sense of the distinctness of periods and encouraging one to think of the reproduction of these discursive structures *across* time. Most important, though, it encourages one to read events in terms of the categories provided by this larger framework. In some cases, this forces one to entertain the rationality of what appears the most horrific and irrational of actors and actions. Most notably, it forces one to see Stalin as not, or not *only*, an insane tyrant; Hanson argues that Stalin's actions are understandable when one considers the intensity of the need in the late 1920s to improvise a new fusion of left and right. Stalin believed the victory of any one of these groups would mean the abandonment of the revolution, since what made the revolution was its fusion of the charismatic and the rational concepts of time.

What Hanson does not discuss is the status of the past within the three dominant discourses embedded in European Marxism. What conceptions of the past are embedded in the left-charismatic, right-rational, and center-orthodox orientations to time? What mode of remembering characterizes each position?

The sense of the past that is easiest to grasp is that of the right-rational concept of time and its acceptance of the unfolding of human activity in the encompassing framework of empty time. European socialists took this concept of time from bourgeois capitalist culture, believing that this borrowing did not contaminate or disqualify socialism in any way. From this perspective, socialism was defined according to the overall structure of ownership in a given society, not with reference to the quality of the subjective experiences of the citizens of that society. In this understanding, the abstract grid of time is the scene of all human existence, with the present being fixed in a position "between" the two identical regions of past and future. One has direct access to neither the past nor the future, yet in order to rationally master the present, one needs to project oneself both back into the past and forward into the future. One appropriates the past in the mode of grasping the past characteristic of the bourgeoisie, namely through historical discourse. The method appropriate to this bourgeois conception is professional historiography, itself founded on the incontrovertible fact that the past is irretrievable and that one can never again be present to it, although one can understand it through textual reconstructions based on documentary evidence. In this reading, history is but one expression of nineteenth-century societies' devotion to the concept of the Real: rational economic planning projects the real into the future, while historical discourse projects it into the past.

The left-charismatic concept of the past is much harder to describe because it is premised on the idea that the "normal," bourgeois concept of time can be "transcended." Thus, a completely different language of analysis is required to describe charismatic time. Transcendence involves passing over limits normally taken for granted, the limits in question being those that box the present between past and future. So, instead of a concept of the past based on a location outside the subject from which to perceive the subject's placement within the empty space of time, the charismatic view stresses the fact that time exists only through the medium of subjective experience. Time is not total and absolute, but rather malleable and variable, and Hanson turns not to philosophy or political economy, but to literature for a characterization of this charismatic time, specifically a passage from Valentin Kataev's novel *Time, Forward*, written during the first five-year plan. Describing the experience of a shock brigade in the new industrial city of Magnitogorsk, Kataev writes, "Time flew through them. They changed in time, as in a campaign. New recruits became fighters, fighters became heroes, heroes became leaders."[10] Instead of subjects occupying the scene of time as in the right-rational concept of time, time temporarily occupies—flies through—the subject. The past is known only as the person you used to be. Past, present, and future are crammed together in the process of a person becoming someone better, with Communism being the scene of this continuous abolishing of the present state of things, to paraphrase the famous statement of Marx. The past simply does not exist as something to be objectively contemplated.

The center-orthodox concept of time draws from certain aspects of both these left and right formations. On the one hand, the center-orthodox accepts time as an abstract grid, but only in order to locate the original, generative revolutionary moment or event. On the other hand, it denies time in a charismatic fashion through a ritual re-presentation of that event, claiming that those who have experienced this ritual have transcended time. It must reject this grid insofar as it represents the possibility of historical accident and contingency. It cannot admit or acknowledge that any founding moment is in fact thoroughly historical, that is, both absolutely removed from the realm of experience and knowable only through the productions of historical discourse. The relevant mode of remembering for orthodoxy is myth, that narrative form that claims to erase temporal or spatial distance in order to make the generative moment immediately meaningful in the present.

Revolution, History, and Myth in the Postwar Period

Given the two schema, which offer a broad overview of essential cultural practices around time and memory in the late Soviet period, one can focus more closely on the composite picture formed by overlaying one on the other. What emerges from this exercise is a view of the centrality of the war both in strengthening the Soviet Union as an object of cultural identification through the 1960s, then in weakening this identification through the late 1980s. The war provided an inexhaustible source for programs of both revolutionary time transcendence and mythical reenactment, and during perestroika it emerged into public discourse as an object of historical inquiry. The transition from one phase to the other might be indexed by the changes that took place in the status of Victory Day, 9 May, in the Soviet Union. In 1947 Stalin decided to downgrade Victory Day from a "state" holiday, which included a day off work, to a "working" holiday; in 1965 Leonid Brezhnev reestablished Victory Day as a state holiday. In examining how the war was given meaning by the discourses that shaped the Soviet worldview, it is important to recall that the war began *after* Stalin had "solved" the problem of how to create a revolutionary but disciplined populace, a solution predicated on planned heroism in the economy and permanent purge in society. But this solution did not prove durable in the long run; it succeeded in creating the basic structures of an industrial economy and in establishing a veneer of legitimacy, yet many Soviet citizens, particularly in the countryside, remained alienated from and even hostile to Soviet power, particularly after the catastrophic upheaval of collectivization, which for many peasants was a preview of the suffering they were to experience during the war. In this situation, Hanson suggests, the Nazi invasion was, "paradoxically, the regime's salvation." The war integrated millions of Soviet citizens into a common national cause. Moreover, the Soviet victory became proof of the correctness of Stalin's solutions to the problem of how to create a charismatic-rational economy; it gave Stalin—and the socio-economic organization of Soviet society that he constructed—a much wider and deeper degree of legitimacy than they had enjoyed before the war.[11]

It did this in part by forcing the party to transform the landscape of representations conveyed in the Soviet press, which supplied to the far flung corners of the Soviet Union a sense of the common experience of the war. Between June 1941, when the Nazis invaded the Soviet Union, and the spring of 1943, when it became clear that the surrender and capture of the German army at Stalingrad meant that the tide of war had shifted in the Soviets' favor, the press reported on events as it had never done before.[12] Stalin retreated from the foreground of the grand tableau of socialist construction, and reporting from both the battlefield and the home front grappled with the catastrophe and the resistance as they unfolded. War correspondents became national heroes by chronicling the sacrifices of individuals who represented the spectrum of the entire population, and between the lines, they revealed how millions of Soviet citizens were taking control over their lives as never before.

At the same time, the party's grid of Marxist discourse produced the war as fully continuous with the process set in motion by the revolution. As Amir Weiner writes regarding the first postwar decades, "The war was not only a part of the revolutionary era but, in more ways than one, the postwar and post-Stalin eras epitomized the undiminished impetus for revolutionary transformation. . . . The war and its aftermath could not be distinguished from the Revolution at large. As long as the revolutionary ethos retained its viability, it was the prism through which Soviet contemporaries made sense of the cataclysmic events that shaped their lives."[13] Because the revolutionary project of time transcendence was defined as the continuous production of transformative experiences, the war was a revolution experienced by the entire population. It was in a sense the perfect revolution, bringing the majority of the population together in a single event for a single, life-altering purpose. In other words, the war was a natural "fit" for the left-charismatic vision of the revolutionary project.

Weiner's recent book, *Making Sense of War*, provides a number of insights into the war's revolutionary character. Because the war fractured the territorial integrity of the Soviet State, it enabled Stalin and the Communist Party to give revolutionary birth to the Soviet Union once again. Weiner focuses on the Soviet Union's western republics and demonstrates how the ethnic and religious heterogeneity of Ukraine in particular ensured the appearance during the war of extremely complex and dynamic relations of domination. It sometimes happened that neighboring villages in the western republics had vastly different experiences of the invasion and occupation depending on their geographic position and ethnic composition. Many Ukrainian nationalists hailed the Nazi invasion as liberation from the Soviet regime, and these groups worked sometimes in cooperation and sometimes in competition with partisans loyal to the Soviet State. The sizable Jewish population in the eastern parts of Poland, in Belorussia, and in Ukraine complicated matters still more. On the one hand, these areas became important sites for the genocidal policies of the Nazi State, policies that resonated with an earlier Slavic anti-Semitism. Weiner makes clear, however, that these overlapping anti-Semitisms did not necessarily lead to alliances; he cites examples of anti-Semitic Ukrainian nationalists protecting local Jews from the Nazis on the basis of their connection to the local community. In such circumstances, a variety of relationships evolved concerning the initially defeated, later victorious Soviet regime. Ukrainian Communists were suspect in the eyes of Russian Communists for having "allowed" the populace to seek a livable relationship with the Germans; and Ukrainian peasants could not quite trust *any* Communist given the Soviet regime's exploitation of the republic in the 1920s. Ukrainian Jews knew that many in the Soviet leadership doubted that members of the Jewish "nationality," no matter how assimilated into Russian society or devoted to the cause of Marxism, could ever be fully trusted with the task of constructing socialism. While the circumstances in Ukraine and Belorussia were to some degree unique, in that these republics were the pathways for first the Nazi invasion from the west and then the Soviet liberation from the east, such heterogeneity represented more the rule than the exception. Thus, while many Soviet citizens experienced the upheaval of the war *as a nation,* they also did so as a part of groups defined in terms of ethnicity and geography, and it is the war's exposure of the Soviet Union's heterogeneity that helps explain the fact that the Soviet victory did not end the revolutionary upheavals. Soviet POWs were sent straight to the camps, party officials were purged in formerly occupied territories, national groups such as the Volga Germans, Chechens, Ingush, and Tatars remained in exile.

Stalin's 1947 decision to downgrade the status of Victory Day is in part understandable in terms of Stalin's own distorted psychology; a prisoner of his own paranoia, Stalin came to fear that the war's greatness would with time eclipse his own. But the decision to downgrade the official status of 9 May can be more fully understood in a wider context as an effort to discipline the population by reminding it of its revolutionary purpose and stressing that while one war had been won, the revolutionary project would have to continue. Any pausing over memory risked giving the impression that the revolution was over, so as Hanson points out, Stalin took up again the policies that had seemed to work in the late 1920s and 1930s. Most sinister, of course, was the rearticulation of discourses around internal enemies, one that perhaps would have led to an anti-Semitic purge in the mid-1950s had Stalin not died of a stroke in March 1953. And yet his approach had neither the consistency nor coherence it once had. During the last years of Stalin's life, the USSR, in Ronald Suny's words, "was isolated, domestically impoverished, with a stagnating economy and a weary population."[14]

Thus, on the one hand, there was a war generation characterized in Weiner's words by "a unique mode of association and sense of self that did not run through the socialization channels provided by the regime," and on the other hand was the party leadership's belief that the war was the next phase of the revolutionary process. On the one hand was an experience that, for the historian Elena Seniavskaia, was a first, preliminary stage of de-Stalinization, preparing the way for the attack on totalitarianism that would occur in the late 1950s, and on the other hand was a resounding confirmation of Soviet power as the most progressive and powerful of world historical forces.[15]

Khrushchev is sometimes portrayed as guiding Soviet society in a completely new direction after he consolidated his power in the mid-1950s, but one should perhaps concentrate more on the continuities with the Stalin period than with those few conspicuous moments where the Stalinist legacy came in for honest and harsh criticism. One must first understand Khrushchev's pursuit of "charismatic Leninism," then place the "thaw" within this overall approach.

The connection between the war and revolutionary transcendence helps explain the emergence of Nikita Khrushchev at the top of the Soviet hierarchy in the middle 1950s. The victory of Khrushchev's left-charismatic alternative after the struggle with the anti–Communist Party group in 1956 may have been due to the fact that Khrushchev articulated more faithfully and sympathetically the revolutionary aspirations of the generation of Soviet citizens who had been transformed by the war. Khrushchev, a voluble and gregarious man who unlike Stalin enjoyed mixing with the masses, recognized just how much the war had changed Soviet citizens, making them, in his eyes, into an entire nation of revolutionary actors. Weiner hints at this when he argues that the millions of peasants-turned-soldiers who fought and won the war after the defeats of 1941–1942, returned to their towns and villages with a heightened sense of their own capabilities and of the magnitude of their achievements. "Returning soldiers displayed uncompromising reluctance to let others—the regime included—articulate for them the defining moment in their lives."[16] This sense of independence contributed, Weiner argues, to a reinvigoration of Soviet power, as these soldiers took over positions of authority in collective farms, schools, and factories. So while Khrushchev completely identified with revolution as the ongoing project of creating a Communist society, he understood that Stalin's "solution" to the problem of how to forge a charismatic-rational system of economic production could not be his own, that it was no longer possible to treat Soviet citizens as individuals whose loyalty to the revolution had to be coerced. The revolution's next task—the achievement of Communism— could only be undertaken by citizens confident that their leading institutions no longer viewed them with suspicion or condescension. One should not overlook the principled nature of this attitude: after such a disastrous upheaval, which touched every Soviet family, Khrushchev came to believe that Communism should not be created through the cynical preying on the population by the People's Commissariat for Internal Affairs (NKVD), the Russian secret police, and a discourse about enemies of the people.

In this light Khrushchev's decision to publicly reject that portion of the Stalinist inheritance focused on coercion and violence appears, in the long perspective of the second half of the twentieth century, to be one of the most consequential decisions made by any national leader. The strategy he chose was to adopt a historical perspective on Stalinism, that is, a historical perspective on what claimed to be outside of historical time. Khrushchev, in attempting to take possession of and redefine Marxism's "left" alternative, deployed a sense of time characteristic of Marxism's "right." Khrushchev's "secret speech" at the 20th Congress in 1956 produced an enormous crack in

the monolithic structure of charismatic-rational time constructed by Stalinism. His assumption was that historical time could operate in the service of
charismatic time.

The significance of the "thaw" in art and literature that constituted the
"liberalization" of the Soviet public sphere under Khrushchev can be traced
to this insinuation of historical discourse into genres of socialist realism.
This involved the promotion of a new kind of realism about aspects of the
Soviet Union's own history, as suggested by two 1962 works: Andrei Tarkov-
sky's film *Ivan's Childhood* (*Detstvo Ivanovo*) and Alexander Solzhenitsyn's
novella *One Day in the Life of Ivan Denisovich*. The former quickly became
one of the most popular World War II films made in the Soviet Union, while
the latter was read by many as symbolizing a dramatic departure from the
canon of Zhdanovian norms in literature. Both works consciously depart
from the conventions of socialist realism in order to be more faithful to the
author or director's personal vision of historical experience. The popularity
of these works at the time of their production and thereafter suggests that
they resonated with the experience of a vast audience. The "thaw" was the
crucible of the first postwar generation, being that moment when Soviet
identity received honest and authentic representation *outside of any connection to Stalin or Stalinism*.

The Khrushchev period was perhaps the most contradictory and complex
decade of the Soviet Union's history. On the one hand, it relied on the
renewal and reinvigoration of the left-charismatic concept of the revolutionary project, but on the other hand, the most famous strategy it employed to
achieve this was to allow a concept of historical time to appear in public
discourse. Even as the Brezhnev leadership turned to the defense of Stalinist
orthodoxy and to the promotion of the past in myth, the memory of having
experienced historical discourse was one shared by millions of Soviet citizens. It continued to exist in the literary productions of dissident circles, and
later reappeared in public with the approval of the Soviet Union's final
leader, Mikhail Gorbachev.

Khrushchev was removed from the Soviet leadership by a group of his
colleagues in November 1964. The widely cited reason for his removal was
that he pursued "hare-brained" schemes that disrupted the operation of the
Soviet economy. Brezhnev and his colleagues condemned the permanent
state of upheaval that Khrushchev had created in the Soviet Union's economic administration by relying so heavily on voluntarist campaigns that
would allegedly achieve great leaps in production. Not only were these campaigns threatening to a key middle level of party leaders, the fanfare they

entailed was also dangerous in promising the Soviet public more than could be realistically delivered. Indeed, after a few years of conspicuous success in the late 1950s, the Soviet economy showed clear signs of a significant slowdown by the early 1960s. Put in the terms of Hanson's structure, Brezhnev's tenure as general secretary represented the triumph of the orthodox center, the position that above all sought stability, consistency, and fidelity to earlier founders and innovators. The center was all that remained, since Khrushchev's policies were viewed as a "revolutionary form of failure" and any right-rational policy, like the brief tactics of Georgy Malenkov in the mid-1950s and Alexey Kosygin in the mid-1960s, promised only a "bourgeois form of success."[17] "Brezhnev's centrist alternative to these positions from 1964 to 1982, like [Grigory] Zinoviev's platform in 1924, was simply to resist all pressures for change from the left and the right, defending the ideological, political, and now also the socioeconomic status quo . . . From 1971 on, Brezhnev's rule became marked by the elite's increasing reluctance to tolerate even the slightest deviation from the theoretical and institutional legacy of Marx, Lenin, and Stalin."[18]

According to Nina Tumarkin, the principal cultural technology for the maintenance of this orthodoxy was the creation of a second major "cult"; just as a cult had been created around Lenin immediately after his death in 1924, so, too, was a vast enterprise of commemoration geared up in the mid-1960s around the Great Fatherland War. A convenient date presents itself as a marker of the cult's founding: 9 May 1965, when the Soviet leadership returned Victory Day to the status of state holiday. From the mid-1960s on, the party expanded its efforts to make the commemoration of the war a sacred duty of every Soviet citizen. This included the promotion of lifestyle rituals like the visit of newlyweds to the Tomb of the Unknown Soldier, the construction of monuments and markers to heroism and sacrifice, and the message that by commemorating the war all Soviet peoples fulfilled their common duty. The party encouraged veterans to take on a new public role as authorized witnesses, to visit schools, clubs, and libraries to tell stories of their heroic exploits.

In Tumarkin's sociological reading the cult of the war was evidence of the estrangement between generations. The first postwar generation was composed of "a new breed of Soviet citizen," whose youth culture was one of "insularity, self-protectiveness, and an unsettling sense of estrangement that sociologists used to call 'anomie.' "[19] This was, after all, the first generation without personal experience of the revolutionary, time-transcendent project that was the Soviet Union. Thus, Tumarkin argues, the cult of the war developed as a utilitarian means of social control, mobilizing shame and guilt in order to make the younger generation feel indebted to the older generation for the peaceful and prosperous lives they enjoyed. "The idealized war experience was a reservoir of national suffering to be tapped again and again to mobilize loyalty, maintain order, and achieve a semblance of energy to counter the growing nationwide apathy and loss of popular resilience of spirit."[20]

The chief problem for the older generation—and for the regime—was that the younger generation saw through these rituals and representations, recognizing them as a means of discipline, if not coercion. The cost of the cult was that it set up a structure of hypocrisy and bad faith: the veterans who came to schools every year to repeat the stories of their exemplary exploits in the war came to expect bouquets of flowers on Victory Day, and the students who pretended to listen to their stories resented the fact that they had no choice but to give them. Tumarkin suggests that during perestroika this resentment bubbled over, as incidents were reported in the press of teenagers vandalizing war monuments, the most holy of Soviet shrines.

Tumarkin's work sheds valuable light on the war cult, although the opposition between the cult and the private cultures of remembrance that provides the implicit structure of her book is too starkly drawn.[21] Her account resonates with Hanson's framework. One could argue, for example, that both the cult and the private reactions against it can be understood in terms of the mode of time that underlay Hanson's concept of the center-orthodox, namely myth. The cult of the Great Fatherland War that arose in the 1960s was an expression of the fact that the leaders who replaced Khrushchev in 1964 employed a concept of mythical time to grasp the Soviet past. The war cult, like the Lenin cult, relied on the proliferation of ritualized performances like medal ceremonies that manifested military symbols, languages, and conventions in daily life, and it authorized the creation of enormous monuments, like the vast memorial complex at Stalingrad (Volgograd), whose sheer size seemed the sculptural equivalent of mythic form. And the war cult sought to mythologize the wartime exploits of the Soviet Union's leaders, Brezhnev's above all.

Myth is an organization of discourse that involves the restaging, the organized rearticulation, of an event from the past in the present. Yet, unlike historical discourse, which is predicated on viewing that past as an object, myth involves a presentation of that narrative in such a way as to erase everything that separates this event from the present, so that the past becomes something experienced, rather than understood or examined. This is one of the purposes of ritual: an event in the past is reenacted in such a way that it takes on the force of a contemporary event. Myth refuses the pastness of the past, even while it is made possible by the absence of what it seeks to make present again. Myth was central to Brezhnevian orthodoxy because through it Brezhnev and his colleagues were able to repeatedly stage the life of Lenin and the heroic unfolding of the war, were able, in other words, to relive the long revolution without having to risk formulating policies that would make revolution more than just a performance. They learned from the experience of Khrushchev that it was dangerous to identify too closely with the charismatic annihilation of time, as this entailed experimenting with policies whose outcomes were far from predictable, especially because it was still far from clear what the achievement of Communism actually meant. But stepping back from the left-charismatic time evoked by Khrushchev made visible again the separation between past and present that charismatic time did not recognize and posed the problem of how to acknowledge this gap. Myth solved this problem by presenting the past as something to be relived, reexperienced through the organized performances of the cult. In this way continuity with the revolution was asserted by the regime; participation in these rituals brought the public into moments of contact with the revolution. It is not enough to view the cult of war in terms of its social function. One also needs to see it in the context of the deeper cultural framework set by the existence of the discourse on revolution going back to Marx.

Noting the centrality of mythic time in the Brezhnev era also helps explain those phenomena that Tumarkin cites as evidence of opposition to the cult. She draws a sharp boundary between those phenomena that represented the regime's opportunistic exploitation of the past and those that showed the effort of individuals to develop their own relation to the past. She pays much attention, for example, to the formation in the 1960s of associations dedicated to the discovery, identification, and burial of soldiers who had been officially listed as missing in action but who in fact were still lying where they had been killed on battlefields abandoned and forgotten decades earlier. Important parts of her book narrate her involvement with these groups, experiences that in her eyes represented personal authenticity and integrity, as against the hypocrisy of the regime's cult of the war. Yet, much of what she identifies as an authentic relation to the past was in fact its mythical nature. She highlights the religious dimension of this search for human remains and implied that the members of these associations, camping out under the stars in the Soviet countryside where decades ago battles raged, felt in the uncanny immediacy the presence of that vanished reality. Remains and artifacts were treated as relics, the activity of recovery as a sacred duty. These are precisely the terms by which myth grasps events in the past in order to make them immediately present to experience. Thus, Tumarkin's rescue of the war from the regime seems to involve a similar relationship to the past. This also justifies the premise of this essay: that each of the positions within a wider politics of memory in the Soviet Union took shape within the cultural framing of time provided by the revolutionary project.

Much like Khrushchev took over from a paranoid, confused, and isolated Stalin, and like Brezhnev took power from an inconsistent and impulsive Khrushchev, Gorbachev was elected general secretary because of the serious displeasure his colleagues felt with the previous style of leadership. During the three years between Brezhnev's death in 1982 and Gorbachev's election in March 1985, the reputation of the Soviet Union had been badly damaged by the image broadcast around the world that one of the world's two global superpowers was ruled by a clique of feeble septuagenarians. It had become clear within the politburo that a new direction and approach was required if Soviet society was to overcome the conspicuous obstacles—slowing economic growth, a disastrous war in Afghanistan that showed no signs of resolution, falling life expectancies, numerous points of pressure and complication in the socialist countries of Eastern Europe, simmering nationalist problems in the Soviet Union's republics, and the reinvigoration of the Cold War in military, technological, and ideological spheres—that had appeared during the development of what Brezhnev had labeled "mature socialism." Gorbachev, who had enjoyed the patronage of Yurii Andropov in the 1970s and was brought by him to Moscow in the early 1980s, represented a significant departure from this model. Fifty-four years old at the time of his election, healthy, vigorous, a skilled politician within the politburo and central-committee bureaucracy, voluble and personable, Gorbachev seemed the ideal choice to reform and reenergize Soviet society. And yet to the surprise of the most-experienced and well-connected observers, within a few years after launching a full-scale reform effort, the Soviet Union's leader handed power to Russia's national leader, Boris Yeltsin, who then declared the dissolution of the Soviet state. The reform process Gorbachev had launched with a call to reinvent socialism led in six short years to the end of the Communist Party's rule, the collapse of the Soviet economy, and the breakup of the union structure of the Soviet state. In its place emerged fifteen separate republics, each of which began the process of grappling with its insertion into a global capitalist market. Russia grasped at capitalism and democracy with help from Western Europe and the United States, and within a couple of years after 1991, had become "just" another two-tiered society, with a tiny, Westernized elite, managing—and profiting from—Russia's massive downsizing and ruling over an impoverished but free populace.

The complexity of this period defies easy explanations, but one must first remember the structures of options within Soviet Marxism that presented themselves to Gorbachev as he began to shape new domestic policies for the Soviet regime. One must also immediately acknowledge the structural analogy with the Khrushchev period. Gorbachev, like Khrushchev, approached the task of reform from within the framework of Hanson's left-charismatic revolutionary transformation. Both men felt they had to decisively break with some aspect of their predecessor, and Gorbachev's problem was Brezhnev's center-orthodoxy. Neither Gorbachev nor Khrushchev seriously considered the right-rational framework and its acceptance of bourgeois time. Only in the Soviet Union's last year did Gorbachev begin to speak about capitalism and far-reaching market reform, that is, *after* the political and institutional changes he had introduced had brought the planned economy to a point of crisis.

Yet, there was an essential difference between the two moments: Gorbachev had no access to a revolutionary experience that would serve as the basis of or as a model for projects of renewal and reform, whereas Khrushchev was able to organize and mobilize Soviet youth to take on vast projects of social and economic transformation, mobilizations that embodied the revolutionary project of constructing a Communist self and society. By 1985, however, it was clear that Soviet society had passed the point when it could be mobilized in the form of campaigns.[22] In the intervening two decades the Soviet Union had become an urbanized, highly educated society with a generation born in the 1960s and 1970s for whom revolution was a story from the deepest past. After existing for two decades in the form of mythical retellings and rituals, the war could no longer serve as any kind of template. The left-charismatic became, therefore, less about production than about discourse, less about heroic campaigns than about communication. Gorbachev's "resources" for the ongoing revolutionary transformation of the society were the memories and the cultural products of the 1960s. Perestroika was in this sense a memory politics, one that tried to make Soviet citizens re-remember their own pasts in a different light.

Perestroika was the result of an analysis that saw the essential weakness of Soviet society not in the quality or design of negative sanctions on Soviet citizens' behavior, but rather in the atrophied connection between individual well-being and collective social purpose. Gorbachev's attention quickly turned to the "spiritual" maladies of Soviet society, where the evident problem was a lack of faith in and understanding of socialism as a morally superior organization of society. From the early policies of *uskorenie*, or acceleration, to perestroika in 1987–88, the concern was ultimately the same: how to change consciousness, how to help Soviet citizens understand what had become masked during Brezhnev's tenure, namely their own position within the collective revolutionary project of Communism. Thus, Gorbachev understood that the left-charismatic orientation toward the cultural transformation of the Soviet Union would require a corresponding transformation of Soviet media. And here Gorbachev and Aleksandr Iakovlev noted a whole range of problems, the most conspicuous of which was the gulf that existed between officially sanctioned representations and the everyday knowledge carried around in people's heads. As long as citizens could not trust the authorized images of their society, they would be unable to view themselves as contributors to the society's progress; as long as Soviet public discourse was characterized by public relations rather than public deliberation, it would be impossible to overcome stagnation.

So Gorbachev began in 1986 to encourage journalists and all media workers to find new ways to help the party reform socialism, and in return the party was to allow journalists more leeway in "covering" Soviet society. This included allowing a practice of reporting that had not been known since the 1960s; journalists could write, for example, about topics such as train wrecks and street crime whose publication had previously been forbidden because negative news was considered detrimental to the spiritual health of the Soviet polity. The combination of an easing of censorship and the encouragement of critical reporting resulted in a situation in which, according to a saying that circulated in Moscow in the late 1980s, "it was more interesting to read than to live."

The Soviet journalistic tradition experienced a revival of sorts. Journalists and editors began to write as if they were taking seriously Lenin's call in the early 1920s for sharp, honest, incisive criticism, and a flood of articles criticizing Soviet institutions and diagnosing their pathologies appeared. Moreover, many editors at the party's central press rededicated themselves to the view that the press was the most important means by which the party could learn the needs and desires of the people; they began to publish in evergreater quantities and with the party's approval letters from readers describing not just their own heart-rending situations but also their diagnoses of the sorry state of Soviet society itself. Other editors interpreted the relaxation of censorship as license to experiment with the basic features of Soviet journalistic practice; they began to remake both the look and content of their publications according to Western models, introducing journalistic values like brevity and timeliness that had previously not been important. By 1989, Western concepts of journalistic practice began to inform many journalists' work, and this affinity for an "international" style of journalism was expressed both on the level of the printed page and on the level of enterprise: one of the most conspicuous, if short-lived, of these highly symbolic joint ventures in publishing was the paper *We/My*, published briefly in 1990–1991 by both Hearst and *Izvestiia*.[23]

The combination of a resurrected agenda of a left-charismatic transformation and a reformation of media practices entailed a significant change in the discursive framework within which the past took shape. Just as Khrushchev had emphasized a left-charismatic perspective of history, Gorbachev sponsored and promoted a sense of the historical past that helped him acknowledge just how far Soviet society was from the achievement of Communism. Gorbachev went so far as to demarcate distinct historical periods, one of the seminal tasks of the historian. The previous twenty years, he wrote, constituted a separate "era of stagnation" that had to be overcome in the course of the future development of socialism. Gorbachev spoke with an unprecedented candor about Stalin's crimes, not stopping in his catalog where Khrushchev had, with the outbreak of war in 1941. He insisted that the new consciousness of perestroika should be able to assimilate this history, could find strength in an honest examination of both the good and the bad aspects of the Soviet past. These references went beyond Khrushchev's "secret speech" in their explicit thematization of a necessary and truthful accounting with the past without which Soviet society could not reform itself. An essential feature of this process was a newfound visibility for the practice of historiography, as a market quickly appeared for detailed, documented accounts of specific events that refuted or at least shed a very different light on the accounts promoted in official texts and rituals. As a result, newspaper stories that referred to previously secret documents or archival research became immensely popular, and scores of reporters began digging into the formerly inaccessible recesses of the Soviet past.

Indeed, one of the perestroika press's most popular genre of articles was the "interview with the historian," such as *Izvestiia*'s March 1988 interview with the historian A. Samsonov, who discussed Stalin's order No. 227 of July 1942, the "not one step back" order, which demanded the execution of any soldier caught retreating. These kinds of articles not only offered truthful data about the past but also publicized the value of historical research for civil society, a value evoked in questions like the one posed by the *Izvestiia* journalist to Samsonov: "Which wartime documents classified as 'Secret' would you personally like to present to the court of public opinion?"[24] From approximately 1987 on, the press was full of revelations: of the "secret lives" of the Soviet leaders, of wartime atrocities conducted by the NKVD (such as the 1940 Katyń Forest massacre of Polish officers), of Soviet killings of suspected collaborators, of Stalin's inept preparations for war, of the fabricated wartime exploits of party leaders, and so on.[25] Gorbachev assumed that by allowing such discussions to appear, the cause of perestroika would be furthered, because Soviet citizens needed a firm orientation toward the past, a historical record they could refer to for the future. Historical discourse was a way of combating the mythical orientation promoted during the era of stagnation, since the past should be a matter of documents not of rituals, of facticity not of feeling. Journalists faithful to Gorbachev's program believed that accurate information circulating in an unrestricted public sphere would contribute to the clarification of collective consciousness. Good information would drive out bad, and political passions would be transformed into reasoned debates. It soon became clear, though, that this outpouring of historical knowledge was hardly making possible prudent public deliberation.

One can only imagine the Gorbachev group's chagrin as they realized that their opening up of the Soviet public sphere, their promotion of historical knowledge, intended as the basis for the reinvigoration of socialism, permitted and in fact provoked articulations of the mythic discourse on the past that the reformers so opposed. On the one hand, the problem was caused by media practitioners who were suspicious of perestroika and who had learned under Brezhnev to always play it safe by continuing to publish articles and reports that perpetuated the cult of the war.[26] And at the same time, Gorbachev's own invocations of Lenin and his treatment of the war resonated with the mythical discourse that had become established during the tenure of his predecessor. At the heart of Gorbachev's articulations of the past, then, was a contradiction between the necessity for historical knowledge as a basis for transformed consciousness and the imperative of continual reference to those events that established the revolutionary credentials of the Soviet Union, namely the 1917 revolution and the Great Fatherland War. Looked at in the large sweep of Russian history, what emerges is yet another Russian leader borrowing from the West, only instead of naval technology or judicial systems, what Gorbachev in fact sought was a modular kind of Vergangenheitsbewältigung, what he or his advisors understood as Germany's cultural technology of simultaneously using the past and putting it to rest.

Perhaps the most consequential aspect of glasnost was the space it gave to other groups in Soviet society to articulate their own relationship to the past. First there were dissident groups, many of whose publications gradually took on greater public visibility as Gorbachev allowed the emergence of a contested political sphere in the late 1980s. But instead of glorifying the originary moment of 1917 and the course of the revolution, they excoriated it; the past they sought to make contemporary was the past of the forced migrations, purges, and terrors. The articulations of the past with the most powerful effect on Soviet government, however, were those giving voice to a range of ethnic nationalisms. While Soviet leaders had always had to manage the aspirations of national groups within the Soviet Union, perestroika changed the conditions of nationalism's possibility. Assertions of national identity fit easily into the mythic frame that had been promoted during the Brezhnev era, hailing originary moments and mystic rituals of belonging. These mythic national discourses appeared in every republic, including the Russian Republic, where perestroika enabled both the growth of mythic discourses of Russian and Soviet nationalism.

The most well-known articulation of orthodox Soviet identity within the mythic frame of the center-orthodox enunciated during perestroika took place with the Nina Andreeva affair of March 1988. What made the publication of a letter by a Leningrad schoolteacher in the paper *Sovetskaia rossiia* an "affair" was the widespread opinion that the letter's appearance had been orchestrated by conservative elements in the Politburo to criticize the ideological effects of Gorbachev's policy of glasnost. And in fact, the letter can be read as the articulation in a popular, everyday idiom of those orthodox principles at the core of which was respect before and deeply felt emotional attachment to the achievements of the Soviet Union. According to Andreeva, the paramount achievement was of course the Soviet victory over the Nazis, which would not have been possible without the other milestones in Soviet history: the revolution, the civil war, and the construction of an industrialized state out of a vast peasant empire. Most worrisome for Andreeva was the media's role in distorting young people's relationship to this common (mythical) past, for it appeared to her to be guided by the worldview of a "left-wing liberal intellectual socialism" that "champions counter proletarian collectivism with the 'intrinsic value of the individual'— modernistic quests in the cultural sphere, God-seeking tendencies, technocratic idols, homilies to the 'democratic' charms of contemporary capitalism, and kowtowing to its real and supposed achievements."[27]

Andreeva was identifying here precisely those elements of Gorbachev's "new thinking" that were circulating widely in the Soviet media at the time. That young people would interest themselves in any aspect of the Soviet past other than that of the achievements of Soviet society baffled Andreeva, and both these distractions and the general climate of cynicism she attributed to the confusing status that Communist ideology had acquired in the contemporary media. Symptomatic in this regard was how Stalin was represented in the official perestroika media. As opposed to being the insane tyrant portrayed in many articles in the popular press, for Andreeva, Stalin was above all the central symbol of the enormous progress made by the Soviet Union in the seventy-some years of its existence. This symbolic presence was felt primarily on an emotional and aesthetic level, and to this extent it was hardly debatable. Yet, in order to show that she, too, could speak the language of history, she supplied some historical documents of her own, countering the widespread image of Stalin as mad autocrat, a modern day Ivan the Terrible, documents that (allegedly) included a description of Stalin written by Winston Churchill, in which he acknowledged Stalin's personal genius and praised his achievements. The problem with the left-liberal socialists, Andreeva asserted, was that they had lost their intellectual and philosophical bearings in the course of their infatuation with the historical record: "Claiming full possession of historical truth, they replace the sociopolitical criterion of society's development with scholastic ethical categories."[28] In other words, their obsession with history leads to the loss of class explanation and an overemphasis on the judgment of actions of individuals, a familiar socialist criticism of "bourgeois" historiography.

Also present in the letter was that other feature of the post-Soviet culture of remembrance that emerged from the cult, namely, the substitution of Russian national categories for what formerly had referred to Soviet ones. This was reflected in Andreeva's concern for what she called the tendency toward "cosmopolitanism" in the left-liberal media; here she used Trotsky as a foil to comment on the present, specifically his negative assessment in the 1920s of the Russian people as possessing adequate revolutionary consciousness. She alluded to one of the themes that would come out in the open in 1989 as Russian nationalist movements began to articulate their own criticisms in the public sphere: that of all the nations who had suffered during the last seventy years and who had sacrificed the most during the war, none could compare with the Russian *narod*. Thus, she supported a mythical consciousness grounded in the nation, one that supports a strong sense of patriotism, the heroic defense of the state, and pride in the nation's achievements.

One way to conceptualize the Nina Andreeva letter is to think of it as representing a transitional moment in the construction of orthodox mythic discourse, from being a product of the cult of Lenin, Stalin, and the war supervised by the state but deeply felt by a broad sector of society, to being an articulated national-type program that would have to compete with other mythic narratives in the rapidly evolving public sphere. The Andreeva affair was a preview of the landscape that would emerge in the early years of post-Soviet Russia in which a so-called "red-brown coalition," claiming possession of an authentic national consciousness, faced a group of reformers whose popularity was based in part on possession of a lack, a purported *absence* of a connection to the Soviet past. All pasts became overtly politicized as both reformers and their opponents struggled over the remains of the Soviet system.

### History and Myth in the Post-Soviet Decade

The end of the Soviet Union in 1991 brought to a close the cycles of Marxist transformation that Hanson so provocatively laid out. No longer was the range of government action limited to the three options of left-charismatic, right-rational, or center-orthodox that derived from European Marxism; no longer was policy informed by the struggle to imagine and define a relationship to the transcendent cause of revolution. The Russian federation began its new life as a capitalist democratic state and was more or less promptly welcomed into the "club" of the West. And yet, as Stephen Kotkin has pointed out, the new Russia in many ways is still the old Soviet Union, and those who assume that 1991 represented a "revolution" have been paying too much attention to the statements of Westernizing Russian politicians and their American and European advisers.[29] Most important, a vast gulf remains between the elites who control the Russian economy and the masses of the population who have born the brunt of Russia's deindustrialization.[30] The war generation is dwindling, although there are still enough veterans around to serve as iconic figures on Victory Day, shuffling along and grasping both walking cane and bouquets. The *shestideciatniki*, or people of the sixties generation, are gradually ceding their places to the second postwar generation, now in their thirties and forties, who are themselves ushering into existence the first post-Soviet generation.

A conspicuous aspect of Soviet culture was how the formation of individuals' relationships to the past took place within the idioms of three different conceptualizations of time inherent in the three political "options" presented by Soviet Marxism. The transmission of this memory problem from generation to generation supplied one of the central social dynamics of the late Soviet period. Insofar as Marxism's senses of time were sustained by the party's struggle to rule the first socialist state, the end of the Soviet Union, and the party's disappearance means that the framing of time is now the province of other discourses and cultural practices. Likewise, one should continue to pay close attention to the war's place in the ongoing transformation of the media in the Soviet Union.

To the degree that the market requires a rational approach to time, one would expect that historical consciousness would quickly take the place of those orientations toward the past that seemed to rely on irrational attitudes to the past, attitudes of transcendence and myth. For this line of thought, the end of party rule and the embrace of the market would have finally allowed what *must have been present* all along in the Soviet Union, the desire among all citizens for a true accounting, a stable record, a known and acknowledged past. The fact that such a desire was and is not present in the way Besançon expects should send one back to the drawing board to do more of what Hanson does, to think more deeply about the specific historical shaping of time in Soviet society.

But the political struggles of the first post-Soviet decade involved what can only be called a mad rush after legitimacy, one key aspect of which was the search for usable pasts. The field of post-Soviet politics during the early and mid-1990s consisted on the one side of those Communist/nationalist parties and groupings that maintained a sense of continuity with concepts of mythic time deriving from the Soviet era, and on the other side of those post-Soviet liberal politicians who grasped for new ways to define and assert their collective identities. The Yeltsin forces, for example, assumed the self-evidence of a historical record that depicted the Soviet Union as the most disastrous episode in Russian history. But the very emptiness of the Soviet past left them in a quandary as they set about constructing a substantive vision of the past that would ensure their legitimacy and could compete with the vision of their principal opponents, the Communists/nationalists. Their search took on an almost pathetic quality when in 1996 Yeltsin, in a speech to a gathering of the Russian intelligentsia, announced a competition for "a new national idea" for Russia, one that would replace Marxism and a narrow, exclusive nationalism. The competition had no winner. This episode revealed the central problem for any liberal ideology in Russia: the fact that

Russia has no history of civic nationalism. There is no counterfund of symbols with which politicians could mobilize the populace around the values of such (Western) abstractions as "civil society," "the rule of law," and "democratic empowerment."

The post-Soviet politician who moved most quickly to remake the public spaces under his jurisdiction, with the goal of evoking a soft, inclusive image of Russian national identity, was the Moscow mayor Yurii Luzhkov. Under his guidance and with his personal involvement in the design and placement of statues and monuments, Moscow became the site of multiple references to the Russian past, some solemn and spectacular, like the reconstructed Christ the Savior Cathedral, and others whimsical and pompous, like the statue of Peter the Great on Krymskii Island.[31]

As far as the memory of the war goes, the post-Soviet era finally saw the completion of Victory Park in Moscow, a project that was first envisioned under Khrushchev in the 1950s and meant to be the most important monument to the Soviet victory in the Great Fatherland War. The project languished for decades until Gorbachev once again took an interest in it in the late 1980s, although it was still not completed when the Soviet Union dissolved in December 1991. As one might have expected, the new custodians of the project, the liberals Luzhkov and Yeltsin, required some serious design changes, such as the removal of all symbols of the Soviet era and their replacement with Russian symbols. Amazingly, the official brochure printed up to describe the park made no mention of the Soviet Union.[32] The park opened in 1995, on the fiftieth anniversary of the end of the war, with Yeltsin and Luzhkov both supervising citywide rituals to commemorate the victory of a country that neither wished to acknowledge—more evidence of the awkwardness of civic nationalism in Russia, with politicians trying to tap into the power of Russia's greatest moment without acknowledging that the society who fought the war did so for the fatherland *and* for Stalin.

Putin appears to be another case altogether. Although he was Yeltsin's hand-picked successor, he has shown himself much less categorical about the need to reject the Soviet past. In 2000 he authorized the erection of a plaque dedicated to his former boss Yurii Andropov on Lubianka Square; he declared that for the time being Lenin would stay put on Red Square; and he decreed that the Russian national anthem was to be the Soviet national anthem with a few new verses added. Moreover, he participated in the symbolic resurrection of Stalin as war hero and state builder by allowing busts and plaques of Stalin to be placed at the Kremlin and Victory Park, and by repeating on 9 May 2000 the opening of the speech Stalin used in 1945 to announce the Soviet victory. A May 2001 *Izvestiia* article entitled "Long Live Ratings, Long Live Stalin!" argued that under Putin, "Victory Day has again become an ideological holiday." This suggests that Putin considers his most pressing task not to consolidate the market and democracy in Russia, but to project a sense of collective identity and purpose that would encompass and not refuse the Soviet past.

## Conclusion

In terms of the larger questions concerning memory, politics, and democratization in the postwar era, the Soviet and Russian case is idiosyncratic. Indeed, the very idea of democratization is one that fits uneasily into the post-Soviet context, for while the Russian Federation is formally governed by a democratically elected parliament and president, it is clear that many Russian politicians and citizens are not at all accustomed to what Western Europeans understand as the culture of democracy. Neither the model of Germany nor the model of South Africa, with its Truth and Reconciliation Commission, seems particularly suited to the post-Soviet context. The commitment to democracy in Germany after 1945 might have taken place on the tabula rasa of burned fields and rubble-strewn streets, and yet it was a table set firmly in a capitalist culture with a history of groups interacting in parliamentary forums. Democracy was by no means a completely foreign or alien object in the hands of the architects of Germany's postwar system, and after twenty or so years of economic growth, German society was able to literally and figuratively afford paying attention to its place in history. It could be argued that the *Wirtschaftswunder* (economic miracle) underwrote Vergangenheitsbewältigung, creating a condition in which acknowledgement of the crimes of the past did not threaten the existence of any of the classes, parties, or actors forced to grapple with the legacy of Nazism. The past later became an addressable problem as a part of Germany's broader assertion of its importance in Europe and in international organizations. In South Africa the door to the past was opened by the desires of a vast majority of the population that had been the object of systemic oppression and exploitation based on race. Its post-apartheid rulers believed that the civil society they sought to build could not work without giving all victims the opportunity to confront their oppressors; nor did they believe that South Africa could continue as Africa's wealthiest state in the post–Cold War era without asserting its identity as an African nation, ruled by Africans. German historians and South African activists had in this sense a "simpler" time of it, in that the German and South African memory problems derived from a moment when morally bankrupt and pseudoscientific assumptions about race constituted the foundation of government.[33] This enabled the drawing of a sharp boundary between a time when these assumptions were believed and a time when they were discredited and condemned. In both cases a confluence of circumstances allowed a singular kind of performance to emerge in the public sphere, a performance that asserted for both domestic and international audiences a particular image of a national experience or process.

The Russian case departs from these in many ways. The crimes of the past are complicated by layers of ideological reinterpretations that undermine any unanimous and unambiguous assertions about a truthful past. Crimes and acts of heroism are embedded in the same historical moment, the same historical process. In these circumstances, memory must remain in objects of everyday life, in gestures and tones of voice of passing generations, and in private rituals of loss and mourning, none of which are amenable to being recast in a public performance.

But just as important, the Russian case is marked by an uncertainty over the fit between discourses of national identity and the international sphere that valorizes and uses these discourses. Given a global circumstance of neoliberal hegemony, defined by both the struggle of national governments to define their autonomy vis-à-vis both America's national-security empire and the opportunistic shuffle of multinational corporations from country to country; and given the legacy of strong national identification supplied by both the Soviet and imperial Russian past, the sense of a distinct break that would enable a judgmental kind of historical vision is unlikely to emerge. The overwhelming problem in Russia is less to account for the past than to interpret the present.

## Postscript

If there is one point that all of the essays in this volume agree on, it is that World War II has in a sense transformed all politics into politics of memory. Any effort to define a collective identity and purpose inevitably stakes out a narrative terrain on which is said, Remember, this happened to us, this is why today we must. . . . The catastrophe of World War II was so enormous that no national narrative can avoid it; every national leader will have to produce and repeat a story about the war, even as the generation who actually fought the war disappears from the scene, as the new generations must be oriented to the past in the course of becoming political subjects. Thus politics, which must continually produce its own spectacles, seizes on commemorations as made-to-order events offering the opportunity to sculpt the past in particular ways. Anniversaries of many of the key events of World War II will recur endlessly, thus filling the future with memories and with significant dates. The recent celebration of the sixtieth anniversary of Victory in Europe Day showed this dynamic with great clarity.

The official American presentation of VE Day was a spectacle of absences —the Baltic states had no fascists or Communists, the Soviets had no non-Russians who fought in the war, the entire postwar history of the Soviet Union and Eastern Europe was simply the experience of tyranny. These absences make some sense if one remembers that according to the world-view of the current president of the United States and his colleagues and teachers, World War II is problematic, since the dominant evil of the age is Communism, not Fascism, and yet Communism is not the flawed ideology in question on 9 May. They understand and process Fascism chiefly through the lens of the Holocaust, not through any frame that would acknowledge the common genealogy of all three of the twentieth century's leading ideo-logical systems in the crisis of democracy, biopolitics, and sovereignty of the nineteenth century.[34] From the perspective of the Bush administration, the fascists and Nazis were just a bunch of ruthless crazies, mad mullahs, terror-ists with no respect for life or freedom who had to be defeated. It was, of course, Russia's (not the Soviet Union's) service to the world to help defeat the Nazis between 1941 and 1945, and generations of U.S. presidents will no doubt recall this sacrifice at the appropriate time. And perhaps they, too, will go to places like Latvia and Georgia, like President George W. Bush did, in order to repeat this story to the Latvian and Georgian publics, lending prestige and authority to a story that helps local elites struggling to establish themselves within the networks of European and Western power.

President Putin, for his part, seized the moment, too, using the anniver-sary as another opportunity to play the memory game he has promoted since coming to power. The game involves time-travel and transplants: his task is to re-present the stability, coherence, and solidarities of 1945 in 2005, to sculpt the images of state and people in such a way as to enable the constant recall of the "greatness" of the Soviet Union. Every five years, the Russian public can expect to be restapled to its Soviet past, whether it wants to or not, through the medium of the Great Patriotic War. Politics as spec-tacles of memory produced and will no doubt continue to produce strange juxtapositions, confusing images, as challenging as the photograph of Presidents Putin and Bush driving in an old 1956 Soviet car, waving out the window. How to interpret this image? It was ostensibly an attempt at "fun," a demonstration that the two men liked each other enough to goof around together, taking each other for a ride. But it is a good idea to remember that in any spectacle of memory politics there is noise in the channel, or more accurate, the channel *is* noise. Symbols and semiotic play, a peeling away of layers of meanings. In this sense, the car was not just the set for elaborately constructed friendship, it was the Cold War lasting into the present, shined up, good as new. The two leaders just took the opportunity to take the Cold War out for a drive. Perhaps both were remembering, each in their own way, something they know well: the utility of fear.

## Notes

I would like to thank Eric Weitz for encouraging me to take up this essay in the first place, as well as the editors of this volume, Ned Lebow, Wulf Kansteiner, and Claudio Fogu, for their patience and assistance in helping me to rework the very different drafts of this essay. They are to be commended, too, for their organization of the two conferences that led up to this volume, which were models of collegiality and intellectual engagement. I would also like to thank all the contributors for their comments on earlier drafts and for the all-around-stimulating intellectual encounter.

1  Suny, *The Soviet Experiment*, 333.

2  The only country that approaches the Soviet case in what one might call its geographic and historical peculiarity would be Switzerland: a small, mountainous country in the center of Europe that avoided the social, economic, and demographic upheaval of total war altogether. Although it also goes without saying that Switzerland's total identification with democracy, capitalism, and the West meant that its modes of dealing with its active nonparticipation in the war can be better understood with reference to the experiences of other West European countries.

3  See Besançon, "Forgotten Communism."

4  Ibid., 27.

5  Merridale, *Night of Stone*.

6  Here I am trying to use the concept in the face of its employment by the advertising industry for which simply being young is enough to justify one's membership in a specific shared universe of experience.

7  To narrow the concept to that cohort of men from the ages of nineteen to twenty-five who actually did the fighting and dying ignores the power of total war in the modern era. It is commonplace to define total war as warfare not of armies but of populations, and indeed it would be hard to say that between 1940 and 1945 one society experienced "more" total war than any other. Americans saw relatively small civilian losses in the European theater, yet the economic dimension of the war

changed the social and cultural circumstances of the vast majority of Americans. On the other hand, the claim that there was in the United States a "war generation" that was the "greatest generation ever" seems ideological, ignoring the divides of race, class, and gender that gave the war many meanings and conflicting histories.

8    I do not want to imply that all Soviet citizens had the *same* experience of the war, for they obviously did not. Indeed, it would be a strange claim to argue that they did or could. And yet I do not think it justified to view the diversity of the population as justifying the same degree of suspicion of the claim for the existence of a wartime "generation" in the Soviet case as is justified in the American case.

9    Marx and Engels, *The German Ideology*, quoted in Hanson, *Time and Revolution*, 54.

10    Kataev, cited in Hanson, *Time and Revolution*, 162.

11    Ibid., 170.

12    See, in particular, Brooks, *Thank You, Comrade Stalin!*, 160.

13    Weiner, *Making Sense of War*, 17.

14    Suny, *The Soviet Experiment*, 391.

15    See Seniavskaia, *Frontovoe Pokolenie 1941–1945*.

16    The generational cohort who experienced the war was less fearful and less passive before the power of the party and NKVD, as shown by the wave of strikes, rebellions, and uprisings led by veterans that took place after the war in a number of camps of the Soviet penal system (Weiner, *Making Sense of War*, 366–67).

17    Hanson, *Time and Revolution*, 177.

18    Ibid.

19    Tumarkin, *The Living and the Dead*, 131.

20    Ibid., 133.

21    For another criticism of this opposition, see Weiner who in the course of surveying the relatively small literature on the Soviet experience of World War II points out that the image in Tumarkin's book of a passive population receiving the collective memory imposed by the state ignores the theoretical issue that a number of historians have recently begun to pay serious attention to, namely, the process by which Soviet citizens adopted the ideological images and practices of the state in the process of creating their own relationship to the state. By stressing an absolute divide between a ritualistic state and an anomic society, between an oppressive public sphere and an individualistic private sphere, what is lost is the fact that operating beneath the cult was a process by which Soviet citizens created their own meanings out of the war, ones that existed in parallel to official meanings. Weiner, *Making Sense of War*, 17–18.

22    This was the lesson of Gorbachev's ill-fated anti-alcohol campaign of 1986, which aroused so much opposition that it was quickly abandoned.

23    *My* is the first-person plural pronoun in Russian.

24    Eisen, *The Glasnost Reader*, 410.

25    In April 1990 Gorbachev himself presented the Polish leader General Jaru-

zelski with a collection of documents proving the NKVD's role in the murder of Polish officers at Katyń in 1940.

26 Like the following brief notice that appeared at the bottom of the front page of *Komsomol'skaia pravda* on 23 July 1988, under the headline "They Saved the World": "Slavutich (Kiev Oblast')—Not far from this young city of energy workers, in the village of Mycy a memorial complex opened that is dedicated to those soldiers who perished during the years of the Great Patriotic War. It was designed and realized during the voluntary labor Saturdays of the Komsomol youth league by the workers of Slavutich."

27 Andreeva, quoted in Eisner, *The Glasnost Reader*, 29.

28 Ibid.

29 See Kotkin, *Armageddon Averted*.

30 See Caroline Humphrey's collection of essays, *The Unmaking of Soviet Life*, for a compelling view of the cultural and economic chaos brought about by the disappearance of the Soviet state.

31 See Grant, "New Moscow Monuments, or, States of Innocence."

32 Forest and Johnson, "Unraveling the Threads of History."

33 For a discussion of the relevance of race for the ethnic purges of the 1930s and 1940s, Weitz, "Racial Politics without the Concept of Race," as well as four responses to his article in the same issue of *Slavic Review*.

34 Agamben, *Homo Sacer*.

CLAUDIO FOGU AND WULF KANSTEINER ⁂

# The Politics of Memory and the Poetics of History

The purpose of this final chapter is to draw some comparative conclusions
from the national case studies presented in this volume and to show how
they contribute to reframing the study of memory. This is not an easy
undertaking, especially for historians whose suspicion of generalizing statements has been reinforced by their scholarly focus on a subject—collective
forms of remembrance—which is highly contested both theoretically and
historiographically.[1] Bearing this cautionary premise in mind, we have approached our task somewhat obliquely. First, we offer an overview of the
current state of memory studies that highlights the specific theoretical-
methodological issues that our case studies address and clarify. Informed by
these preliminary reflections, we then turn to the case studies to illustrate
what we believe to be the most generalizable traits which they reveal about
the institutionalization of the memory of Nazism and World War II in
Europe from 1945 to the present.

Our analysis dispels any temptation to generalize about patterns of institutionalization that neatly reflect the categories of victors, losers, and
bystanders; while that assumption informed our initial research design, it
has not been confirmed in the course of the project. Our investigation
highlights, instead, two historically specific contributions that our case studies offer to the most vexing theoretical issues characterizing the debate on
memory: the relationship between individual and collective memory, and
that between history and memory. On the one hand, we present a specific
generational dynamic as the primary agent affecting the most dramatic
changes in the politics of memory observed between the late 1960s and the
mid-1980s across Europe. On the other, we underscore how, in some national contexts this dynamic was affected by a peculiar culture of history that
framed it from the beginning. Though it is impossible to isolate any generalizable causal factor, it appears that the politics of memory always interacts
with specific poetics of history whose intensity may constitute *the* major
variable in the evolution of collective memories.

The Memory Wave

The memory wave of the past two decades has changed the field of cultural history and raised serious questions about the methodological and institutional status quo. As "memory has become a central and organizing concept in the humanities and certain branches of the social sciences," it remains unclear to what extent this convergence reflects actual common intellectual, methodological, and political interests.[2] Are we dealing with a fad that introduces a new name for an old field of study, or do memory studies offer an opportunity to confront important social problems in sophisticated and original ways that transcend the debilitating limits of academic specialization?[3]

Students of collective memory are indeed grappling with a slippery phenomenon. It is not history, least of all in the academic sense, but it is sometimes made from similar material. It is a collective phenomenon, but it primarily manifests itself in the actions and statements of individuals. It can take hold of historically and socially remote events but often privileges the interests of the contemporaries of the events under description. It is as much a result of conscious manipulation as unconscious absorption. It arises from a peculiar interplay of consensus and conflict, and it is always mediated: it can only be observed in roundabout ways, more through its effects than its characteristics. In essence, collective-memory studies represent a new approach to "that most elusive of phenomena, 'popular consciousness.' "[4]

Although the phrase *collective memory* is the most widely used definitional term for this phenomenon, scholars have coined terms such as *collective remembrance*, *social memory*, and *cultural memory*, or altogether rejected the need for new terminology in favor of the old-fashioned concept of "myth."[5] In addition, some of the more unusual phrases used to designate collective memories are *memory work*, *popular history making*, and *historical culture*.[6] The multitude of terms has further increased as scholars seek to develop expressions that illuminate the social base or social function of the collective memories under consideration. Therefore the range of vocabulary includes *national memory*, *public memory*, *vernacular memory*, and *counter-memory*, among many others.[7] Finally, there is the conceptual opposite of collective memory, which has been alternatively called "social forgetting," "social amnesia," and "*lieux d'oubli*."[8] Most recently, there seems to be a tendency to forego further terminological fine-tuning and to simply refer to "memory" when discussing collective memories. While such shorthand might reduce terminological overkill, it also indicates an increasing insecurity about the academic community's abilities to determine the sociological base of any given representation of the past with some precision.

As a result of this conceptual haziness, inquiries into collective memory have been hardly distinguishable from research on topics such as tradition, popular history, historical identities, and historical consciousness. Differences in terminology often reflect different tastes and research customs rather than clearly distinguishable analytical foci, research objectives, or conceptual strategies. Consequently, many of the scholarly traditions that have preceded and informed collective-memory studies have shown substantial overlap with their successful successor. That applies in particular to the history of mentalities, oral history, the history of everyday life and popular culture, and inquiries into historical consciousness.[9] Many of the titles to emerge from these research traditions could carry the epitaph "memory" without misleading the audience about their content and methods.[10] In this respect, the astonishing quantitative dimension of the memory wave also attests to large-scale editorial "relabeling." Memory studies bring together an impressive range of intellectual interests that hitherto sailed under separate colors; that explains both the relatively sudden popularity and the methodological inconsistency of the field.

Despite an impressive range of subject matter, memory studies have thrived on catastrophes and trauma, and the Holocaust is still the primary, archetypal topic in memory studies.[11] Every imaginable type of Holocaust representation has by now been analyzed, and a continuous string of recent publications indicates that this trend will not abate any time soon.[12] In fact, Holocaust studies have reached a phase of metacriticism and anti-memory as many Holocaust experts are focusing on the critique of Holocaust memory and representation.[13] Due to its exceptional breadth and depth, Holocaust studies illustrate the full range of methods and perspectives in event-oriented studies of collective memory, but we find similar works analyzing the memory of other exceptionally destructive, criminal and catastrophic events—for instance, World War II and Fascism, slavery, and recent genocides and human-rights abuses.[14] Especially with regard to human-rights abuses, attempts to establish the historical record of the events in question and the desire to facilitate collective remembrance and mourning often overlap. In comparison, the legacy of relatively benign events is only rarely considered in contemporary studies of collective memory.[15]

Quite aside from the question of imbalance between studies of positive legacies and studies of the lingering memory of negative events, the preeminence of the latter has had theoretical consequences that cannot be overlooked. The emphasis given to traumatic events, *ipso facto*, has opened the way to a very slippery articulation of the relationship between the concepts of individual and collective memory. At first glance, recent psychological and neurological studies give ample reason for the conflation of individual and collective memory because such research has time and again emphasized the social nature of individual remembering and forgetting. Even on a neurological level one's ability to store, recall, and reconfigure verbal and nonverbal experiences and information is significantly shaped by neural pathways that one has laid down in response to previous stimuli and learning from the immediate and wider social environment.[16] The very language and narrative patterns that one uses to express memories, even autobiographical memories, are inseparable from the social standards of plausibility and authenticity that they embody.[17] In this sense, "there is no such thing as individual memory."[18]

This neurological definition of the collective nature of memory confirms the insights of the French sociologist Maurice Halbwachs, who may be credited with being both the inventor of the concept of "collective memory" and the primary theoretical reference point for historians working on this phenomenon.[19] Following Halbwachs, who was a student of Emile Durkheim, historians have understood collective memories as collectively shared representations of the past. Halbwachs's emphasis on the function of everyday communication for the development of collective memories and his interest in the imagery of social discourse, especially in commemorations, resonate very well with recent historiographical themes, including oral history, the history of mentalities, and questions of historical representation. The impressive convergence of neuropsychological, sociological, historical, and artistic perspectives on the social character of individual memory seems to confirm Halbwachs's view, who insisted as far back as 1925 that "the idea of an individual memory, absolutely separate from social memory, is an abstraction almost devoid of meaning."[20] Yet some historians have grown uncomfortable with Halbwachs's determined anti-individualism. They object that Durkheim's disciples have held too tenaciously to the notion "that individual memory was entirely socially determined," thereby writing the role of the individual out of the history of collective memory.[21] Accordingly, while most historians of memory have continued to pay homage to Halbwachs in their texts and footnotes, they have also increasingly distanced themselves from his theories by reinserting into the study of memory their traditional concerns with the objectives and actions of individuals.

This distancing of historians from the sociological tradition in which the concept of individual memory is negated and socialized has helped highlight some of the theoretical imprecision in Halbwachs's work. In the first place, even if one were to admit that all individual memories are formed and transmitted within social collectives of all sorts, the term *collective* becomes entirely misleading when applied to images derived from the representational artifacts in which these socially constructed memories are institutionalized. There is no easy way to determine if a collectively constructed memorial image, once institutionalized into a specific representational site, translates into an equivalent mental image held by a collectivity of viewers. Everything about mental images is mediated, by the ritual politics of commemoration, by the modes and media of representation, by the codes and processes of reception. And yet, most sociologically inspired studies tend to elide the difference between the two planes: that of the collective *construction* of all mental memories, where *collective* stands for "social" rather than "non-individual," and that of the collective *use* of institutionalized memories, where *collective* simply refers to a multiplicity of addressees (viewers, participants, visitors, etc.), but does not imply at all a correspondent collectively *received*, *held*, or even *constructed* mental image. If one wants to identify such collectively held believes about the past, the study of collective memory on the basis of cultural artifacts—films, books, exhibits, and the like—involves the challenge of relating the artifacts in question to their effects on producers and audiences. Collective memories might indeed be reflected in products of historical culture, but only if these products can be shown to have had similar effects, at the level of form and/or content, on the historical identities of their users.

It might be interesting to note at this point how the translation of Halbwachs's writings on *Les cadres sociaux de la memoire* into English has completely transfigured the French emphasis on the collective *as* synonymous with social, into the Anglo-American obsession with the collective *as* the opposite of the individual. In fact, a marked tendency in English-language studies of collective memory is that of making the direction between the individual and the collective *tout court* reversible. The fact that individual memory cannot be conceptualized and studied without recourse to its social context does not necessarily imply the reverse, that is, that collective memory can only be imagined and accessed through its manifestation in individuals. At the very least, one must differentiate between different types of "social" memory—autobiographical memory on the one hand and collective memory on the other. For lack of such differentiation, many inquiries into collective memories commit a tempting, yet potentially grave, methodological error: they perceive and conceptualize collective memory exclusively in terms of the psychological and emotional dynamics of individual remembering.

Since the threshold between the individual and the collective is often crossed without any adjustments in method, collectives are found to remember, forget, and repress the past without any awareness that such language is at best metaphorical and at worst misleading about the phenomenon under study. Historians rationalize this conflation and sidestep the theoretical and methodological challenge of thinking in terms of collectives as distinct from individuals by emphasizing the role of human agency in the construction of collective memories. They focus on acts of memorialization —for instance, in museum design—assuming the realized object and its meaning is prescribed by its maker's conscious or unconscious objectives.[22]

These category mistakes stem from a subtle but decisive confusion about the difference between "collected memory" and "collective memory."[23] A collected memory would be an aggregate of individual memories that behaves and develops just like its individual composites and which can therefore be studied with the whole inventory of neurological, psychological, and psychoanalytical methods and insights concerning the memories of individuals. Unfortunately, collective memories might not behave according to such rules but might have their own dynamics and rules of engagement for which one must find appropriate methods of analysis.

For instance, it might make sense to argue with Freud that an individual's failure to work through his/her past results in unwanted symptoms of psychological illness; that the self relies on a sense of continuity which makes it impossible to repress the past without having to pay a psychological price for this repression. On a collective scale, especially on the scale of larger collectives, such assumptions are misleading.[24] Nations can repress with psychological impunity; their collective memories can be changed without a return of the repressed. Therefore, "when speaking of social forgetting, we are best advised to keep psychological or psychoanalytical categories at bay and to focus, rather, on the social, political, and cultural factors at work."[25]

Reservations about the use of psychoanalytical methods in collective-memory studies extend to the concept of trauma, which has particular relevance for understanding of the legacy of collective catastrophes. However, unlike the concepts of the unconscious and repression that inappropriately individualize and psychologize collective-memory processes, the use of the concept of trauma has had an opposite yet equally misleading effect. Some recent works in trauma theory invoke the example of the Holocaust as illustration for a more general postmodern claim about incommensurability in language and representation. The very specific and unusual experiences and memory challenges of survivors, who find that their memories of the Final Solution form a volatile, independent realm of memory that remains painfully irreconcilable with subsequent experiences, are offered as proof for the general traumatic characteristics of the postmodern condition.[26] In this vein Cathy Caruth has argued with regard to the Holocaust that such "a crisis of truth extends beyond the question of individual cure and asks how we in this era can have access to our own historical experience, to a history that is in its immediacy a crisis to whose truth there is no simple access."[27] Not surprisingly, such obliteration of historical specificity has met with determined criticism, even from theorists who are very sympathetic to the use of psychoanalytical methods in memory studies.

Dominick LaCapra, who has systematically and extensively worked on trauma and memory, pointed out that "there is a great temptation to trope away from specificity and to generalize hyperbolically, for example, through an extremely abstract mode of discourse that may at times serve as a surrogate for a certain form of deconstruction, elaborate an undifferentiated notion of all history (or at least all modernity) as trauma, and overextend the concept of victim and survivor."[28] One could add to this that specific visions of the past might originate in traumatic experiences but that they do not retain that quality if they become successful collective memories. The concept of trauma, as well as the concept of repression, neither captures nor illuminates the forces that contribute to the making and unmaking of collective memories. Even in cases of so-called delayed collective memory (as with the Holocaust or Vietnam), the delayed onset of public debates about the meaning of negative pasts has more to do with political interest and opportunism than with the persistence of trauma or any "leakage" in the collective unconscious.[29] Small groups whose members have directly experienced such traumatic events (veterans' or survivors' groups) have a chance to shape the national memory only if they command the means to express their visions and if their vision meets with compatible social or political objectives and inclinations among other important social groups (for instance, political generations or parties). Past events can only be recalled in a collective setting "if they fit within a framework of contemporary interests."[30]

The critique of undue emphasis on the individual in psychoanalytically informed approaches to collective memory, as well as the frustration with postmodern disregard for historical specificity, have led to attempts to rethink intentionality in ways that are perhaps best described as post-postmodern methodological reflections. Nancy Wood delineated such an approach in her remarks on collective memory, the unconscious, and intentionality: "While the emanation of individual memory is primarily subject to the laws of the unconscious, public memory—whatever its unconscious vicissitudes—testifies to a will or desire on the part of some social group or disposition of power to select and organize representations of the past so that these will be embraced by individuals as their own. If particular representations of the past have permeated the public domain, it is because they embody an intentionality—social, political, institutional and so on—that promotes or authorizes their entry."[31]

Wood addressed a number of possible sources that "purposefully" shape public memory, ranging from social groups to institutions and dispositions of power. In this way she politely and diplomatically summarized the different notions of intentionality and power that have informed collective-memory studies and that run the gamut from conventional historical accounts of human agency to theoretically informed inquiries into the limits of memorial culture as they are reflected in specific traditions and practices of historical representation. The most interesting interventions in collective-memory studies seek to profit from poststructural insights into cultural systems of representation but also hope to reconcile these insights with conventional methods of historical studies without returning to simplistic notions of human agency (including those of Freudian origins).

While all remembering might take place in the minds of individuals, the factors that inform the form and content of that process are shaped elsewhere beyond the reach of individual and perhaps even collective intent.[32] Although collective memories have no organic basis and do not exist in any literal sense, the term *collective memory* is not simply a metaphorical expression. Collective memories originate from shared communications about the meaning of the past that are anchored in the life-worlds of individuals who partake in the communal life of the respective collective. As such, collective memories are based on the society and its inventory of signs and symbols: "Memory seems to reside not in perceiving consciousness but *in the material*: in the practices and institutions of social or psychic life, which function within us, but, strangely, do not seem to require either our participation or our explicit allegiance."[33] Such collective memories exist on the level of families, professions, political generations, ethnic and regional groups, social classes, and nations. These examples indicate that one is always part of several mnemonic communities and that collective remembering can be explored on very different scales; it takes place in very private settings as well as in the public sphere. On the one side of the spectrum one might pursue collective memories of small groups, such as families whose members weave a common vision of the family's origin and identity.[34] On the other hand, we are beginning to consider supranational collective memories, as in the case of the dubious entity of a collective European memory.[35] On any level, however, "collective memory works by subsuming individual experiences under cultural schemes that make them comprehensible and, therefore, meaningful."[36]

Methodologically speaking, memories are at their most collective when they transcend the time and space of the event's original occurrence. As such they take on a powerful life of their own, "unencumbered" by actual individual memory, and become the basis of all collective remembering as disembodied, omnipresent, low-intensity memory. This point has been reached, for instance, with regard to the memory of the Holocaust in American society. The Holocaust has become one of the icons of the American "memory of the modern."[37] As a result, millions of people share a limited range of stories and images about the Holocaust, although few of them have any personal link to the actual events. For many consumers the stories and images do not constitute particularly intense or overpowering experiences, but they nevertheless shape people's identities and worldviews.[38]

Collective memories evolve through an interesting dialectic of conflict and consensus; but while memory debates have enjoyed ample attention in memory studies, the more routine and more pervasive forms of collective memory remain underexplored. Concern with low-intensity collective memories shifts the focus from the politics of memory and its excess of scandal and intrigue to rituals and representations of the past that are produced and consumed routinely without causing much disagreement. Most groups settle temporarily on such collective memories and reproduce them for years and decades until they are questioned and overturned, often in the wake of generational turnover. These repetitive representations form the backbone of collective memories. They represent the common denominator in questions of historical taste that are disseminated widely and frequently enough to create and maintain group identities.

The complex interdisciplinary space occupied by collective-memory studies sustains three intertwined conclusions against which we will seek to evaluate this volume's collection of studies. First, collective-memory studies are largely content-oriented, but this orientation has been occupied primarily by negative-traumatic events. Second, as a result of the application of psychological and psychiatric concepts such as the unconscious, repression,

and trauma, collective-memory studies have not yet sufficiently conceptualized collective memory as distinct from individual memory; the nature
and dynamics of collective memories are frequently misrepresented through
the facile use of psychological categories, while little or no attention is paid
to the problem of reception both in terms of methods and sources. Third,
despite these shortcomings, collective-memory studies constitute an ingenious intellectual hybrid that integrates seemingly contradictory epistemol-
ogies from classical hermeneutics to postmodern theory in a very productive
fashion.

## Comparative Analysis

In focusing on the memory of World War II and Nazism, this collection
belongs to the tradition of collective-memory studies that deals with the
legacy of exceptionally destructive events; however, we were concerned with
the relational and institutional dynamics of collective memories as well as
their content. We specifically asked our authors to pay close attention to the
processes, the agents, and the media that informed the institutionalization
of memory over time in the respective national contexts. This national
framework of analysis has per force limited and informed the results of our
comparisons. On the one hand, our conclusions cannot address the dialectic
between local and national levels of institutionalization of memory (even
though some of the case studies highlight its importance); on the other, they
cannot exhaustively measure the impact of international events, relations,
and organizations on national politics of memory. Nevertheless, at least
indirectly, our case studies provide important insights into the transnational
dimension of collective-memory formation. All the authors acknowledge,
for instance, that the fall of the Berlin Wall has had an impact on the national politics of memory across Europe. The results of this impact, however,
can neither be generalized nor typologized. It is not simply that changes in
the politics of memory in nations such as France or Austria in the 1990s were
much less intense than those registered in Germany, the USSR/Russia, or
Poland. What is more striking and worth underscoring is that even in the
cases of the last three countries, the direction of change preceded the collapse of Communism, and in the case of Germany, the resulting change was
not even as dramatic as the one that preceded it in the mid-1980s. Clearly,
the first result of our comparative analysis is that politics of memory take
place *primarily* within a national framework of reference that does not
wither even before historic events of supranational magnitude.

This first conclusion is not a mere reflection of the analytical framework adopted for our study. It is the result of an inductive, comparative analysis that has not identified any shared periodization, theme, or memory-image ascribable either in the whole sample or in any group of nations characterized by similar relations to the events themselves. At the level of content, until very recently, there has never been a "European" collective memory of World War II, nor is there any generalizable similarity in the phases identified by our authors as characteristics of each nation's politics of memory. Furthermore, this conclusion holds true not only when we divide our sample according to Cold War criteria among Western-capitalist nations (Austria, France, Germany, Italy, Switzerland) and Eastern-Communist nations (Poland, the USSR), but, more important, even when we look at the results in terms of the selection criteria we adopted at the beginning of our study. We have found no appreciable similarity among the nations that—from the sole and simplified point of view of their official role in the war effort—we typologically cast as victors (France, the USSR), losers (Germany, Italy), and neutrals (Poland, Austria, Switzerland). Our comparative analysis thus highlights the *dominant* relevance of the national—as opposed to the international or role-dependent—framing of politics of memory. This conclusion is particularly relevant for the study of global processes of memory formation that have received much attention in recent years.[39]

Our focus on the national level of collective memory does not preclude the possibility of applying other comparative frameworks to our material or of designing studies specifically aimed at registering the impact of international factors. On one hand, our collection offers comprehensive national surveys and periodizations, which can be fruitfully integrated into historical accounts of postwar Europe. On the other, our results offer important historical material for the advancement of related research agendas in the social sciences.[40] Our primary hope—articulated also in Ned Lebow's introductory essay in this volume—is that scholars working on topics such as processes of collective identity-formation, democratization, and European unification will find in the material presented here a valid stimulus to include the institutionalization of collective forms of memory within the range of variables bearing on the phenomena they analyze.

Disciplines such as social psychology, which for the last thirty years have been characterized by an almost exclusive focus on cognitive processes, are now reintegrating content and emotions into their analyses. Yet, current experiments designed to test the existence, formation, or institutionalization of a European form of identity have not given any consideration to the variable of collective memory. Furthermore, the whole scholarship on European identity is generally polarized between social psychologists intent on registering the entativity (the extent to which a group is perceived as a real entity) of this supranational form of identity and intellectual-cultural historians intent on contesting the theoretical validity of the concept itself or pointing out the constructed notion of Europeanness.[41] It seems to us that our inquiry offers the potential of fostering some dialogue between these seemingly antithetical positions. For example, the role of national collective memories in processes of identity-formation could constitute a key moderating factor in experiments that analyze the concept of European identity from other vantage points. By the same token, social psychology experiments conducted on the entativity of collective memories of World War II and Nazism might advance the agendas of historians by offering important insights into the processes of reception of memory images, which remain the most important limitation in all historical studies of collective memory.

The case studies in this volume may also contain some useful research data for scholars in political science and sociology. Scholars of democratization, for example, might find of particular interest the fact that the revision of World War II collective memory in Eastern Europe started in the mid-1980s, well before the fall of the Berlin Wall, and therefore anticipated and accompanied the breakdown of the Soviet system in both Poland and Russia. As we shall highlight below, this process of revision was the result of a particular generational dynamic. Doesn't this observation suggest that changes in the politics of memory that appear to assume a generational dimension could be studied by political scientists as early indicators of a political earthquake in the making? All these, of course, are but research suggestions offered in the hope that scholars in sociology, political science, and social psychology will develop them.

In this respect, the verification of our success lies beyond the confines of this volume. There are, however, a number of contributions that our collection of studies makes to the field of memory studies that merit immediate attention. Content-oriented approaches to collective memory are usually distinguished from inquiries into the structure and history of institutionalized memory as a way of knowing the past. Works in this last category have established how specific intellectual traditions and societies have thought about memory and how particular social practices and institutional settings shape and facilitate collective memory.[42] For instance, scholars have studied the construction of collective memories through museums and collecting, architecture and city planning, religion, postcolonial capitalism, and the politics of international atonement for past crimes.[43] These works are particularly helpful in revealing the institutional agents and social infrastructures of collective memory. Our collection also fits in this latter category of works, not only because all the essays focus on institutional sites of memory but also because the chapters collectively address the central theoretical question of the relationship between "the individual" and "the collective" in memory studies as a whole. Our comparative analysis isolates one common denominator among our case studies: more or less explicitly, all the essays reveal the importance of a *generational* level of agency standing between the hermetically insulated individual and the unspecified collective. We are not, however, speaking of a primary or single cause, but rather of a historically specific dynamic of change.

All of the case studies in this volume point to the decade and a half between the late 1960s and the mid-1980s as the period in which the most profound changes in the politics of memory took place in each of the nations observed. In France and Italy, after decades of resistance-dominated memory, a process of demystification-desecration of antifascist mythology began in the early 1970s and continues in both nations today. In neighboring Austria, au contraire, a sudden re-evaluation of anti-Nazi resistance took place. In Germany, the most open phase in coming to terms with the Holocaust started in the mid 1970s. In Switzerland and Poland, beginning in the 1970s and in the 1980s, respectively, this was a period in which intellectuals began to challenge the mythic images that crushed all living memory of the war under the rock of uninterrupted historical continuity. Lastly, in the former Soviet Union, the Brezhnev era (1964–1982) represented the key phase in the formation of both official and popular memories of the war, with the creation of an official myth of the Great Patriotic War by the Soviet leadership matched by the equally mythic manifestations of a popular-religious cult of the war dead. In sum, the major turning points in the politics of memory analyzed by our case studies took place between the late 1960s and the mid-1980s.

The years between 1968 and 1985 correspond to the period of overlap between the coming of age of the first postwar generation and the passing of the last prewar generation that had participated actively in the war or resistance effort. In some cases very early on (the late 1960s to mid-1970s in Soviet Russia, France, Italy, and Switzerland), in other cases toward the latter part of the period (early to mid-1980s in Germany, Austria, and Poland), everywhere in Europe, and irrespective of any specific political situation, the first postwar generation came to assert a collective challenge to the memories that were collectivized, officialized, and institutionalized by the survivors of the war. Naturally, the forms, the content, and the institutional shapes this challenge assumed varied from nation to nation, but the authors in this volume are unanimous in noting that the changes registered in that period were of an intensity and quality very different from those characterizing earlier ones; and in the unrelated cases of Austria and Poland the turning point in the 1980s were virtually the first noticeable changes in collective memory formation. Even where some of our authors are not particularly explicit—that is, Fogu, Orla-Bukowska, and Ludi—the absence of any other factor capable of accounting for the ubiquitous occurrence of change or explaining why it occurred roughly at the same time in Soviet Russia and Switzerland, or Poland and Germany, unmistakably points to the importance of generational relay during this fifteen-year period.

Theoretically, the isolation of a generational level of memory-collectivization is neither new nor original. Many studies have illustrated the generational dynamics of collective memory in a number of different contexts.[44] Following Karl Mannheim's 1926 definition of political generations, scholars have shown that the worldview shared by the members of a cohort is shaped by a number of formative historical experiences in their youth, which later in life resurface as memories with which the members of the group tend to identify.[45] Kansteiner's study of the 1986 historians' debate (Historikerstreit), for example, shows how certain "disturbing utterances" by some of the protagonists were "not so much part of a political program as they mark[ed] the resurfacing of bits and pieces of troubled memory."[46] Confirming these conclusions on a larger scale, this volume also offers two specific insights that could not be provided by other, more narrowly conceived projects.

In the first place, the study of fifty years of memory politics permits observation of four overlapping age cohorts, each united by common experience rather than by age: the war generation proper, that is, men and women who were in their thirties and forties or older during the war and thus politically responsible for it; the war-youth generation, those born before the war but too young to be responsible for the war and Nazism; the first postwar generation, those born during or right after the war and coming of age between the late 1960s and early 1980s; and the second postwar, or boom, generation, those born in the 1960s and currently coming of age. Although Kansteiner's contribution to this volume shows how sensitive the whole German process of "coming to terms with the past" has been to each generational coming of age, this is not the case in any of the other countries observed. From our comparative point of observation, it is the interaction and dynamic conflict between the socially dominant war-youth generation and the first postwar generation coming of age, rather than the sole agency of either of them, that produced the sort of paradigmatic shifts observed by all authors between the late 1960s and the mid-1980s. Although a prediction can be only tentative, the ubiquity of this dynamic in every national context examined suggests that changes of similar intensity might well be observable in the same period in all other European and non-European nations in which the memory of World War II played a major cultural-political role.

This conclusion finds paradoxical support in the second comparative element resulting from this study: the fact that generational dynamics are specifically and independently highlighted by Kansteiner, Golsan, Uhl, and Wolfe, and *not* explicitly by Fogu, Orla-Bukowska, and Ludi. Although all national communities examined exhibit signs of a generational dynamic at play in the changes taking place between the late 1960s and the mid-1980s, our sample is split down the middle when we look at the larger picture. Why do the national communities of Germany, Austria, France, and Soviet Russia display continuous signs of generational agency in their politics of memory throughout the fifty-year period, while Italy, Poland, and Switzerland do not? Methodological preferences may have played a role in attracting some authors to this specific level of collective agency, but a more plausible and interesting explanation emerges from the perspective of the three authors who do not stress generational patterns of change. The evolution of memory in Switzerland, Poland, and Italy seems to have followed a different trajectory than the developments in the four other nations. The politics of memory in these three national communities were shaped more by the persistence and popular diffusion of preexisting historical images, tropes, and paradigms than by the succession of different political generations. Here the archetypal image of Poland as a "Noble Camelot"—forever the unrecognized but self-conscious martyr to the cause of democracy, tolerance, and united Europa—there, the Swiss cultivation of historical "neutrality" identified with a perennial commitment to "humanitarianism." And, in Italy, the eternal return of the myth of "resurgence." In all three cases a historical culture predating the events of World War II clearly informs the formation, the evolution, and the institutionalization of its memory. It would thus appear that while in some national communities collective memories turn to the tick of the generational clock, in others the politics of memory are framed by long-lasting poetics of history. This observation raises the second theoretical issue: that of the relationship between history and memory in all its multifaceted forms.

## The Politics of Memory and the Poetics of History

The differentiation between history and memory is a recent invention. As part of large-scale relabeling efforts, many representations of the past that were previously studied under the rubrics of popular history, folk history, or history in everyday life have been rediscovered as collective memories.[47] At first this terminological shift seems relatively meaningless until one considers its political and epistemological implications. As long as popular representations of the past were conceptualized as histories, they were explicitly or implicitly measured against academic histories and often found wanting on epistemological grounds. However, as more and more representations of the past, including academic histories, are reconceptualized as memories they are removed from the judgmental and arbitrary standards of scholarship and have gained new respect as meaningful explanations in their own right. The liberation of representations of the past from the gravitational pull of professional scholarship and the concurrent rise of memory studies is an important result of the postmodern critique of academic history and its ideological foundation.[48]

Among historians the rise of memory studies, as well as the postmodern challenge, has caused considerable disagreement. On one hand, a number of historians argue that it would be misleading to distinguish between history and memory in any radical sense on epistemological grounds, because, as Peter Burke remarked in 1989, "neither memories nor histories seem objective any longer. In both cases we are learning to take account of conscious or unconscious selection, interpretation and distortion. In both cases this selection, interpretation and distortion is socially conditioned."[49] At the same time, many historians do not share this self-critical assessment. They assume that memory and history represent two related modes of knowing the past that nevertheless differ with regard to their respective social function and malleability. As David Lowenthal put it, while "memories continually change to conform with present needs . . . the historical record to some extent resists deformation."[50] Therefore, historians occasionally insist on the epistemological integrity of their craft, arguing that, "in its demand for proof, history stands in sharp opposition to memory."[51] But within memory studies the differentiation between history and memory serves a very different purpose.

Here the dividing line is frequently defined as the difference between events that are still remembered by contemporaries and events that have irretrievably passed into history because living memory of them no longer exists.[52]

The difference between history and memory in this diachronic sense is well illustrated by Jan Assmann's juxtaposition of communicative and cultural memory. He designates the former as everyday communications about the meaning of the past characterized by instability, disorganization, and non-specialization. These everyday communications have a limited temporal horizon of eighty to one hundred years at the most; they are by definition strongly influenced by contemporaries of the events in question. In contrast, cultural memory "comprises that body of reusable texts, images, and rituals specific to each society in each epoch, whose 'cultivation' serves to stabilize and convey that society's self-image."[53] Cultural memory consists of objectified culture, that is, the texts, rites, images, buildings, and monuments that are designed to recall fateful events in the history of the collective. As the officially sanctioned heritage of a society they are intended for the long durée.

Assmann's concepts point to the fact that collective memories are not limited to the constantly retreating horizon of contemporaneity; most events that happen in one's lifetime never enter any institutional form of collective memory, and many collective memories retain vibrant "recollections" of events that happened a long time ago or that never happened at all, at least not in the way that they are collectively remembered. However, despite their power to transmit concern for historical events to future generations, collective memories have a strong bias toward the present; they dedicate disproportionate amounts of time, space, and resources to communications about events that happened within the lifetimes of its producers and consumers. Or, to use Lutz Niethammer's words, collective memories are primarily located on this side of the "floating gap" between memory and history.[54]

Seen against the background of Assmann's discussion of cultural memory, the case studies focusing on Italy, Poland, and Switzerland not only prove that the membrane between history and memory is permeable but also suggest that the institutionalization of collective memory can at times situate itself *on the other side*—history's side—of the floating gap. The direction of influence in these case studies is curiously inverted: it is the remote past (history) that seems to have more agency than the present (political generations) over the institutionalization of the recent past into communicative memory. "New Camelot," the "Rütli," and the "Risorgimento" constitute the historical molds out of which Polish, Swiss, and Italian collective memories of World War II were shaped, as well as the tracks along which ran—and are still partially running—the politics of memory in these national communities. One could conceptualize these historical images as the semipermanent tropes that provide a sense of historical continuity between lived memory (present) and national history (past), or, in Assmann's terms, as the codes that oversee the transformation of communicative into cultural memory. In this respect, these three case studies confirm Pierre Nora's famous thesis concerning the replacement of lieux de memoire by "historicized" forms of memory in the twentieth century, but they also offer a different perspective on the phenomena.[55]

As one of the most distinguished practitioners of memory studies, Nora has advanced the most ambitious historicization of the memory phenomenon, dividing it in three phases: a premodern, modern, and postmodern condition. A natural, unselfconscious relation between people and their past characterizes premodern times. Their environments of memory sustain traditions and rituals that provide a stable sense of being in time for the members of local memory communities. For Nora, the fall from memory grace occurred in the nineteenth century with the acceleration of everyday life through industrial and social modernization. As old traditions and affiliations lost their meaning, the relation between people and their past was reconstructed through first-order simulations of natural memory. Elites produced sites of memory in language, monuments, and archives which had one common referent—the nation-state—and which strove to secure the future of the nation-state through compelling inventions of its traditions. With the supposed collapse of the ideology and reality of the nation-state in the late twentieth century, these first-order simulations have been replaced by second-order simulations of natural memory. The media culture of the late twentieth century spews out identities and representations of the past which have little relation to any shared traditions, life worlds, or political institutions other than the frantic pace of media consumption itself.[56]

According to Nora, a further characteristic of our age—meaning the second half of the twentieth century to the present—is "memory sized by history," that is, collective forms of memory that are no longer "spontaneous" but are "transformed by their passage through history" and become "deliberate" and "experienced as a duty."[57] For Nora, postmodern "memory is above all archival": "it exists only through its exterior scaffolding and outward signs."[58] It is "individualized," insofar as each social group feels impelled to "redefine its identity through the revitalization of its own history."[59] And finally, it has made all past "distant," "invisible," and forever retreating from the horizon of the expanded present. "Archive-memory," "duty-memory," and "distance-memory" represent the postmodern replacements for nineteenth-century "memory-history" aimed at counteracting the "regime of historical discontinuity" in which we live.[60]

This collection of studies per se confirms the gist of Nora's analysis of postmodern "historicized memory" by participating in the "history of memory," which Nora identifies as the academic counterpart of the processes he describes. Yet, the articulation of the relationship between history and memory we derived from our comparative analysis is very different from the one illustrated by Nora. According to Nora, history stands for "the opposite" of memory: the "representation of the past" as opposed to "the bond tying us to the eternal present," or "the process that carries us forward and our representation of that process" rather than "a perpetually actual phenomenon."[61] The movement of Nora's argument is inflected by this tautology: positing a priori memory and history as opposite modes of relating to the past, the history of their relationship cannot but be one of mutual hostility and subordination. "Memorized" history in the nineteenth-century *milieux de memoire* gradually yields to historicized memory in the discontinuous *milieux d'histoire* of the postmodern age.

Looking at "history" from a more cultural perspective than the one advocated by Nora, the studies of Poland, Italy, and Switzerland underscore that, far from being "prosaic," history comes with its own poetic arsenal and relation to the present. As the national case studies prove, this relation may assume precisely the form of a rhetorical enframing of the memory of recent events by tropes derived from an already institutionalized historical culture. Thus conceived, historicized memory may function under certain historical conditions as an antidote, rather than a parallel, to the postmodern experience of historical discontinuity. But it can do so precisely because the boundary between history and memory is by nature porous, and has always turned on a poetic axis. Thus, even the most remote, historicized past may become instrumental in keeping a particular regime of patriotic wartime memory alive for several decades (Switzerland), or shape symmetrically opposed but complementary regimes of official and hidden memory (Poland), or even provide a never-ending reservoir of tropes to keep the present anchored to a never-fulfilled past (Italy). It appears, therefore, that in addition to rendering the recent living past more voluntary, individual, and distant, the historicization of memory can also make it more natural, collectively meaningful, and present.

This volume then presents two sets of countries and dynamics: first, Austria, France, Germany, and Russia, wherein generational agency operates particularly at the political level but also extends to high culture and popular culture; second, Italy, Poland, and Switzerland, with poetic agents such as Catholic rhetorical codes (Italy and Poland), or, more simply, national traditions iconized in a historic site (Switzerland). Once again, however, even among the countries of the latter group, there is no clearly unifying factor. At the level of both content and modality of change, the resilience and popular diffusion of "wartime patriotic memory" in Switzerland between the early 1950s and the early 1990s has very little to do with either the endemic split between public and private characterizing the collectivization of Polish memory until the early 1980s, or the tropical transfigurations that characterize the four phases in the Italian politics of memory. In fact, these three countries related very differently to the events of the war and developed different political cultures in the postwar era. Switzerland, the neutral nation par excellence, transformed itself comfortably into a militant anti-Communist cold warrior; Italy, fascist aggressor turned resistant ally in the last two years of the war, harbored the most successful Communist party in the West; and Poland, official first victim of both Nazi and Soviet totalitarianisms, became the first site of successful resistance to the latter.

In the final analysis, no single factor seems to account for the similarities among Italy, Poland, and Switzerland and their dissimilarity from Austria, France, Germany, and Russia. Both similarities and dissimilarities might reflect partially the authors' sensitivities or correspond to underlying patterns that only become visible through a more complete and detailed study of European memory. In addition, the dialectic between permanence and change, the poetics of history and the politics of memory that we uncovered might depend on specific social, political, and cultural factors that cannot be generalized. For example, the striking contrast between the German "coming to terms with the past" and the succession of Catholic tropes in Italian memory culture derived from fascist historical culture itself cannot be explained by the special status the Italians acquired after September 1943 as a defeated and Nazi-occupied nation or by the collective guilt supposedly felt by all Germans about the destruction caused by Nazism. A more plausible hypothesis is that the Nazis had abruptly severed the German people from the critical roots of their culture of history, thereby preparing the field for a rebirth of German historical culture which, in its new incarnation, proved to be much more sensitive to generational relay. By contrast, the continuities between prefascist and fascist historical culture in Italy were so strong that generational changes in collective memory have been almost imperceptible, hidden under the cloth of a never-ending series of iconic replacements. Similarly, it is certainly not the case that the different revolutionary temporalities identified by Tom Wolfe in his study of the USSR and Russia were totally absent in Communist Poland. More plausibly, it was the peculiar longevity and persistence of the Catholic poetics of history that tempered generational dynamics and tensions in Polish politics of memory until the early 1980s.

As we reach the end of our comparative journey, we cannot help noticing that our inquiry may have landed in bed with an unusual and notorious fellow. Our analysis leads us to reflect on the relationship between history and memory as articulated by Friedrich Nietzsche in 1872. In his well-known but rarely discussed untimely meditation "On the Advantages and Disadvantages of History for Life," Nietzsche argued that history was an "occidental prejudice," that is, a peculiarly Western way of responding to the universal fact that men cannot help remembering.[62] In discussing the various historical senses (monumental, antiquarian, and critical) that individuals or cultures had developed to organize their memory of the past, Nietzsche focused specifically on the monumental and the critical—despising altogether the antiquarian, which he identified with historical knowledge for knowledge's sake. Of the monumental he wrote that it corresponded most closely to the ancient conception of history, *historia magistra vitae*, that is, history as a collection of examples to be remembered for the moral edification of leaders and people. Of the critical Nietzsche wrote that it was born of the desire of certain generations to reject the past handed down to them by their fathers and to create a new one. This, he added, was always a dangerous affair, for it meant to further distort the past for the sake of the present. Yet, Nietzsche hastened to conclude, a consolation remained for the critical individual or generation: that the past that the previous generation had intended to pass on to them had itself been the construction of older generations. We are not suggesting—nor do we believe that Nietzsche did—that some cultures of history live in a monumental state of repetition, while others change with Kantian precision at every critical turn of the generational clock. What we advocate in closing is that scholars in all fields of memory studies pay more attention to the dialectic between the politics of memory and the poetics of history.

Notes

Parts of this conclusion have been previously published in Kansteiner, "Finding Meaning in Memory." We wish to thank the editors and publishers of *History and Theory* for their permission to reprint them here.

1  The methodological and terminological variety of the case studies in this one volume sufficiently illustrates the fact that "memory" lacks even that stable and

intuitive reference that notions such as "society," "politics," or "economy" have retained despite all methodological, ideological, and terminological redefinitions.

2  Radstone, "Working with Memory," 1.

3  See, for example, A. Assmann, *Erinnerungsräume*, 17; and compare to Geary, "The Historical Material of Memory," 17.

4  Dower, *Embracing Defeat*, 25.

5  Regarding the phrase *collective remembrance*, see ibid. Regarding the phrase *social memory*, see Fentress and Wickham, *Social Memory*. Regarding the term *cultural memory*, see Bal, Crewe, and Spitzer, *Acts of Memory*; the term *cultural memory* has also been preferred by scholars who specifically embrace Halbwachs's anti-individualism but want to stress the role of culture in the transmission of collective memories (see, for example, Ben-Amos and Weissberg, *Cultural Memory and the Construction of Identity*; and especially Sturken, *Tangled Memories*); see also the discussion of Jan Assmann's definition of *cultural memory* below. Also see Gedi and Elam, "Collective Memory."

6  Regarding the phrase *memory work*, see Irwin-Zarecka, *Frames of Remembrance*, 13; Irwin-Zarecka's terminology is not an allusion to Freud but an acknowledgment that the construction of collective memories takes a serious commitment of scarce resources of time, energy, and money. Regarding the phrase *popular history making*, see Rosenzweig and Thelen, *The Presence of the Past*, 3. Regarding the phrase *historical culture*, see Füssmann, Grütter, and Rüsen, *Historische Faszination*.

7  The term *countermemory* is derived from Foucault (see Hutton, *History as Art of Memory*, 106–23). *Public memory* vs. *vernacular memory* designate officially endorsed or produced memories as distinct from grassroots memories, for instance in Bodnar, *Remaking America*. Other phrases for the same phenomenon are "elite memory and popular memory" (see Gillis, "Memory and Identity," 6).

8  The blessings of social forgetting are often elaborated by reference to Nietzsche's "On the Uses and Disadvantages of History for Life." For a recent analysis of Nietzsche's political philosophy in relation to history and memory, see Dienstag, "*Dancing in Chains*." The phrase "social amnesia" is already used by Benedict Anderson in *Imagined Communities*. For the use of the phrase "lieux d'obli," the "counter-concept" to Pierre Nora's "lieux de mémoire," see Yerushalmi, *Usages de l'oubli*; N. Wood, *Vectors of Memory*, 10; and compare to Todorov, "The Uses and Abuses of Memory," 12.

9  In the case of the history of mentalities the connection dates back to Halbwachs himself, who was closely associated with the Annales School and especially Marc Bloch in Strasbourg. See also LeGoff, *History and Memory*. In the context of the memory wave, oral history has undergone a subtle transformation from the inquiry into past life-worlds through biographical interviews into the study of perceptions of the past from the perspective of the individuals who experienced it. The connection to memory studies is aptly illustrated by the 1980 title edited by Lutz Niethammer, *Lebenserfahrung und kollektives Gedächtnis*. See in particular the excellent volumes Straub, *Erzählung, Identität und historisches Bewusstsein*; Rüsen and Straub, *Die*

*dunkle Spur der Vergangenheit*; and Lutz, *Das Geschichtsbewusstsein der Deutschen*. More recently, the German conception of historical consciousness has crossed the Atlantic (see Seixas, *Theorizing Historical Consciousness*).

10  To give just one example, Jim Cullen's *The Civil War in Popular Culture: A Reusable Past* could have been subtitled with equal validity "A Reusable Memory."

11  The survey is limited to recent publications in English and German. For publications in English, see also the excellent introduction to the field by Jeffrey Olick and Joyce Robbins, "Social Memory Studies."

12  See, for example, these recent publications concerning literature: Schlant, *The Language of Silence*; Leak and Paizis, *The Holocaust and the Text*. Concerning television, see Shandler, *While America Watches*; Classen, *Bilder der Vergangenheit*. Concerning photography, see Zelizer, *Remembering to Forget*; Liss, *Trespassing through Shadows*. Concerning film, see Avisar, *Screening the Holocaust*. Concerning theater, see Patraka, *Theatre, Fascism, and the Holocaust*; Schumacher, *Staging the Holocaust*. Concerning architecture, see Young, *At Memory's Edge*. Concerning museums, see Linenthal, *Preserving Memory*. Concerning national memories in general, see Steinlauf, *Bondage to the Dead*; Segev, *The Seventh Million*; Zerubavel, *Recovered Roots*.

13  See, for example, Novick, *The Holocaust in American Life*; Cole, *Selling the Holocaust: From Auschwitz to Schindler* (New York: Routledge, 1999); and the already infamous Finkelstein, *The Holocaust Industry*. See also Bartov, *Mirrors of Destruction*; Diner, *Beyond the Conceivable*.

14  With regard to Fascism and World War II, new publications present collaborative surveys as well as in-depth analysis of the afterlife of specific events. For the collaborative surveys, see, for example, Peitsch et al., *European Memories of the Second World War*; Deak et al., *The Politics of Retribution in Europe*; Lagrou, *The Legacy of Nazi Occupation in Western Europe*; Bosworth and Dogliani, *Italian Fascism*. For analyses of specific events, see especially works on Hiroshima such as Yoneyama, *Hiroshima Traces*; Bird and Lifschultz, *Hiroshima's Shadow*; Yamamoto, *Nanking*; Molasky, *The American Occupation of Japan and Okinawa*; Dower, *Embracing Defeat*. Memory scholars have also studied the legacy of other wars, albeit much less frequently, as well as revolutions (see, for example, Edwards, *To Acknowledge a War*; Benjamin, *La Revolucion*). Regarding slavery, see M. Wood, *Blind Memory*; Osagie, *The Armistad Revolt*. Regarding genocide and human-rights abuses, see, for example, Berry and Berry, *Genocide in Rwanda*; Amadiume and An-Na'im, *The Politics of Memory*, which deals especially with Biafra; Roniger and Sznajder, *The Legacy of Human-Rights Violations in the Southern Cone*; Recovery of Historical Memory Project, *Guatemala*.

15  See, for example, Beckwith, *Charting Memory*; Behlmer and Leventhal, *Singular Continuities*; Schwartz, *Abraham Lincoln and the Forge of National Memory*; Bradley and Cahill, *Habsburg Peru*; Filene, *Romancing the Folk*.

16  That is one of the many interesting results of neuropsychological research on memory distortion (see, for example, recent research in Schacter, *The Cognitive Neuropsychology of False Memory*; Schacter, *Searching for Memory*).

17 For psychological research on autobiographical memory, see Polkinghorne, *Narrative Knowing and the Human Sciences*; Neisser and Winograd, *Remembering Reconsidered*; Shotter and Gergen, *Texts of Identity*; Neisser and Fivush, *The Remembering Self*; Conway et al., *Theoretical Perspectives on Autobiographical Memory*; Rubin, *Remembering Our Past*; and, more generally, Conway, Gathercole, and Cornoldi, *Theories of Memory*.

18 Schudson, "Dynamics of Distortion in Collective Memory," 346.

19 Halbwachs, *Les cadres sociaux de la memoire*; Halbwachs, *La topographie legendaire des Evangiles en Terre Sainte*; Halbwachs, *La memoire collective* (published posthumously by Jeanne Alexandre). See also the discussion of Halbwachs' work in Hutton, *History as an Art of Memory*, 73–90. For a general introduction and contextualization of social constructivism, see Spivey, *The Constructivist Metaphor*, chap. 1, esp. 17–26.

20 Connerton, *How Societies Remember*, 37. For applications of the consensus, see the excellent discussion of neurological and psychological research for purposes of cultural history in Domansky and Welser, *Eine offene Geschichte*, 11–23; Winter and Sivan, *War and Remembrance in the Twentieth Century*, 10–19; and the interdisciplinary volume edited by Schacter, *Memory Distortion*.

21 Winter and Sivan, *War and Remembrance in the Twentieth Century*, 23.

22 Crane, "Writing the Individual Back into Collective Memory"; Winter and Sivan, *War and Remembrance in the Twentieth Century*.

23 See Jeffrey Olick's excellent discussion in "Collective Memory."

24 This tacit, yet misleading assumption is nicely spelled out in Edwards, *To Acknowledge a War*: "When nations, like individuals, try to rewrite the past in such a way as to ignore its impact, they are likely to become sick, and their affirmations to become obsessions" (18).

25 Irwin-Zarecka, *Frames of Remembrance*, 116. This also explains why a number of scholars have strongly objected to the use of methods of individual psychology and psychoanalysis for the study of collective memories, including Marc Bloch as early as 1925 ("Mémoire collective, tradition, et coutume"), and why some classics of Vergangenheitsbewältigung literature in Germany are methodologically (but not morally) problematic (see especially Mitscherlich and Mitscherlich, *The Inability to Mourn*).

26 See, for example, Gillian Banner, *Holocaust Literature*; and especially Langer, *Holocaust Testimonies*.

27 Caruth, *Unclaimed Experience*, 6. See also Caruth, "Introduction"; and compare to Antze and Lambek, *Tense Past*.

28 LaCapra, *History and Memory after Auschwitz*, 23. See also LaCapra, *Representing the Holocaust*, 18 n.10.

29 See on this point also Kansteiner, "Genealogy of a Category Mistake."

30 Weissberg, Introduction, 15. See also Yael Zerubavel, who argues, "Collective memory continuously negotiates between available historical records and current social and political agendas" (*Recovered Roots*, 5).

31  N. Wood, *Vectors of Memory*, 2.

32  This insight has been best expressed by Amos Funkenstein, who reminded us that "just as a nation cannot eat or dance it cannot speak or remember" and less entertaining prolepsis about the individual's exclusive ability to remember abound in the study of collective memory (see Funkenstein, *Perceptions of Jewish History*, 4).

33  Terdiman, *Present Past*, 34. See also A. Assmann, *Erinnerungsräume*, 132. Or, as Barbie Zelizer put it, "Collective memories have texture, existing in the world rather than in a person's head" (*Remembering to Forget*, 4).

34  Keppler, *Tischgespräche*.

35  We are doubtful about the existence of a European collective memory because it is not as yet reproduced in a similar fashion across Europe. With the exception of intellectuals and bureaucrats who convene as colleagues and are paid to discuss and administer European concerns (including the question of a European collective memory), a common European collective memory does not yet exist. See Passerini, *The Question of European Identity*; Mcdonald, *Approaches to European Historical Consciousness*; Koshar, *From Monuments to Traces*, 286–96. Regardless of the level at which collective memories are analyzed, it is important to consider the interdependencies between different levels of collective identity. The larger the collective in question the more important it is that its memory be reflected and reproduced on a lower level of numeric complexity. For instance, national memories need to be reproduced on the level of families, professions, or in other locations where people form emotional attachments in their everyday lives (see, for instance, Confino, *The Nation as Local Metaphor*).

36  Schwartz, *Abraham Lincoln and the Forge of National Memory*, xi.

37  A phrase borrowed from Matsuda, *The Memory of the Modern*.

38  Media events such as *Schindler's List* and Goldhagen are just the tip of the iceberg, and they differ from more routine and more prevalent representations of the Holocaust in that they have elicited more intense emotional reactions. For discussions of these media events, see, for example, Loshitzky, *Spielberg's Holocaust*; Heil and Erb, *Geschichtswissenschaft und Öffentlichkeit*.

39  Levy and Sznaider, *Erinnerung im globalen Zeitalter*.

40  Several recent edited volumes address the legacy of World War II in Europe from a historical or interdisciplinary perspective. None of the volumes is based on a compelling conceptual framework, nor do they offer a synthetic overview of the politics of memory in Europe. Two collections recently published by Duke University Press—Olick, *States of Memory*, and Walkowitz and Knauer, *Memory and the Impact of Political Transformation in Public Space*—offer, respectively, national perspectives on politics of memory but on a global-comparative scale and medium-related essays concerned with the political value of memorialization in museums, monuments, cityscapes, commemorations, and other memory sites. Istvan Deak, Jan Gross, and Tony Judt, in *The Politics of Retribution in Europe*, do a good job of describing the politics of justice in postwar Europe precisely because they focus specifically on the history of collaboration during World War II and postwar attempts to come to terms

with that legacy. Their book is of great interest to experts but of limited value as a teaching tool because only very few contributors try to contextualize the question of collaboration and justice within an overall history of European memory. *European Memories of the Second World War*, edited by Helmut Peitsch, Charles Burdett, and Claire Gorrara, offers a rich collection of primarily literary case studies on the representation of resistance, Fascism, and World War II in Germany, France, Italy and Japan. Each of the many short chapters analyzes only one specific literary text or film. As a result, the volume is an inspiration for comparative, interdisciplinary work, but it lacks both the conceptual strategies and the methodological rigor that a more systematic study of European collective memories requires. Finally, *Memory and Power in Post-War Europe: Studies in the Presence of the Past*, edited by Jan Werner Müller, includes thought-provoking methodological reflections in the introductory chapters, but the chapters that follow do not live up to the conceptual ambition of the introductions. The different contributions that address the memory of World War II in selected European countries engage the question of collective memory, but each chapter does so on a different sociopolitical level and with incompatible methods. As a result, the volume is not particularly suitable for comparative, interdisciplinary studies.

41 See, for example, Malmborg and Stråth, *The Meaning of Europe*; Passerini, *Europe in Love, Love in Europe*.

42 On the concept of memory in modern philosophy, see, for example, Grosz, *Becomings*; Comay and McCumber, *Endings*. On memory in late antiquity, see Hedrick, *History and Silence*. There is a particularly insightful body of work on concepts and practices of memory in the middle ages (see, for example, the contributions and bibliographies in del Alamo and Pendergast, *Memory and the Medieval Tomb*).

43 With regard to museums and collecting, see, for example, Maleuvre, *Museum Memories*; Kavanagh, *Dream Spaces*; Crane, *Collecting and Historical Consciousness in Early Nineteenth-Century Germany*. With regard to architecture and city planning, see, for example, Koshar, *Germany's Transient Pasts*; Koshar, *From Monuments to Traces: Artifacts of German Memory*; Rosenfeld, *Munich and Memory*; Murphy, *Memory and Modernity*. With regard to religion, see, for example, Hervieu-Leger, *Religion as Chain of Memory*, a work in the sociology of religion that follows in the tradition of Halbwachs. With regard to postcolonial capitalism, see Speyer, *The Memory of Trade*. With regard to the politics of international atonement, see Barkan, *The Guilt of Nations*.

44 See Wulf Kansteiner's discussion of the issue in "Between Politics and Memory," especially 108–12. See also Bude, *Bilanz der Nachfolge*; Kohlstruck, *Zwischen Erinnerung und Geschichte*; Marcuse, *Legacies of Dachau*.

45 Mannheim, "Das Problem der Generationen."

46 Kansteiner, "Between Politics and Memory," 109.

47 For an excellent example of this approach to popular history, see Schörken, *Geschichte in der Alltagswelt*.

48 See especially the work of Hayden White, particularly his *Metahistory*, *Tropics*

of *Discourse*, *The Content of the Form*, and *Figural Realism*. See also LaCapra, *Rethinking Intellectual History*; Cohen, *Historical Culture*; Cohen, *Passive Nihilism*; Kellner, *Language and Historical Representation*.

49  Burke, "History as Social Memory," 98.

50  Lowenthal, *The Past Is a Foreign Country*, 214.

51  Megill, "History, Memory, Identity," 56. See also the nuanced assessment in LaCapra, *History and Memory after Auschwitz*, 19–21.

52  The terms *history* and *memory* are used in this sense in the festschrift for Saul Friedländer edited by Gulie Ne'man Arad, *Passing into History: Nazisms and the Holocaust beyond Memory* (the festschrift appeared as a special issue, volume 9, numbers 1 and 2, of *History and Memory*). See also Young, *At Memory's Edge*.

53  J. Assmann, "Collective Memory and Cultural Identity," 132. See also J. Assmann, *Das kulturelle Gedächnis*.

54  Niethammer, "Diesseits des 'Floating Gap.' "

55  Nora, "Between Memory and History," 14.

56  Nora, *Realms of Memory*. For lucid discussions of Nora's project and methodology, see also N. Wood, "Memory's Remains," republished in N. Wood, *Vectors of Memory*; and Carrier, "Places, Politics and the Archiving of Contemporary Memory in Pierre Nora's *Les Lieux de mémoire*"; Radstone, *Memory and Methodology*, 37–57.

57  Nora, *Realms of Memory*, 1:13.

58  Ibid.

59  Ibid., 1:15.

60  Ibid., 1:14–17.

61  Ibid., 1:8–9.

62  Nietzsche, "On the Advantages and Disadvantages of History for Life."

# Bibliography

Absalom, R. "Peasant Memory and the Italian Resistance, 1943–1945." In *Italian Fascism: History, Memory, and Representation*, edited by R. J. B. Bosworth and P. Dogliani, 31–44. London: Macmillan, 1999.

Adams, W. "War Stories: Movies, Memory, and the Vietnam War." *Comparative Social Research* 11 (1989): 165–89.

Adorno, T. *Erziehung zur Mündigkeit*. Frankfurt: Suhrkamp, 1970.

———. *Minima Moralia*. London: Verso, 1978.

———. *Negative Dialectics*. New York: Continuum, 1973.

———. *Prisms*. Cambridge, Mass.: MIT Press, 1988.

Adorno, T., and M. Horkheimer. *Dialectic of Enlightenment*. New York: Continuum, 1988.

Agamben, Giorgio. *Homo Sacer: Sovereign Power and Bare Life*. Translated by Daniel Heller-Roazen. Palo Alto, Calif.: Stanford University Press, 1998.

Ahonen, P. *After the Expulsion: West Germany and Eastern Europe 1945–1990*. Oxford: Oxford University Press, 2003.

Ahren, Y., et al., eds. *Das Lehrstück "Holocaust": Wirkungen und Nachwirkungen eines Medienereignisses*. Opladen: Westdeutscher Verlag, 1982.

Albrich, T. "Holocaust und Schuldabwehr: Vom Judenmord zum kollektiven Opferstatus." In *Österreich im 20. Jahrhundert*, edited by R. Steininger and M. Gehler, 2:39–106. Vienna: Böhlau, 1997.

Alexander, J. C. " 'On the Social Construction of Moral Universals': The 'Holocaust' from War Crime to Trauma Drama." *European Journal of Social Theory* 5, no. 1 (2002): 5–58.

Alexandre, J., ed. *La Memoire collective*. Paris: Presses Universitaires, 1950.

Allport, G., and L. Postman. *Psychology of Rumor*. New York: H. Holt, 1947.

Aly, G. *Macht, Geist, Wahn: Kontinuitäten deutschen Denkens*. Berlin: Fischer, 1997.

Amadiume, I., and A. An-Na'im, eds. *The Politics of Memory: Truth, Healing, and Social Justice*. London: Zed, 2000.

"Amtliches Bulletin der Bundesversammlung." *Nationalrat*, 1988, 1710–67.

———. *Nationalrat*, 1989, 779–817.

"Amtliches Stenographisches Bulletin der Bundesversammlung." *Nationalrat*, 30 January 1958, 16–39.

———. *Nationalrat*, 7 October 1965, 550–79.

Anderson, B. *Imagined Communities: Reflections on the Origin and Spread of Nationalism*. London: Verso, 1983.

Andics, H. *Der Staat, den keiner wollte: Österreich 1918–1943*. Vienna: Herder, 1962.

Antze, P., and M. Lambek, eds. *Tense Past: Cultural Essays in Trauma and Memory.* New York: Routledge, 1996.

Arbeitskreis Gelebte Geschichte, ed. *Erpresste Schweiz: Zur Auseinandersetzung um die Haltung der Schweiz im Zweiten Weltkrieg und die Berichte der Bergierkommission: Eindrücke und Wertungen von Zeitzeugen.* Stäfa: Th. Gut Verlag, 2002.

Arning, M. *Späte Abrechnung: Über Zwangsarbeiter, Schlussstriche und Berliner Verständigungen.* Frankfurt: Fischer, 2001.

Assmann, A. *Erinnerungsräume: Formen und Wandlungen des kulturellen Gedächnisses.* Munich: Beck, 1999.

Assmann, A., and U. Frevert. *Geschichtsvergessenheit/Geschichtsversessenheit: Vom Umgang mit deutschen Vergangenheiten nach 1945.* Stuttgart: Deutsche Verlags-Anstalt, 1999.

Assmann, J. "Collective Memory and Cultural Identity." *New German Critique* 65 (1995): 125–33.

——. *Das kulturelle Gedächnis: Schrift, Erinnerung und politische Identität in den frühen Hochkulturen.* Munich: Beck, 1992.

"Asyl in der Schweiz nach den Revolutionen von 1848." *Studien und Quellen* 25 (1999).

Augstein, R., et al. *Historikerstreit: Die Dokumentation der Kontroverse um die Einzigartigkeit der nationalsozialistischen Judenvernichtung.* Munich: Piper, 1987.

Authers, J., and R. Wolffe. *The Victim's Fortune: Inside the Epic Battle over the Debts of the Holocaust.* New York: HarperCollins, 20002.

Avisar, I. *Screening the Holocaust: Cinema's Images of the Unimaginable.* Bloomington: Indiana University Press, 1988.

Aymé, M. *Uranus.* Paris: Gallimard, 1948.

Bacher, G. "Die Gegenwart leben helfen." In *Österreich II: Die Wiedergeburt unseres Staates,* edited by H. Portisch, 7–8. Vienna: Kremayr und Scheriau, 1985.

Baddeley, A. "Is Memory All Talk?" *The Psychologist* 5 (1992): 447–48.

Baier, L. *Die Früchte der Revolte: Über die Veränderung der politischen Kultur durch die Studendenbewegung.* Berlin: Wagenbach, 1988.

Bailer, B. *Wiedergutmachung kein Thema: Österreich und die Opfer des Nationalsozialismus.* Vienna: Löcker, 1993.

Bailer-Galanda, B. *Die Entstehung der Rückstellungs- und Entschädigungsgesetzgebung: Die Republik Österreich und das in der NS-Zeit entzogene Vermögen.* Vienna: Oldenbourg, 2003.

——. *Haider wörtlich: Führer in die Dritte Republik.* Vienna: Löcker, 1995.

——. "Wolfgang Neugebauer: Das Dokumentationsarchiv des österreichischen Widerstandes (1963–1983)." In *40 Jahre Dokumentationsarchiv des österreichischen Widerstandes 1963–2003,* edited by Dokumentationsarchiv des österreichischen Widerstandes, 26–70. Vienna: Dokumentationsarchiv des österreichischen Widerstandes, 2003.

Baioni, M. "Predappio." In *Simboli e miti dell'Italia unita,* edited by M. Isenghi, 501–12. Bari: La Terza, 1997.

Bajohr, F. *"Aryanisation" in Hamburg: The Economic Exclusion of the Jews and the*

*Confiscation of Their Property in Nazi Germany.* Translated by G. Wilkes. New York: Berghahn, 2002.

Bajt, V. "Invisible Nationalism." In *Reformulations: Markets, Policies, and Identities in Central and Eastern Europe,* edited by S. Kapralski and S. C. Pearce. Warsaw: IFIS Publishers, 2000.

Bal, M., J. Crewe, and L. Spitzer, eds. *Acts of Memory: Cultural Recall in the Present.* Hanover, N.H.: University Press of New England, 1999.

Baldissara, L., and P. Pezzino, eds. *Crimini e memorie di Guerra.* Rome: L'Ancora del Mediterraneo, 2004.

Balzli, B. *Treuhänder des Reichs: Die Schweiz und die Vermögen der Naziopfer: Eine Spurensuche.* Zurich: Werd Verlag, 1997.

Banner, G. *Holocaust Literature: Schulz, Levi, Spiegelman and the Memory of the Offense.* London: Vallentine Mitchell, 2000.

Barclay, C. R. "Composing Protoselves through Improvisation." In *The Remembering Self,* edited by U. Neisser and R. Fivush, 55–77. Cambridge: Cambridge University Press, 1994.

Barkan, E. *The Guilt of Nations: Restitution and Negotiating Historical Injustices.* Baltimore: Johns Hopkins University Press, 2000.

Barth, K. *Eine Schweizer Stimme 1938–1945.* Zurich: Theologischer Verlag, 1985.

Bartlett, F. C. *Remembering: A Study in Experimental and Social Psychology.* New York: Macmillan, 1932.

Bartoszewski, W. *The Convent at Auschwitz.* London: Bowerdean Press, 1990.

Bartov, O. *Mirrors of Destruction: War, Genocide, and Modern Identity.* Oxford: Oxford University Press, 2000.

Basso, K. H. "Stalking with Stories: Names, Places and Moral Narratives among the Western Apaches." In *Text, Play, and Story: The Construction and Reconstruction of Self and Society,* edited by E. M. Bruner and S. Plattner, 19–55. Washington: American Ethnological Society, 1984.

Baumgärtner, U. *Reden nach Hitler: Theodor Heuss: Die Auseinandersetzung mit dem Nationalsozialismus.* Stuttgart: Deutsche Verlagsanstalt, 2001.

Bazyler, M. J. *Holocaust Justice: The Battle for Restitution in America's Courts.* New York: New York University Press, 2003.

Becker, W., and N. Schöll. *In jenen Tagen: Wie der deutsche Nachkriegsfilm die Vergangenheit bewältigte.* Opladen: Leske and Budrich, 1995.

Beckwith, S., ed. *Charting Memory: Recalling Medieval Spain.* New York: Garland, 2000.

Béguin, P. *Le balcon sur l'Europe. Petite histoire de la Suisse pendant la guerre 1939–1945.* Neuchâtel: La Baconnière, 1951.

Behlmer, G., and F. Leventhal, eds. *Singular Continuities: Tradition, Nostalgia, and Identity in Modern British Culture.* Stanford, Calif.: Stanford University Press, 2000.

Bellone, A. "La Resistenza." In *Strutture ed eventi dell'Italia unita,* edited by M. Isnenghi, 403–38. Bari: La Terza, 1997.

Ben-Amos, D., and L. Weissberg, eds. *Cultural Memory and the Construction of Identity*. Detroit: Wayne State University Press, 1999.

Bendix, R. "National Sentiment in the Enactment and Discourse of Swiss Political Ritual." *American Ethnologist* 19, no. 4 (1992): 768–90.

Ben-Ghiat, R. *Fascist Modernities: Italy 1922–1945*. Los Angeles: University of California Press, 2001.

———. "Liberation: Italian Cinema and the Fascist Past, 1945–1950." In *Italian Fascism: History, Memory and Representation*, edited by R. J. B. Bosworth and P. Dogliani, 83–101. London: Macmillan Press, 1999.

———. "The Secret Histories of Roberto Benigni's *Life Is Beautiful*." *Yale Journal of Criticism* 14, no. 1 (2001): 253–66.

Benjamin, T. *La Revolucion: Mexico's Great Revolution as Memory, Myth and History*. Austin: University of Texas Press, 2000.

Berg, J. *Hochhuths "Stellvertreter" und die "Stellvertreter"-Debatte: "Vergangenheitsbewältigung" in Theater und Presse der sechziger Jahre*. Kronberg: Scriptor, 1977.

Berger, F., et al. *Zeiten, Völker und Kulturen: Ein Lehr und Arbeitsbuch für den Geschichtsunterricht an Haupt- und Untermittelschulen*, vol. 4. Vienna: Österreichischer Bundesverlag, 1957.

Berger, S. *The Search for Normality: National Identity and Historical Consciousness in Germany since 1800*. Providence, R.I.: Berghahn, 1997.

Bergier, J.-F. *Guillaume Tell*. Paris: Fayard, 1988.

Bergmann, W. *Antisemitismus in öffentlichen Konflikten: Kollektives Lernen in der politischen Kultur der Bundesrepublik 1949–1989*. Frankfurt: Campus, 1997.

Bergmann, W., R. Erb, and A. Lichtblau. "Die Aufarbeitung der NS-Zeit im Vergleich: Österreich, die DDR und die Bundesrepublik Deutschland." In *Schwieriges Erbe: Der Umgang mit Nationalsozialismus und Antisemitismus in Österreich, der DDR und der Bundesrepublik Deutschland*, edited by W. Bergmann, R. Erb, and A. Lichtblau, 11–17. Frankfurt: Campus, 1995.

Bernd, U. *Besucher einer Ausstellung: Die Ausstellung "Vernichtungskrieg, Verbrechen der Wehrmacht 1941 bis 1944" in Interview und Gespäch*. Hamburg: Hamburger Edition, 1998.

Berry, J., and C. P. Berry, eds. *Genocide in Rwanda: A Collective Memory*. Washington: Howard University Press, 1999.

Besançon, A. "Forgotten Communism." *Commentary* 105, no. 1 (1 Jan. 1998): 24–28.

Bidussa, D. *Il mito del bravo italiano*. Rome: Il Saggiatore, 1994.

Bird, K., and L. Lifschultz, eds. *Hiroshima's Shadow*. Stony Creek, Conn.: Pamphleteer's Press, 2000.

Bischof, G. *Austria and the First Cold War, 1945–55: The Leverage of the Weak*. Basingstoke, U.K.: Macmillan, 1999.

———. "Die Instrumentalisierung der Moskauer Erklärung nach dem 2. Weltkrieg." *Zeitgeschichte* 29 (1993): 345–66.

———. "Victims? Perpetrators? 'Punching Bags' of European Historical Memory? The

Austrians and Their World War II Legacies." *German Studies Review* 1 (2004): 17–32.

——. " 'Opfer' Österreich? Zur moralischen Ökonomie des österreichischen historischen Gedächtnisses." In *Die politische Ökonomie des Holocaust: Zur wirtschaftlichen Logik von Verfolgung und "Wiedergutmachung,"* edited by D. Stiefel, 305–32. Vienna: Verlag für Geschichte und Politik, Oldenbourg, 2001.

Bischof, G., and A. Pelinka, eds. *Austrian Historical Memory and National Identity.* New Brunswick, N.J.: Transaction, 1997.

Bloch, M. "Memoire collective, tradition, et coutume." *Revue de Synthese Historique* 40 (1925): 73–83.

Bock, P., and E. Wolfrum, ed. *Umämpfte Vergangenheit.* Göttingen: Vandenhoeck und Ruprecht, 1999.

Bodek, J. *Die Fassbinder-Kontroversen: Entstehung und Wirkung eines literarischen Textes.* Frankfurt: Lang, 1991.

Bodemann, M. *Gedächtnistheater: Die jüdische Gemeinschaft und ihre deutsche Erfindung.* Hamburg: Rotbuch, 1996.

——. *In den Wogen der Erinnerung: Jüdische Existenz in Deutschland.* Munich: dtv, 2002.

Bodnar, J. *Remaking America: Public Memory, Commemoration, and Patriotism in the Twentieth Century.* Princeton, N.J.: Princeton University Press, 1992.

Bohannon, J. N., and V. L. Symons. "Flashbulb Memories: Confidence, Consistency, and Quantity." In *Affect and Accuracy in Recall,* edited by E. Winograd and U. Neisser, 65–91. New York: Cambridge University Press, 1992.

Böhler, I. " 'Wenn die Juden ein Volk sind, so ist es ein mieses Volk': Die Kreisky-Peter-Wiesenthal Affäre 1975." In *Politische Affären und Skandale in Österreich: Von Mayerling bis Waldheim,* edited by M. Gehler and H. Sickinger, 502–31. Thaur: Kulturverlag, 1995.

Bonhage, B., H. Lussy, and M. Perrenoud. *Nachrichtenlose Vermögen bei Schweizer Banken.* Edited by Independent Commission of Experts Switzerland–Second World War. Zurich: Chronos, 2001.

Böning, H. *Der Traum von Freiheit und Gleichheit: Helvetische Revolution und Republik (1798–1803): Die Schweiz auf dem Weg zur bürgerlichen Demokratie.* Zurich: Orell Füssli, 1998.

Bonjour, E. *Geschichte der schweizerischen Neutralität.* Vols. 4–6. Basel: Helbing und Lichtenhahn, 1970.

——. *Die schweizerische Neutralität. Ihre geschichtliche Wurzel und gegenwärtige Funktion.* Bern: Peter Lang, 1946.

Borkowicz, J., et al., eds. *Thou Shalt Not Kill: Poles on Jedwabne.* Warsaw: Więź, 2001.

Bosworth, R. J. B. "Film Memories of Fascism." In *Italian Fascism: History, Memory and Representation,* edited by R. J. B. Bosworth and P. Dogliani, 103–23. London: Macmillan, 1999.

——. "The Italian 'Second Republic' and the History of Fascism: Finding (and Losing) a Usable Past." In *The Italian Dictatorship: Problems and Perspectives in the Interpretation of Mussolini and Fascism*. New York: Oxford University Press, 1998.

Bosworth, R. J. B., and P. Dogliani, eds. *Italian Fascism: History, Memory, and Representation*. New York: St. Martin's Press, 1999.

"Botschaft des Bundesrates vom 25. Mai 1988." *Schweizerisches Bundesblatt* 2 (1988): 975.

Botz, G. "Eine deutsche Geschichte 1938 bis 1945?" *Zeitgeschichte* 14, no. 1 (1986): 19–38.

Botz, G., and G. Sprengnagel, eds. *Kontroversen um Österreichs Zeitgeschichte: Verdrängte Vergangenheit, Österreich-Identität, Waldheim und die Historiker*. Frankfurt: Campus, 1994.

Bourgeois, D. *Business helvétique et Troisième Reich*. Lausanne: Page Deux, 1998.

———. *Le Troisième Reich et la Suisse, 1933–1941*. Neuchâtel: Editions de la Baconnière, 1974.

Bower, T. *The Blood Money: The Swiss, the Nazis and the Looted Billions*. London: Pan Books, 1997.

Bradley, P., and D. Cahill. *Habsburg Peru: Images, Imagination and Memory*. Liverpool: Liverpool University Press, 2000.

Braese, S. *Deutsche Nachkriegsliteratur und der Holocaust*. Frankfurt: Campus, 1998.

Bravo, A. "Gli scritti di memoria della deportazione dall'Italia (1944–1993): I significati dell'accoglienza." In *Storia e memoria della deportazione*, edited by P. M. Levi, 61–78. Florence: La Giuntina, 1996.

Bretscher-Spindler, K. *Vom heissen zum Kalten Krieg: Vorgeschichte und Geschichte der Schweiz im Kalten Krieg 1943 bis 1968*. Zurich: Orell Füssli, 1997.

Breuer, J., and S. Freud. *Studies in Hysteria*. Translated by A. A. Brill. New York: Nervous and Mental Disease Publishing, 1936.

Breuss, S., K. Liebhart, and A. Pribersky. *Inszenierungen: Stichwörter zu Österreich*. Vienna: Sonderzahl, 1995.

Brewer, W. F. "What Is Autobiographical Memory?" In *Autobiographical Memory*, edited by D. C. Rubin, 24–49. Cambridge: Cambridge University Press, 1986.

Brink, C. *Ikonen der Vernichtung: Öffentlicher Gebrauch von Fotografien aus nationalsozialistischen Konzentrationslagern nach 1945*. Berlin: Akademie Verlag, 1998.

Brix, E., E. Bruckmüller, and H. Stekl. "Das kulturelle Gedächtnis Österreichs: Eine Einführung." In *Memoria Austriae 1: Menschen, Mythen, Zeiten*, edited by E. Brix, E. Bruckmüller, and H. Stekl, 9–25. Vienna: Verlag für Geschichte und Politik, 2004.

Brochhagen, U. *Nach Nürnberg: Vergangenheitsbewältigung und Westintegration in der Ära Adenauer*. Hamburg: Junius, 1994.

Brodmann, R., et al., eds. *Unterweg zu einer Schweiz ohne Armee. Der freie Gang aus der Festung*. Basel: Z-Verlag, 1986.

Brooks, J. *Thank You, Comrade Stalin! Soviet Public Culture from Revolution to Cold War*. Princeton, N.J.: Princeton University Press, 1999.

Brown, R., and J. Kulik. "Flashbulb Memories." *Cognition* 5 (1977): 73–99.

Bruckmüller, E. *Nation Österreich: Kulturelles Bewusstsein und gesellschaftlich-politische Prozesse.* 2nd ed. Vienna: Böhlau, 1996.

———. *Österreichbewußtsein im Wandel: Identität und Selbstverständnis in den 90er Jahren.* Vienna: Signum Verlag, 1994.

Brüggemeier, F. J., and J. Kocka, eds. *"Geschichte von unten, Geschichte von innen": Kontroversen um die Alltagsgeschichte.* Hagen: Fernuniversität.

Brumlik, M., H. Funke, and L. Rensmann, eds. *Umkämpftes Vergessen: Walser-Debatte, Holocaust-Mahnmal und neuere deutsche Geschichtspolitik.* Berlin: Das Arabische Buch, 2000.

Brusto, M. *Im schweizerischen Rettungsboot.* Munich: Starczewski, 1967.

Büchel, R. *Der deutsche Widerstand im Spiegel von Fachliteratur und Publizistik seit 1945.* Munich: Bernard und Graefe, 1975.

Bucher, E. *Zwischen Bundesrat und General: Schweizer Politik und Armee im Zweiten Weltkrieg.* Zurich: Orell Füssli, 1993.

Bude, H. *Das Altern einer Generation: Die Jahrgänge 1938–1948.* Frankfurt: Suhrkamp, 1995.

———. *Bilanz der Nachfolge: Die Bundesrepublik und der Nationalsozialismus.* Frankfurt: Suhrkamp, 1992.

———. *Deutsche Karrieren: Lebenskonstruktionen sozialer Aufsteiger aus der Flakhelfer-Generation.* Frankfurt: Suhrkamp, 1987.

Bude, H., and M. Kohli, eds. *Radikalisierte Aufklärung: Studentenbewegung und Soziologie in Berlin 1965 bis 1970.* Weinheim: Juventa, 1989.

Bukey, E. B. *Hitler's Austria: Popular Sentiment in the Nazi Era, 1938–1945.* Chapel Hill: University of North Carolina Press, 2000.

———. *Hitlers Österreich: "Eine Bewegung und ein Volk."* Hamburg: Europa Verlag, 2001.

Bundeskanzleramt, ed. *Rot-Weiss-Rot-Buch: Gerechtigkeit für Österreich: Darstellungen, Dokumente und Nachweise zur Vorgeschichte und Geschichte der Okkupation Österreich.* Vienna: Verlag der Österreichischer Staatsdruckerei, 1946.

Burke, P. "History as Social Memory." In *History, Culture, and the Mind*, edited by T. Butler, 97–113. London: Blackwell, 1998.

Cała, A. "Kształtowanie się polskiej i żydowskiej wizji martyrologicznej po II wojnie światowej." *Przegląd socjologiczny* 49, no. 2 (2000): 167–80.

Caracciolo, N. *Uncertain Refuge: Italy and the Jews during the Holocaust.* Urbana: University of Illinois Press, 1995.

Carpi, D. *Between Mussolini and Hitler: The Jews and Italian Authorities in France and Tunisia.* Hanover, N.H.: University Press of New England, 1994.

Carrier, P. "Places, Politics and the Archiving of Contemporary Memory." In *Memory and Methodology*, edited by S. Radstone, 37–57. Oxford: Berg, 2000.

Caruth, C. Introduction. In *Trauma: Explorations in Memory*, edited by C. Caruth, 3–12. Baltimore: Johns Hopkins University Press, 1995.

———. *Unclaimed Experience: Trauma, Narrative, and History.* Baltimore: Johns Hopkins University Press, 1996.

Cenci, C. "Rituale e memoria: Le celebrazioni del 25 Aprile." In *Le memorie della repubblica*, edited by L. Paggi, 335–78. Florence: La Nuova Italia, 1999.

Charlesworth, A. "Contesting Places of Memory: The Case of Auschwitz." *Environment and Planning D: Society and Space* 12 (1994): 579–93.

Chiquet, S. "Der Anfang der Auseinandersetzung: Zu den Fakten, Zusammenhängen und Interpretationen in der Debatte um die 'Übung Diamant' 1989." *Studien und Quellen* 24 (1998): 193–228.

Christie, N. "Answers to Atrocities." In *The Moral Fabric in Contemporary Societies*, edited by G. Skąpska, A. Orla-Bukowska, and K. Kowalski, 335–56. Leiden: Brill, 2003.

Classen, C. *Bilder der Vergangenheit: Die Zeit des Nationalsozialismus im Fernsehen der Bundesrepublik Deutschland*. Cologne: Böhlau, 1999.

Cohen, S. *Historical Culture*. Berkeley: University of California Press, 1986.

———. *Passive Nihilism*. New York: St. Martin's Press, 1998.

Cole, T. *Selling the Holocaust: From Auschwitz to Schindler*. New York: Routledge, 1999.

Comay, R., and J. McCumber, eds. *Endings: Questions of Memory in Hegel and Heidegger*. Evanston, Ill.: Northwestern University Press, 1999.

Conan, É., and H. Rousso. *Vichy: An Everpresent Past*. Hanover, N.H.: University Press of New England, 1998.

Confino, A. *The Nation as Local Metaphor: Württemberg, Imperial Germany, and National Memory, 1871–1918*. Chapel Hill: University of North Carolina Press, 1997.

Connerton, P. *How Societies Remember*. Cambridge: Cambridge University Press, 1989.

Contini, G. *La memoria divisa*. Milan: Rizzoli, 1997.

Conway, M. *Autobiographical Memory: An Introduction*. Buckingham, U.K.: Open University Press, 1990.

Conway, M., et al., eds. *Theoretical Perspectives on Autobiographical Memory*. Dordrecht: Kluwer, 1992.

Conway, M., S. Gathercole, and C. Cornoldi, eds. *Theories of Memory*. Vol. 2. Hove, U.K.: Psychology Press, 1998.

Conway, M., and D. C. Rubin. "The Structure of Autobiography Memory." In *Theories of Memory*, edited by A. E. Collins, S. E. Gathercole, M. A. Conway, and P. E. M. Morris, 103–37. Hillsdale, N.J.: Lawrence Erlbaum, 1993.

Crainz, G. "The Representation of Fascism and the Resistance in the Documentaries of Italian State Television." In *Italian Fascism: History, Memory and Representation*, edited by R. J. B. Bosworth and P. Dogliani, 124–40. London: Macmillan, 1999.

Crane, S. *Collecting and Historical Consciousness in Early Nineteenth-Century Germany*. Ithaca, N.Y.: Cornell University Press, 2000.

———. "Writing the Individual Back into Collective Memory." *American Historical Review* 102, no. 5 (1997): 1372–85.

Csáky, E. *Der Weg zu Freiheit und Neutralität: Dokumentation zur österreichischen Außenpolitik 1945–1955*. Vienna: Braumüller, 1980.

Cullen, J. *The Civil War in Popular Culture: A Reusable Past*. Washington: Smithsonian Institution Press, 1995.

Czernin, H. "Die Folgen von Krumpendorf." *Profil*, 30 Dec. 1995, 11.

———, ed. *Wofür ich mich meinetwegen entschuldige: Haider, beim Wort genommen*. Vienna: Czernin, 2000.

Dainotto, R. "'Tramonto' and 'Risorgimento': Gentile's Dialectics and the Prophecy of Nationhood." In *Making and Unmaking Italy: The Cultivation of National Identity around the Risorgimento*, edited by A. R. Ascoli and K. von Henneberg, 241–56. Oxford: Berg, 2001.

"Dank an Innsbruck." *Die Furche* (5 March 1958): 2.

Danyel, J., ed. *Die geteilte Vergangenheit: Zum Umgang mit Nationalsozialismus und Widerstand in beiden deutschen Staaten*. Berlin: Akademie Verlag, 1995.

Davies, N. *Europe*. London: Pimlico, 1997.

———. *God's Playground*. Oxford: Oxford University Press, 1981.

———. "O historii prawdziwej." In *Rozmowy na nowy wiek, tom 1*, edited by M. Janion, K. Janowska, and P. Mucharski. Kraków: Znak, 2001.

———. *Rising '44: The Battle for Warsaw*. New York: Viking Press, 2004.

Deak, I., et al., eds. *The Politics of Retribution in Europe: World War II and Its Aftermath*. Princeton, N.J.: Princeton University Press, 2000.

de Baecque, A., and S. Toubiana. *François Truffaut*. Paris: Gallimard, 2001.

De Felice, R. *Interpretations of Fascism*. Boston: Harvard University Press, 1976.

———. *The Jews in Fascist Italy: A History*. New York: Enigma Books, 2001.

———. *Rosso e nero*. Milan: Baldini e Castoldi, 1995.

Degen, B. *Sozialdemokratie: Gegenmacht? Opposition? Bundesratspartei? Die Geschichte der Regierungsbeteiligung der schweizerischen Sozialdemokraten*. Zurich: Orell Füssli, 1993.

Dejung, C., and R. Stämpfli, eds. *Armee, Staat und Geschlecht: Die Schweiz im internationalen Vergleich*. Zurich: Chronos, 2003.

del Alamo, V., and C. S. Pendergast, eds. *Memory and the Medieval Tomb*. Aldershot, U.K.: Ashgate, 2000.

del Boca, Angelo. "L'impero." In *Simboli e miti dell'Italia unita*, edited by M. Isenghi, 417–38. Bari: La Terza, 1997.

de Luna, G. "I fatti di luglio 1960." In *Personaggi e date dell' Italia unita*, edited by M. Isenghi, 359–72. Bari: La Terza, 1997.

de Luna, G., and M. Revelli. *Fascismo, antifascismo: Le idee, le identità*. La Florence: Nuova Italia, 1995.

Deutsch, K. W. *Nationalism and Social Communication*. Cambridge, Mass.: MIT Press, 1953.

di Cori, P. "Le leggi razziali." In *Simboli e miti dell'Italia unita*, edited by M. Isenghi, 461–76. Bari: La Terza, 1997.

Diem, P. *Die Symbole Österreichs: Zeit und Geschichte in Zeichen*. Vienna: Kremayr und Scheriau, 1995.

Dienstag, J. F. *"Dancing in Chains": Narrative and Memory in Political Theory*. Stanford, Calif.: Stanford University Press, 1997.

Diggelmann, W. M. *Die Hinterlassenschaft*. 2nd ed. Zurich: Limmat, 1982.

Diner, D. *Beyond the Conceivable: Studies on Germany, Nazism, and the Holocaust*. Berkeley: University of California Press, 2000.

——, ed. *Ist der Nationalsozialismus Geschichte? Zu Historisierung und Historikerstreit*. Frankfurt: Fischer, 1987.

——, ed. *Zivilisationsbruch: Denken nach Auschwitz*. Frankfurt: Fischer, 1998.

Di Rienzo, E. *Un dopoguerra storiografico: Storici Italiani tra Guerra civile e Repubblica*. Florence: Le Lettere, 2004.

Doehring, K., B. J. Fehn, and H. G. Hockerts. *Jahrhudertschuld, Jahrhundertsühne: Reparationen, Wiedergutmachung, Entschädigung für nationalsozialistisches Kriegs- und Verfolgungsunrecht*. Munich: Olzog, 2001.

Dogliani, P. "Constructing Memory and Anti-Memory: The Monumental Representation of Fascism and Its Denial in Republican Italy." In *Italian Fascism: History, Memory and Representation*, edited by R. J. B. Bosworth and P. Dogliani, 11–30. London: Macmillan, 1999.

——. "The Debate on the Historiography of Fascism." *Differentia: Review of Italian Thought* 3–4 (1989): 243–58.

Dokumentationsarchiv des österreichischen Widerstandes, ed. *"Anschluß" 1938: Eine Dokumentation*. Vienna: Österreichischer Bundesverlag, 1998.

——, ed. *Gedenken und Mahnen in Wien 1934–1945: Gedenkstätten zu Widerstand und Verfolgung, Exil, Befreiung: Eine Dokumentation*. Vienna: Deuticke, 1998.

Domansky, E. " 'Kristallnacht,' the Holocaust and German Unity: The Meaning of November 9 as an Anniversary in Germany." *History and Memory* 4, no. 1 (spring/summer 1992): 60–94.

Domansky, E., and H. Welser, eds. *Eine offene Geschichte: Zur kommunikativen Tradierung der nationalsozialistischen Vergangenheit*. Tübingen: Edition discord, 1999.

Domenico, R. P. *Italian Fascists on Trial, 1943–1948*. Chapel Hill: University of North Carolina Press, 1991.

Dondi, M. "The Fascist Mentality after Fascism." In *Italian Fascism: History, Memory and Representation*, edited by R. J. B. Bosworth and P. Dogliani, 141–56. London: Macmillan, 1999.

——. "Piazzale Loreto." In *Simboli e miti dell'Italia unita*, edited by M. Isenghi, 3:487–500. Bari: La Terza, 1997.

"Doświadczenia wrześniowego." *Przegląd socjologiczny* 49, no. 2 (2000): 53–68.

Doumanis, N. "The Italian Empire and *brava gente*: Oral History and the Dodacanase Islands." In *Italian Fascism: History, Memory and Representation*, edited by R. J. B. Bosworth and P. Dogliani, 161–77. London: Macmillan, 1999.

Dower, J. *Embracing Defeat: Japan in the Wake of World War II*. New York: Norton, 1999.

Dubiel, H. *Niemand ist frei von der Geschichte: Die nationalsozialistische Herrschaft in den Debatten des Deutschen Bundestages.* Munich: Carl Hanser, 1999.

Dudek, P. *"Der Rückblick auf die Vergangenheit wird sich nicht vermeiden lassen": Zur pädagogischen Verarbeitung des Nationalsozialismus in Deutschland (1945–1990).* Opladen: Westdeutscher Verlag, 1995.

Dumont, H. *Leopold Lindtberg und der Schweizer Film 1935–1953.* Neu-Ulm: Knorr, 1981.

Dürrenmatt, P. *Schweizer Geschichte.* Bern: Hallwag, 1957.

Durrer, M. *Die schweizerisch-amerikanischen Finanzbeziehungen im Zweiten Weltkrieg: Von der Blockierung der schweizerischen Guthaben in den USA über die "Safehaven"-politik zum Washingtoner Abkommen (1941–1946).* Bern: Paul Haupt, 1984.

Dwork, D., and R. van Pelt. "Reclaiming Auschwitz." In *Holocaust Remembrance: The Shapes of Memory,* edited by G. H. Hartman, 232–51. Oxford: Basil Blackwell, 1994.

Eberan, B. *Wer war an Hitler schuld? Die Debatte um die Schuldfrage 1945–1949.* 2nd ed. Munich: Minerva, 1985.

Edwards, D., and J. Potter. "The Chancellor's Memory: Rhetoric and Truth in Discursive Remembering." *Applied Cognitive Psychology* 6, no. 3 (1992): 187–215.

Edwards, D., J. Potter, and D. Middleton. "Toward a Discursive Psychology of Remembering." *The Psychologist* 5 (1992): 441–46.

Edwards, P. *To Acknowledge a War: The Korean War in American Memory.* Westport, Conn.: Greenwood, 2000.

Eisen, J. *The Glasnost Reader.* New York: New American Library, 1990.

Eizenstat, S. E. *Imperfect Justice: Looted Assets, Slave Labor, and the Unfinished Business of World War II.* New York: Public Affairs, 2003.

Eley, G. "Labor History, Social History, Alltagsgeschichte: Experience, Culture, and the Politics of the Everyday: A New Direction for German Social History?" *Journal of Modern History* 61, no. 2 (1989): 297–343.

Eliot, T. S. *The Complete Poems and Plays, 1909–1950.* New York: Harcourt, Brace, 1952.

Elsaesser, T. *New German Cinema: A History.* New Brunswick, N.J.: Rutgers University Press, 1989.

Embacher, H. *Neubeginn ohne Illusionen: Juden in Österreich nach 1945.* Vienna: Picus Verlag, 1995.

Endlich, S., et al. *Gedenkstätten für die Opfer des Nationalsozialismus.* Vol. 2. Bonn: Bundeszentrale für politische Bildung, 1999.

English, R. D. *Russia and the Idea of the West: Gorbachev, Intellectuals and the End of the Cold War.* New York: Columbia University Press, 2000.

Erikson, E. *Adulthood.* New York: Norton, 1975.

——. *Childhood and Society.* New York: Norton, 1950.

Evangelista, M. *Unarmed Forces: The Transnational Movement to End the Cold War.* Ithaca, N.Y.: Cornell University Press, 1999.

Facchinelli, E. "Il fenomeno fascista." In *La freccia ferma: Tre tentativi di annullare il tempo*. Milan: Adelphi, 1992.

Fahlbusch, M. *Wissenschaft im Dienst der nationalsozialistischen Politik?* Baden-Baden: Nomos, 1999.

Fanta, W., and V. Sima. *"Stehst mitten drin im Land": Das europäische Kameradentreffen auf dem Kärntner Ulrichsberg von den Anfängen bis heute*. Klagenfurt/Celovec: Drava, 2003.

Farassino, A. "Mediologia della Resistenza, radio e televisione." In *La Resistenza italiana nei programmi della* RAI, edited by G. Cranz, A. Farrassino, E. Forcella, and N. Gallerano, 89–124. Rome: RAI, 1996.

Favez, J. *The Red Cross and the Holocaust*. Cambridge: Cambridge University Press, 1999.

Favez, J.-C. "Le Don Suisse et la politique étrangère." In *Des archives de la mémoire*, edited by B. Roth-Lochner and W. Neuenschwander, 327–39. Geneva: Société d' histoire, 1995.

"Federal Council Determines May 5 as Commemorative Day against Violence and Racism." *Parlamentskorrespondenz*, no. 785 (20 Nov. 1997).

Fehrenbach, H. *Cinema in Democratizing Germany: Reconstructing National Identity after Hitler*. Chapel Hill: University of North Carolina Press, 1995.

Feinberg, A. *Wiedergutmachung im Programm: Jüdisches Schicksal im deutschen Nachkriegsdrama*. Cologne: Prometheus, 1988.

Fels, G. *Der Aufruhr der 68er: Zu den geistigen Grundlagen der Studentenbewegung und der RAF*. Bonn: Bouvier, 1998.

Fentress, J., and C. Wickham. *Social Memory*. London: Blackwell, 1992.

Filene, B. *Romancing the Folk: Public Memory and American Roots Music*. Chapel Hill: University of North Carolina Press, 2000.

Finkelstein, N. *The Holocaust Industry: Reflections on the Exploitation of Jewish Suffering*. London: Verso, 2000.

Finkelstein, N., and R. B. Birn, eds. *A Nation of Trial: The Goldhagen Thesis and Historical Truth*. New York: Holt, 1998.

Fisch, J. *Reparationen nach dem Zweiten Weltkrieg*. Munich: Beck, 1992.

Fitzgerald, J. M. "Vivid Memories and the Reminiscence Phenomenon." *Human Development* 31 (1988): 261–73.

Fogu, C. "Fascismo-Stile." *Spectator* 21, no. 2 (spring 2001): 56–67.

———. *The Historic Imaginary: Politics of History in Fascist Italy*. Toronto: University of Toronto Press, 2003.

———. " 'To Make History': Gatibaldianism and the Formation of a Fascist Historic Imaginary." In *Making and Unmaking Italy: The Cultivation of National Identity around the Risorgimento*, edited by A. R. Ascoli and K. von Henneberg, 203–40. Oxford: Berg, 2001.

Forest, B., and J. Johnson. "Unraveling the Threads of History: Soviet-Era Monuments and Post-Soviet National Identity in Moscow." *Annals of the Association of American Geographers* 92, no. 3 (2002): 524–47.

Forgacs, D. "Days of Sodom: The Fascism-Perversion Equation in Films of the 1960s and 1970s." In *Italian Fascism: History, Memory and Representation*, edited by R. J. B. Bosworth and P. Dogliani, 217–36. London: Macmillan, 1999.

Forgion, L. P. *Il libro della memoria: Gli ebrei deportati dall'Italia (1943–1945)*. Milano: Mursia, 1991.

Förster, A., and B. Beck. "Post-Traumatic Stress Disorder and World War II: Can a Psychiatric Concept Help Us Understand Postwar Society?" In *Life after Death: Approaches to a Cultural and Social History of Europe During the 1940s and 1950s*, edited by R. Besse and D. Schumann, 15–35. Cambridge: Cambridge University Press, 2003.

Forster, D. *Wiedergutmachung in Österreich und der BRD im Vergleich*. Innsbruck: Studienverlag, 2001.

Foucault, M. "Anti-Rétro: Entretien avec Michel Foucault." *Cahiers du Cinéma*, nos. 251–52 (July–August 1974): 5–15.

———. *The Archaeology of Knowledge*. Translated by A. M. Sheridan Smith. New York: Pantheon, 1972.

Fox, T. *Stated Memory: East Germany and the Holocaust*. Rochester, N.Y.: Camden House, 1999.

Franklin, H. C., and D. H. Holding. "Personal Memories at Different Ages." *Quarterly Journal of Experimental Psychology* 29 (1977): 527–32.

Franzielli, M. "L'8 settembre." In *Personaggi e date dell Italia unita*, edited by M. Isnenghi, 241–70. Bari: La Terza, 1997.

———. "25 luglio." In *Personaggi e date dell Italia unita*, edited by M. Isnenghi, 219–40. Bari: La Terza, 1997.

Franzinelli, M. *Le stragi nascoste: L'armadio della vergogna: Impunità e rimozione dei crimini di Guerra nazifascisti 1943–2001*. Milan: Mondadori, 2002.

Frei, D. *Die Förderung des schweizerischen Nationalbewusstseins nach dem Zusammenbruch der Alten Eidgenossenschaft 1798*. Zurich: Juris Verlag, 1964.

Frei, N. "Auschwitz und Holocaust: Begriff und Historiographie." In *Holocaust: Die Grenzen des Verstehens*, edited by H. Loewy, 101–9. Reinbek: Rowohlt, 1992.

———. "Der Frankfurter Auschwitz-Prozess und die deutsche Zeitgeschichtsforschung." In *Auschwitz: Geschichte, Rezeption, Wirkung*, edited by Fritz Bauer Institut, 123–36. Frankfurt: Campus, 1996.

———. *1945 und wir: Das Dritte Reich im Bewusstsein der Deutschen*. Munich: Beck, 2005.

———. *Vergangenheitspolitik: Die Anfänge der Bundesrepublik und die NS-Vergangenheit*. Munich: Beck, 1996.

———. "Von deutscher Erfindungskraft: Oder, Die Kollektivschuldthese in der Nachkriegszeit." In *Hannah Arendt Revisited: "Eichmann in Jerusalem" und die Folgen*, edited by G. Smith, 163–76. Frankfurt: Suhrkamp, 2000.

———, ed. *Karrieren im Zwielicht: Hitlers Eliten nach 1945*. 2nd ed. Frankfurt: Campus, 2002.

Frei, N., D. van Laak, and M. Stolleis, eds. *Geschichte vor Gericht*. Munich: Beck, 2000.

Freud, S. *Moses and Monotheism*. Translated by K. Jones. New York: Vintage Books, 1939.

Friedländer, S. *Memory, History, and the Extermination of the Jews in Europe*. Bloomington: Indiana University Press, 1993.

——. *Reflets du nazisme*. Paris: Le Seuil, 1982.

——. "Trauma, Memory, and Transference." In *Holocaust Remembrance: The Shapes of Memory*, edited by G. H. Hartman, 252–63. Oxford: Basil Blackwell, 1994.

Friedrich, J. *Die kalte Amnestie: NS-Täter in der Bundesrepublik*. Frankfurt: Fischer, 1984.

Frisch, M. *Blätter aus dem Brotsack*. Zurich: Atlantis, 1974.

——. *Dienstbüchlein*. Frankfurt: Suhrkamp, 1974.

——. *I'm Not Stiller*. Translated by M. Bullock. San Diego: Harcourt Brace, 1994.

Fritsche, C. *Vergangenheitsbewältigung im Fernsehen: Westdeutsche Filme über den Nationalsozialismus in den 1950er und 1960er Jahren*. Munich: Meidenbauer, 2003.

Funkenstein, A. *Perceptions of Jewish History*. Berkeley: University of California Press, 1993.

Füssmann, K., H. T. Grütter, and J. Rüsen, eds. *Historische Faszination: Geschichtskultur heute*. Cologne: Böhlau, 1994.

Gabriel, J. M. *Sackgasse Neutralität*. Zurich: Hochschuleverlag, 1997.

Gallerano, N. "I programmi: Dagli anni settanta agli anni novanta." In *La Resistenza italiana nei programmi della RAI*. Rome: RAI, 1996.

Galli della Loggia, E. *La morte della patria*. Bologna: Il Mulino, 1996.

Garscha, W. R. "Entnazifizierung und gerichtliche Ahndung von NS-Verbrechen." In *NS-Herrschaft in Österreich: Ein Handbuch*, edited by E. Tálos, E. Hanisch, W. Neugebauer, and R. Sieder, 852–83. Vienna: öbv und hpt, 2000.

——. "Die verhinderte Re-Nazifizierung: Herbert Steiner und das Österreich des 'Herrn Karl.'" In *Erinnern und Vergessen als Denkprinzipien*, edited by H. Arlt, 27–44. St. Ingbert: Röhrig Universitätsverlag, 2002.

Gast, U. *Von der Kontrolle zur Abwehr: Die eidgenössische Fremdenpolizei im Spannungsfeld von Politik und Abwehr*. Zurich: Chronos, 1997.

Gautschi, W. *General Henri Guisan: Die schweizerische Armeeführung im Zweiten Weltkrieg*. Zurich: Verlag NZZ, 1989.

Geary, P. "The Historical Material of Memory." In *Art, Memory, and Family in Rennaissance Florence*, edited by G. Ciappelli and P. L. Rubin, 17–25. Cambridge: Cambridge University Press, 2000.

Gedi, N., and Y. Elam. "Collective Memory: What Is It?" *History and Memory* 8, no. 1 (1996): 30–50.

Gehler, M. "Die Affäre Waldheim: Eine Fallstudie zum Umgang mit der NS-Vergangenheit in den späten achtziger Jahren." In *Österreich im 20. Jahrhundert*, edited by R. Steininger and M. Gehler, 2:355–414. Vienna: Böhlau, 1997.

Gehrig-Straube, C. *Beziehungslose Zeiten: Das schweizerisch-sowjetische Verhältnis* zwischen Abbruch und Wiederaufnahme der Beziehungen (1918–1946) aufgrund schweizerischer Akten. Zurich: Hans Rohr, 1997.

Geiser, C. "Der Schweizer Soldat." Neutralität 45 (April 1970): 8.

Geisler, M. "The Disposal of Memory: Fascism and the Holocaust on West German Television." In Framing the Past: The Historiography of German Cinema and Television, edited by B. Murray and C. Wickham, 220–60. Carbondale: Southern Illinois University Press, 1992.

Gemeinde Wien, ed. "'Niemals vergessen!' Ein Buch der Anklage, Mahnung und Verpflichtung. Vienna: Jugend und Volk, 1946.

Gentile, E. The Sacralization of Politics in Fascist Italy. Cambridge, Mass.: Harvard University Press, 1996.

Gergen, K. J. "Mind, Text, and Society: Self-Memory in Social Context." In The Remembering Self: Construction and Accuracy in the Self Narrative, edited by U. Neisser and R. Fivush, 78–103. Cambridge: Cambridge University Press, 1994.

Giesen, B., and C. Schneider, eds. Tätertrauma: Nationale Erinnerung im öffentlichen Diskurs. Konstanz: UVK, 2004.

Gillis, J. "Memory and Identity: The History of a Relationship." In Commemorations: The Politics of National Identity, edited by J. Gillis, 3–24. Princeton, N.J.: Princeton University Press, 1994.

Giordano, R. Die zweite Schuld oder von der Last Deutscher zu sein. Hamburg: Rasch und Röhrig, 1987.

Göhring, W., and F. Stadlmann. Start in den Abgrund: Österreichs Weg 1918–1945. Vienna: Verlag des Österreichischen Gewerkschaftsbundes, 1978.

Golsan, R., ed. Memory, the Holocaust, and French Justice: The Bousquet and Touvier Affairs. Hanover, N.H.: University Press of New England, 1996.

——. The Papon Affair: History and Memory on Trial. New York: Routledge, 2000.

Görlich, E. J., and F. Romanik. Geschichte Österreichs. Innsbruck: Tyrolia Verlag, 1970.

Goschler, C. Schuld und Schulden: Die Politik der Wiedergutmachung für NS-Verfolgte seit 1945. Göttingen: Wallstein, 2005.

Goschler, C., and P. Ther, eds. Raub und Restitution: "Arisierung" und Rückerstattung des jüdischen Eigentums in Europa. Frankfurt: Fischer, 2003.

Grabitz, H. "Die Verfolgung von NS-Verbrechen in der Bundesrepublik Deutschland, der DDR und Österreich." In Umgang mit dem Holocaust: Europa, USA, Israel, edited by R. Steininger, 198–220. Vienna: Böhlau, 1994.

Gramsci, A. Prison Notebooks. New York: Columbia University Press, 1991.

Grant, B. "New Moscow Monuments, or, States of Innocence." American Ethnologist 28, no. 2 (May 2001): 332–62.

Greschat, M., ed. Im Zeichen der Schuld: 40 Jahre Stuttgarter Schuldbekenntnis. Neukirchen: Neukirchener Verlag, 1985.

Greven, M., and O. Wrochem, eds. Der Krieg in der Nachkriegszeit. Opladen: Leske und Budrich, 2000.

——. Sąsiedzi. Sejny: Pogranicze, 2000.

Gross, L., and M. E. Barnes, eds. *Talk That Talk: An Anthology of African-American Story-Telling*. New York: Simon and Schuster, 1989.

Grosz, E., ed. *Becomings: Explorations in Time, Memory, and Futures*. Ithaca, N.Y.: Cornell University Press, 1999.

Grumke, T., and B. Wagner, eds. *Handbuch Rechtsradikalismus: Personen–Organisationen–Netzwerke vom Neonazismus bis in die Mitte der Gesellschaft*. Poladen: Leske und Budrich, 2002.

Guéry, C. "Une interrogation après le procès Touvier: Le crime contre l'humanité existe-t-il?" *Le genre humain* 28 (Nov. 1994): 119–37.

Guggenbühl, A. *Die Schweizer sind anders: Die Erhaltung der Eigenart: Eine Frage der nationalen Existenz*. Zurich: Schweizer Spiegel Verlag, 1967.

Gutte, R., and F. Huisken. *Alles bewältigt, nichts begriffen! Nationalsozialismus im Unterricht: Eine Kritik der antifaschistischen Erziehung*. Berlin: Edition Ost, 1997.

Haas, G. *"Wenn man gewusst hätte, was sich drüben im Reich abspielte" 1941–1943: Was man in der Schweiz von der Vernichtungspolitik wusste*. Basel: Helbing und Lichtenhahn, 1994.

Habermas, J. "Grenzen des Neohistorismus." In *Die nachholende Revolution*. Frankfurt am Main: Suhrkamp, 1990.

———. "Historical Consciousness and Post-Traditional Identity: The Federal Republic's Orientation to the West." In *The New Conservatism: Cultural Criticism and the Historians' Debate*. Cambridge, Mass.: MIT Press, 1989.

Hacker, W., ed. *Warnung an Österreich: Neonazismus: Die Vergangenheit bedroht die Zukunft*. Vienna: Europa Verlag, 1966.

Halbwachs, M. *Les cadres sociaux de la memoire*. Paris: Alcan, 1925.

———. *La memoire collective*. Paris: Presses Universitaires, 1950.

———. *La topographie legendaire des Evangiles en Terre Sainte: Etude de memoire collective*. Paris: Presses Universitaires, 1941.

Haltiner, K. W., L. Bertossa, and K. Spillmann. *Sicherheit '97*. Zürcher Beiträge zu Sicherheitspolitik und Konfliktforschung, vol. 42. Zurich: Forschungsstelle für Sicherheitspolitik der ETH Zürich, 1997.

Hanisch, E. "Gab es einen spezifisch österreichischen Widerstand?" *Zeitgeschichte* 12, nos. 9–10 (1985): 339–50.

———. *Der lange Schatten des Staates: Österreichische Gesellschaftsgeschichte im 20. Jahrhundert*. Vienna: Ueberreuter, 1994.

———. "Der Ort des Nationalsozialismus in der österreichischen Geschichte." In *NS-Herrschaft in Österreich: Ein Handbuch*, edited by E. Tálos, E. Hanisch, W. Neugebauer, and R. Sieder, 11–25. Vienna: öbv und hpt, 2001.

Hanson, S. *Time and Revolution*. Chapel Hill: University of North Carolina Press, 1997.

Hartman, G., ed. *Bitburg in Moral and Political Perspective*. Bloomington: Indiana University Press, 1986.

Häsler, A. A. *The Lifeboat Is Full: Switzerland and the Refugees, 1933–1945*. Funk and Wagnalls, 1969.

Haug, W. F. *Vom hilflosen Antifaschismus zur Gnade der späten Geburt*. 2nd ed. Hamburg: Argument, 1987.

Hayes, C. J. H. *Essays on Nationalism*. New York: Macmillan, 1926.

Hedrick, C. *History and Silence: Purge and Rehabilitation of Memory in Late Antiquity*. Austin: University of Texas Press, 2000.

Heer, H., ed. *War of Extermination: The German Military in World War II, 1941–1944*. New York: Berghahn, 2000.

Heer, H., W. Manoschek, A. Pollak, and R. Wodak, eds. *Wie Geschichte gemacht wird: Zur Konstruktion von Erinnerungen an Wehrmacht und Zweiten Weltkrieg*. Vienna: Czernin, 2003.

Heer, H., and K. Naumann, eds. *Vernichtungskrieg: Verbrechen der Wehrmacht*. Hamburg: Hamburger Edition, 1995.

Heil, J., and R. Erb, eds. *Geschichtswissenschaft und Öffentlichkeit: Der Streit um Daniel J. Goldhagen*. Frankfurt: Fischer, 1998.

Hein, L., and M. Selden, eds. *Censoring History: Citizenship and Memory in Japan, Germany and the United States*. Armonk, N.Y.: M. E. Sharpe, 2000.

Heiniger, M. *Dreizehn Gründe warum die Schweiz im Zweiten Weltkrieg nicht erobert wurde*. Zurich: Limmat, 1989.

Henke, K.-D. "Die Trennung von Nationalsozialismus: Selbstzerstörung, politische Säuberung, 'Entnazifizierung,' Strafverfolgung." In *Politische Säuberung in Europa*, edited by K.-D. Henke and H. Woller, 21–83. Munich: Deutscher Taschenbuch Verlag, 1991.

Herbert, U. "Nicht entschädigungsfähig? Die Wiedergutmachungsansprüche der Ausländer." In *Wiedergutmachung in der Bundesrepublik Deutschland*, edited by L. Herbst and C. Goschler, 272–302. Münich: Oldenbourg, 1989.

———. "Vernichtungspolitik: Neue Antworten und Fragen zur Geschichte des Holocaust." In *Nationalisozialistische Vernichtungspolitik 1939–1945*, edited by U. Herbert, 9–66. Frankfurt: Fischer, 1998.

———, ed. *National-Socialist Extermination Policies: Contemporary German Perspectives and Controversies*. New York: Berghahn, 2000.

Herbst, K. *Didaktik des Geschichtsunterrichts zwischen Traditionalismus und Reformismus*. Hanover, Germany: Schroedel, 1977.

Herdt, G. H. *Guardians of the Flutes: Idioms of Masculinity*. New York: McGraw-Hill, 1981.

Herf, J. *Divided Memory: The Nazi Past and the Two Germanies*. Cambridge, Mass.: Harvard University Press, 1997.

Herodotus. *The Histories*. Translated by G. Rawlinson. New York: Knopf, 1997.

Hervieu-Leger, D. *Religion as Chain of Memory*. New Brunswick, N.J.: Rutgers University Press, 2000.

Herz, T., and M. Schwab-Trapp. *Umkämpfte Vergangenheit: Diskurse über den Nationalsozialismus seit 1945*. Opladen: Westdeutscher Verlag, 1997.

Hettling, M. "Das Fähnlein der Treffsicheren: Die eidgenössischen Schützenfeste im 19. und 20. Jahrhundert." In *Männerbund und Bundesstaat: Über die politische Kultur der Schweiz*, edited by L. Blattmann and I. Meier, 97–119. Zurich: Orell Füssli, 1998.

——. "Geschichtlichkeit: Zwerge auf den Schultern von Riesen." In *Eine kleine Geschichte der Schweiz: Der Bundesstaat und seine Traditionen*. Frankfurt: Suhrkamp, 1998.

Heulenkamp, U. *Deutsche Erinnerung*. Berlin: Schmidt, 2000.

Hicketheir, K. "Der zweite Weltkrieg und der Holocaust im Fernsehen der fünfziger und frühen sechziger Jahre." In *Der Krieg in der Nachkriegszeit*, edited by M. Greven and O. Wrochem, 93–112. Opladen: Leske und Budrich, 2000.

Hindels, J. "Nazivergangenheit und Gegenwart." *Zukunft* 9 (1987): 20–22.

Histor, M. *Willy Brandts vergessene Opfer: Geschichte und Statistik der politisch motivierten Berufsverbote in Westdeutschland, 1971–1988*. Freiburg: Ahriman, 1989.

Höbelt, L. *Defiant Populist: Jörg Haider and the Politics of Austria*. West Lafayette, Ind.: Purdue University Press, 2003.

Hobsbawm, E., and T. Ranger, eds. *The Invention of Tradition*. Cambridge: Cambridge University Press, 1993.

Hockerts, H. G., and C. Kuller, eds. *Nach der Verfolgung: Wiedergutmachung nationalsozialistischen Unrechts in Deutschland?* Göttingen: Wallstein, 2003.

Hofer, W. *Neutralität als Maxime der schweizerischen Aussenpolitik*. Berlin: Hochschulverlag, 1956.

Hoffmann, H., and W. Schober, eds. *Zwischen Gestern und Morgen: Westdeutscher Nachkriegsfilm 1946–1962*. Frankfurt: Deutsches Filmmuseum, 1989.

Hoffmann, S. "Cinquante ans après, quelques conclusions essentielles." *Esprit* 181 (May 1992): 38–42.

Hohls, R., and K. Jarausch, eds. *Versäumte Fragen: Deutsche Historiker im Schatten des Nationslsozialismus*. Stuttgart: Deutsche Verlagsanstalt, 2000.

Holler, R. *20. Juli 1944: Vermächtnis oder Alibi*. Munich: Saur, 1994.

Höllwart, R., C. Martinez-Turek, N. Sternfeld, and A. Pollak, eds. *In einer Wehrmachtsausstellung Erfahrungen mit Geschichtsvermittlung*. Vienna: Turia und Kant, 2003.

Hornung, E. "Trümmermänner: Zum Schweigen österreichischer Soldaten der Deutschen Wehrmacht." In *Inventur 45/55: Österreich im ersten Jahrzehnt der Zweiten Republik*, edited by W. Kos and G. Rigele, 232–50. Vienna: Sonderzahl, 1996.

Horowitz, M. J. *Stress Response Syndromes*. New York: Jacob Aronson, 1976.

Huener, J. *Auschwitz, Poland, and the Politics of Commemoration, 1945–1979*. Athens: Ohio University Press, 2003.

Hug, P. *Schweizer Rüstungsindustrie und Kriegsmaterialhandel zur Zeit des Nationalsozialismus: Unternehmensstrategien Marktentwicklungpolitische Überwachung*. Edited by Independent Commission of Experts Switzerland–Second World War. Zurich: Chronos, 2002.

———. "Verhinderte oder verpasste Chancen? Die Schweiz und die Vereinten Nationen, 1943–1947." In *Die Schweiz im internationalen System der Nachkriegszeit 1943–1950* (Itinera, vol. 18), edited by G. Kreis, 84–87. Basel: Schwabe, 1996.

———. "Vom Neutralismus zur Westintegration: Zur schweizerischen Aussenpolitik in der Nachkriegszeit." In *"Goldene Jahre": Zur Geschichte der Schweiz seit 1945*, edited by W. Leimgruber and W. Fischer, 59–100. Zurich: Chronos, 1999.

Hug, P., and M. Kloter, eds. *Aufstieg und Niedergang des Bilateralismus: Schweizerische Aussen- und Aussenwirtschaftspolitik, 1930–1960*. Zurich: Chronos, 1999.

Hug, P., and M. Perrenoud. *In der Schweiz liegende Vermögenswerte von Nazi-Opfern und Entschädigungsabkommen mit Oststaaten*. Bern: Schweizerisches Bundesarchiv, 1997.

Hughes, M. *Shouldering the Burdens of Defeat: West Germany and the Reconstruction of Social Justice*. Chapel Hill: University of North Carolina Press, 1999.

Humphrey, C. *The Unmaking of Soviet Life*. Ithaca, N.Y.: Cornell University Press, 1992.

Huonker, T. *Anstaltseinweisungen, Kindswegnahmen, Eheverbote, Sterilisationen, Kastrationen*. Zurich: Sozialdepartement der Stadt Zürich, 2002.

Hurdes, F. "Von Friedrich bis Hitler: Totentanz Österreichs." In *"Niemals vergessen!" Ein Buch der Anklage, Mahnung und Verpflichtung*, edited by Gemeinde Wien, 72–74. Vienna: Jugend und Volk, 1946.

Hutton, P. *History as an Art of Memory*. Hanover, N.H.: University Press of New England, 1993.

Hyman, I. E., Jr. "Multiple Approaches to Remembering." *The Psychologist* 5 (1992): 450–51.

Hymans, J. "What Counts as History and How Much Does History Count? The Case of French Secondary Education." In *The Nation, Europe, the World: Textbooks and Curricula in Transition*, edited by H. Schissler and Y. Soysal, 61–81. New York: Berghahn, 2005.

Iggers, G. G. *Geschichtswissenschaft im 20. Jahrhundert*. Göttingen: Vandenhoek und Ruprecht, 1993.

Imboden, M. *Helvetisches Malaise*. Zurich: EVZ-Verlag, 1964.

Imhof, K. "Wiedergeburt der geistigen Landesverteidigung: Kalter Krieg in der Schweiz." In *Konkordanz und Kalter Krieg: Analyse von Medienereignissen in der Schweiz der Zwischen- und Nachkriegszeit*, edited by K. Imhof, H. Kleger, and G. Romano, 173–247. Zurich: Seismo Verlag, 1996.

Imhof, K., et al. *Die Flüchtlings- und Aussenwirtschaftspolitik der Schweiz im Kontext der öffentlichen politischen Kommunikation 1938–1950*. Edited by Independent Commission of Experts Switzerland–Second World War. Zurich: Chronos, 2002.

Imhof, K., H. Kleger, and G. Romano, eds. *Vom Kalten Krieg zur Kulturrevolution: Analyse von Medienereignissen in der Schweiz der 50er und 60er Jahre*. Zurich: Seismo Verlag, 1999.

Im Hof, U. *Mythos Schweiz: Identität, Nation, Geschichte 1291–1991*. Verlag NZZ, 1991.

Independent Commission of Experts Switzerland–Second World War. *Final Report.* Zurich: Pendo Editions, 2002.

——. *Switzerland and Gold Transactions in the Second World War: Interim Report.* Bern: EDMZ, 1998.

——. *Switzerland and Refugees in the Nazi Era.* Bern: EDMZ, 1999.

——. *Switzerland, National Socialism and the Second World War: Final Report.* Zurich: Pendo, 2002.

Institut für Zeitgeschichte, ed. *Alltagsgeschichte der NS-Zeit: Neue Persektive oder Trivialisierung?* Munich: Oldenbourg, 1984.

Irwin-Zarecka, I. *Frames of Remembrance: The Dynamics of Collective Memory.* New Brunswick, N.J.: Transaction, 1994.

Isnenghi, M. Conclusione. In *Strutture ed eventi dell'Italia unita*, edited by M. Isnenghi, 515–62. Bari: La Terza, 1997.

——. "Memoria pubblica della Resistenza." In *L'Italia nella seconda guerra mondiale e nella Resistenza*, edited by F. Ferratini Tosi, G. Grassi, and M. Legnani, 559–66. Milan: Franco Angeli, 1999.

——, ed. *I luoghi della memoria.* 3 vols. Bari: La Terza, 1997.

——, ed. *Personaggi e date dell Italia unita.* Volume 3 of *I luoghi della memoria.* Bari: La Terza, 1997.

——, ed. *Simboli e miti dell'Italia unita.* Volume 1 of *I luoghi della memoria.* Bari: La Terza, 1997.

——, ed. *Strutture ed eventi dell'Italia unita.* Volume 2 of *I luoghi della memoria.* Bari: La Terza, 1997.

Jacobs, N. "Der Streit um Dr. Hans Globke in der öffentlichen Meinung der Bundesrepublik Deutschland 1949–1973." PhD diss., University of Bonn, 1992.

Jaspers, K. *Die Schuldfrage: Von der politischen Haftung Deutschlands.* Munich: Piper, 1987.

Jeismann, M. *Auf Wiedersehen Gestern: Die deutsche Vergangenheit und die Politik von morgen.* Stuttgart: Deutsche Verlagsanstalt, 2001.

Jellinek, G. "Die Geschichte der österreichischen Wiedergutmachung." In *The Jews of Austria*, edited by J. Fraenkel, 395–426. London: Vallentine Mitchell, 1967.

Jochum, M., and F. Olbort, eds. *80 Jahre Republik: 1918 bis 1938 und 1945 bis 1998 in Reden und Statements.* Vienna: Verlag Eugen Ketterl, 1998.

Johnson, L. R. "Die österreichische Nation, die Moskauer Deklaration und die völkerrechtliche Argumentation: Bemerkungen zur Problematik der Interpretation der NS-Zeit in Österreich." In *Jahrbuch 1988*, edited by Dokumentationsarchiv des österreichischen Widerstandes, 78. Vienna: Globus Verlag, 1987.

Jost, H. U. *Politik und Wirtschaft im Krieg: Die Schweiz 1938–1948.* Zurich: Chronos, 1998.

Judt, T. "Die Vergangenheit ist ein anderes Land: Politische Mythen im Nachkriegseuropa." *Transit*, no. 6 (autumn 1993): 87–120.

Kaes, A. *From Hitler to Heimat: The Return of History as Film.* Cambridge, Mass.: Harvard University Press, 1989.

Kägi-Fuchsmann, R. *Das gute Herz genügt nicht: Mein Leben und meine Arbeit.* Zurich: Ex Libris, 1968.

Kaldor, M. *The Imaginary War: Understanding the East-West Conflict.* Oxford: Blackwell, 1990.

Kannonier-Finster, W., and M. Ziegler. "Einleitung und Ausgangspunkte." In *Österreichisches Gedächtnis: Über Erinnern und Vergessen der NS-Vergangenheit*, edited by M. Weiterschan, 21–26. Vienna: Böhlau, 1993.

Kansteiner, W. "Between Politics and Memory: The Historikerstreit and the West German Historical Culture of the 1980s." In *Fascism's Return: Scandal, Revision, Ideology*, edited by R. J. Golsan, 86–129. Lincoln: University of Nebraska Press, 1998.

——. "Entertaining Catastrophe: The Reinvention of the Holocaust on German Television." *New German Critique*, no. 90 (2003): 135–62.

——. "Finding Meaning in Memory: A Methodological Critique of Collective Memory Studies." *History and Theory* 41, no. 2 (2002): 179–97.

——. "Genealogy of a Category Mistake: A Critical Intellectual History of the Cultural Trauma Metaphor." *Rethinking History* 8, no. 2 (summer 2004) 193–221.

——. *In Pursuit of German Memory: History, Television, and Politics after Auschwitz.* Athens: Ohio University Press, 2006.

——. "Nazis, Viewers, and Statistics: Television History, Television Audience Research, and Collective Memory in West Germany." *Journal of Contemporary History* 39, no. 4 (October 2004): 575–98.

——. "The Radicalization of German Memory in the Age of Its Commercial Reproduction: Hitler and the Third Reich in the TV Documentaries of Guido Knopp." In *Atlantic Communications: Media in American and German History*, edited by U. Lehmkuhl, 335–72. Providence, R.I.: Berg, 2004.

——. "The Rise and Fall of Metaphor: German Historians and the Uniqueness of the Holocaust." In *Is the Holocaust Unique? Perspectives on Comparative Genocide*, 2nd ed., edited by A. Rosenbaum, 221–44. Boulder, Colo.: Westview, 2001.

Kaplan, A. *The Collaborator: The Trial and Execution of Robert Brasillach.* Chicago: University of Chicago Press, 2000.

Kapralski, S. "Oświęcim: Konflikt pamięci czy kryzys tożsamości?" *Przegląd Socjologiczny* 49, no. 2 (2000): 141–66.

Kapuściński, R. *Lapidaria.* Warsaw: Czytelnik, 1997.

Kasemir, G. "Spätes Ende für 'wissenschaftlich' vorgetragenen Rassismus: Die Affäre Borodajkewycz." In *Politische Affären und Skandale in Österreich: Von Mayerling bis Waldheim*, edited by M. Gehler and H. Sickinger, 486–501. Thaur: Kulturverlag, 1995.

Kattago, S. *Ambiguous Memory: The Nazi Past and German National Identity.* Westport, Conn.: Praeger, 2001.

Kavanagh, G. *Dream Spaces: Memory and the Museum.* London: Leicester University Press, 1999.

Keilbach, J. "Fernsehbilder der Geschichte: Anmerkungen zur Darstellung des Nationalsozialismus in den Geschichtsdokumentationen des ZDF." *1999: Zeitschrift für Sozialgeschichte des 20. und 21. Jahrhunderts* 17, no. 2 (2002): 104–13.

Keller, S. *Grüningers Fall: Geschichten von Flucht und Hilfen.* Zurich: Rotpunkt, 1993.

Kellner, H. *Language and Historical Representation.* Madison: University of Wisconsin Press, 1989.

Keppler, A. *Tischgespräche: Über Formen kommunikativer Vergemeinschaftung am Beispiel der Konversation in Familien.* Frankfurt: Suhrkamp, 1994.

Keyserlingk, R. H. *Austria in World War II: An Anglo-American Dilemma.* Kingston: McGill-Queen's University Press, 1988.

Kinkel, L. "Viele Taten, wenig Täter: Die Wehrmacht als Sujet neuerer Dokumentationsserien des öffentlich-rechtlichen Rundfunk." In *Der Krieg in der Nachkriegszeit,* edited by M. Greven and O. Wrochem, 113–30. Opladen: Leske und Budrich, 2000.

Kirsch, J.-H. *Nationaler Mythos oder historische Trauer? Der Streit um ein zentrales "Holocaust-Mahnmal" für die Berliner Republik.* Köln: Böhlau, 2003.

——. *"Wir haben aus der Geschichte gelernt": Der 8. Mai als politischer Gedenktag in Deutschland.* Cologne: Böhlau, 1999.

Kittel, M. *Die Legende von der "Zweiten Schuld": Vergangeheitsbewältigung in der Ära Adenauer.* Berlin: Ullstein, 1993.

Klein, E. *The Battle of Auschwitz: Catholic-Jewish Relations under Strain.* London: Vallentine Mitchell, 2001.

Klein, K. L. "On the Emergence of Memory in Historical Discourse." *Representations* 69 (winter 2000): 127–50.

Klingenstein, G. "Über Herkunft und Verwendung des Wortes 'Vergangenheitsbewältigung.'" *Geschichte und Gegenwart* 4 (1988): 301–12.

Klinkhammer, L. "La politica di repressione della Wehrmacht in Italia: Le stragi ai danni della popolazione civile nel 1943–1944." In *La memoria del nazismo nell'Europa di oggi.* Florence: La Nuova Italia, 1997.

Knigge, V., and N. Frei, eds. *Verbrechen erinnern: Die Auseinandersetzung mit Holocaust und Völkermord.* Munich: Beck, 2002.

Knight, R., ed. *"Ich bin dafür, die Sache in die Länge zu ziehen": Die Wortprotokolle der österreichischen Bundesregierung von 1945–52 über die Entschädigung der Juden.* Frankfurt: Athenäum, 1988.

Knoch, H. *Die Tat als Bild: Fotografien des Holocaust in der deutschen Erinnerungskultur.* Hamburg: Hamburger Edition, 2001.

Koch, G., ed. *Bruchlinien: Tendenzen der Holocaustforschung.* Cologne: Böhlau Verlag, 1999.

Koch, P. F. *Geheim-Depot Schweiz: Wie die Banken am Holocaust verdienen.* Munich: Paul List, 1997.

Koebner, T. "Die Schuldfrage: Vergangenheitsverweigerung und Lebenslügen in der Diskussion 1945–1949." In *Deutschland nach Hitler: Zukunftspläne im Exil und aus der Besatzungszeit 1939–1949,* edited by T. Koebner et al., 301–29. Opladen: Westdeutscher Verlag, 1987.

Kohlstruck, M. *Zwischen Erinnerung und Geschichte: Der Nationalsozialismus und die jungen Deutschen.* Berlin: Metropol, 1997.

Kohn, H. *Prophets and Peoples: Studies in Nineteenth Century Nationalism.* New York: Macmillan, 1946.

Koller, G. "Entscheidungen über Leben und Tod: Die behördliche Praxis in der schweizerischen Flüchtlingspolitik während des Zweiten Weltkrieges." *Studien und Quellen* 22 (1996): 17–136.

Komitee Schluss mit dem Schnüffelstaat, ed. *Schnüffelstaat Schweiz: Hundert Jahre sind genug.* Zurich: Limmat, 1990.

König, H., M. Kohlstruck, and A. Wöll, eds. *Vergangenheitsbewältigung am Ende des zwanzigsten Jahrhunderts.* Opladen: Westdeutscher Verlag, 1998.

König, M., et al. *Dynamisierung und Umbau: Die Schweiz in den 60er und 70er Jahren.* Zurich: Chronos, 1998.

Kos, W. "Die Schau mit dem Hammer: Zur Planung, Ideologie und Gestaltung der antifaschistischen Ausstellung 'Niemals Vergessen!' " In *Eigenheim Österreich: Zu Politik, Kultur und Alltag nach 1945,* 7–58. Vienna: Sonderzahl, 1994.

Koshar, R. *From Monuments to Traces: Artifacts of German Memory, 1870–1990.* Berkeley: University of California Press, 2000.

———. *Germany's Transient Pasts: Preservation and National Memory in the Twentieth Century.* Chapel Hill: University of North Carolina Press, 1998.

Kotkin, S. *Armageddon Averted: The Soviet Collapse, 1970–2000.* Oxford: Oxford University Press, 2001.

Kraushaar, W. *1968: Das Jahr, das alles verändert hat.* Munich: Piper, 1998.

Kreis, G. "Der 'homo alpinus helveticus': Zum Rassendiskurs der 30er Jahre in der Schweiz." In *Erfundene Schweiz: Konstruktionen nationaler Identität—La Suisse imaginée: Bricolages d'une identité nationale,* edited by G. P. Marchal and A. Mattioli, 175–90. Zurich: Chronos, 1992.

———. "Introduction: Four Debates and Little Consensus." In *Switzerland and the Second World War,* edited by G. Kreis, 1–18. London: Frank Cass, 2000.

———. "Philipp Etter." In *Intellektuelle von Rechts: Ideologie und Politik in der Schweiz 1918–1939,* edited by A. Mattioli, 185–213. Zurich: Orell Füssli, 1995.

———. *Die Rückkehr des J-Stempels: Zur Geschichte einer schwierigen Vergangenheitsbewältigung.* Zurich: Chronos, 2000.

———. *Die Schweiz unterwegs: Schlussbericht des NFP 21 "Kulturelle Vielfalt und nationale Identität."* Basel: Helbing und Lichtenhahn, 1993.

———. *Staatsschutz in der Schweiz: Die Entwicklung von 1935–1990.* Bern: Paul Haupt, 1993.

Kris, E. *Selected Papers of Ernst Kris.* New Haven, Conn.: Yale University Press, 1975.

Król, M. "Pamięć i historia." *Res Publica Nowa* 7, no. 154 (July 2001): 5.

Krzemiński, I. *Antysemitizm w Polsce i na Ukrainie.* Warsaw: Wydawnictwo Naukowe Scholar, 2004.

———. *Czy Polacy są antysemitami?* Warsaw: Oficyna Naukowa, 1996.

Kubik, J. *The Power of Symbols against the Symbols of Power*. University Park: Pennsylvania University Press, 1994.

*Das kulturelle Gedächtnis: Schrift, Erinnerung and politische Identität in den frühen Hochkulturen*. Munich: Beck, 1999.

Kunz, M. *Aufbruchstimmung und Sonderfall-Rhetorik: Die Schweiz im Übergang von der Kriegs- zur Nachkriegszeit in der Wahrnehmung der Parteipresse 1943–1950*. Bern: Schweizerisches Bundesarchiv, 1998.

Kuretsidis-Haider, C. "Verdrängte Schuld, vergessene Ahndung: NS-Prozesse in Österreich." In *Die Lebendigkeit der Geschichte: (Dis-)Kontinuitäten in Diskursen über den Nationalsozialismus*, edited by E. Lappin and B. Schneider, 91–104. St. Ingbert: Röhrig Universitätsverlag, 2001.

Kuroń, J., and J. Żakowski. *PRL dla początkujących*. Wrocław: Wydawnictwo Dolnośląskie, 1999.

LaCapra, D. *History and Memory after Auschwitz*. Ithaca, N.Y.: Cornell University Press, 1998.

———. *Representing the Holocaust: History, Theory, Trauma*. Ithaca, N.Y.: Cornell University Press, 1994.

———. *Rethinking Intellectual History*. Ithaca, N.Y.: Cornell University Press, 1983.

Laermann, K. " 'Nach Auschwitz ein Gedicht zu schreiben, ist barbarisch': Überlegungen zu einem Darstellungsverbot." In *Kunst und Literatur nach Auschwitz*, edited by M. Köppen, 11–15. Berlin: Schmidt, 1993.

Lagrou, P. *The Legacy of Nazi Occupation: Patriotic Memory and National Recovery in Western Europe 1945–1965*. Cambridge: Cambridge University Press, 2000.

———. "The Victims of Genocide and National Memory: Belgium, France and the Netherlands, 1945–1965." *Past and Present* 154 (Feb. 1997): 181–222.

Lahodynsky, O. "Trend zum Revisionismus: Der Streit darüber, ob Österreich am 8. Mai befreit oder besetzt wurde, spaltet 57 Jahre nach Kriegsende noch immer die Republik." *Profil*, 13 May 2002, 28–32.

Lambelet, J.-C. *Le mobbing d'un petit pays: Onze thèse sur la Suisse pendant la deuxième guerre mondiale*. Lausanne: L'Age d'homme, 1999.

Landsgesell, G. "Sind wir alle Nazis?" *Format* 41 (1991): 40–46.

Langer, L. *Holocaust Testimonies: The Ruins of Memory*. New Haven, Conn.: Yale University Press, 1991.

Leak, A., and G. Paizis, eds. *The Holocaust and the Text: Speaking the Unspeakable*. New York: St. Martin's, 2000.

LeGoff, J. *History and Memory*. New York: Columbia University Press, 1992.

Lehmann, A. *Im Fremden ungewollt zuhaus: Füchtlinge und Vertriebene in Westdeutschland 1945–1990*. 2nd ed. Munich: Beck, 1993.

Leimgruber, W., T. Meier, and R. Sablonier. *Das Hilfswerk für die Kinder der Landstrasse*. Bern: Bundesarchiv, 1998.

Leisi, E. *Freispruch für die Schweiz*. Frauenfeld: Huber, 1997.

Leonhard, N. *Politik- und Geschichtsbewusstsein im Wandel: Die politische Bedeutung der nationalsozialistischen Vergangenheit im Verlauf von drei Generationen in Ost- und Westdeutschlend*. Münster: Lit, 2002.

Lepsius, M. R. "Das Erbe des Nationalsozialismus und die politische Kultur der Nachfolgestaaten des 'Großdeutschen Reiches.'" In *Kultur und Gesellschaft: Verhandlungen des 24. Deutschen Soziologentags, des 11. Österreichischen Soziologentags und des 8. Kongresses der Schweizerischen Gesellschaft für Soziologie in Zürich 1988*, edited by M. Haller, H. Hoffmann-Nowotny, and W. Zapf, 247–64. Frankfurt am Main: Campus-Verlag, 1989.

Leser, N., and M. Wagner, eds. *Österreichs politische Symbole: Historisch, ästhetisch und ideologiekritisch beleuchtet*. Vienna: Böhlau, 1994.

Lévesque, J. *The Enigma of 1989: The USSR and the Liberation of Eastern Europe*. Translated by K. Martin. Berkeley: University of California Press, 1997.

Levy, D., and N. Sznaider. *Erinnerung im globalen Zeitalter: Der Holocaust*. Frankfurt: Fischer, 2001.

Lichtenstein, H. (1979). *Majdanek: Reportage eines Prozesses*. Frankfurt: Europäische Verlagsanstalt, 1979.

———. *Im Namen des Volkes: Eine persönliche Bilanz der NS-Prozesse*. Cologne: Bund, 1984.

Linenthal, E. *Preserving Memory: The Struggle to Create America's Holocaust Museum*. New York: Viking, 1995.

Linn, A. *"Noch heute ein Faszinosum": Philipp Jenninger zum 9. November 1938 und die Folgen*. Münster: Lit, 1991.

Liss, A. *Trespassing through Shadows: Memory, Photography and the Holocaust*. Minneapolis: University of Minnesota Press, 1998.

Łodziński, S. "'Battles for Monuments and Memory': Controversies about the National Minorities' Places of Commemoration in Poland after 1989." In *Dominant Culture as a Foreign Culture: Dominant Groups in the Eyes of Minorities*, edited by J. Mucha, 195–208. New York: East European Monographs, 1999.

Longerich, P. *Politik der Vernichtung: Eine Gesamtdarstellung der nationalsozialistischen Judenverfolgung*. Munich: Piper, 1998.

Loshitzky, Y., ed. *Spielberg's Holocaust: Critical Perspectives on "Schindler's List."* Bloomington: Indiana University Press, 1997.

Lottman, H. *The Purge*. New York: Morrow, 1986.

*Louis Malle par Louis Malle*. Paris: Lathanor, 1978.

Lowenthal, D. *The Past Is a Foreign Country*. New York: Cambridge University Press, 1985.

Lübbe, H. "Der Nationalsozialismus im deutschen Nachkriegsbewusstsein." *Historische Zeitschrift* 236, no. 3 (1983): 579–99.

———. "Verdrängung? Über eine Kategorie zur Kritik des deutschen Vergangenheitsverhältnisses." In *Die Gegenwart der Vergangenheit*, edited by H. Wiebe, 94–106. Bad Segeberg: Wäser, 1989.

Ludi, R. "Gendering Citizenship and the State in Switzerland after 1945." In *Nation and Gender in Contemporary Europe: Exploring the East-West Divide*, edited by S. Booth and V. Tolz. Manchester, U.K.: Manchester University Press, 2004.

——. "Die Parzellierung der Vergangenheit: Schweizer NS-Opfer und die Grenzen der Wiedergutmachung." *Studien und Quellen* 29 (2003): 101–28.

Ludi, R., and A. A. Speck. "Swiss Victims of National Socialism: An Example of How Switzerland Came to Terms with the Past." In *Remembering for the Future: The Holocaust in an Age of Genocide*, edited by J. K. Roth and E. Maxwell, 2:907–22. London: Palgrave, 2001.

Lüdke, A. "Einleitung: Was ist und wer treibt Alltagsgeschichte?" In *Alltagsgeschichte: Zur Rekonstruktion historischer Erfahrungen und Lebensweisen*, edited by A. Lüdtke, 9–47. Frankfurt: Campus, 1989.

Lüthi, H. J. *Max Frisch*. Tübingen: Francke, 1997.

Lutz, F. P. *Das Geschichtsbewusstsein der Deutschen: Grundlagen der politischen Kultur in Ost und West*. Cologne: Böhlau, 2000.

Luzzatto, S. *Il corpo del duce: Un cadavere tra immaginazione, storia e memoria*. Turin: Einaudi, 1998.

——. *La crisi dell'antifascsmo*. Torino: Einaudi, 2004.

Lyotard, F. *The Postmodern Condition: A Report on Knowledge*. Minneapolis: Minnesota University Press, 1984.

Machcewicz, P., and K. Persak, eds. *Wokół Jedwabnego*. Warsaw: Instytut Pamięci Narodowej, 2002.

Mächler, S. "Kampf gegen das Chaos: Die antisemitische Bevölkerungspolitik der eidgenössischen Fremdenpolizei und Polizeiabteilung 1917–1954." In *Antisemitismus in der Schweiz 1848–1960*, edited by A. Mattioli, 357–421. Zurich: Orell Füssli, 1998.

Maciejewska, I. *Męczeństwo i zagłada Żydów w zapisach literatury polskiej*. Warsaw: Krajowa Agencja Wydawnicza, 1988.

Maleuvre, D. *Museum Memories: History, Technology, Art*. Stanford, Calif.: Stanford University Press, 1999.

Malinowski, B. "The Role of Myth in Life." In *Sacred Narrative*, edited by A. Dundes, 193–206. Berkeley: University of California Press, 1984.

Malmborg, M., and B. Stråth, eds. *The Meaning of Europe: Variety and Contention within and among Nations*. Oxford: Berg, 2002.

Manig, B.-O. *Die Politik der Ehre: Die Rehabilitierung der Berufssoldaten in der frühen Bundesrepublik*. Göttingen: Wallstein, 2004.

Mannheim, K. "Das Problem der Generationen." In *Wissenschaftssoziologie: Auswahl aus dem Werk*. Berlin: Luchterhand, 1964.

Manoschek, W. "Verschmähte Erbschaft: Österreichs Umgang mit dem Nationalsozialismus 1945 bis 1955." In *Österreich 1945–1995: Gesellschaft, Politik, Kultur*, edited by R. Sieder, H. Steinert, and E. Tálos, 94–106. Vienna: Verlag für Gesellschaftskritik, 1995.

Marboe, E., ed. *Das Österreich-Buch*. Vienna: Verlag der Österreichischen Staatsdruckerei, 1948.

Marchal, G. P. "Die 'Alten Eidgenossen' im Wandel der Zeiten: Das Bild der frühen Eidgenossen im Traditionsbewusstsein und in der Identitätsvorstellung der Schweizer vom 15. bis ins 20. Jahrhundert." In *Innerschweiz und frühe Eidgenossenschaft- Jubiläumsschrift 700 Jahre Eidgenossenschaft*. Vol. 2. Olten: Walter Verlag, 1990.

Marchal, G. P., and A. Mattioli, eds. *Erfundene Schweiz: Konstruktionen nationaler Identität—La Suisse imaginée: Bricolages d'une identité nationale*. Zurich: Chronos, 1992.

Marchart, O., V. Öhner, V., and H. Uhl. " 'Holocaust' Revisited: Lesarten eines Medienereignisses zwischen globaler Erinnerungskultur und nationaler Vergangenheitsbewältigung." *Tel Aviver Jahrbuch für deutsche Geschichte 2003*, 283–310. Göttingen: Wallstein, 2003.

Marcuse, H. *Legacies of Dachau: The Use and Abuses of a Concentration Camp*. Cambridge: Cambridge University Press, 2001.

Marrus, M. "Reflections on the Historiography of the Holocaust." *Journal of Modern History* 66 (March 1994): 92–116.

Märtesheimer, P., and I. Frenzel, eds. *Im Kreuzfeuer: Der Fernsehfilm Holocaust: Eine Nation ist betroffen*. Frankfurt: Fischer, 1979.

Matejka, V. *Widerstand ist alles: Notizen eines Unorthodoxen*. Vienna: Löcker, 1984.

Matsuda, M. *The Memory of the Modern*. New York: Oxford University Press, 1996.

Matustik, M. *Postnational Identity: Critical Theory and Existential Philosophy in Habermas, Kierkegaard, and Havel*. New York: Guilford, 1993.

Mayer, H. F. *Lexikon der populären Irrtümer Österreichs*. Vienna: Buchgemeinschaft Donauland, 2002.

Mazower, M. *Dark Continent: Europe's Twentieth Century*. New York: Knopf, 1998.

Mcdonald, S., ed. *Approaches to European Historical Consciousness: Reflections and Provocations*. Hamburg: Edition Körber, 2000.

Megill, A. "History, Memory, Identity." *History of the Human Sciences* 11, no. 3 (1998): 37–62.

Meienberg, N. "Bonsoir, Herr Bonjour." In *Vielleicht sind wir morgen schon bleich u. tot*. Zurich: Limmat, 1989.

———. *Die Erschiessung des Landesverräters Ernst S.* Darmstadt: Luchterhand, 1977.

———. *Reportagen aus der Schweiz*. Darmstadt: Luchterhand, 1974.

Meier, M., et al. *Schweizerische Aussenwirtschaftspolitik 1930–1948*. Edited by Independent Commission of Experts Switzerland–Second World War. Zurich: Chronos, 2002.

Menasse, R. *Das Land ohne Eigenschaften: Essay zur österreichischen Identität*. Vienna: Sonderzahl, 1993.

Merridale, C. *Night of Stone: Death and Memory in Twentieth Century Russia*. London: Penguin, 2000.

Merseburger, P. *Willy Brandt 1913–1992: Visionär und Realist*. Stuttgart: Deutsche Verlagsanstalt, 2002.

Meyer, A. *Anpassung oder Widerstand: Die Schweiz zur Zeit des deutschen Nationalso-zialismus*. Frauenfeld: Huber, 1965.

Meyer-Seitz, C. *Die Verfolgung von NS-Straftaten in der Sowjetischen Besatzungszone*. Berlin: Arno Spitz, 1998.

Mezzana, D. *La memoria storica della Resistenza nelle nuove generazioni*. Milan: Murzia, 1997.

Michman, D., ed. *Remembering the Holocaust in Germany, 1945–2000: German Strategies and German Responses*. New York: Lang, 2002.

Miłosz, C. *The Captive Mind*. New York: Vintage, 1990.

Miquel, M. von. *Ahnden oder Amnestieren? Westdeutsche Justiz und Vergangenheitsbewältigungpolitik in den sechziger Jahren*. Göttingen: Wallstein, 2004.

Mitscherlich, M. "Die Unfähigkeit zu trauern in Ost- und Westdeutschland: Was Trauerarbeit heissen könnte." *Psyche* 46, no. 7 (July 1992): 406–18.

———. *Erinnerungsarbeit: Zur Psychoanalyse der Unfähigkeit zu trauern*. Frankfurt: Fischer, 1993.

Mitscherlich, M., and A. Mitscherlich. *The Inability to Mourn*. New York: Grove, 1975.

Mitten, R. *The Politics of Prejudice: The Waldheim Phenomenon in Austria*. Boulder, Colo.: Westview Press, 1992.

Möckli, D. (2001). "Neutralität, Solidarität, Sonderfall: Die Konzeptionierung der schweizerischen Aussenpolitik der Nachkriegszeit, 1943–1947." *Zürcher Beiträge zur Sicherheitspolitik und Konfliktforschung* 55 (2001). See http://e-collection.eth bib.ethz.ch.

Moeller, R. O. *War Stories: The Search for a Usable Past in the Federal Republic of Germany*. Berkeley: University of California Press, 2001.

———. "What Has Coming to Terms with the Past Meant? From History to Memory to the History of Memory in Germany." *Journal of Central European History* (forthcoming).

Mohler, A. *Der Nasenring: Die Vergangenheitsbewältigung vor und nach dem Fall der Mauer*. Munich: Langen Müller, 1991.

Molasky, M. *The American Occupation of Japan and Okinawa: Literature and Memory*. London: Routledge, 1999.

Molden, O. *Der Ruf des Gewissens: Der österreichische Freiheitskampf 1938–1945: Beiträge zur Geschichte der österreichischen Widerstandsbewegung*. Vienna: Herold, 1958.

Moller, S. *Die Entkonkretisierung der NS-Herrschaft in der Ära Kohl*. Hanover, Germany: Offizin, 1998.

Mommsen, H. "Holocaust und die Deutsche Geschichtswissenschaft." In *The Historiography of the Holocaust Period*, edited by Y. Gutman and G. Greif, 79–97. Jerusalem: Yad Vashem, 1988.

Montavi, M. *Schweizerische Sicherheitspolitik im Kalten Krieg 1947–1963: Zwischen angelsächsischem Containment und Neutralitäts-Doktrin*. Zurich: Orell Füssli, 1999.

Mooser, J. " 'Spiritual National Defence' in the 1930s: Swiss Political Culture between the Wars." In *Switzerland and the Second World War*, edited by G. Kreis, 236–53. London: Frank Cass, 2000.

Morris, A. *Collaboration and Resistance Reviewed: Writers and the Mode Rétro in Post-Gaullist France.* New York: Berg, 1992.

Müller, I. *Hitler's Justice: The Courts of the Third Reich.* Cambridge, Mass.: Harvard University Press, 199.

Müller, J.-W. *Another Country: German Intellectuals, Unification and National Identity.* New Haven, Conn.: Yale University Press, 2000.

——, ed. *Memory and Power in Post-War Europe: Studies in the Presence of the Past.* Cambridge: Cambridge University Press, 2002.

Müller-Hohagen, J. *Verleugnet, verdrängt, verschwiegen: Die seelischen Auswirkungen der Nazizeit.* Munich: Kösel, 1988.

Murphy, K. *Memory and Modernity: Voillet-le-Duc at Vezelay.* University Park: Pennsylvania State University Press, 2000.

Muschg, A. *Wenn Auschwitz in der Schweiz liegt: Fünf Reden eines Schweizers an seine und keine Nation.* Frankfurt: Suhrkamp, 1997.

Naumann, K., ed. *Nachkrieg in Deutschland.* Hamburg: Hamburger Edition, 2001.

Neisser, U. "John Dean's Memory: A Case Study." *Cognition* 9, no. 1 (February 1981): 1–22.

——. *Memory Observed: Remembering in Natural Contexts.* San Francisco: Freeman, 1982.

——. "The Psychology of Memory and the Socio-Linguistics of Remembering." *The Psychologist* 5 (1992): 451–52.

——. "Self-Narratives: True and False." In *The Remembering Self: Construction and Accuracy in the Self Narrative*, U. Neisser and R. Fivush, 1–18. Cambridge: Cambridge University Press, 1994.

——, ed. *The Perceived Self: Ecological and Interpersonal Sources of Self-Knowledge.* Cambridge: Cambridge University Press, 1993.

Neisser, U., and R. Fivush. *The Remembering Self: Construction and Accuracy in the Self Narrative.* Cambridge: Cambridge University Press, 1994.

Neisser, U., and E. Winograd, eds. *Remembering Reconsidered: Ecological and Traditional Approaches to the Study of Memory.* Cambridge: Cambridge University Press, 1988.

Ne'man Arad, G. *America, Its Jews, and the Rise of Nazism.* Bloomington: Indiana University Press, 2000.

Neues Österreich, ed. *Pflichterfüllung: Ein Bericht über Kurt Waldheim.* Vienna: Löcker, 1986.

Neugebauer, W. "Widerstand und Opposition." In *NS-Herrschaft in Österreich: Ein Handbuch*, edited by E. Tálos, E. Hanisch, W. Neugebauer, and R. Sieder, 187–213. Vienna: öbv und hpt, 2000.

Neugebauer, W., and P. Schwarz. *Der Wille zum aufrechten Gang: Offenlegung der Rolle des BSA bei der gesellschaftlichen Reintegration ehemaliger Nationalsozialis-*

*ten*. Edited by Bund sozialdemokratischer Akademiker Innen. Vienna: Czernin, 2005.

Niethammer, L. "Diesseits des 'Floating Gap': Das kollektive Gedächnis und die Konstruktion von Identität im wissenschaftlichen Diskurs." In *Deutschland danach: Postfaschistische Gesellschaft und nationales Gedächnis*. Bonn: Dietz, 1999.

———. *Kollektive Identität: Heimliche Quellen einer unheimlichen Konjunktur*. Reinbek: Rowohlt, 2000.

———. *Lebenserfahrung und kollektives Gedächnis: Die Praxis der "Oral History."* Frankfurt: Syndikat Autoren- und Verlagsgesellschaft, 1980.

———. *Die Mitläuferfabrik: Die Entnazifizierung am Beispiel Bayerns*. 2nd ed. Berlin: Dietz, 1982.

Nietzsche, F. "On the Advantages and Disadvantages of History for Life." In *Untimely Meditations*. Cambridge, Mass.: Hackett Publishing, 1980.

Niggli, P., and J. Frischknecht. *Rechte Seilschaften: Wie die "unheimlichen Patrioten" den Zusammenbruch des Kommunismus meisterten*. Zurich: Rotpunktverlag, 1998.

Niven, B. *Facing the Nazi Past: United Germany and the Legacy of the Third Reich*. London: Routledge, 2002.

Noiriel, G. *Le Origines républicaines de Vichy*. Paris: Hachette, 1999.

Nora, P. "Between Memory and History: Les Lieux de Mémoire." *Representations* 26 (spring 1989): 7–25.

———. "Czas pamięci." *Res Publica Nowa* 7, no. 154 (July 2001): 37–43.

———. *The State*. Vol. 1 of *Les Lieux de Mémoire*. Chicago: University of Chicago Press, 2001.

———, ed. *Realms of Memory: Rethinking the French Past*. 3 vols. New York: Columbia University Press, 1996–1998.

Novick, P. *The Holocaust in American Life*. New York: Houghton-Mifflin, 1999.

Olick, J. "Collective Memory: The Two Cultures." *Sociological Theory* 17, no. 4 (1999): 333–48.

———, ed. *States of Memory: Continuities, Conflicts and Transformations in National Retrospect*. Durham, N.C.: Duke University Press, 2003.

Olick, J., and J. Robbins. "Social Memory Studies: From 'Collective Memory' to the Historical Sociology of Mnemonic Practices." *Annual Review of Sociology* 24 (1998): 105–40.

Orla-Bukowska, A. "Presenting and Representing the Shoah in the Post-Communist World." In *Enteignet, Vertrieben, Ermordet: Beiträge zur Genozidforschung*, edited by D. J. Schaller, R. Boyadin, V. Berg, and H. Scholtz, 319–47. Zurich: Chronos, 2004.

———. "Representing the Shoah in Poland and Poland in the Shoah." In *Re-presenting the Shoah for the Twenty-first Century*, edited by R. Lentin, 179–94. Oxford: Berghahn, 2004.

Orwell, G. *Nineteen Eighty-Four*. London: Milestone, 1949.

Ory, P. "Comme de l'an quarante: Dix ans de 'rétro satanas.'" *Le Débat* 16 (Nov. 1981): 109–17.

Osagie, I. F. *The Armistad Revolt: Memory, Slavery, and the Politics of Memory in the United States and Sierra Leone.* Athens: University of Georgia Press, 2000.

Otto, K. *Vom Ostermarsch zur Apo: Geschichte der ausserparlamentarischen Opposition in der Bundesrepublik 1960–1970.* Frankfurt: Campus, 1977.

Paggi, L. "La repubblica senza Pantheon: Politica e memoria dell'antifascismo (1945–1978)." In *Le memorie della repubblica*, edited by L. Paggi, 247–68. Florence: La Nuova Italia, 1999.

——. "Storia di una memoria anti-partigiana." In *La memoria del nazismo nell'Europa di oggi.* Florence: La Nuova Italia, 1997.

Pape, M. *Ungleiche Brüder: Österreich und Deutschland 1945–1965.* Cologne: Böhlau, 2000.

Passerini, L. *Europe in Love, Love in Europe: Imagination and Politics between the Wars.* New York: New York University Press, 1999.

——. *Fascism in Popular Memory: The Cultural Experience of the Turin Working Class.* London: Cambridge University Press, 1984.

——. *Mussolini immaginario.* Bari: Laterza, 1986.

——. "Il '68." In *Personaggi e date dell Italia unita*, edited by M. Isnenghi, 373–88. Bari: La Terza, 1997.

——, ed. *The Question of European Identity: A Cultural Historical Approach.* Florence: European Historical Institute, 1998.

Paszkowski, R. "Przedmowa do czwartego wydania." In *Przewodnik po upamiętnionych miejscach walk i męczeństwa lata wojny 1939–1945*, edited by Rada Ochrony Pomników Walki i Męczeństwa. Warsaw: Wydawnictwo Sport i Turystyka, 1988.

Patraka, V. *Theatre, Fascism, and the Holocaust.* Bloomington: Indiana University Press, 1998.

Pavone, C. "L'eredità della guerra civile e il nuovo quadro istituzionale." In *Lezioni sull' italia repubblicana*, 59–84. Rome: Donzelli, 1994.

——. *Una guerra civile: Saggio storico sulla moralità nella Resistenza.* Torino: Bollati Bordighieri, 1994.

——. "Le idee della Resistenza: Antifascisti e fascisti di fronte alla tradizione del Risorgimento." *Passato e Presente* 7 (January–February 1959): 59–84.

——. "La resistenza in Italia: Memoria e rimozione." *Rivista di storia contemporanea* 33–34, no. 2 (1994–1995): 484–92.

Paxton, R. Foreword. *Vichy: An Everpresent Past*, by É. Conan and H. Rousso, ix–xiii. London: University Press of New England, 1998.

Paxton, R., et al. "Symposium on Mitterrand's Past." *French Politics and Society* 13, no. 1 (winter 1995): 19–21.

Peitsch, H., et al., eds. *European Memories of the Second World War.* New York: Berghahn, 1999.

Pelinka, A. *Austria: Out of the Shadow of the Past.* Boulder, Colo.: Westview Press, 1998.

———. "Der verdrängte Bürgerkrieg." In *Das große Tabu: Österreichs Umgang mit seiner Vergangenheit*, edited by A. Pelinka and E. Weinzierl, 143–53. Vienna: Verlag der Österreichischen Staatsdruckerei, 1987.

Pennebaker, J. W. "Confession, Inhibition and Disease." In *Advances in Experimental Social Psychology*, edited by L. Berkowitz, 22:211–40. San Diego: Academic Press, 1989.

Pennebaker, J. W., and B. L. Banasik. "On the Creation and Maintenance of Collective Memories: History as Social Psychology." In *Collective Memory of Political Events: Social Psychological Perspectives*, edited by J. W. Pennebaker, D. Paez, and B. Rimé, 3–20. Mahwah, N.J.: Lawrence Erlbaum, 1997.

Pennebaker, J. W., and K. Harber. "A Social Stage Model of Collective Coping: The Loma Prieta Earthquake and the Persian Gulf War." *Social Issues* 49, no. 4 (1993): 125–45.

Perels, J. *Das juristische Erbe des "Dritten Reiches": Beschädigung der demokratischen Rechtsordnung*. Frankfurt: Campus, 1999.

Perz, B. *Die KZ-Gedenkstätte Mauthausen 1945 bis zur Gegenwart*. Innsbruck: Studienverlag, 2005.

Pestalozzi, H. A., ed. *Rettet die Schweiz: Schafft die Armee ab*. Bern: Zytglogge, 1982.

Pezzino, P. "Guerra ai civili: Le stragi tra storia e memoria." *Passato e Presente* 21, no. 58 (2003): 111–31.

Picard, J. "Eine Politik der Erinnerung: Anmerkungen zu den schweizerischen Erinnerungsfeierlichkeiten zum Ende des Zweiten Weltkrieges in Europa." *Traverse* 8, no. 2 (1996): 7–17.

———. *Die Schweiz und die Juden, 1933–1945*. Zurich: Chronos, 1994.

———. "Switzerland as a 'Bystander' of History: On Neutrality in a Time of Global Crises and Genocidal Wars." In *Remembering for the Future: The Holocaust in an Age of Genocide*, edited by J. K. Roth and E. Maxwell, 1:71–89. London: Palgrave, 2001.

Pick, H. *Guilty Victim: Austria from the Holocaust to Haider*. London: I. B. Tauris Publishers, 2000.

Plack, A. *Hitlers langer Schatten*. Munich: Langen Müler, 1993.

Pogany, I. *Righting Wrongs in Eastern Europe*. Manchester, U.K.: Manchester University Press, 1997.

Poliakov, L., and J. Sabille. *The Jews under the Italian Occupation*. New York: Howard Fertig, 1983.

Polkinghorne, D. E. "Narrative and Self-Concept." *Journal of Narrative and Life History* 1, nos. 2–3 (1991): 135–53.

———. *Narrative Knowing and the Human Sciences*. Albany: State University of New York Press, 1988.

Polonsky, A., ed. *My Brother's Keeper: Recent Polish Debates on the Holocaust*. Oxford: Routledge, 1990.

Polonsky, A., and J. B. Michlic, eds. *The Neighbors Respond: The Controversy over the Jedwabne Massacre in Poland*. Princeton, N.J.: Princeton University Press, 2004.

Portelli, A. "Uchronic Dreams: Working-Class Memory and Possible Worlds." In *The Death of Luigi Trastulli and Other Stories: Form and Meaning in Oral History.* Albany: State University of New York Press, 1991.

Preece, J. *The Life and Work of Günter Grass: Literature, History, Politics.* New York: Palgrave, 2001.

Preuss-Lausitz, U., ed. *Kriegskinder, Konsumkinder, Krisenkinder: Zur Sozialisationsgeschichte seit dem Zweiten Weltkrieg.* 2nd ed. Weinheim: Beltz, 1991.

Prinz, M., and R. Zitelmann, eds. *Nationalsozialismus und Modernisierung.* Darmstadt: Wissenschaftliche Buchgesellschaft, 1994.

Prokop, J. *Universum polskie: Literatura, wyobraźnia zbiorowa, mity polityczne.* Krakow: Universitas, 1993.

Pugliese, S., ed. *The Most Ancient of Minorities: The Jews of Italy.* Westport, Conn.: Greenwood Press, 2002.

Putz, E. " 'Zuviel der Mahnung': Das Gedenken an den Kriegsdienstverweigerer Franz Jägerstätter." In *Steinernes Bewusstsein II,* edited by H. Uhl. Forthcoming.

Puvogel, U., and M. Stankowski, M. *Gedenkstätten für die Opfer des Nationalsozialismus.* Vol. 1. 2nd ed. Bonn: Bundeszentrale für politische Bildung, 1995.

Quack, S. *Auf dem Weg zur Realisierung: Das Denkmal für die ermordeten Juden Europas und der Ort der Information: Architektur und historisches Konzept.* Stuttgart: Deutsche Verlagsanstalt, 2002.

Qualtinger, H. " 'Der Herr Karl' und andere Texte fürs Theater." In *Werkausgabe,* vol. 1. Vienna: Deuticke, 1995.

Rabinbach, A. "Response to Karen Brecht, 'In the Aftermath of Nazi Germany: Alexander Mitscherlich and Psychoanalysis: Legend and Legacy.' " *American Imago* 52, no. 3 (1995): 313–28.

Rada Ochrony Pomników Walki i Męczeństwa, ed. *Przewodnik po upamiętnionych miejscach walk i męczeństwa lata wojny 1939–1945.* Warsaw: Sport i Turystyka, 1988.

Raddatz, F. J. *Summa Inuiria oder Durfte der Papst schweigen: Hochuth's Stellvertreter in der öffentlichen Kritik.* Reinbek: Rowohlt, 1964.

Radstone, S. "Working with Memory: An Introduction." In *Memory and Methodology,* edited by S. Radstone, 1–22. Oxford: Berg, 2000.

——, ed. *Memory and Methodology.* Oxford: Berg, 2000.

Raissig, W. *Geistige Landesverteidigung: Erklärungen vor dem Nationalrat am 18.9.1963.* Bern: Zentralsekretariat des Schweizerischen Aufklärungsdienstes, 1964.

Ranzato, G. "La guerra di Spagna." In *Strutture ed eventi dell'Italia unita,* edited by M. Isnenghi, 331–44. Bari: La Terza, 1997.

Rathkolb, O., ed. *Revisiting the National Socialist Legacy: Coming to Terms with Forced Labor, Expropriation, Compensation, and Restitution.* Innsbruck: Transaction, 2002.

Ravetto, K. *The Unmaking of Fascist Aesthetics.* Minneapolis: University of Minnesota Press, 2001.

Recovery of Historical Memory Project, ed. *Guatemala: Never Again!* Maryknoll, N.Y.: Orbis, 1999.

Reichel, P. *Erfundene Erinnerung: Weltkrieg und Judenmord in Film und Theater.* Munich: Hanser, 2004.

———. *Politik mit der Erinnerung: Gedächnisorte im Streit um die nationalsozialistische Vergangenheit.* Munich: Hanser, 1995.

———. *Vergangenheitsbewältigung in Deutschland: Die Auseinandersetzung mit der NS-Diktatur von 1945 bis heute.* Munich: Beck, 2001.

Reisman, M., and C. Antoniou. *The Laws of War: A Comprehensive Collection of Primary Documents on International Laws Governing Armed Conflict.* New York: Vintage, 1994.

Rensmann, L. *Demokratie und Judenbild: Antisemitismus in der politischen Kultur der Bundesrepublik Deutschland.* Wiesbaden: Verlag für Soziolwissenschaften, 2004.

Rentschler, E. *The Ministry of Illusion: Nazi Cinema and Its Afterlife.* Cambridge, Mass.: Harvard University Press, 1996.

———, ed. *West German Filmmakers on Film: Visions and Voices.* New York: Holmes and Meier, 1988.

Richter, F. *Günter Grass: Die Vergangenheitsbewältigung in der Danziger-Trilogie.* Bonn: Bouvier, 1979.

Rickman, G. J. *Swiss Banks and Jewish Souls.* New Brunswick, N.J.: Transaction, 1999.

Ridolfi, M. *Le feste nazionali.* Bologna: Il Mulino, 2003.

Rings, W. *Raubgold aus Deutschland: Die "Golddrehscheibe" Schweiz im Zweiten Weltkrieg.* Zurich: Artemis, 1985.

Robinson, J. A. "Sampling Autobiography." *Cognitive Psychology* 8, no. 4 (October 1976): 588–95.

Rochat, G. "La guerra di Grecia." In *Strutture ed eventi dell'Italia unita*, edited by M. Isnenghi, 345–64. Bari: La Terza, 1997.

Rogers, D. *Politics after Hitler: The Western Allies and the German Party System.* New York: University Press New York, 1995.

Rokuszewska-Pawełek, A. "Pożoga wojenna: O niektórych właściwościach doświadczenia wrześniowego." *Przegląd socjologiczny* 49, no. 2 (2000): 64–65.

Roniger, L., and M. Sznajder, eds. *The Legacy of Human-Rights Violations in the Southern Cone.* Oxford: Oxford University Press, 2000.

Rosenfeld, G. *Munich and Memory: Architecture, Monuments, and the Legacy of the Third Reich.* Berkeley: University of California Press, 2000.

Rosenzweig, R., and D. Thelen. *The Presence of the Past: Popular Uses of History in American Life.* New York: Columbia University Press, 1998.

Roth, W., and B. Rusinek, eds. *Verwandlungspolitik: NS-Eliten in der westdeutschen Nachkriegsgesellschaft.* Frankfurt: Campus, 1998.

Rother, B. "Willy Brandt: Der Kniefal von Warschau." In *Engagierte Demokraten: Vergangenheitspolitik in kritischer Absicht*, edited by C. Fröhlich and M. Kohlstruck, 299–308. Münster: Westfälisches Dampfboot, 1999.

Rousso, H. *The Haunting Past.* Philadelphia: University of Pennsylvania Press, 2001.

———. "Une justice impossible: L'épurarion et la politique antijuive de Vichy." *Annales* 48, no. 3 (May–June 1993): 745–70.

———. *Le Syndrome de Vichy de 1944 à nos jours*. Paris: Le Seuil, 1987.

———. *Vichy: L'événement, la mémoire, l'histoire*. Paris: Gallimard, 2001.

———. *The Vichy Syndrome: History and Memory in France since 1944*. Translated by A. Goldhammer. Cambridge, Mass.: Harvard University Press, 1991.

Rubin, D., ed. *Remembering Our Past: Studies in Autobiographical Memory*. Cambridge: Cambridge University Press, 1996.

Rubin, D. C., S. E. Wetzler, and R. D. Nebes. "Autobiographical across the Lifespan." In *Autobiographical Memory*, edited by D. C. Rubin, 202–21. Cambridge: Cambridge University Press, 1986.

Rückerl, A. *NS-Verbrechen vor Gericht: Versuch einer Vergangenheitsbewältigung*. 2nd ed. Heidelberg: C. Müller, 1984.

Rüegg, S. *"Ich hasse nicht die Schweiz, sondern die Verlogenheit": Das Schweiz-Bild in Max Frischs Werken "Graf Öderland," "Stiller" und "Achtung: Die Schweiz" und ihre zeitgenössische Kritik*. Zurich: Chronos, 1998.

Rüsen, J., and J. Straub, eds. *Die dunkle Spur der Vergangenheit: Psychoanalytische Zugänge zum Geschichtsbewusstsein*. Frankfurt: Suhrkamp, 1998.

Rybicka, A. *Instytut Niemieckiej Pracy Wschodniej: Kraków 1940–45*. Warsaw: Wydawnictwo DiG, 2002.

Saathoff, G. "Entschädigung für Zwangsarbeiter? Entstehung und Leistungen der Bundestiftung 'Erinnerung, Verantwortung und Zukunft' im Kontext der Debatte um die 'vergessenen Opfer.'" In *Nach der Verfolgung: Wiedergutmachung nationalsozialistischen Unrechts in Deutschland*, edited by H. G. Hockerts and Kuller, 241–73. Göttingen: Wallstein, 2003.

Sabrow, M., ed. *Verwaltete Vergangenheit: Geschichtskultur und Herrschaftslegitimation in der DDR*. Leipzig: Akademische Verlagsanstalt, 1997.

Saburo, I. *Japan's Past/Japan's Future: One Historian's Odyssey*. Translated by R. H. Minear. New York: Littlefeld, 2001.

Sacks, J. *Studies in Renewal 1: From Integration to Survival to Continuity*, June 1993. See http://www.chiefrabbi.org.

Salis, J.-R. von. "Die Schweiz im Kalten Krieg." In *Schwierige Schweiz. Beiträge zu einigen Gegenwartsfragen*. Zurich: Orell Füssli, 1968.

Santomassimo, P. *Antifascismo e dintorni*. Rome: Manifestolibri, 2004.

Sapir, E. "Language." In *Selected Writings of Edward Sapir in Language, Culture, and Personality*, edited by D. G. Mandelbaum, 7–32. Berkeley: University of California Press, 1949.

Sartre, J.-P. "Qu'est-ce qu'un collaborateur?" In *Situations 3*. Paris: Gallimard, 1949.

Satzman, L., and A. Kiefer. *Anselm Kiefer and Art after Auschwitz*. Cambridge: Cambridge University Press, 1999.

Schaal, G., and A. Wöll, eds. *Vergangenheitsbewältigung: Modelle der politischen und sozialen Integration in der bundesdeutschen Nachkriegsgeschichte*. Baden-Baden: Nomos, 1997.

Schacter, D. *Searching for Memory: The Brain, the Mind and the Past.* New York: Basic Books, 1996.

——, ed. *The Cognitive Neuropsychology of False Memory.* New York: Psychology Press, 1999.

Schafft, G. E., and G. Zeidler. *Die KZ-Mahn- und Gedenkstätten in Deutschland.* Berlin: Dietz, 1996.

Schillinger, R. "Der Lastenausgleich." In *Die Vertreibung der Deutschen aus dem Osten: Ursachen, Ereignisse, Folgen,* edited by W. Benz, 183–92. Frankfurt: Fischer, 1985.

Schindler, D. "Fragen des Neutralitätsrechts im Zweiten Weltkrieg." In *Die Schweiz, der Nationalsozialismus und das Recht. I. Öffentliches Recht.* Veröffentlichungen der Unabhängigen Experten Kommission, 18:79–126. Zurich: Chronos, 2001.

Schirrmacher, F. *Die Walser-Bubis-Debatte: Eine Dokumentation.* Frankfurt: Suhrkamp, 1999.

Schivelbusch, W. *In a Cold Crater: Cultural and Intellectual Life in Berlin 1945–1948.* Berkeley: University of California Press, 1998.

Schlant, E. *The Language of Silence: West German Literature and the Holocaust.* New York: Routledge, 1999.

Schlant, E., and T. Rimer, eds. *Legacies and Ambiguities: Postwar Fiction and Culture in West Germany and Japan.* Baltimore: Johns Hopkins University Press, 1991.

Schläppi, E., and W. Kälin. *Schweizerische Aussenwirtschaftshilfe und Menschenrechtspolitik: Konflikte und Konvergenzen.* Chur: Rüeggger, 2001.

Schmidlin, A. *Eine andere Schweiz: Helferinnen, Kriegskinder und humanitäre Politik, 1933–1942.* Zurich: Chronos, 1999.

Schmidt, D. J. *On Germans and Other Greeks: Tragedy and Ethical Life.* Bloomington: Indiana University Press, 2001.

Schmidt, T., E. Mittig, and V. Böhm, eds. *Nationaler Totenkult: Die neue Wache: Eine Streitschrift zur zentralen deutschen Gedenkstätte.* Berlin: Karin Kramer Verlag, 1995.

Schneider, M. *"Den Kopf verkehrt aufgesetzt": Die melancholische Linke.* Darmstadt: Luchterhand, 1981.

Schneider, U., ed. *Auschwitz: Ein Prozess.* Cologne: Papyrosa, 1993.

Schoenberner, G. *Der gelbe Stern.* Hamburg: Rütten and Loening, 1960.

Schoeps, J., ed. *Ein Volk von Mördern? Die Dokumentation zur Goldhagen-Kontroverse um die Rolle der Deutschen im Holocaust.* Hamburg: Hoffmann und Campe, 1996.

Schörken, R. *Geschichte in der Alltagswelt: Wie uns Geschichte begegnet und was wir aus ihr machen.* Stuttgart: Klett-Cotta, 1981.

——. *Jugend 1945: Politisches Denken und Lebensgeschichte.* Opladen: Leske und Budrich, 1990.

Schöttler, P., ed. *Geschichtsschreibung als Legitimationswissensschaft.* Frankfurt: Suhrkamp, 1997.

Schudson, M. "Dynamics of Distortion in Collective Memory." In *Memory Distor-*

*tion: How Minds, Brains, and Societies Reconstruct the Past*, edited by D. Schacter, 346–64. Cambridge, Mass.: Harvard University Press, 1995.

Schulze, W., ed. *Sozialgeschichte, Alltagsgeschichte, Mikro-Historie*. Göttingen: Vandenhoek und Ruprecht, 1994.

Schulze, W., and O. G. Oexle, eds. *Deutsche Historiker im Nationalsozialismus*. Frankfurt: Fischer, 1999.

Schumacher, C., ed. *Staging the Holocaust: The Shoah in Drama and Performance*. Cambridge: Cambridge University Press, 1998.

Schuman, H., and J. Scott. "Generations and Collective Memories." *American Sociological Review* 54, no. 3 (June 1989): 359–81.

Schwabb-Trapp, M. *Konflikt, Kultur und Interpretation: Eine Diskursanalyse des öffentlichen Umgangs mit dem Nationalsozialismus*. Opladen: Westdeutscher Verlag, 1996.

——. *Kriegsdiskurse: Die politische Kultur des Krieges im Wandel 1991–1999*. Opladen: Leske und Budrich, 2002.

Schwan, G. *Politik und Schuld: Die zerstörerische Macht des Schweigens*. Frankfurt: Fischer, 1997.

Schwartz, B. *Abraham Lincoln and the Forge of National Memory*. Chicago: University of Chicago Press, 2000.

——. "The Social Context of Commemoration: A Study in Collective Memory." *Social Forces* 61, no. 2 (1982): 374–402.

Schwarz, G. "Gli ebrei italiani e la memoria della persecuzione fascista (1945–1955)." *Passato e presente* 17, no. 47 (1999): 109–30.

Segev, T. *The Seventh Million: The Israelis and the Holocaust*. New York: Hill and Wang, 1993.

Seiler, D. "Im Labyrinth der Geschichtspolitik: Die Erinnerung an die Shoa im öffentlichen österreichischen Gedächtnis." *Zeitgeschichte* 24, no. 9–10 (1997): 281–301.

Seixas, P. *Theorizing Historical Consciousness*. Toronto: University of Toronto Press, 2004.

Seniavskaia, E. *Frontovoe Pokolenie 1941–1945*. Moscow: Institut rossiiskoi istorii RAN, 1995.

Seuthe, R. *"Geistig-moralische Wende"? Der politische Umgang mit der NS-Vergangenheit in der Ära Kohl am Beispiel von Gedenktagen, Museums- und Denkmalprojekten*. Frankfurt: Lang, 2001.

Shafir, S. *The American Jewish Community and Germany since 1945*. Detroit: Wayne State University Press, 1999.

Shandler, J. *While America Watches: Televising the Holocaust*. New York: Oxford University Press, 1999.

Shandley, R., ed. *Unwilling Germans? The Goldhagen Debate*. Minneapolis: University of Minnesota Press, 1998.

Shotter, J., and K. J. Gergen. *Texts of Identity*. London: Sage, 1989.

Siebert, R. "Don't Forget: Fragments of a Negative Tradition." *International Yearbook of Oral History and Life Stories* 1 (1992): 165–77.

Silver, R. L., C. Boon, and M. H. Stones. "Searching for Meaning in Misfortune: Making Sense or Incest." *Journal of Social Issues* 39 (1980): 81–202.

Singer, J. L., ed. *Repression and Dissociation*. Chicago: University of Chicago Press, 1990.

Sluga, G. "Italian National Memory, National Identity, and Fascism." In *Italian Fascism: History, Memory and Representation*, edited by R. J. B. Bosworth and P. Dogliani, 178–93. London: Macmillan, 1999.

Smith, A. D. *National Identity*. London: Penguin, 1991.

Spann, G. "Staatswappen und Bundeshymne der Republik Österreich." In *26. Oktober: Zur Geschichte des österreichischen Nationalfeiertages*, edited by Bundesministerium für Unterricht, Kunst und Sport, 35–41. Vienna: Bundesministerium für Unterricht, Kunst und Sport, 1999.

Spence, D. P. *Narrative Truth and Historical Truth: Meaning and Interpretation in Psychoanalysis*. New York: Norton, 1982.

Speyer, P. *The Memory of Trade: Modernity's Entanglement on an Eastern Indonesian Island*. Durham, N.C.: Duke University Press, 2000.

Spiliotis, S. *Verantwortung und Rechtsfrieden: Die Stiftungsinitiative der deutschen Wirtschaft*. Frankfurt: Fischer, 2003.

Spivey, N. N. *The Constructivist Metaphor: Reading, Writing and the Making of Meaning*. San Diego: Academic Press, 1997.

*Staatsgesetzblatt für die Republik Österreich*. Vienna: Österreichische Staatsdruckerei, 1945.

Stachel, P. *Mythos Heldenplatz*. Vienna: Pichler Verlag, 2002.

Stamm, L. *Kniefall der Schweiz*. Zofingen: Zofinger Tagblatt, 1998.

Stavginski, H. G. *Das Holocaust-Denkmal: Der Streit um das "Denkmal für die ermordeten Juden Europas" in Berlin (1988–1999)*. Paderborn, Germany: Schöningh, 2002.

Steinberg, J. *All or Nothing: The Axis and the Holocaust*. London: Routledge, 1990.

——. *Why Switzerland?* Cambridge: Cambridge University Press, 1996.

Steiner, I. "Kostümierte Interessen: Österreichische Identität als Travestie in Wolfgang Liebeneiners 1. April 2000." In *1. April 2000*, edited by E. Kieninger, Nikola Langreiter, Armin Loacker, and Klara Löffler, 149–86. Vienna: Filmarchiv Austria, 2000.

Steinlauf, M. C. *Bondage to the Dead: Poland and the Memory of the Holocaust*. Syracuse, N.Y.: Syracuse University Press, 1997.

Stephan, C. *Der Betroffenheitskult: Eine politische Sittengeschichte*. Berlin: Rowohlt, 1993.

Stern, F. *The Whitewashing of the Yellow Badge: Antisemitism and Philosemitism in Postwar Germany*. Oxford: Pergamon, 1992.

Stiefel, D. *Entnazifizierung in Österreich*. Vienna: Europaverlag, 1981.

Stille, A. *Benevolence and Betrayal*. New York: Summit Books, 1991.

Stourzh, G. *Um Einheit und Freiheit: Staatsvertrag, Neutralität und das Ende der Ost-West-Besetzung Österreichs 1945–1955.* Vol. 4. Vienna: Böhlau, 1998.

Strasser, C. " 'The Sound of Music,' Ein unbekannter Welterfolg: Die virtuelle Trapp-Emigrantensaga als globale Kultur-Ikone mit Widersprüchen." In *"The Sound of Music" zwischen Mythos und Marketing,* edited by U. Kammerhofer-Aggermann and A. G. Keul, 267–302. Salzburg: Salzburger Landesinstitut für Volkskunde, 2000.

Straub, J., ed. *Erzählung, Identität und historisches Bewusstsein: Die psychologische Konstruktion von Zeit und Geschichte.* Frankfurt: Suhrkamp, 1996.

Streit, C. *Keine Kameraden: Die Wehrmacht und die sowjetischen Kriegsgefangenen 1941–1945.* Stuttgart: Deutsche Verlagsanstalt, 1978.

Sturken, M. *Tangled Memories: The Vietnam War, the Aids Epidemic, and the Politics of Remembering.* Berkeley: University of California Press, 1997.

Suedfeld, P., ed. *Light from the Ashes.* Ann Arbor: University of Michigan Press, 2001.

Suny, R. *The Soviet Experiment.* London: Oxford, 1998.

Suter, A. "Neutralität: Prinzip, Praxis und Geschichtsbewusstsein." In *Eine kleine Geschichte der Schweiz: Der Bundesstaat und seine Traditionen.* Frankfurt: Suhrkamp, 1998.

Tanner, J. *Bundeshaushalt, Währung und Kriegswirtschaft: Eine finanzsoziologische Analyse der Schweiz zwischen 1938 und 1953.* Zurich: Limmat, 1986.

——. "Die Krise der Gedächtnisorte und die Havarie der Erinnerungspolitik: Zur Diskussion um das kollektive Gedächtnis und die Rolle der Schweiz während des zweiten Weltkrieges." *Traverse,* no. 16 (1999): 16–37.

——. "Militär und Gesellschaft in der Schweiz." In *Militär und Gesellschaft im 19. und 20. Jahrhundert,* edited by U. Frevert, 314–40. Stuttgart: Klett-Cotta, 1997.

——. " 'Réduit national' und Aussenwirtschaft: Wechselwirkungen zwischen militärischer Dissusasion und ökonomischer Kooperation mit den Achsenmächten." In *Raubgold, Reduit, Flüchtlinge. Zur Geschichte der Schweiz im Zweiten Weltkrieg,* edited by P. Sarasin and R. Wecker, 81–104. Zurich: Chronos, 1998.

——. "Die Schweiz in den 1950er Jahren: Prozesse, Brüche, Widersprüche, Ungleichzeitigkeiten." In *Achtung: die 50er Jahre! Annäherungen an eine widersprüchliche Zeit,* edited by J.-D. Blanc and C. Luchsinger, 19–50. Zurich: Chronos, 1994.

Tanner, J., and S. Weigel. "Gedächtnis, Geld und Gesetz in der Politik mit der Vergangenheit." In *Gedächtnis, Geld und Gesetz: Vom Umgang mit der Vergangenheit des 2. Weltkriegs,* edited by J. Tanner and S. Weigel, 7–18. Zurich: Hochschulverlag, 2002.

Terdiman, R. *Present Past: Modernity and the Memory Crisis.* Ithaca, N.Y.: Cornell University Press, 1993.

Teschke, J. *Hitler's Legacy: West Germany confronts the Aftermath of the Third Reich.* New York: Peter Lang, 1999.

Thiele, M. *Publizistisch Kontroversen über den Holocaust im Film.* Münster: Lit, 2001.

Thoma, S. *Vergangenheitsbewältigung am Beispiel der Auseinandersetzungen um die Neue Wache.* Berlin: Scheibel, 1995.

Thomas, D. C. *The Helsinki Effect: International Norms, Human Rights, and the Demise of Communism.* Princeton, N.J.: Princeton University Press, 2001.

Tocqueville, Alexis de. *Democracy in America.* 2 vols. The Henry Reeve text as revised by Francis Brown. New York: Knopf, 1945.

Todorov, T. "The Uses and Abuses of Memory." In *What Happens to History: The Renewal of Ethics in Contemporary Thought,* edited by H. Marchitello, 11–22. New York: Routledge, 2001.

Torpey, J. "'Making Whole What Has Been Smashed': Reflections on Reparations." *Journal of Modern History* 73, no. 2 (June 2001): 308–49.

Tramontana, R. "Spruch heil: NS-Prozesse in der Zweiten Republik." *Profil,* 18 July 1979, 25–28.

Tranfaglia, N. "Fascismo e mass media: Dall'intervista di De Felice agli sceneggiati televisivi." *Passato e presente* 3 (January–June 1983): 135–48.

——. *Un passato scomodo: Fascismo e postfascismo.* Bari: Laterza, 1996.

——. "La repubblica." In *Personaggi e date dell Italia unita,* edited by M. Isenghi, 291–318. Bari: La Terza, 1997.

Tschuy, T. *Dangerous Diplomacy: The Story of Carl Lutz, Rescuer of 62,000 Hungarian Jews.* Grand Rapids, Mich.: W. B. Erdmans, 2000.

Tumarkin, N. *The Living and the Dead: The Rise and Fall of the Cult of World War II in Russia.* New York: Basic, 1994.

Uhl, H. (2000). "Gedächtnisraum Graz: Zeitgeschichtliche Erinnerungszeichen im öffentlichen Raum von 1945 bis zur Gegenwart." In *Erinnerung als Gegenwart: Jüdische Gedenkkulturen,* edited by S. Hödl and E. Lappin, 211–32. Berlin: Philo Verlagsgesellschaft, 200.

——. "Konkurrierende Gedächtnislandschaften: Widerstand gegen das NS-Regime, Zweiter Weltkrieg und Holocaust in der Denkmalkultur der Zweiten Republik." In *Steinernes Bewusstsein II: Die öffentliche Repräsentation staatlicher und nationaler Identität Österreichs in seinen Denkmälern,* edited by H. Uhl. Vienna: Böhlau, forthcoming.

——. "Der Staatsvertrag: Ein Gedächtnisort der Zweiten Republik." In *Souverän, Neutral, Europäisch: 1945 1955 1995 2005, Informationen zur Politischen Bildung 22,* edited by N. Frei, 67–78. Innsbruck: Studienverlag, 2004.

——, ed. *Steinernes Bewusstsein: Die öffentliche Repräsentation staatlicher und nationaler Identität Österreichs in seinen Denkmälern.* Vol. 2. Vienna: Böhlau, forthcoming.

——, ed. (2003). *Zivilisationsbruch und Gedächniskultur.* Innsbruck: Studienverlag, 2003.

"Unified Germany: Stabilizing Influence or Threat." Special edition, *Partisan Review* 62, no. 4 (1995).

Urner, K. "Die schweizerische Aussenhandelspolitik 1939–1945." In *Schwedische und schweizerische Neutralität im Zweiten Weltkrieg,* edited by R. L. Bindschedler et al., 250–92. Basel: Helbing und Lichtenhahn, 1985.

——. *"Let's Swallow Switzerland": Hitler's Plans against the Swiss Confederation.* Translated by L. N. Eichhorn. Lanham, Mass.: Lexington Books, 2002.

U.S. Department of State, ed. *U.S. and Allied Efforts to Recover and Restore Gold and Other Assets Stolen or Hidden by Germany During World War II.* Washington: U.S. Department of State, 1997.

Utgaard, P. *Remembering and Forgetting Nazism: Education, National Identity, and the Victim Myth in Postwar Austria.* New York: Berghahn, 2003.

van Dongen, L. *La Suisse face à la Seconde Guerre mondiale 1945–1948: Emergence et construction d'une mémoire publique.* Geneva: Librairie Droz, 1998.

Varon, J. *Bringing the War Home: The Weather Underground, the Red Army Faction, and Revolutionary Violence in the Sixties and Seventies.* Berkeley: University of California Press, 2004.

Verein Volksumfrage, ed. *Die Schweiz hält durch.* Zurich: Verein Volksumfrage, 1948.

Vidal-Naquet P. *Le Trait empoisonné: Réflexions sur l'affaire Moulin.* Paris: La Découverte, 1993.

Vogt, J. *Erinnerung ist unsere Aufgabe: Über Literatur, Moral und Politik 1945–1990.* Opladen: Westdeutscher Verlag, 1991.

Voigt, L. *Aktivismus und moralischer Rigorismus: Die politische Romantik der Studentenbewegung.* Wiesbaden: Deutscher Universitätsverlag, 1991.

*Vorkommnisse im EJPD: Bericht der Parlamentarische Untersuchungskommission vom 22. November 1989.* Bern: EDMZ, 1989.

Vygotsky, L. S. *Mind in Society: The Development of Higher Psychological Processes.* Edited by M. Cole. Cambridge, Mass.: Harvard University Press, 1978.

Wachs, P.-C. *Der Fall Theodor Oberländer (1905–1998): Ein Lehrstück deutscher Geschichte.* Frankfurt: Campus, 2000.

Walkowitz, D. J., and L. M. Knauer, eds. *Memory and the Impact of Political Transformation in Public Space.* Durham, N.C.: Duke University Press, 2004.

Walston, J. "History and Memory of the Italian Concentration Camps." *Historical Journal* 40, no. 1 (1997): 169–83.

Wassermann, H. P. *"Zuviel Vergangenheit tut nicht gut!" Nationalsozialismus im Spiegel der Tagespresse der Zweiten Republik.* Innsbruck: Studienverlag, 2000.

Webber, J. *The Future of Auschwitz: Some Personal Reflections.* Yarnton, U.K.: Oxford Centre for Postgraduate Hebrew Studies, 1992.

Weber, J., and P. Steinbach, eds. *Vergangenheitsbewältigung durch Strafverfahren: NS-Prozesse in der Bundesrepublik Deutschland.* Munich: Olzog, 1984.

Wegner, D. M. *White Bears and Other Unwanted Thoughts.* New York: Viking, 1989.

Weinbaum, L. *The Struggle for Memory in Poland: Auschwitz, Jedwabne and Beyond.* Jerusalem: Institute of the World Jewish Congress, 2001.

Weiner, A. *Making Sense of War.* Princeton, N.J.: Princeton University Press, 2001.

——. *Die Verfolgung von NS-Tätern im geteilten Deutschland: Vergangenheitsbewältigungen 1949–1969 oder: Eine deutsch-deutsche Beziehungsgeschichte im Kalten Krieg.* Paderborn, Germany: Schöningh, 2002.

Weishaupt, M. *Bauern, Hirten und "frume edle puren": Bauern- und Bauernstaat-sideologie in der spätmittelalterlichen Eidgenossenschaft und der nationalen Geschichtsschreibung*. Basel: Helbing und Lichtenhahn, 1992.

Weissberg, L. Introduction. *Cultural Memory and the Construction of Identity*, edited by D. Ben-Amos and L. Weissberg, 7–26. Detroit: Wayne State University Press, 1999.

Weitz, E. "Racial Politics without the Concept of Race: Reevaluating Soviet Ethnic and National Purges." *Slavic Review* 61, no. 1 (spring 2002): 1–29.

Welzer, H., S. Moller, and K. Tschuggnall. *"Opa war kein Nazi": Nationalsozialismus und Holocaust im Familiengedächtnis*. Frankfurt: Fischer, 2002.

Wenke, H. " 'Bewältigte Vergangenheit' und 'Aufgearbeitete Geschichte': Zwei Schlagworte, kritisch beleuchtet." *Geschichte in Wissenschaft und Unterricht* 11, no. 2 (1960): 65–70.

Wenzel, E. *Gedächnisraum Film: Die Arbeit an der deutschen Geschichte in Filmen seit den sechziger Jahren*. Stuttgart: Metzler, 2000.

Werle, G., and T. Wandres. *Auschwitz vor Gericht: Völkermord und bundesdeutsche Strafjustiz*. Munich: Beck, 1995.

White, H. *The Content of the Form*. Baltimore: Johns Hopkins University Press, 1987.

——. *Figural Realism*. Baltimore: Johns Hopkins University Press, 1999.

——. *Metahistory*. Baltimore: Johns Hopkins University Press, 1973.

——. *Tropics of Discourse*. Baltimore: Johns Hopkins University Press, 1978.

White, R. T. "Recall of Autobiographical Events." *Applied Cognitive Psychology* 3, no. 2 (April–June 1989): 127–35.

*Widerstand und Verfolgung in Wien 1934–1945: Eine Dokumentation*. 2 vols. Vienna: Österreichischer Bundesverlag, 1984.

Wiell, N. "Penser le procès Papon." *Le Débat* 103 (Jan.–Feb. 1999): 100–110.

Wiesen, J. *West German Industry and the Challenge of the Nazi Past*. Chapel Hill: University of North Carolina Press, 2001.

Wiesenthal, S., ed. *Projekt: Judenplatz Wien, Zur Konstruktion von Erinnerung*. Vienna: Zsolnay, 1000.

Wieviorka, A. *Déportation et génocide: Entre la Mémoire et l'oubli*. Paris: Plon, 1992.

Wieviorka, O. *Nous entrerons dans la carrière*. Paris: Le Seuil, 1994.

Wilke, J., B. Schenk, A. Cohen, and T. Zemach. *Holocaust und NS-Prozesse: Die Berichterstattung in Israel und Deutschland zwischen Aneignung und Abwehr*. Cologne: Böhlau, 1995.

Winter, J., and E. Sivan, eds. *War and Remembrance in the Twentieth Century*. Cambridge: Cambridge University Press, 1999.

Winterhalter, C. "L'immagine della Resistenza nella radio e nella televisione. Una analisi quantitative." In *La Resistenza italiana nei programmi della RAI*. Rome: RAI, 1996.

Wodak, R., et al. *"Wir sind alle unschuldige Täter": Diskurshistorische Studien zum Nachkriegsantisemitismus*. Frankfurt: Suhrkamp, 1990.

Wodak, R., and A. Pelinka, eds. *The Haider Phenomenon in Austria*. New Brunswick, N.J.: Transaction, 2002.

Wolfrum, E. *Geschichtspolitik in der Bundesrepublik Deutschland: Der Weg zur bundesrepublikanischen Erinnerung 1948–1990*. Darmstadt: Wissenschaftliche Buchgesellschaft, 1999.

Wolgast, E. *Die Wahrnehmung des Dritten Reiches in der unmittelbaren Nachkriegszeit*. Heidelberg: Winter, 2001.

Wolin, R. Introduction. *The New Conservatism: Cultural Criticism and the Historians' Debate*, by J. Habermas, vii–xxxi. Cambridge, Mass.: MIT Press, 1989.

Wood, M. *Blind Memory: Visual Representations of Slavery in England and America 1780–1865*. New York: Routledge, 2000.

Wood, N. "Memory's Remains: Les lieux de memoire." *History and Memory* 6, no. 1 (1994): 123–49.

———. *Vectors of Memory: Legacies of Trauma in Postwar Europe*. Oxford: Berg, 1999.

Wylie, N. "Pilet-Golaz and the Making of Swiss Foreign Policy: Some Remarks." In *Switzerland and the Second World War*, edited by G. Kreis, 158–70. London: Frank Cass, 2000.

Wyman, D., ed. *The World Reacts to the Holocaust*. Baltimore: Johns Hopkins University Press, 1996.

Yamamoto, M. *Nanking: Anatomy of an Atrocity*. Westport, Conn.: Praeger, 2000.

Yerushalmi, Y., ed. *Usages de l'oubli*. Paris: Le Seuil, 1988.

Yoneyama, L. *Historical Traces: Time, Space, and the Dialectics of Memory*. Berkeley: University of California Press, 1999.

Young, J. *At Memory's Edge: After-Images of the Holocaust in Contemporary Art and Architecture*. New Haven, Conn.: Yale University Press, 2000.

Zahn, G. C. *In Solitary Witness: The Life and Death of Franz Jägerstätter*. New York: Holt Rinehart and Winston, 1964.

Żakowski, J. *Pół wieku pod włos*. Kraków: Znak, 1999.

Zala, S. *Gebändigte Geschichte: Amtliche Historiographie und ihr Malaise mit der Geschichte der Neutralität 1945–1961*. Schweizerisches Bundesarchiv, vol. 7. Bern: Schweizerisches Bundesarchiv, 1998.

———. "Governmental Malaise with History: From the White Paper to the Bonjour Report." In *Switzerland and the Second World War*, edited by G. Kreis, 312–32. London: Frank Cass, 2000.

Zblewski, Z. *Leksykon PRLu*. Kraków: Znak, 2001.

Zeidler, M. *Stalinjustiz contra NS-Verbrechen: Die Kriegsverbrecherprozesse gegen deutsche Kriegsgefangene in der UDSSR in den Jahren 1943–1952*. Dresden: Hannah-Arendt-Institut, 1996.

Zelizer, B. *Remembering to Forget: Holocaust Memory through the Camera's Eye*. Chicago: University of Chicago Press, 1998.

Zerubavel, Y. *Recovered Roots: Collective Memory and the Making of Israeli National Tradition*. Chicago: University of Chicago Press, 1995.

Zimmer, O. " 'A Unique Fusion of the Natural and the Man-made': The Trajectory of Swiss Nationalism 1933–1939." *Journal of Contemporary History* 39, no. 1 (2004): 5–24.

Zippe, H. *Bildband zur Geschichte Österreichs*. Innsbruck: Pinguin Verlag, 1967.

Zöchling, C. *Haider: Eine Karriere*. Munich: Econ, 2000.

Zuccotti, S. *Under His Very Windows: The Vatican and the Holocaust in Italy*. New Haven, Conn.: Yale University Press, 2000.

———. *The Italians and the Holocaust*. New York: Basic Books, 1987.

Zumbansen, P., ed. *Zwangsrabeit im Dritten Reich: Erinnerung und Verantwortung*. Baden-Baden: Nomos, 2002.

Zunino, P. *La Repubblica e il suo passato: Il fascismo dopo il fascismo, il comunismo, la democrazia: Le origini dell'Italia contemporanea*. Bologna: Il Mulino, 2003.

"Zürcher Forschungsstelle für Sicherheitspolitik und Konfliktanalyse." *Sicherheit: Aussen-, sicherheits- und verteidigungspolitische Meinungsbildung im Trend*. 1999–2003. See http://www.ssn.ethz.ch.

# Contributors

CLAUDIO FOGU teaches in the Italian and French Department at the University of California, Santa Barbara. He has taught in the history departments of Ohio State University and the University of Southern California. Trained in both cultural historiography and the history and philosophy of history, he has studied in particular the transformations of historical consciousness in relation to the development of mass-visual culture in the twentieth century. In addition to essays published in the *Journal of Contemporary History*, *Representations*, and *History and Theory*, he is the author of *The Historic Imaginary: Politics of History in Fascist Italy* (2003). He is currently working on "A Study of Cultural Articulations of Mediterranean-ness in Fascist Italy."

RICHARD J. GOLSAN is a professor of French and head of the Department of European and Classical Languages and Cultures at Texas A&M University. In addition to editing *The Papon Affair* (2001) and other works dealing with the history and memory of Vichy France, he is the author of *Vichy's Afterlife* (2000) and of the forthcoming *French Writers and the Politics of Complicity: Crises of Democracy in the 1940s and 1990s* (2006).

WULF KANSTEINER is an associate professor of history and Judaic studies at Binghamton University, SUNY, where he teaches German history, Holocaust studies, and historical theory. He has published essays on collective memory, trauma theory, and German intellectual and media history in *History and Theory*, *German Politics and Society*, *New German Critique*, *Rethinking History*, *History of the Human Sciences*, and the *Journal of Contemporary History*. He is the author of *In Pursuit of German Memory: History, Television, and Politics after Auschwitz* (2006) and is currently working on a monograph on the representation of Nazism and World War II in German television.

RICHARD NED LEBOW is James O. Freedman Presidential Professor of Government at Dartmouth College. He is past president of the International Society of Political Psychology and a fellow of the Centre of International Relations at Cambridge University. His most recent books include *The Tragic Vision of Politics: Ethics, Interests and Orders* (2003) and two coedited volumes: *Ending the Cold War* (2004) and *Unmaking the West: Alternative Histories of the Creation, Rise, and Fall of Western Civilization* (2006).

REGULA LUDI teaches in the Department of History, University of Zurich, and is a researcher at the Center for Interdisciplinary Women's and Gender Studies, University of Bern. Until 2000 she was a staff historian and head of a research team of the

Independent Commission of Experts Switzerland–Second World War, and coauthor of several commission reports. Since then she has held fellowships at the Minda de Gunzburg Center for European Studies at Harvard University; the Center for European and Eurasian Studies at the University of California, Los Angeles; and the Center for Advanced Holocaust Studies, U.S. Holocaust Memorial Museum. Her main publications include *Die Fabrikation des Verbrechens: Zur Geschichte der modernen Kriminalpolitik 1750-1850* (1999); and, with Thomas Huonker, *Roma, Sinti und Jenische: Schweizerische Zigeunerpolitik zur Zeit des Nationalsozialismus*, Publications of the Independent Commission of Experts Switzerland–Second World War, vol. 23 (2001). Her recent work has also appeared in *Jewish Social Studies* and in *Nation and Gender in Contemporary Europe: Exploring the East-West Divide*, edited by St. Booth and V. Tolz (2005).

ANNAMARIA ORLA-BUKOWSKA is a social anthropologist in the Institute of Sociology at the Jagiellonian University in Krakow; her general field of research is majority-minority relations. She lectures extensively not only for various departments at the Jagiellonian but also for the postgraduate programs at the State Museum Auschwitz-Birkenau and the Centre for Social Studies in Warsaw, among others. She has guest-lectured in the United States, the Czech Republic, Belgium, Greece, and Australia. She was a 1999 Koerner Holocaust Fellow at the Oxford Centre for Hebrew and Jewish Studies and a 2004 Yad Vashem Fellow in Israel. Her most recent publications include essays in *Enteignet, vertrieben, ermordet: Beiträge zur Genozidforschung*, edited by H. Scholz and R. Bodyjian (2004) and in *POLIN*, edited by A. Polonsky (2004).

HEIDEMARIE UHL is a senior researcher and lecturer at the University of Graz. Since 2001 she has been contributing to the research program on the sites of memory run by Kommission für Kulturwissenschaften und Theatergeschichte der Österreichischen Akademie der Wissenschaften in Vienna. From 1994 to 2000 she conducted research for the project "Moderne: Wien und Zentraleuropa um 1900." Her major interest is in memory politics, theory of cultural studies, and modernity, culture, and identity in Central Europe. She is the author of *Zwischen Versöhnung und Verstörung: Eine Kontroverse um Österreichs historische Identität fünfzig Jahre nach dem Anschluß* (1992); coeditor, with S. Riesenfellne, of *Todeszeichen: Zeitgeschichtliche Denkmalkultur in Graz und in der Steiermark vom Ende des 19. Jahrhunderts bis zur Gegenwart* (1994); editor of *Kultur, Urbanität, Moderne: Differenzierungen der Moderne in Zentraleuropa um 1900* (1999); and coeditor, with A. Senarclens De Grancy, of *Moderne als Konstruktion: Debatten, Diskurse, Positionen um 1900* (2001).

THOMAS C. WOLFE is an associate professor in the Department of History at the University of Minnesota and holds adjunct appointments in the Department of Anthropology, the Institute for Global Studies, and the School of Journalism and Mass Communications. He teaches a variety of courses on twentieth-century European history, communications, media, culture, and ideas. He is author of *Governing Soviet Journalism* (2005) and is beginning work on a project about mass media and the politics of European integration.

# Index

Miłosz, Czesław, 14, 183, 191, 194
Mitscherlich, Alexander, 105
Mitscherlich, Margaret, 105, 108
Mitterrand, François, 6, 73, 75, 78, 83–85, 97–98
Modiano, Patrick, 77, 85–89
Molotov-Ribbentrip Pact, 182
Monte Cassino, 187
Morgenstern, Janusz, 188
Morris, Alan, 77
Moscow, 249
Moscow Declaration (October 1943), 41, 44–45, 58
Moulin, Jean, 26, 79, 84, 94
Museum of Modern Art (New York), 64
Mussolini, Benito, 148–49, 151, 160
Mussolini, Rachaele, 155, 219

Nałkowska, Zofia, 183
Nanjing massacre, 1, 18
Napoleonic Wars, 17–18, 21
Narrative, 3, 6, 15, 33
Nascita di una dittatura, 154, 158
Nazi Germany, 27, 107, 109, 110, 111, 112–14, 116, 122, 130. See also Nazi regime
Nazi regime, 1, 5, 22–23, 27; in Austria, 31, 33, 40, 41–43, 44, 46, 47–49, 59, 62, 63–65; in Belgium, 73; in France, 73, 91–92, 93, 94–95, 97; in Germany (see Nazi Germany); in Italy, 149, 151–52, 165; in Netherlands, 73; in Poland, 20, 177
Negrin, Alberto, 159
Neither Right nor Left, 77
Netherlands, 19, 73, 87
Nicholas II (Russia), 250
Niethammer, Lutz, 300
Nietzsche, Friedrich, 167, 304
Night Porter, 154
Noiriel, Gérard, 74
Nora, Pierre, 81, 301–2
Nord, 86
North Atlantic Treaty Organizaton (NATO), 29, 194
North Korea, 13

Norway, 21
Norwid, Cyprian, 191
Novecento, 154–55
Nowa Huta, 196
Nuremberg trials, 107, 113, 182

Oberländer, Theodor, 118
Occupation, German, 19. See also individual countries
October Revolution, 167
Oder-Neisse line, 120, 189
L'oeil de Vichy, 90
Oil crisis (1973), 121
One Day in the Life of Ivan Denisovitch, 264
Open City, 147
Operation Reinhard, 48
Ophuls, Marcel, 35, 74, 85–88, 90
Oral history, 286
Orban, Victor, 2
Orla-Bukowska, Annamaria, 20, 23–24, 32, 297–98
Orwell, George, 14
Ory, Pascal, 82–83
Ottoman Empire, 17

Pan Tadeusz, 196
Papon, Maurice, 36, 75, 90, 93, 97–99
Parlament, Das, 55
Partisans, 19, 148, 149, 151, 152, 153, 154, 156–57
Pasolini, Pier Paolo, 34, 154
Passerini, Luisa, 147, 161
Paul VI (pope), 47
Pavone, Claudio, 158
Paxton, Robert, 74–75, 90
Pearl Harbor, 9
Pelt, Robert van, 185
Perestroika, 269–70
Pétain, Henri-Philippe, 73, 84, 87, 91
Peter, Friedrich, 59–60
Peter and Paul Cathedral, 250
Pilat-Golaz, Marcel, 211
Pius XII (pope), 117, 169, 195
Place de l'Étoile, La, 86